TERRORISM

Documents of International and Local Control

VOLUME 97

TERRORISM

Documents of International and Local Control

VOLUME 97

USE OF CONTRACTORS IN THE WAR AGAINST TERRORISTS

Douglas C. Lovelace Jr., Esquire
Senior National Security Strategist

Oceana®
NEW YORK

OXFORD
UNIVERSITY PRESS

Oxford University Press, Inc., publishes works that further Oxford University's objective of excellence in research, scholarship, and education.

Published by Oxford University Press, Inc.
198 Madison Avenue, New York, New York 10016

Cataloging-in-Publication information is available from the Library of Congress.

ISSN 1062-4007
Terrorism: Documents of International and Local Control

ISBN: 978-0-19-538309-6 (v. 97)

Note to Readers:

This publication is designed to provide accurate and authoritative information in regard to the subject matter covered. It is based upon sources believed to be accurate and reliable and is intended to be current as of the time it was written. It is sold with the understanding that the publisher is not engaged in rendering legal, accounting, or other professional services. If legal advice or other expert assistance is required, the services of a competent professional person should be sought. Also, to confirm that the information has not been affected or changed by recent developments, traditional legal research techniques should be used, including checking primary sources where appropriate.

(Based on the Declaration of Principles jointly adopted by a Committee of the American Bar Association and a Committee of Publishers and Associations.)

TABLE OF CONTENTS

VOLUME 97

USE OF CONTRACTORS IN THE WAR AGAINST TERRORISTS

DOCUMENTS

C. CONTRACTOR ACCOUNTABILITY

D. ADDITIONAL CONCERNS

PREFACE

USE OF CONTRACTORS IN THE WAR AGAINST TERRORISTS

We devote this volume of *Terrorism: Documents of International and Local Control* to an assessment of the use of contractors to help wage the war against terrorists, particularly by the Department of Defense, but also by the Department of State and other agencies of the U.S. government. This is an exceptionally important area of analysis for several reasons. As Matthew Uttley notes in the lead-off document of this volume, the use of contractors to help prosecute war is not new; but, two trends have developed to draw our attention to the practice. They involve the increasing prevalence of contractors on the battlefield and the ever expanding roles and missions they perform. These trends have combined to raise significant legal, ethical, economic, and professionalism issues. The documents presented in this volume highlight many and describe measures taken, contemplated, and needed to address them.

The use of contractors to assist in the waging of war has increased dramatically over the past several decades and has become a highly contentious issue. It seems that their use has correlated inversely with the commitment of the American public to various war efforts. The unpopular Vietnam War, for example, especially in its later stages, featured a substantial rise in the use of contractors, for support functions such as facilities and equipment maintenance, line-haul transport of supplies and equipment, and administrative support. Operation Iraqi Freedom, the war conducted on what many claim to be "the central front against terrorism" continues to become increasingly unpopular among the U.S. public. Perhaps then, it should not be surprising that it involves proportionally more contractors than any war the United States has ever fought. Additionally, contractors in Iraq, such as those provided by Blackwater Worldwide (formerly Blackwater USA) provide services and perform functions previously reserved almost exclusively for military personnel.

Notwithstanding the apparent inverse relationship between public commitment to a war effort and the level of contractors used and their roles, other factors possibly help explain the increased resort to contractors. Former Secretary of Defense Donald Rumsfeld assumed office with a business model perspective and a bias toward relying more on the commercial sector for key services to support U.S. national security efforts. His "outsourcing" policies diverted significant defense funding that would have gone toward service members' salaries, benefits, supplies, and equipment to contractors who promised to provide the same service cheaper and better. But, Mr. Rumsfeld's outsourcing never really passed the business analysis test, nor did it consider the second and third order effects of withdrawing tasks performed by military members and Department of Defense civilian employees and awarding them to contractors. In many cases, the contractors ultimately proved more expensive, sometimes far more, and produced lower levels of service. In some cases, the very companies with which DoD contracted competed with DoD for the highly skilled service members in whom DoD had made significant training and development investment, thus driving up DoD's cost for retaining such personnel. In essence, DoD manufactured a bidding war against itself that drove up costs considerably.

Beyond the questionable economic advantages promised by the increased use of contractors in the war against terrorists lie professional and legal accountability issues. It is true that many contractors are former service members, who were imbued with service to the nation values when in uniform. Nonetheless, as contractors their actions and conduct rapidly become derived from a business ethic based on profit and economic advantage. They are not expected to serve selflessly and lay down their lives for their country. They are not expected to show the same loyalty to their superiors, peers and subordinates or to the constitution that is instilled in service members. In short, they are no longer bound by the professional ethic that guides members of the U.S. armed forces. The waging of war is one of the most challenging and serious of human endeavors. That is why it is left to disciplined, highly trained, dedicated service members who are led by professional noncommissioned officers and commissioned officers. It should come as no surprise that when contractors are assigned missions traditionally and prudently reserved for members of the military profession, problems, such as those which arose in the Nisour Square shooting in Iraq, follow.

In addition to professionalism challenges, the increased use of contractors in the war against terrorists has raised legal challenges, as well. Traditionally, contractors were beyond the reach of the U.S. judicial system when deployed in a foreign country and generally beyond the reach of the judiciaries of those countries. In essence, they were unaccountable. The U.S. Congress has addressed such accountability issues, with varying efficacy, at least as observed to date. We devote a section of this volume to describing and discussing some of those legislative measures. Related legal challenges concern the status of contractors on the battlefield, with respect to the law of armed conflict, a consideration made more challenging given the difficulty of defining the boundaries of the battlefield for the war against terrorists. One should note that this is not a uniquely American problem; many nations that use contractors in war zones face the same dilemmas.

This volume begins by presenting an historical context for considering the use of contractors on the battlefield, albeit from a United kingdom perspective. It then moves directly into the most salient case study of the use of contractors in the war against terrorists, by presenting four excellent documents on the use of contractors in Iraq. Next the volume addresses contractor accountability through the presentation of three documents that address establishment of proper accountability. The volume continues its discussion of the use of contractors in the war against terrorists by providing documents that discuss important related topics such as contractor conflicts of interests, over-reliance on contractors, use of contractors to contract with other contractors, and employment of former government employees as or by contractors. The diversity of topics in this volume demonstrates how complex and varied the issues are for the use of contractors in the war against terrorists.

BACKGROUND FOR UNDERSTANDING THE USE OF CONTRACTORS ON THE BATTLEFIELD

Commentary

By
Douglas C. Lovelace, Jr.

While this volume focuses on the U.S. Department of Defense's use of contractors on the battlefield, many other nations have increased their use of contractors as well. One of the best historical assessments is that provided by Professor Matthew Uttley in the first document of this volume. Professor Uttley astutely points out that since the United Kingdom (U.K.) and the United States will remain allies in future conflicts, U.S. readers can learn much from the U.K. Ministry of Defense's experience in using contractors to support military operations. Professor Uttley's monograph, *Contractors on Deployed Military Operations: United Kingdom Policy and Doctrine*, provides informative background for this contentious issue, "tees-up" issues, and provides U.S. national security strategists and legal professionals important insights useful for understanding the many dimensions of contractor use.

Professor Uttley accurately points out the similarity in U.K. MoD and U.S. DoD reasons for and approaches to the use of private contractors in lieu of uniformed military for many tasks and missions. He also correctly notes, however, that contractor substitution has not been nearly as contentious in the United Kingdom, as it has been in the United States. The concerns of the U.S. public and policy making elites could derive partially from the somewhat differing view they have of their armed forces than that possessed by their U.K. counterparts. It may also be partially explained by the U.S. history of contractor abuse and fraud and the public's general distrust of profit motivated commercial enterprises. The fact that contractor use in military operations is more controversial in the United States makes the U.K. experience and the lessons it has learned even more salient for U.S. strategists and policy makers.

Professor Uttley points out that while both the U.K. and U.S. governments have claimed economic and operational advantages to using contractors in military operations and generally seek to increase the practice, a community of critics has formed who argue that resort to contractors has become too pervasive and must be arrested or even reversed. Testing the two hypotheses, Professor Uttley makes broad observations. The U.K. MoD appears to have developed and implemented effective policies and procedures for employing contractors at acceptable level of risk. Nonetheless, a serious assessment of the true impact of using contractors has been hampered by a dearth of data in the public domain. The lack of such an assessment, as Professor Uttley accurately observes, raises unanswered questions concerning the actual cost-effectiveness of using contractors vice uniformed military personnel. Those questions remain largely unanswered by U.S. analysts, as well. Anecdotal information suggests in some instances, it may be far less cost-effective to use contractors.

Professor Uttley summarizes several main premises upon which of the U.K. MoD bases its argument (orthodoxy) for the use of contractors on the battlefield. First, as suggested above, contractors can provide certain military support functions more cost-effectively than service members. That claim has yet to be proven in the United Kingdom's case as well as in the United States' experience. Secondly, the MoD argues that the manpower and cost savings realized by the use of contractors can be applied to increase and enhance the effectiveness of "front line" military personnel. Again, that claim rests on unproven cost savings. The third premise, that contractors can provide support functions with no adverse result on operational effectiveness, rests on some rather questionable assumptions: 1) the presence of relatively safe and secure areas from which contractors can operate; 2) contractors can be integrated into military operational planning, and command and control without disrupting such planning and the execution of such plans; and 3) contractors will enhance the morale, cohesion, combat effectiveness, and ethos of the armed services by performing the more mundane support missions and projecting a "corporate ethos" very compatible with the military ethos.

U.S. policy makers would be well advised to look deeply into the assumptions underlying the third premise. Contemporary operations demonstrate that the nature of battle has changed such there are no clearly defined secure rear areas and front lines. The military operations planning culture has developed over centuries and is not an innate characteristic of a commercial enterprise. Contractors who are not required to adhere to the strict discipline of military units nor bear the same burdens of sacrifice borne by military personnel may actually have deleterious effects on morale, unit cohesion, ethos, and ultimately combat effectiveness.

The MoD premise summarized by Professor Uttley is that because contractors provide cost-effective support to military operations, the "inevitable global trend" is for the increased use of contractors. Consequently, the MoD sees itself as a trend setter. Clearly, there has been trend toward the increased use of contractors in military operations over the past half-century, but it has drawn sharp criticism in recent years. Consequently, it cannot be logically argued as a reason for attempts to perpetuate it.

Professor Uttley moves through his analysis of the use of contractors in military operations by summarizing the arguments for their increased use and for reducing reliance on them and discusses derivative policy issues addressing bureaucratic, resource, and operational considerations. He ends his analysis with an excellent discussion of the relevance of the United Kingdom experience with the use contractors in military operations to the challenges faced by U.S. policy makers and defense planners. His monograph sets the stage nicely for the documents that follow.

DOCUMENT NO. 1

CONTRACTORS ON DEPLOYED MILITARY OPERATIONS: UNITED KINGDOM POLICY AND DOCTRINE

Strategic Studies Institute Report
By Matthew Uttley

September 2005

*****

The views expressed in this report are those of the author and do not necessarily reflect the official policy or position of the Department of the Army, the Department of Defense, or the U.S. Government. This report is cleared for public release; distribution is unlimited.

*****

This manuscript was funded by the U.S. Army War College External Research Associates Program. Information on this program is available on our website, *http://www.carlisle.army.mil/ssi/*, at the Publishing button.

*****

The author would like to thank the many individuals whose comments on previous drafts or briefings have improved the final monograph, particularly Mr. Andy Higginson, Lieutentant Colonel James Greaves, Professor Joyce Kaufman, Dr. Antulio Echevarria, Dr. Paul Williams, and Dr. Christopher Spearin. Any errors of fact or interpretation are the responsibility of the author.

*****

Comments pertaining to this report are invited and should be forwarded to: Director, Strategic Studies Institute, U.S. Army War College, 122 Forbes Ave, Carlisle, PA 17013-5244.

*****

All Strategic Studies Institute (SSI) monographs are available on the SSI Homepage for electronic dissemination. Hard copies of this report also may be ordered from our Homepage. SSI's Homepage address is: *www.StrategicStudiesInstitute.army.mil*

*****

The Strategic Studies Institute publishes a monthly e-mail newsletter to update the national security community on the research of our analysts, recent and forthcoming publications, and upcoming conferences sponsored by the Institute. Each newsletter also provides a strategic commentary by one of our research analysts. If you are interested in receiving this newsletter, please subscribe on our homepage at *www.StrategicStudiesInstitute.army.mil*.

Foreword

Department of Defense (DoD) initiatives to use contractors on deployed military operations remains a contentious issue in U.S. military transformation. Despite the intense debates surrounding the benefits and costs of DoD outsourcing, little attention has focussed on similar Ministry of Defence (MoD) initiatives underway in the United Kingdom (UK). Since the UK and United States are likely to remain close allies in future expeditionary deployments, the MoD's approach to contractor support is a salient case study for the DoD and U.S. armed services.

This monograph, by Professor Matthew Uttley, examines the controversies surrounding deployed contractor support, the ways that the MoD has harnessed private sector capacity, and the lessons this provides for U.S. policymakers and military planners. In doing so, the author provides important insights into a significant theme in contemporary defense and security policy.

DOUGLAS C. LOVELACE, JR.
Director
Strategic Studies Institute

Biographical Sketch of the Author

MATTHEW UTTLEY holds the Chair in Defence Studies at King's College London (KCL). He is currently the Head of the Defence Studies Department: a KCL department of 50 academics supporting military education at the UK Joint Services Command and Staff College, Shrivenham. He has previously held posts at the Royal Naval College, Greenwich, the University of York and Lancaster University. Professor Uttley has published widely on the historical and contemporary dimensions of defence economics, weapons acquisition, and UK defence policy. His authored/edited books include *Westland and the British Helicopter Industry, 1945–1960* (Frank Cass, 2001), *Britain and Defence 1945–2000* (Longman, 2001, with S. Croft, A. Dorman and W. Rees), *The Changing Face of Maritime Power*, (Macmillan, 1999), and *The Changing Face of Military Power* (Palgrave, 2002). He has published in a variety of journals including *Intelligence and National Security, Defense Analysis, Public Policy and Administration*, and *Defence and Peace Economics.* Professor Uttley has acted as an advisor for a number of UK bodies including the National Audit Office, European Commission, the Ministry of Defence and the Economic and Social Research Council.

Summary

Since the Cold War, the U.S. and UK armed services have undergone significant transformation in response to the radically altered threat environment, new operational demands, and reduced defense budgets. Central to this transformation in both states is an expanded role for private contractors in providing deployed support functions traditionally conducted by uniformed personnel. Despite the similar direction of military reform, the U.S. armed services' approach to battlefield outsourcing has undergone extensive public scrutiny and debate, whereas UK Ministry of Defence (MoD) initiatives have hitherto attracted comparatively little independent assessment. Close U.S.-UK military cooperation over recent years in Afghanistan and Iraq, and the likelihood that both states will remain close allies in future interventions, suggest that the UK MoD's approach to deployed contractor support is a salient issue for U.S. military planners. This monograph analyses the MoD's outsourcing strategy and identifies those aspects of UK policy and doctrine that warrant consideration by the Department of Defense (DoD) and U.S. armed services.

The monograph surveys the evolution and content of the MoD's "public private partnership" program. This reveals the scale and scope of MoD initiatives to date, and the managerial, operational, and technological factors that have shaped the MoD's approach to organizing and managing private sector involvement. It also surveys why, despite the DoD's and MoD's widespread use of contractors on deployed operations, military outsourcing remains a controversial aspect of defense policy in the United States and UK. The DoD and MoD have been keen to articulate the financial and operational gains that the private sector can provide. Correspondingly, this "government orthodoxy" has been under sustained attack from those critics claiming the UK and U.S. armed services have gone "too far" with ideologically motivated privatization policies, and others who argue they have done "too little" to harness private sector capacity. The utility of this survey of claims and counterclaims is that it generates testable hypotheses against which the financial and operational performance of MoD and DoD outsourcing policies can be evaluated.

Evaluation of the performance of MoD outsourcing policy and doctrine against these testable hypotheses reveals two broad observations. On the one hand, the MoD has developed a number of novel command and control mechanisms that have succeeded in rationalizing and removing the risk in commercial battlefield support. On the other, the data necessary to evaluate the real impact of deployed outsourcing have yet to enter the public domain. Despite internal MoD reforms intended to ensure in-house and contractor alternatives are assessed on a "level playing field," limited information has emerged on how this works in practice. Similarly, questions remain about the relative cost-effectiveness of organic military provision and contractor alternatives, and whether purported savings from contracting out are actually being reinvested in additional front-line capability. Moreover, the MoD confronts a range of personnel issues before it can optimize the management of deployed contractor assets and ensure that outsourcing does not erode military cohesion.

Comparative analysis indicates that there are no fundamental differences in overarching MoD and DoD outsourcing philosophy. To the extent that variations do exist, this reflects differing national military structures, contractual practices and legal frameworks within which deployed contractor support has been engaged. Despite the similarities in overall approach, the analysis points to specific MoD initiatives that could enhance the U.S. armed services' ability to manage their deployed contractor support.

The monograph generates three primary conclusions and associated recommendations. The first is that military outsourcing will remain a controversial element of defense transformation unless the MoD and DoD release more detailed information policy on performance into the public domain. Second, given the current U.S. and UK commitment to outsourcing, the MoD and DoD need to address a range of implementation questions to ensure that contractors are engaged on deployed operations in the most efficient and cost-effective manner. And third, there are aspects of outsourcing "best practice" that the MoD and DoD have developed, and both organizations have specific lessons to learn from each other.

Introduction

Over the last decade, the use of private contractors to support U.S. deployed military operations significantly has increased in scale and scope. Private industry's expanded role is evident from the headline statistic that the ratio of military personnel to contract workers was 10:1 in Iraq during 2003, compared to a ratio of 100:1 in the 1991 Gulf War.[1] The broadening scope of outsourcing is reflected in the extension of Department of Defense (DoD) contracting from domestic training and base maintenance functions to include logistical and operational support needs during combat operations, peacekeeping missions, and humanitarian assistance missions, that have ranged from Somalia and Haiti to Bosnia, Kosovo, Afghanistan, and Iraq.[2] The perspective of contemporary U.S. policymakers has become that:

> The use of contractors to support military operations is no longer a "nice to have." Their support is no longer an adjunct, ad hoc add-on to supplement a capability. Contractor support is an essential, vital part of our force projection capability—and increasing in its importance.[3]

One outcome is that DoD outsourcing has attracted extensive debate and scrutiny from the U.S. policymaking and academic communities.[4]

In the United Kingdom (UK), the Ministry of Defence (MoD) also has contracted for commercial sector support under its "Contractors On Deployed Operations" (CONDO) policy and "public private partnership" programs. Reflecting DoD trends, MoD's objective is to incorporate the private sector "so firmly into the doctrine for deployed operations that Planning Staffs and their Commanders will take it for granted that their task force will include a contract support element."[5] However, in contrast to DoD outsourcing, MoD initiatives have attracted comparatively little scrutiny or independent assessment to date.

This monograph provides an in-depth analysis of MoD's approach to deployed contractor support, and highlights those aspects of UK policy and doctrine that warrant consideration by the U.S. armed services. The content and direction of MoD outsourcing is relevant to the U.S. armed services for four reasons. First, since the Cold War, the UK has been one of the few states to join the United States in developing a joint expeditionary power projection capability across the spectrum of conflict types, ranging

[1] M. Dobbs, "Iraq: Halliburton Reaping Huge Profits," *Washington Post*, August 28, 2003.

[2] See, for example, H. Keeter, "Army Launches $12 Million Outsourcing Review," *Defense Daily*, February 11, 1999, pp. 1–2. For a discussion of the U.S. Army's recent decision to contract out as many as 214,000 military and civilian jobs, see C. Lee, "Army Outsourcing Plan Decried, Thousands of Jobs Could Be Affected," *Washington Post*, December 21, 2002; and *Military Operations: Contractors Provide Vital Services to Deployed Forces but Are Not Adequately Addressed in DOD Plans*, GAO-03-695, Washington, DC: U.S. General Accounting Office, June 2003, p. 4.

[3] G. L. Campbell, "Contractors on the Battlefield: The Ethics of Paying Civilians to Enter Harm's Way and Requiring Soldiers to Depend Upon Them," paper presented at the Joint Services Conference on Professional Ethics, Springfield, VA, January 2000, cited in C. Spearin, "American Hegemony Incorporated: The Importance and Implications of Military Contractors in Iraq," *Contemporary Security Policy*, Vol. 24, No. 3, December 2003, p. 32.

[4] See P. W. Singer, *Corporate Warriors: The Rise of the Privatized Military Industry*, New York: Cornell University Press, 2003.

[5] Speech by UK Minister of State for the Armed Forces John Spellar, Royal United Services Institute, February 8, 2000, *http://www.news.mod.uk/news/press*.

from high-intensity warfare to lower-intensity humanitarian and peace support. The MoD has also followed DoD trends in seeking to acquire "network centric warfare" capabilities that link sensors, command and control, and weapons delivery platforms via common digital communications networks. These similarities in defense transformation strategies mean all aspects of British military reform are salient for U.S. policymakers.[6]

Second, the UK and United States remain key allies, as evidenced in their close political and military cooperation in Afghanistan and Iraq. Britain's defence policy is predicated on the assumption that in "the most demanding operations" in the future, its armed services "will be operating alongside the U.S. and other allies."[7] As Britain is likely to be a key member of future U.S.-led coalitions, its approach to contractor support is directly relevant to DoD operational planners. Third, analysis of international defense outsourcing statistics indicates that the MoD most closely matches DoD trends. As Figure 1 shows, the number of UK MoD "public private partnerships" (PPP) significantly exceeds those in other European countries, which suggests that the U.S. armed services are more likely to draw policy-relevant lessons from the UK experience than from comparisons with other allies.

Figure 1: International Statistics on Public Private Partnerships (PPP) in Defense

Country	Number of Defence PPP Projects
UK	1,181
Ireland	62
Italy	55
Netherlands	40
Portugal	21
Finland	7
Spain	6
Sweden	6
France	3
Norway	3

Source: Statistics presented in S-E Bakke, *What is PPP About, With Main Focus on Outsourcing*, 2nd Annual Nordic Defence Industry Summit, Oslo, April 27, 2004.

[6] For an extended discussion, see A. Dorman, *European Adaptation to Expeditionary Warfare: Implications for the U.S. Army*, Carlisle PA: U.S. Army War College, Strategic Studies Institute, November 2002.

[7] Ministry of Defence, *Defence White Paper: Delivering Defence in a Changing World*, Cm 6041-I, London: HMSO, December 2003, p. 7.

Finally, similar controversies and debates surround government initiatives to employ "contractors on the battlefield" in the UK and United States. According to MoD and DoD, contractor support reduces defense costs and provides a crucial "force multiplier" to meet the needs of contemporary military deployments. Despite this shared "government orthodoxy," military outsourcing remains emotive, and two contending critiques have emerged. One claims that MoD and DoD risk going "too far" with "obtuse" forms of privatization that could increase defense support costs and erode operational effectiveness.[8] Correspondingly, another critique starts with the premise that "there are no military core competencies, and that all functions (including combat) are candidates for private sector involvement,"[9] and criticizes MoD and DoD for employing "too little" commercial sector support on deployed operations.[10] In this context, an in-depth assessment of MoD's approach provides a mechanism to evaluate controversies surrounding military outsourcing in both Britain and America.

This monograph is divided into five sections. The first surveys the evolution, content, scale and scope of MoD's "public private partnerships" program. The second analyses the premises underpinning the "government orthodoxy" and the counterclaims of the "too far" and "too little" perspectives. This generates contrasting hypotheses against which the performance of MoD outsourcing policy can be assessed. The third evaluates the evidence on MoD policy towards battlefield contractor support, and the fourth identifies those aspects of the UK approach that warrant consideration by the DoD and U.S. armed services. The final section summarizes the main conclusions and recommendations.

An Overview of "Public Private Partnerships" in UK Defence

Contemporary commentators tend to assume that defense outsourcing is a post-Cold War phenomenon and that the presence of "contractors on the battlefield" marks a recent departure from a paradigm of military self-sufficiency. In the UK case, neither assumption is accurate. As this section shows, MoD initiatives to harness contractor support on deployed operations mark the latest phase of a privatization program stemming from the early 1980s. It was the legacy of 2 decades of outsourcing that provided the impetus for contractor battlefield support and shaped MoD's assessment of how private sector involvement should be organized and managed.

---

[8] G. Frost, "How to Destroy an Army: The Cultural Subversion of Britain's Armed Forces," in A. Alexandrou, R. Bartle, and R. Holmes, eds., *New People Strategies for the British Armed Forces*, London: Frank Cass, 2001, p. 41.

[9] E. Pint and R. Hart, *Public-Private Partnerships: Proceedings of the US-UK Conference on Military Installation Assets, Operations, and Services April 14–16, 2000*, Santa Monica, CA: RAND, 2001, p. 42.

[10] J. Stokoe, "A Fine Division," *Defence Management Journal*, Vol. 4, Issue 4, Autumn 2001, p. 11.

Until 1980, a key tenet of UK defence policy was that MoD and the armed services provided directly all the services for which they were responsible and owned the main resources necessary to provide those services. Comprehensive in-house self-sufficiency across the spectrum of "front line" and support functions was considered essential for operational effectiveness, and:

> There was little or no scope, or perceived need, for private, commercial organizations to contribute to national defence. Moreover, the armed forces were increasingly likened to a "total institution," one in which all the functions and activities of those concerned were internally geared to achieve the goals of the institution to the exclusion of all else.[11]

Between 1980 and 1997, MoD gradually extended the scale and scope of competitive tendering and private sector involvement in nondeployed defense support under successive Conservative administrations. This started modestly in 1981 when government-imposed Civil Service manpower targets led MoD to consider the possibility of "putting work out to contract."[12] By 1983, Defence Secretary Heseltine introduced the more systematic approach that henceforth:

> . . . the only work which is carried out within our own defence support organization should be that which is essential for clearly proven operational reasons, or where there is financial advantage for the taxpayer.[13]

Policy became to "market test" selected in-house defense support functions against private sector bids and to contract-out where industry offered cheaper alternatives. A more intensive phase followed with the 1991 *Competing for Quality* (CFQ) White Paper,[14] which exposed Third and Fourth line logistic support to external competition and led to multiactivity facilities management contracts where tasks "did not impinge directly on the services' operational roles."[15]

In parallel, after 1992, MoD explored the scope for capital items traditionally purchased through the defence budget and run in-house to be financed and operated by industry under the UK government's wider Private Finance Initiative (PFI). By 1997, the results of outsourcing policies under the Conservative administrations were that £2.2 billion, or approximately

[11] M. Edmonds, "Defence Privatization: From State Enterprise to Commercialism, *Cambridge Review of International Affairs*, Vol. XIII, No. 1, Autumn-Winter 1999, p. 117.

[12] Ministry of Defence, Statement on the Defence Estimates 1981, *Cmnd. 8212*, London: HMSO, 1981, p. 68.

[13] *Ibid.*, p. 18.

[14] HM Treasury, Competing for Quality: Buying Better Public Services, Cm. 1730, London: HMSO, 1991.

[15] C.R. Pickard, "Competing for Quality in Defence," *Economic Affairs*, December 1997, p. 35.

25 percent of the defence support budget, was market tested and MoD estimates were that CFQ had "realized significant efficiency savings."[16]

After June 1997, the new Labour Government criticized its predecessor for assuming that the best solution to public sector problems was "simply to transfer as much of the activity as quickly as possible to the private sector."[17] However, the Blair administration actually set about increasing private contractor involvement in defence under a banner of government "modernization" and "publicprivate partnerships," and sought to build "upon the successes of contracting out support services that formed the basis of the early program."[18]

Launched in 1998, the *Better Quality Services* (BQS) initiative assessed all MoD support functions in terms of whether they should be abolished, internally restructured, strategically contracted out, or privatized.[19] The BQS initiative has formed one part of the Labour administration's pan-government PPP program, which is intended to replace "adversarial" relationships between MoD and its suppliers with "alignment" of mutual objectives.[20] The PPP philosophy is predicated on competitive tendering in the allocation of long-term contracts, open discussion between MoD and suppliers on the allocation of project risk, "framework agreements" that allow MoD to place separate tasking orders, and opportunity for "gain-share" between MoD and suppliers if contractors can provide innovative solutions to requirements. The PPP program emphasises that:

> With industry increasingly involved in providing long-term services to MoD, we have recognized that a partnership approach–building reliable links with our suppliers–is often the best way of achieving the required performance. This does not mean creating privileged or monopoly suppliers: selection of a long-term partner is competitive wherever possible.[21]

The PPP initiative significantly has increased the scale and scope of private sector involvement in defence support. In practical terms, the program contains five generic types of customer-supplier relationships between MoD and industry (see Figure 2).

The first PPP category covers the outsourcing of support services. The trend has been towards new large-scale multiactivity contracts with "industrial prime vendors," typically of 5–7 years' duration. Illustrative is the "Defence High Frequency Communications Service" (DHFCS) contract

[16] Cabinet Office, *Competing for Quality Policy Review: An Efficiency Unit Scrutiny*, London: HMSO, 1996, p. 6.
[17] HM Treasury, *Public Private Partnerships: The Government's Approach*, London: HMSO, 2000, p. 25.
[18] Sir Roger Jackling, "Public Private Partnerships in MoD," *World Defence Systems*, July 2001, p. 93.
[19] Cabinet Office, *Better Quality Services: A Handbook on Creating Public/Private Partnerships Through Market Testing and Contracting Out*, London: HM Government, 1998, p. 9.
[20] Jackling, p. 94.
[21] Ministry of Defence, *The Smart Acquisition Handbook*, Ed. 5, London: HMSO, 2004, p. 42.

Figure 2: Elements of the UK PPP Program

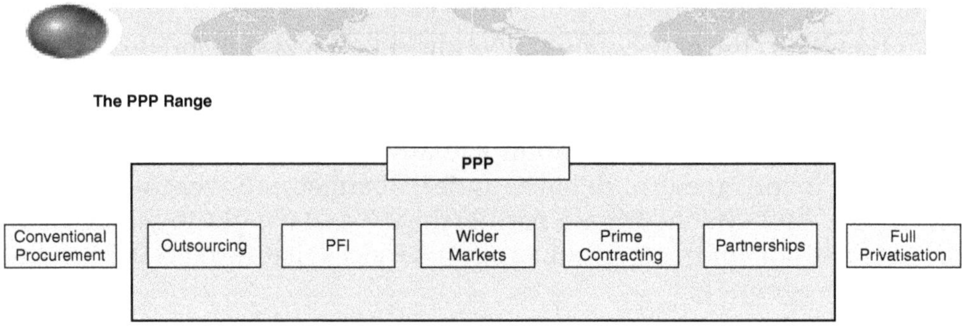

covering operation of long distance strategic communication between Army units, Royal Air Force (RAF) aircraft, Royal Navy (RN) warships, and UK headquarters.[22]

The second category covers PFI contracts. Between 1997 and 2000, the Joint Services Command and Staff College, the Medium Support Helicopter Aircrew Training Facility, the Attack Helicopter Training Package, the Hawk Training Simulator, and the Tornado GR4 Training Simulator were contracted for under PFI arrangements.[23] During 2000, following the publication of the *Ministry of Defence Investment Strategy*, MoD policy became that "before funds are made available for any new investment, private financing must be shown to be inappropriate, unworkable or uneconomic."[24] Subsequent PFI deals have included commercial provision of support vehicles ("White Fleet" project), new e-business systems, a Royal Navy communications service, Lynx and E3D Sentry aircraft simulator-based training and Tri-Service Materials Handling services.

The third PPP category covers commercial marketing of irreducible spare capacity in MoD facilities, which commenced in 1998 under the pan-Government *Wider Markets Initiative*.[25] Practical developments have included "equity joint ventures" between the former Defence Evaluation and Research Agency (renamed QinetiQ) and the private sector to market speech-recognition technology,[26] and the Navy Recruitment and Training

[22] Editorial, "Partnerships in Progress," *Defence Management Journal*, Issue 22, April 2003, p. 16.

[23] See V. Doyle, "Fresh Private Sector Investment," *Defence Management Journal*, Vol. 3, Issue 2, Spring 2000, pp. 88–89.

[24] M. Harte, "A New Strategy for Investment," *Defence Management Journal*, Vol. 4, Issue 3, Summer 2001.

[25] For more details, see M. Emmerich, "Generating Enterprise in Government," *Defence Management Journal*, Vol. 3, Issue 2, Spring 2000, pp. 80–81; and J. Williams and N. Holland, "Developing Wider Market Opportunities Through Public Private Partnerships," *Defence Management Journal*, Issue 18, February 2002, pp. 62–63.

[26] See L. Peace, "A Public Private Partnership for DERA," *Defence Management Journal*, Vol. 4, Issue 3, Summer 2001, p. 13.

Agency's (NRTA) partnership with Flagship Training Ltd. to exploit MoD estate and training facilities.

The fourth PPP category is "Prime Contracting." Here, MoD retains ownership and responsibility for the full capital costs of new facilities, but prime contractors manage entire project design, construction, and final delivery supply chains. The fifth category covers "partnership agreements" between MoD and "key suppliers" under loose contractual frameworks intended to encourage the private sector partner to identify the scope for potential innovation and value for money improvements in defense support delivery.

The PPP program significantly has increased the scale and scope of private sector involvement in defence support. By 2000, some £10 billion, or 45 percent of MoD's "annual business," had been reviewed for potential private sector involvement under the BQS initiative.[27] The MoD currently has 42 PFI projects in operation covering military training facilities, logistics functions, and communications that bring in £2 billion of private sector investment, and another 40 projects in procurement that could ultimately generate £12 billion of additional defence investment. By 2000, the situation was that MoD and the armed services had assessed most nondeployable nonequipment support for partnering potential, and private companies were now:

> involved in the management of property, the provision of services to military establishments and, increasingly, in the delivery of operational support to Forces overseas–a continuum of support from the home base in the UK to deployed military units.[28]

This experience provided impetus for MoD to pursue the next logical progression: the development of systematic policies for the spatial movement of logistic support already provided by private industry nearer to the front line of deployed military operations. Though industry supported deployed forces in theatres of operation on an *ad hoc* basis during the 1990–91 Gulf War, and the Bosnia and Kosovo campaigns, MoD "lacked a coherent and agreed policy for its use."[29] Systematic policies have emerged since the 1998 *Strategic Defence Review*–the UK's policy blueprint to transform the armed services for post-Cold War operational deployments–stated that "wherever appropriate" MoD "will consider the use of contractors to assist with logistic support."[30] This new imperative manifested itself in 2003 with

[27] Ministry of Defence, *Performance Report 2000/2001*, London: HMSO, *Cm 5290*, November 2001, Para. 105.
[28] Stokoe, p. 11.
[29] R. Tripp, "Contractors on Deployed Operations CONDO," *World Defence Systems*, Vol. 3, Issue 3, p. 94.
[30] Ministry of Defence, *Strategic Defence Review*, *Cmnd. 3,999*, London: HMSO, 1998.

MoD directives to "maximise the use of contractors" during UK military operations in Iraq.

In parallel, weapons acquisition reviews suggested benefits from closer "partnering" between MoD and equipment suppliers in the "through-life" design, development, manufacture, in-service support and disposal of weapons platforms.[31] The MoD's "Smart Acquisition" initiative attempts to achieve this through "integrated project teams" involving industry at all stages of weapons projects to achieve "faster, cheaper, and better equipment."[32] This has provided an imperative for acquisition officials to draw manufacturers "further and further forward in the operational area in support of their equipment," as prime contractors have assumed greater responsibility for Integrated Logistic Support (ILS).[33] Building on the PPP philosophy, the trend here has been towards "an outsourcing of procurement from MoD with the prime taking ever greater responsibility, and risk and reward, for what is becoming a service rather than the provision of an asset."[34]

Five discrete types of deployed operational support contracts have emerged that reflect a combination of MoD's overarching PPP approach, and operational and acquisition imperatives. "Original equipment manufacturer" (OEM) and "contractor logistic support" (CLS) contracts, signed when new equipment is brought into service, cover maintenance and upgrade of deployed equipment. The OEM contracts normally specify the provision and maintenance of "proprietary" equipment (e.g., combat aircraft, armoured fighting vehicles); CLS contracts provide the armed services with options to contract out some or all aspects of the deployed support and maintenance function to a commercial supplier. Available statistics suggest that 10–15 percent of the total value of equipment contracts is spent on through-life support to make the equipment available on deployed operations. Since 2001, some 30 CLS contracts to support systems and platforms have been invoked in support of British forces in Afghanistan and Iraq.[35]

"Urgent Operational Requirements" (UORs) are one-off (short term for individual items) and time-limited contracts established as circumstances

[31] For a detailed analysis of the "Smart Acquisition" initiative, see B. Kincaid, "Smart Procurement: Revolution or Regression?" in R. Matthews and J. Treddenick, eds., *Managing the Revolution in Military Affairs*, London: Palgrave, 2001, pp. 175–190.

[32] Summarized from Ministry of Defence, *The Acquisition Handbook: A Guide to Smart Procurement*, London: Ministry of Defence, 1999.

[33] P. Smart, "Support to the Front Line," *RUSI Journal*, February 2000, p. 67.

[34] B. Hedley and I. Busby, "The Impact on Industry," in *The Outcome of the Strategic Defence Review*, RUSI Whitehall Paper, Series 44, 1998, p. 37.

[35] A. Higginson, *MoD Contractors' Support to Deployed Operations: Industry Perceptions of Contracting for Availability on Deployed Operations*, Presentation at the DMA MoD Contractors' Support to Deployed Operations Seminar, London, March 15, 2005.

require, and typically cater for logistic functions or equipment upgrades not already covered by OEM and CLS contracts. Approximately £50 million per annum was spent on UORs before the UK's interventions in Afghanistan and Iraq.[36] Of the £800 million UOR expenditure to meet the UK's Iraq intervention cost, approximately £350–£400 million was spent on deployed contractor services.[37] These UOR contracts were placed with over 100 UK and non-national companies, which deployed 2,500 employees in support of UK military forces in the Iraq Joint Operations Area.

"Equipment-based Private Finance Initiative" contracts, which currently include the Army's Heavy Equipment (Tank) Transporter (HET) and the Royal Navy's Roll-on/Roll-off vessels, cover complete private sector provision of deployed equipment.

Finally, deployed capability is provided through MoD's overarching "Contractor Logistics" (CONLOG) Contract, a "one-stop-shop" for packages of commercial support not already covered by OEM, CLS and PFI contracts. CONLOG is intended to reduce the number of *ad hoc* UOR contracts[38] and has been awarded to Kellogg Brown and Root (KBR) under 7-year partnering arrangements. The MoD pays KBR £1.5 million per annum to provide planning and advice about potential contractor capability, and additional payments for specific "task orders" where KBR actually delivers capabilities on deployed operations.

The current scale of MoD deployed contractor support, and the extent to which the UK armed services have shifted from their pre 1980 self-sufficiency paradigm, is evident from contracting data. Before operations in Iraq during 2003, MoD did not collect statistics systematically on the value of contracts placed with firms or data on contractor personnel deployed on operations. Since 2003, the UK Permanent Joint Headquarters (PJHQ)–the organization responsible for command and coordination of UK joint operations–has collected extensive data intended to inform operational planning and decisionmaking.[39] PJHQ and Defence Manufacturers Association (DMA)[40] figures suggest that approximately £11 billion of the UK annual £24 billion defence budget is spent with industry on support services and the provision, operation, and maintenance of equipment. Of this £11 billion, some £2.3 billion of MoD expenditure on equipment and services is "contracted for availability and capability" on deployed operations.

---

[36] Interview, SO1 J4 Contractor Logistics CONLOG, Permanent Joint Headquarters, January 28, 2004.

[37] Interview, Defence Manufacturers Association CONDO Representative, Joint Services Command and Staff College, January 20, 2004.

[38] See "Troops to Get Better Support in the Field," *Preview: The Journal of the Defence Procurement Agency*, September 2003, p. 10.

[39] Interview, SO1 J4 Contractor Logistics CONLOG.

[40] Interview, Defence Manufacturers Association CONDO Representative.

The number of contractors' employees that have supported UK military operations since 1996 also demonstrates the scale in the shift from MoD's traditional self-sufficiency paradigm. Available statistics indicate that somewhere between 21,000 and 27,000 contractor personnel, including locally employed civilians and locally recruited workers, have sustained UK military deployments.[41] Of these, between 15,000 and 20,000 have supported "service contracts" on operations in the Balkans, Afghanistan, West Africa, and the Middle East. A further 1,100 to 1,500 personnel have been involved with CLS-type contracts, and up to 1,200 have acted as consultants or technical advisers. Specific contracts for the Afghanistan and Iraq deployments have involved 3,500 contractor personnel.[42] An indication of the scale of contemporary private sector support is the MoD estimate that contractor personnel have accounted for approximately 25 percent of the UK's total deployed force since combat operations commenced in Iraq during 2003.[43]

Contending Perspectives and Criteria for Evaluating MoD Outsourcing Policies

As MoD has entered into contracts for deployed operational support, it has articulated its rationale for assuming that private sector involvement provides benefits for the UK armed services. This rationale closely resembles orthodoxies shared by other national defense departments pursuing outsourcing strategies. Correspondingly, this "government orthodoxy" has been under sustained challenge from "too far" and "too little" critics. This section reviews the contending perspectives and generates testable hypotheses to evaluate the performance of MoD policy and doctrine.

MoD Orthodoxies

The MoD's stated justification for employing contractors on deployed operations has six main premises. The first is that private firms can provide certain military support functions more cost effectively than the armed services. The assumption here is that military units traditionally have conducted numerous support functions with "close civil analogues and where comparisons of cost and productivity between Services and the private sector should present few insuperable technical problems."[44] Consequently, MoD has a range of "make or buy" options to meet its deployed support needs.

[41] Higginson.
[42] *Ibid.*
[43] Deputy Assistant Chief of Staff J4, Permanent Joint Headquarters UK, Presentation at the DMA MoD Contractors' Support to Deployed Operations Seminar, London, March 15, 2005.
[44] M. S. Levitt, "Need Defence Costs Keep Rising?" in F. Terry, ed., *Managing the Costs of Defence*, London: Public Finance Foundation, 1985, p. 40.

According to MoD, contractor provision may be cheaper than military units for several reasons. In-house military provision "removes, to a significant extent, the incentives and constraints that apply to firms operating under competitive market conditions."[45] Under such monopoly-supply arrangements, there are few incentives for in-house units to seek lower cost methods of work because operating costs are met from defense budget allocations, and policymakers lack comparative cost data on alternative sources of supply ("information asymmetry"). According to MoD, competitive tendering between military units and private firms should resolve these deficiencies because it enables policymakers to compare competitively-determined bids from potential suppliers.

Private firms may also have particular attributes that enable them to provide more cost-effective support capability than military units. According to the UK Treasury, the "realities of the private sector market place," the need to generate profit, innovation incentives to meet customer demand, and skill in running service delivery activities "exert a powerful discipline on private sector management and employees to maximise efficiency."[46] Correspondingly, the "risk averse culture" of the public sector means "these disciplines can never be fully replicated," so in-house provision can be "less equipped to challenge inefficiency and outdated working practices, and to develop imaginative approaches" to delivering defence support services and managing MoD-owned assets.[47] Here, MoD's assumptions reflect a wider literature that concludes transferring activities to the private sector allows "innovative thinking and adjustments, especially about the use of technology and labour, to maximise the chances of success, which are not available to the fixed hierarchies of militaries."[48]

Finally, MoD assumes that battlefield outsourcing can simultaneously be "profitable for the contractor while demonstrating value for money" for MoD.[49] Central here is the notion that "partnership" and "partnering" between MoD and private suppliers enables the development of mutual products/services in a relationship where risks, costs, and benefits are shared, and where "mutual added value" can be achieved.[50] From MoD's perspective, a combination of competitive tendering and "appropriate benchmarking" can ensure that private suppliers provide cost-effective

---

[45] S. Domberger, S. A. Meadowcroft, and D. J. Thompson, "Competitive Tendering and Efficiency: The Case of Refuse Collection," *Fiscal Studies*, Vol. 7, No. 4, November 1986, p. 69.

[46] HM Treasury, *Public Private Partnerships*, p. 11.

[47] *Ibid.*

[48] C. Kinsey, *The Rise of the Corporate Soldier: The Role of Private Military Companies in International Security*, unpublished Ph.D. thesis, University of Wales Aberystwyth, September 2003, p. 182.

[49] Ministry of Defence, Contractors on Deployed Operations CONDO Policy, *JSP 567*, November 20, 2003, para. 101.

[50] E-H. Klijn and G. R. Teisman, "Institutional and Strategic Barriers to Public-Private Partnerships: An Analysis of Dutch Cases," *Public Money and Management*, Vol. 23, No. 3, July 2003, p. 137.

Figure 3: Complementary Contributions in Defence Partnering Arrangements

Private Sector Contribution	Defence Ministry Contributions
Marketing expertise	User needs, users "Frontline" knowledge
Access to capital	"Frontline" knowledge and experience
Access to leading-edge technology	Property, buildings, equipment, and specialized areas
Operating expertise	Operating systems
Increased use of spare capacity	Access to restricted zones, passage through restricted areas Scientific expertise, databases, patents Sharing of communications bandwidth

Source: Adapted from material presented in S-E Bakke, *What is PPP About, With Main Focus on Outsourcing*, 2nd Annual Nordic Defence Industry Summit, Oslo, April 27, 2004.

deployed support solutions. Through mutual trust, the combining of complementary assets and the identification of shared objectives, "public private partnerships" can draw on "complementary contributions to compose a package that makes good business sense and offers benefits" to MoD and the contractors.[51] The types of "complementary contributions" MoD envisages from partnerships are summarized in Figure 3.

The second premise is that MoD can reinvest resources released by outsourcing into operational enhancements in the form of additional front line military personnel, extra equipment, or access to private sector expertise. According to former UK Secretary of State for Defence George Robertson, cost reductions from outsourcing and other efficiency initiatives form "an integral part of our plans to drive down costs to pay for the modernization of our forces."

The MoD also assumes the process of substituting uniformed combat support units with civilian contractors releases trained military personnel for front-line tasks. The MoD's 1998 *Strategic Defence Review* (SDR)[52] marked the first systematic attempt to transform the armed services from their Cold War threat-based posture into a capability-based expeditionary force configured for mission types ranging from humanitarian assistance and peacekeeping, to high-intensity conventional warfighting.[53] The SDR recognized

[51] I. Chan, S. Galing, C. Wong, H. Yee, E. I. Axelband, M. Onesi, and K. P. Horn, *Use of Public-Private Partnerships to Meet Future Army Needs*, Santa Monica, CA: RAND, 1999, p. xiv.

[52] Ministry of Defence, *The Strategic Defence Review, Cm 3999*, July 1998.

[53] A. Dorman, M. L. Smith and M. R. H. Uttley, "Joint and Combined Operations in an Expeditionary Era: Defining the Issues," *Defense Analysis*, Vol. 14, No. 1, 1998, p. 3.

that this spectrum of mission types would require UK forces to deploy to conflicts over longer lines of communication than during the Cold War and conduct concurrent operations, potentially of differing intensities. At the same time, the SDR also acknowledged that:

> The increased operational pressures of the last few years have shown up weaknesses in our ability to sustain forces deployed overseas, particularly where local facilities are limited . . . To remedy these weaknesses and ease overstretch, we plan a package of logistic enhancements . . . Where this is appropriate, we will consider the use of contractors to assist with logistics support.[54]

In this context, MoD planners assess that outsourcing reduces "overstretch" by releasing "those assets, in rouelment, that are still army owned to be available for additional operations that may come along in the meantime."[55]

In addition, MoD assumes the armed services can acquire private sector expertise for support requirements where the generation of in-house military capability is less cost-effective. Outsourcing can provide access to high-technology skills where small numbers of military specialists are required, and where the armed services' retention of training infrastructure is uneconomic. In this regard, outsourcing is seen as a way for the armed services to "to keep pace with technology, retain access to the best that industry can offer, and apply increasingly scarce resources to high value combat systems."[56]

The third major premise is that contractors can provide deployed support functions with no adverse result on operational effectiveness. According to Secretary of State for Defence Geoff Hoon, the main driver for outsourcing "is the better use of resources in defence and the maintenance or enhancement of operational effectiveness." Considerations of private sector involvement must take that aspect into account before proceeding to such issues as "the impact on the chain of command and service discipline."[57] This premise rests on five assumptions.

1. There will invariably be readily identifiable safe and secure areas on any operational deployment where private contractors can operate. The MoD draws a distinction between "benign" and "nonbenign" areas within theatres of operation that are demarked by a "benign edge" behind the "front line."[58] In "benign" areas, "there is minimal risk of [contractor] personnel and equipment sustaining injury or damage through the effects

[54] Ministry of Defence, *The Strategic Defence Review*, Para. 98–99.
[55] Smart, p. 67.
[56] See D. W. Reeve, "Contractors in British Logistic Support," *Army Logistician*, May–June 2001, p. 3.
[57] MoD, "Public Private Partnerships: Changing the way we do business," *http://www.mod.uk/business/ppp/intro.htm*.
[58] Tripp.

of . . . hostile activity," and "adequate [security] means are in place to ensure [personnel and equipment] safety."[59] According to MoD doctrine, "benign" areas represent a safe and secure environment in which contractors can operate. Though "benign conditions are found at different geographical locations and at different times as an operation develops," MoD assumes that there will always be a range of circumstances where "commercial capability could be interchangeable with military capability throughout an operation" behind the "benign edge" (Figure 4).[60]

2. The MoD assumes contractors can enhance significantly the armed services' logistics and equipment support capabilities up to the "benign edge" of deployed operations. Capability enhancements can take various forms. Contractors can provide logistics capabilities that the armed services do not have that might include temporary base and infrastructure provision or the expertise to support new and complex technologies on the battlefield. Contractor-delivered capabilities therefore:

> . . . augment that provisioned by purely military means (as determined by extant Defence Planning Assumptions). [It can provide] . . . functions that may be required to enable extended operations in Joint Operations Areas (JOA), additional (unplanned) concurrency of operations, such as the maintenance of more than two deployed Lines of Communication, or access to the most modern technologies.[61]

Figure 4: Contractor Support and the "Benign Edge"

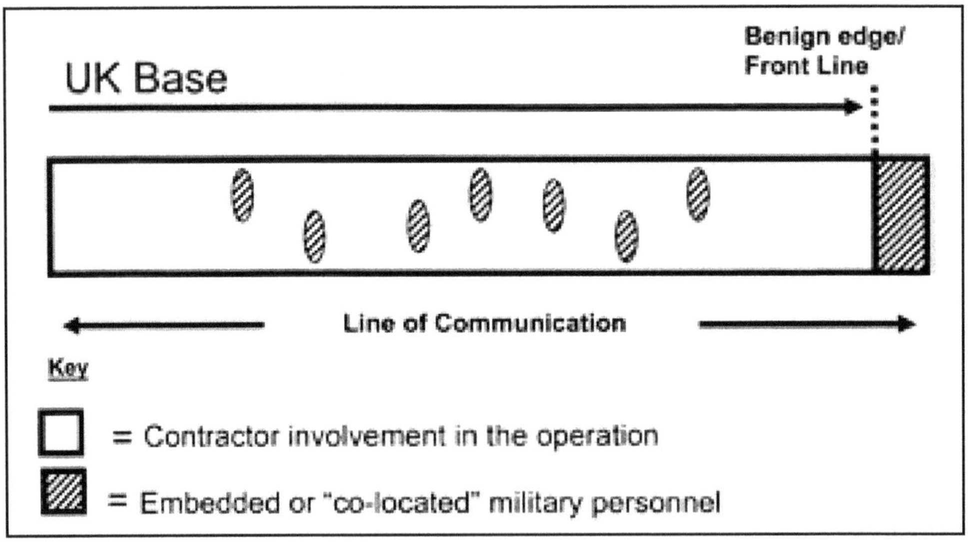

[59] Ministry of Defence, "Contractors on Deployed Operations CONDO," *Joint Doctrine Pamphlet 4/01*, December 2001, para. 107.
[60] *Ibid.*
[61] Ministry of Defence, *JSP 567*, para. 101.

3. Contractors providing deployed support can be integrated into military operational planning, and command and control (C^2) arrangements without disruption. The MoD assessment is that contractors can effectively "interface with and operate within the bounds of military doctrine and the operational commander's concept of operations," and meet "the requirements of the military logistics support plan."[62] Finally, MoD assumes contractor support can be harnessed without undermining the armed services' core military capabilities. The MoD has stated that contractor support "is not intended to replace core military manpower in the Order of Battle," but rather to augment it.[63] Consequently, it is assumed that criteria can be employed to ensure that contractors can safely be employed to "enhance military capability in a cost-effective way, taking advantage of the skills and capabilities available in the commercial environment."[64]

4. The reliability of private firms to deliver the deployed support they are contracted to is ensured by "gain-share." The MoD assumes that its "partnering" philosophy enables relationships with its suppliers that build on "trust, confidence, mutual alignment, [and] mutual understanding of what each party can and cannot do."[65] Consequently, firms providing battlefield support functions offer the same assured service as direct military provision because contractual "partnerships" enshrine common "understanding of constraints and imperatives faced by all parties."[66]

5. Outsourcing can enhance the morale, cohesion, combat effectiveness, and ethos of the armed services themselves. According to MoD, these gains accrue on two levels. On one level, contractors can relieve military personnel of mundane support missions, enabling soldiers to focus on mission critical activities that can improve their "quality of life significantly and, ultimately, impact [positively] on training and retention."[67] On a more fundamental level, it has been suggested that the "corporate ethos" of defence contractors themselves leads to close cooperation with the armed services on operational deployments. The contention here is that UK defence contractors tend to recruit ex-military personnel "predisposed" to "ways of acting, based on values drawn from their experiences of military service," and who operate "to the same high standards" of the armed services "while exhibiting the same moral values which

[62] Ministry of Defence, "Defence Council Instructions Joint Service, Contractors on Deployed Operations," *DCI JS 62 2003*, April 11, 2003, para. 6.
[63] Ministry of Defence, "The Current MoD Policy for Using Contractors on Deployed Operations," *http://www.ams.mod.uk/ams/contents/docs/condo.htm*, October 1, 2003.
[64] Ministry of Defence, *JSP 567*, para. 101.
[65] Smart, p. 69.
[66] *Ibid.*
[67] J. A. Fortner, "Institutionalising Contractor Support on the Battlefield," *Army Logistician*, July–August, 2000.

were first instilled in them in the military."[68] Consequently, it is assumed that contractors working with military personnel "generally share the same experiences, hardships, enjoyment, and problems, eroding further any cultural barriers that exist between them" in a mutually beneficial relationship where "values pass easily between both environments, shaping attitudes and work practices."[69] This suggests a new form of "military ethos" transcending the traditional military/civilian divide that replicates what the UK government sees as a new "public service" ethos and the sharing of "best practice" in other areas where the in-house monopoly provision has been replaced with a mix of public and private service delivery.[70]

The final premise is that because PPPs self-evidently provide a cost-effective mechanism to meet defence support requirements, then MoD policy is in the vanguard of an inevitable global trend. The MoD claims PPPs are successful and proven management tools that have improved defence support without offending traditional military values.[71] It has been keen to point out that PPPs in defence are adopted only after politically "neutral" cost-effectiveness calculations, rather than in response to any ideological commitment to forms of privatization. The MoD claims its:

> approach [to PPPs on deployed operations] is pragmatic, with the emphasis of encouraging innovations through commercial and in-house solutions depending on whichever is better placed to deliver required services at best value. There is no predisposition towards either public or private sector.[72]

As such, MoD sees itself at the cutting edge of defence management innovation because:

> There is huge international interest in the UK's approach to developing partnerships between the public and private sectors. It is an area of public policy where the UK leads the world. Over 50 countries have consulted the Treasury about the PFI. Some, like Italy, Ireland, Japan and the Netherlands are following us in the way we organise within government to deliver partnerships. Some are legislating to enable them to happen.[73]

Consequently, MoD assumes it is a world leader in harnessing private sector support to enhance defense affordability and effectiveness to the extent

---

[68] Kinsey, pp. 244, 273.
[69] *Ibid.*, p. 166.
[70] For a discussion, see M. Brereton and M. Temple, "The New Public *Service* Ethos: An Ethical Environment for Governance," *Public Administration*, Vol. 7, No. 3, 1999, pp. 455–474.
[71] A. Gray and B. Jenkins, "From Public Administration to Public Management: Reassessing a Revolution?" *Public Administration*, Vol. 73, Spring 1995, p. 81.
[72] MoD, "Public Private Partnerships: Changing the way we do business," *http://www.mod.uk/business/ppp/intro.htm.*
[73] HM Treasury, *Public Private Partnerships*, p. 9.

that "the pressures of the modern age will eventually oblige everyone to follow suit."[74]

"Too Far" Critique

The MoD has acknowledged there are "several conflicting points of view" about contractor battlefield support, and that some remain "cautious about possible impact on fighting capability."[75] This alludes to the criticism that MoD risks going "too far" with "unreflective" outsourcing schemes[76] that fail to reduce defense costs and risk degrading combat capability by placing the armed services "at the mercy of a private agent[s]."[77] This "too far" perspective raises concerns about each of the six main premises underpinning MoD's case for deployed contractor support.

The challenge to MoD's assumption that outsourcing is necessarily cheaper than in-house military provision employs two modes of analysis. One is the "Theory of Agency," concerned with understanding conflicting goals between contract providers and contract purchasers.[78] Because it occurs under nonprofitmaking "public service conditions," direct military provision of support functions is assumed to take place in an environment where policymakers have full visibility and control over service delivery.[79] Correspondingly, the "Theory of Agency" suggests that outsourcing introduces inherent tensions between the armed services' security goals and a contractor's imperative to maximise profits, under new circumstances where the armed services' visibility and control are reduced. "Too far" critics argue that opportunistic contractors can exploit this reduced visibility and control, in stark contrast to the situation when the armed services "had the position of a permanent monopoly."[80]

"Too far" critics tend to accept that the scope for contractor opportunism is minimised when markets for military contracts are "contestable," namely, where competitive tendering allows military customers to select between competitively determined bids, and when precise output requirements can

---

[74] C. Pollitt, "Convergence: The Useful Myth?" *Public Administration*, Vol. 79, No. 4, 2001, p. 935.
[75] Speech by UK Minister of State for the Armed Forces, John Spellar.
[76] Frost, p. 41.
[77] Singer, p. 158.
[78] For an extended discussion, see Singer; E. Fredland and A. Kendry, "The Privatization of Military Force: Economic Virtues, Vices and Government Responsibilities," *Cambridge Review of International Affairs*, Autumn-Winter 1999, Vol. XIII, No. 1, pp. 147–164; and, D. Braddon, P. Dowdall and A. Kendry, "Organizational Reform, Market Testing and Defence," in D. Braddon andD. Foster, eds., *Privatization: Social Science Themes and Perspectives*, Aldershot: Dartmouth, 1996, pp. 95–127.
[79] On "public service ethos," see, for example, B. J. O'Toole, "The Loss of Purity: The Corruption of Public Service in Britain," *Public Policy and Administration*, Vol. 8, 1993, p. 3.
[80] G. Boyne, "Comparing the Performance of Local Authorities: An Evaluation of the Audit Commission Indicators," *Local Government Studies*, Vol. 23, No. 4, 1997, p. 701.

be specified.[81] Here, MoD can agree on fixed price contracts with a chosen supplier and impose rigid performance indicators to monitor contractor compliance.

However, "too far" critics point out that contestability rarely applies to contracting for deployed operational activities. On the one hand, the supplier base for battlefield equipment maintenance, logistics, and support functions is often limited to original equipment manufacturers or a small number of large specialized firms with niche expertise.[82] On the other, uncertainties about precise requirements for future operational contingencies mean that the armed services rarely can impose fixed price arrangements when signing contracts.[83] The concern here is that profit-seeking contractors have scope for "expost rent extraction" by exploiting uncertainties to increase the price of service delivery in ways not originally envisaged by the armed services at the contracting stage, thereby increasing the overall cost of service delivery. [84]

The other analytical perspective employed is "Transaction Cost" theory. This emerged to explain why organizations conduct functions in-house so extensively, given the widely acknowledged optimal resource allocating properties of competitive markets. Transaction Cost theory suggests in-house production can be more cost-effective when any additional "transaction costs" of planning, bargaining, modifying, and enforcing a contract with an external supplier outweigh the savings from competitive tendering. "Too far" critics claim that "hidden" costs, including contractor protection and other military support to contractor personnel during deployments, are seldom included in MoD comparisons of armed service and outsourced provision.[85]

Combining Theory of Agency and Transaction Cost perspectives, "too far" critics claim there is no systematic evidence to prove outsourcing is cheaper than military provision,[86] and that military provision might be more cost-effective precisely for deployed operational support functions where contractors have incentives to behave opportunistically, future requirements are uncertain, and the number of potential external suppliers is small.

81 E. Pint and R. Hart, *Public-Private Partnerships: Proceedings of the US-UK Conference on Military Installation Assets, Operations, and Services April 14–16, 2000*, Santa Monica, CA: RAND, 2001, p. 53.

82 J. R. Withers, "Contracting for Depot-Level Maintenance," *Army Logistician*, January/February 2000, p. 5.

83 On cost plus contracting and monitoring issues, see Singer, Ch 10. For a wider treatment of the difficulties in making rigorous connections between quantitative performance measures and the objectives of outsourcing, see Boyne.

84 For an extended discussion, see Singer, pp. 155–157; and Fredland and Kendry, p. 156.

85 M. F. Pausch, "Air Force Deployments and Support Services Contracts," *Air Force Journal of Logistics*, Vol. XXIV, No. 1, Spring 2000, p. 10.

86 E. A. Orsini and G. T. Bublitz, "Contractors on the Battlefield: Risks on the Road Ahead," *Army Logistician*, January-February 1999, p. 1.

These conclusions reflect a wider critique of public sector contracting out, which holds that the implications of outsourcing are:

> . . . often assumed or promised, but not well-documented. Relations between cause and effect are contested; for example, indicators of efficiency and effectiveness are often elusive, side effects are hard to trace and the methodology used in evaluating . . . [outsourcing] . . . is often inadequate. The gap between an emphasis on evaluation and performance assessment in the reform model on the one hand, and the lack of real evaluation of the reform models themselves on the other, is especially striking...because their legitimacy is based on results.[87]

Second, "too far" critics question MoD claims that outsourcing necessarily releases resources for defense modernization and enhances front line capability. In the absence of systematic evidence to prove that private firms can provide battlefield support more cheaply than military alternatives, it has been suggested that the resource redistribution anticipated by MoD is illusory. Critics also challenge MoD claims that safe and secure "benign" areas for contractors exist. Instead, they claim the reality of the contemporary battlespace is "more complex, more dynamic and non-linear" which means that there is a less well-defined "front line" or "rear area."[88] Moreover, the extended range of contemporary weapons systems and threats of enemy interdiction suggest the vulnerability of civilian personnel is significantly greater than MoD policy implies.[89] On this basis, critics suggest that the use of civilian personnel on deployed operations is more likely to tie up the military with contractor protection rather than releasing soldiers for front line duties.[90] They also claim that, as battlefield support functions are increasingly outsourced, then the residual military forces for contractor protection are likely to dwindle, further overstretching scarce military assets.

Third, "too far" critics question MoD assumptions that the private sector can perform battlefield support without undermining operational effectiveness. Instead, they contend that outsourcing generates inherent risks to mission effectiveness. This concern stems from the assumption that "military institutions" are optimized to provide combat and deployed support. As legally recognized organizations controlled directly by the state, armed

[87] T. Christensen, P. Laegreid, and L. Wise, "Transforming Administrative Policy," *Public Administration*, Vol. 80, No. 1, 2002, p. 154.

[88] D. Moore and P. Antill, "British Army Logistics and Contractors on the Battlefield," *RUSI Journal*, February 2000, p. 51.

[89] See D. Moore and P. Antill, "Focused Logistics: Holy Grail or Poisoned Chalice? *RUSI Journal*, October 1999, p. 30.

[90] See Reeve, p. 4. For example, it has been suggested that if contractors are required for deployments where a nuclear, biological, or chemical (NBC) threat emerges, then contractor protection is likely require additional money and force structure. See Lieutenant Colonel M. A. Brown, *Implications of Outsourcing on Network Centric Warfare*, USAWC Strategy Research Project, Carlisle PA: U.S. Army War College, 2002, p. 14.

services have a legal mandate to deliver lethal force and are accorded "combatant" status under international law. The armed services' organizational characteristics, that include rank structures, discipline and training regimes, military doctrine, and structures that combine formal hierarchy and functional specialization (the "line and staff" system), are designed specifically to foster group cohesion and "effectiveness in battle."[91] Finally, armed service personnel have unique conditions of employment that include subjugation to military law and "unlimited liability" to obey legal orders.[92] From this starting point, "too far" critics identify various ways that outsourcing risks mission accomplishment by diluting the proven operational benefits of direct military provision.[93]

Critics point to operational constraints that arise because the military cannot "command and control contractors in the sense that it commands and controls (C^2) military units and soldiers.[94] One C^2 concern here is that a system of "contract management rather than command" erodes the armed services' ability "to adapt logistics structures and procedures to changing situations, missions and concepts."[95] Castillo, for example, claims that:

> A commander's freedom and ability to improvise quickly in using tactics, employing weapons, and deploying personnel have long been considered essential to victory in combat. A contract–a legal, binding document–even when written with the best of intentions, cannot cover every possible contingency in advance. To stop during wartime, no matter how briefly, to rewrite or renegotiate a contractor's obligations severely limits a commander's ability to accomplish the mission.[96]

Another C^2 concern arises from inherent difficulties in measuring contractor readiness and ability to deploy. Readiness states of military units are measured systematically in terms their ability to achieve mission tasks, and logistics units maintain excess capacity to meet potential surge requirements for unplanned contingencies. Conversely, critics argue that contractors are unlikely to maintain such excess capacity because it is costly and cuts into their profit margins.[97] As military commanders lack direct control over contractor functions, then deficiencies in contractor readiness might be difficult to detect, undermining the commander's ability to answer the

---

[91] S. Deakin, *British Civil-Military Relations: An Introduction*, June 1997, p. 13.
[92] *Ibid.*, p. 12.
[93] Orsini and Bublitz, p. 1.
[94] J. A. Fortner, "Managing, Deploying, Sustaining, and Protecting Contractors on the Battlefield," *Army Logistician*, September–October 2000, p. 1.
[95] Orsini and Bublitz, p. 2.
[96] L. A. Castillo, "Waging War with Civilians: Asking the Unanswered Questions," *Aerospace Power Journal*, Fall 2000, p. 3.
[97] Withers, p. 5.

question, "How are we fixed for war?"[98] Analyses of contractor support to British Army combat units, for example, suggest:

> It is unlikely that in a normal situation, civilian production facilities, support assets, and transport assets will be available [within the deployment timetable of Army units] unless they remain uncommitted to other ventures and earmarked solely for MoD use, which in all probability will command a premium price. It may therefore be more cost effective in certain situations to rely on military assets rather than civilian ones.[99]

A further cluster of "operational inflexibilities" identified by critics stem from the legal status of contractors, which, it is argued, impose constraints that are absent with military provision.[100] Military commanders have less direct control over a contractor's workforce than military personnel, and contractors cannot be disciplined for violations of the Uniform Code of Military Justice.[101] Moreover, a fundamental difference is that "contractors are not soldiers, and they cannot be exposed to the same risks as soldiers."[102] This means that contractors are precluded from performing purely military functions that include occupying defensive positions or providing direct support to hostile operations.

According to "too far" critics, these legal factors create a range of operational rigidities and C^2 complications that are absent with military personnel. For example, a problem for commanders is determining the boundaries of "direct support of hostile operations," as:

> A system contractor employee who travels to the area of operations to perform minor technical maintenance on a weapon system that is still operational and capable of performing its intended mission may be violating the constraints against support to hostile operations. On the other hand, the same person performing the same maintenance on the same item in a maintenance facility in a safe area may not be in violation of the constraint.[103]

These complexities generate potential problems that are absent with direct military provision: on the one hand, "by having a contractor accomplish a particular job, field commanders may be asking them to give up their

[98] Orsini and Bublitz, p. 2.
[99] Moore and Antill, 1999, p. 32.
[100] Under the Laws of the Hague and the Laws of Geneva, contractors on deployed operations are not categorized as "combatants" because they are not subject to the armed service's internal disciplinary system, are not trained to conduct operations in compliance with the laws of armed conflict, and are not subordinate to the field commanders. Instead, they are accorded a special interim status between combatants and noncombatants categorized as "civilians authorised to accompany the force." Like noncombatants, contractors cannot be deliberately targeted for military action, but the functions they are supporting can, which means that if they are killed or wounded, this is regarded legally as legitimate collateral damage. For an extended discussion, see S. J. Zamparelli, "Competitive Sourcing and Privatization: Contractors on the Battlefield: What have we Signed up for?" *Air Force Journal of Logistics*, Fall 1999, Vol. 23, Issue 3, p. 8.
[101] *Ibid.*, p. 9.
[102] Fortner, p. 5.
[103] *Ibid.*

protected status if captured"; on the other, the military commander may be violating the law of war by having a contractor participate in an activity that is *de facto* in direct support of hostile operations.[104]

A final series of operational concerns surround MoD claims that contractors are used only to "augment" deployed forces rather than "replace" core tasks that must be performed by military personnel. According to "too far" critics, MoD's failure to define "core functions" or distinguish between "augmentation" and "replacement"[105] has meant that "augmentation" merely describes "outsourced functions without any reference to potential impact on warfighting."[106] The conclusion here is that the armed services may now lack the military personnel to fill mission critical roles if contractors are not present.

Accordingly, the "too far" critics argue that if the armed services lack personnel to fill mission critical functions, the MoD premise that contractors can be relied upon to deliver these functions is questionable. Instead, critics claim the armed services' reliance on private firms can create "critical dependencies" that arise because contractors are inherently less reliable than military units. Whereas military personnel can be compelled to perform mission requirements:

> The Services cannot ensure that the contractor will be there when hostilities begin. Legally, contractors cannot be compelled to go into harm's way, even when under contract, unless there is a formal declaration of war.[107]

The risk that contractors might refuse to service contracts is not limited to those firms directly in receipt of MoD contracts, as prime contractors often rely on an extensive array of potentially unreliable subcontractors to meet deployed operational requirements.[108] "Too far" critics argue this risk is far from theoretical, citing a case during the 1990 Gulf War where a contractor, fearing missile attacks against its employees, withdrew its personnel from Saudi Arabia because "the company alleged that the risk of death or injury to its employees outweighed the profit motive for the company."[109] In the same vein, a more "insidious" risk is that "in a contractor-rich, deployed environment," multinational corporations contracted to support military deployments might decide that the loss of MoD business "is less of a business risk than the loss of more vital business interests [e.g., contracts with other governments] or personal safety in other areas."[110]

---

104 Zamparelli, p. 9. For a more detailed discussion, see A. Faite, "Involvement of Private Contractors in Armed Conflict: Implications under International Humanitarian Law," *Defence Studies*, Vol. 2, No. 4, pp. 166–183.
105 See Withers, p. 2; and Zamparelli, p. 11.
106 Zamparelli, p. 4.
107 *Ibid.*, p. 5.
108 Orsini and Bublitz, p. 2.
109 Brown, p. 15.
110 Pausch, p. 10.

The net effect, critics argue, is that the armed services might lose mission critical support capability as a result of outsourcing. Equally significant, the concern is that outsourcing has left the armed services without the capacity to fill in if contractors are not present,[111] to the extent that the option of "turning to military members in times of contractor failure will become less of an option."[112] Consequently, in contrast to direct military provision, the "no looking back" nature of contractor support means there are potentially significant critical capability shortfalls if contractors withdraw their support.[113] Consequently, the crux of the "too far" operational concerns is that the UK armed services have inadequate mechanisms to evaluate whether management by contract rather than command affects the delivery of military capability.

In contrast to MoD assumptions that outsourcing enhances the cohesion of the armed services, "too far" critics claim that it erodes their morale, combat effectiveness, and professionalism. At the general level, the claim is that reliance on civilians for deployed operational support appears to threaten "the traditional separation of military and civilian society that has been central to the organizational ethos of the armed forces,"[114] which

> risks turning the military vocation into a trade, thereby eroding the moral content of military service and diminishing the serviceman in his own eyes. The end result of this process will [be] . . . the destruction of the ethos which enables men to fight wars with courage and honour.[115]

A central claim is that by "relying excessively on partnerships and by contracting out an increasing portion of what were once in-house defence activities . . . there is a danger that the clear division between military and civilian spheres may continue to blur."[116]

Concerns about the impact of a blurring of military and civilian spheres broadly reflect concerns raised in Charles Moskos's "institution/occupation" thesis.[117] According to Moskos, traditional notions of military service as a "calling or vocation, to the nation by its citizens, legitimated by broadly based national values" ["institutional military"] has been giving way to a subjective definition of military service as an occupation in the labor market, involving the performance of work for civilian types of rewards under specified contractual conditions ["occupational military"]." Moskos, and

[111] *Ibid.*, p. 9.
[112] Castillo, p. 5.
[113] *Ibid.*, p. 3.
[114] D. Detomasi, "The New Public Management and Defense Departments: The Case of Canada, *Defense and Security Analysis*, Vol. 18, No. 1, p. 66.
[115] C. Coker, 'Selling the Regimental Silver: The Dangers of Privatization," in G. Frost, ed., *Not Fit to Fight: The Cultural Subversion of the Armed Services in Britain and America*, London: Social Affairs Unit, 1999, p. 19.
[116] Detomasi, p. 65.
[117] For a discussion, see C. C. Moskos and F. R. Wood, *The Military: More than Just a Job?* Pergamon-Brassey's: London, 1988.

subsequent analysts, claim that forms of civilianization have exacerbated a relative shift from "institutional" to "occupational" armed services, which risks a diminution of their military effectiveness. This erosion of military effectiveness, it is argued, stems from a perception that if support functions can be transferred to the private sector, then there is nothing distinctive about the military function, and "the armed services must not underestimate the effect on morale and discipline if their personnel see contractors responding to different codes of conduct and enjoying a better quality of life in a theatre of operation."[118] As service personnel can compare their terms and conditions with civilian contractors, then incentives for trained military personnel to seek potentially more lucrative employment with private firms might increase military outflow to industry.[119]

More specifically, critics argue that civilianization of home based support functions can have further adverse effects. One claim is that contractorization throughout the logistic pipeline means that uniformed personnel are "increasingly relegated to militarily essential, deployable activities," and limited homebase posting opportunities have negative impacts on force retention and morale.[120] Related concerns are that outsourcing erodes the armed services' skills base, reduces valuable training opportunities,[121] and erodes "core skills and low-level expertise and experience among military personnel...[that would] would require several years."[122]

Given these concerns about the economic and operational implications of outsourcing, some "too far" critics question why MoD and other defense departments have pursued private sector solutions with such vigor.[123] Frost is illustrative of those who claim it reflects a conspiracy between:

> . . . cost-cutting governments enthusiastic to implement innovations that have led to greater efficiency in the private sector, but which cut across the

[118] Moore and Antill, 2000, p. 50.
[119] Castillo, p. 5.
[120] Pausch, p. 11.
[121] See Orsini and Bublitz, p. 3; and U.S. General Accounting Office, *Military Operations: Contractors Provide Vital Services to Deployed Forces but Are Not Adequately Addressed in DOD Plans*, p. 9.
[122] Reeve, p. 4.
[123] See, for example, N. Brunsson and J. P. Olson, *The Reforming Organization*, London and New York: Routledge, 1993; C. Pollitt and G. Bouckaert, eds., *Public Management Reform: A Comparative Analysis*, Oxford: OUP, 2000; C. Hood, "Exploring variations in public management reform of the 1980s," in H. Bekke, J. Perry, and T. Toonen, *Civil Service Systems in Comparative Perspective*, Bloomington: Indiana University Press, 1996; B. Peters and D. Savoie, eds., *Taking Stock: Assessing Public Sector Reforms*, Montreal: McGill-Queens University Press, 1998; P. Keraudern and H. Van Mierlo, "Theories of Public Management Reform and their Practical Implications," in T. Verheijen and D. Coombes, eds., *Innovation in Public Management*, Cheltenham: Edward Elgar, 1998; C. Pollitt, "Justification by work or by faith," *Evaluation*, 1995, Vol. 1, No. 2, pp. 133–54; C. Pollitt, "Is the Emperor in his Underwear? An Analysis of the Impact of Public Management Reform," *Public Management: An International Journal of Theory and Research*, 2000, Vol. 2, No. 2, pp. 181–99; G. Boyne, "Bureaucratic Theory Meets Reality: Public Choice and Service Contracting in U.S. Government," *Public Administration Review*, Vol. 58, November/December 1998, pp. 474–84; D. Kettl, *The Global Public Management Revolution: A Report on the Transformation of Governance*, Washington DC: Brookings, 2000; and J. Kelsey, *The New Zealand Experiment*, Auckland: Auckland University Press, 1997.

> grain of military culture . . . The accomplices in this process of institutional subversion are those at the senior levels within the Armed Forces who, for a variety of reasons, have failed to distinguish adequately between those reforms which are compatible with the military culture, those which are bound to damage it, and those who know perfectly well what is at stake but have chosen to remain silent.[124]

Other critics argue that because the UK government is ideologically committed to an expanded role for the private sector and as officials with "a stake in the process"[125] are tasked to implement outsourcing policies, then there are incentives and opportunities for government to overstate the financial and operational gains from military outsourcing. Several reasons have been suggested as to why MoD and other defence departments might pursue outsourcing strategies that "do not necessarily have anything to do with . . . gains in efficiency and effectiveness."[126] As Pollitt points out, officials might be required to respond to coercive central government imposition of outsourcing policies. Where direct coercion does not apply, officials might conclude that the safest strategy is to "copy whatever is in fashion" within other national defense departments ["mimic isomorphism"], or officials responsible for managing support capabilities may have been educated to assume outsourcing is more efficient than in-house alternatives during their professionalization and institutionalization ["normative isomorphism"]. There might also be individual or unit incentives for officials to be seen to be in the vanguard of outsourcing policy that could take the form of enhanced promotion prospects within the armed services or the enticement of subsequent "rolling door" employment with private firms in receipt of outsourcing contracts.[127] Given the political and bureaucratic market place in which outsourcing policies have been formulated and implemented, "too far" critics conclude that contractors on the battlefield are far from being an inevitable global trend.

"Too Little" Critique

From the opposite extreme, MoD has also been criticized doing "too little" to harness the potential economic and operational gains from far more extensive private sector involvement in defense.[128] This "too little" perspective starts with the premise that the private sector could provide most defense support functions and concludes that bureaucratic barriers within the MoD and armed services have militated against outsourcing being pursued to its logical extreme. The outcomes of these bureaucratic barriers,

[124] Frost, pp. 38–39.
[125] *Inside the Air Force* 1997, cited in J. M. Brower, "Outland: The Vogue of DOD Outsourcing and Privatization," *Acquisition Review Quarterly*, Fall 1997, p. 390.
[126] Pollitt, pp. 933–947.
[127] *Ibid.*
[128] Stokoe, p. 11.

it is argued, have been missed financial and operational opportunities to the armed services themselves and, ultimately, to the UK taxpayer.

The intellectual basis of the "too little" perspective is the sustained attack on government bureaucracy as a mechanism for public service delivery mounted by "Public Choice" theories.[129] Public Choice theorists share the assumption that all individuals and groups are self-interested maximizers of their own utility, and that fundamental differences in utility maximizing behavior exist between private firms and public sector organizations. They identify the motive force for managers of firms in competitive markets to be profits' maximization. Correspondingly, it is assumed that, in the absence of a profit motive, the instrumental goal for public sector bureaucrats is to maximize their bureau's budget. Public choice theorists claim that budget maximizing provides bureaucrats with instrumental gains that might include improved promotion prospects, enhancement of their agency's reputation among the bureaucrat's peer group, and the creation of organizational slack that provides extra resources that can be used to meet unusual risks or crises when they occur.[130] Moreover, bureaucrats are able to pursue budget maximizing strategies because they enjoy a near monopoly of information on the costs of service provision in their area of public service delivery, and because the politicians responsible for their bureau will generally support budgetary increases in their area.

"Too little" critics adapt Public Choice assumptions to assert that the MoD and armed services are fundamentally no different from all other public sector bureaucracies in that "they are goal-seeking and concerned primarily with growth, improvement, and, ultimately, their own survival."[131] In doing so, they tend to regard the "noninstrumental" variables of military organization and culture as a disguise for the armed services to maximise the instrumental goals of budget maximization and the preservation of monopoly in-house delivery of defense capability.[132]

According to "too little" critics, the inherent budget maximizing tendencies of "military bureaucrats" have a number of implications. First, the monopoly of information the "military bureaucracy" has on the costs of delivering defense capability enables defense officials to lobby central government for funding levels that "characteristically produce a radical oversupply of agency outputs."[133] Second, there are few incentives for the "military bureaucracy" to seek efficiency improvements in defense

[129] The summary of "Public Choice" economics in this section draws extensively from P. Dunleavy, *Democracy, Bureaucracy and Public Choice*, London: Harvester Wheatsheaf, 1991.
[130] *Ibid.*, p. 155.
[131] M. Edmonds, *Armed Services and Society*, Boulder, CO: Westview Press, 1990, p. 81.
[132] M. Zafirovski, "Administration and Society: Beyond Public Choice," *Public Administration*, Vol. 79, No. 3, p. 666.
[133] Dunleavy, p. 159.

delivery because any savings could lead to overall defense budget reductions. Third, the "military bureaucracy's" budget maximizing opportunities are enhanced when the armed services provide defense functions under inhouse monopoly conditions because officials have a monopoly on information of delivery costs when negotiating budgets with policymakers. On this basis, critics claim that the in-house military provision is "axiomatically less efficient than market processes" because there are inherent disincentives for defense officials to look for cheaper modes of service delivery.

Consequently, according to critics, any central government-imposed requirement to outsource defense activities:

> . . . clearly threatens . . . [the "military bureaucracy"] . . . by greatly increasing uncertainty and risk for budget-maximizing officials, and creating a much more hostile and turbulent environment for them to operate in. Competition with private firms forces [military bureaucrats] to specify detailed trade-offs between budgets and outputs and explicitly to justify previously customary service standards. It enhances sponsors' power and erodes agencies' capacity to oversupply outputs.[134]

Under these circumstances, "too little" critics infer that if the "military bureaucracy" confronts externally imposed imperatives to outsource functions, officials are likely to respond with minimalist policies that imply compliance as a strategy to deflect government away from genuinely radical budget cutbacks.

"Too little" critics point to various manifestations of "façade privatization" in MoD's approach to outsourcing. They claim that, despite rhetoric to the contrary, MoD has done little to change the market structure of defense support provision leading to a perpetuation of "excessive" in-house supply monopoly. This assessment is indicative of MoD's *Competing for Quality* program:

> Despite all the hype and promises, the program has been far too shallow in application and has not lived up to the expectations of industry. Most of the defence activities under scrutiny have remained on MoD premises, under MoD guise in one form or another. . . . Constrained by Whitehall rules and regulations the CFQ concept has lacked adventure, imagination, innovation and entrepreneurial spirit . . . There has been no real privatization, nor meaningful transfer of activities to industrial bases . . . [in-house provision flourishes] if without a true comparison against industrialization options. . . . This [is] a tragedy, for though MoD can point to having met identified financial savings targets, it has failed to reach possible and achievable goals that full integration with industry might bring.[135]

[134] *Ibid.*, p. 231.
[135] Pickard, pp. 37–38.

Similarly, others claim that, though competition between in-house units and the private sector has occurred:

> The opportunities for competition are far from exhausted. The possibilities include . . . the greater use of market testing, including its extension to activities traditionally excluded from such competition. Ultimately, the aim would be to identify those "core" functions of the armed forces which cannot be contracted out.[136]

In addition, critics claim that MoD exaggerated operational "necessities" as a strategy to retain the vast majority of support functions within the military chain of command.[137] The conclusion they draw is that MoD has pursued such a "façade privatization" program that has limited the scale and scope of outsourcing, along with the economies, efficienciess and operational gains that greater private sector involvement could generate.

It could be argued that the force of the "too little" critique has been eroded by the scale of MoD's program of market testing and PPPs since the early 1980s, and more recent initiatives to use contractors for deployed operational support. However, since private sector delivery of defence support functions remains the exception rather than the rule, and given the "too little" proposition that "anything not directly involved in warfighting should be outsourced," then analysis is required into whether MoD policies and procedures deliberately militate against private sector involvement.[138]

MoD Policy Implementation: Evidence and Issues

The survey of MoD orthodoxies, and the "too far" and "too little" perspectives, identify the major claims and counterclaims surrounding contractor support to deployed operations. In doing so, they reveal the general areas of controversy and the questions that need to be addressed if the performance of MoD outsourcing policy is to be evaluated (Figure 5). Despite these major controversies, no systematic and independent assessment of MoD policy has yet emerged. In part, this reflects the newness of contractors on deployed operations and MoD's acknowledgement that it is still "feeling [its] way on this."[139] It also reflects the limited amount of information on the cost and performance of contractors that has so far entered the public domain. However, sufficient detail is available for a preliminary assessment of the key issues in the debate.[140]

---

[136] K. Hartley, "Defense Markets," *Economic Affairs*, Vol. 17, No. 4, December 1997, p. 26.

[137] See, for example, E. Mellon, "Executive Agencies: Leading Change from the Outside-in," *Public Money and Management*, Vol. 13, No. 2, April–June 1993, pp. 5–11.

[138] Withers.

[139] House of Commons Defence Select Committee, Fourth Report, Session 2001–02, July 3, 2002, Para. 54.

[140] This section draws from interviews with PJHQ and Defence Manufacturers Association personnel.

Figure 5: Criteria for Evaluating MoD Outsourcing Initiatives

The Bureaucratic Dimension: Have bureaucratic factors within MoD and armed services encouraged or militated against PPPs in UK defence?

The Financial Dimension: Are PPPs cheaper or more expensive than direct military provision of defence support function?

Can cost savings be attributed to competitive tendering, contractorization and "partnerships" with private sector?

How effective are MoD measures to minimize the scope for ex post rent extraction on defence support contracts?

How are transaction costs factored into MoD assessments of financial effects outsourcing?

The Resource Redistribution Dimension: What are MoD assessments of the funding and military personnel that have been released/re-directed as a direct result of outsourcing?

What form has the redistribution of funds/personnel taken?

Has resource redistribution reduced military "overstretch"?

The Operational Dimension: How effective are MoD C2 arrangements to manage contractors on deployed operations?

Has MoD outsourcing "augmented" or "replaced" in-house military capabilities, and how effective are MoD measures to manage the operational risks of potential contractor withdrawal?

How effective are MoD procedures to evaluate the impact of defence PPPs on the morale, cohesion, ethos, and professionalism of the armed services?

The Bureaucratic Dimension

Have bureaucratic factors within the MoD and armed services encouraged or militated against PPPs in UK defence? As the previous section demonstrates, MoD has been under sustained criticism from those claiming it has pursued ill-conceived privatization schemes and others who consider it has failed to exploit outsourcing potential. However, actually assessing whether MoD has gone "too far" or done "too little" is fraught with theoretical and empirical difficulties. At the theoretical level, there is a range of inherent difficulties in producing criteria to measure any optimum level of outsourcing that MoD should undertake. At the empirical level, "commercial-in-confidence" caveats surrounding MoD contracting processes preclude a detailed case-by-case analysis of how officials have resolved whether to outsource or retain functions in-house. However, what can be said is that a broad program of UK defence management reforms since the 1980s appear to have created structures, a "corporate culture" and organizational incentives for MoD officials at all levels to evaluate the scope for private sector involvement across the defense support sector.

Until 1980, MoD's management philosophy had two key tenets. First, as former Secretary of State Malcolm Rifkind observes:

> . . . resources were bid for on a very strong single-Service basis, and success in the annual Long Term Costing (LTC) exercise was judged on the ability to protect the level of budget, or ideally increase it at the expense of the other Services. There was little attempt to measure the cost of individual elements of the [UK defence] program and relate this directly to outputs. Thus we were in no position properly to judge the *value for money* of our annual investment in defence; nor could we assess whether everything we did contributed to the delivery of front line forces.[141]

Second, it was assumed that MoD should retain in-house capabilities across the spectrum of front-line and defense support functions.

Since the early-1980s, MoD concerns about a "funding gap" between defence budgets and stated military commitments[142] have been reflected in programs intended to ensure "more efficient management" of defence resources. The MoD's strategy to achieve "more efficient management" has followed a UK central government-imposed "New Public Management" (NPM) reform agenda, emphasising performance management, devolved financial management, greater decentralization of authority and responsibility within government departments, greater recourse to the use of market-type mechanisms such as internal markets and contracting out, and privatization of market-oriented public enterprises.[143]

In MoD's case, the imperative to adopt NPM-style reforms has been particularly acute. Inherent difficulties in defining the final outputs of defense expenditure, post-Cold War pressures to realize a "peace dividend," and the scale of MoD capital expenditure compared to other government departments have created incentives for MoD to be in the vanguard of UK public sector management reform and a "culture of continuous improvement."[144] As a former MoD Permanent Under Secretary acknowledges:

> The degree to which we [MoD] can demonstrate efficiency is important to us when we make the case for the defence budget in the public expenditure survey each year; we have to show that we are spending it wisely. We need to continue to pursue efficiency therefore, *first*, to produce the cash savings needed under the government's wider efficiency program; *second*, to sustain the maximum output within a given level of resources; and *third*, to underpin

141 M. Rifkind, "Front Line First," *RUSI Journal*, December 1994, p. 3.

142 For a discussion, see K. Hartley, *The Economics of Defence Policy*, London: Brassey's, 1991, Ch. 1; and D. Greenwood, "Expenditure and Management," in P. Byrd, ed., *British Defence Policy: Thatcher and Beyond*, London: Philip Allan, 1991, pp. 36–66.

143 See T. Bovaird, "The Changing Context of Public Policy," in T. Bovaird and E. Loffler, eds., *Public Management and Governance*, London: Routledge, 2003, p. 17.

144 I. Andrews, "Managing Change," *Defence Management Journal*, Issue 22, April 2003, p. 26. Ian Andrew is MoD's Second Permanent Under Secretary.

> our budgetary case in competition with other government departments, for the scarce resource of taxpayer's money.[145]

Evidence suggests that MoD's NPM-style reform program has created the managerial context, organizational framework, and culture to provide incentives for officials to pursue private sector involvement when it is assessed to be more efficient than in-house provision. This has been achieved through MoD's adoption and consolidation of six key central government-imposed NPM-style reforms.

First was the imposition of a quasi-contract between MoD and central government, whereby MoD delivers an agreed defence strategy, program, and military capabilities ("defence outputs") in exchange for its budget allocation ("defence inputs"). The MoD's output targets are currently codified in a "Public Service Agreement" (PSA), or "a contract between MoD and the centre" which contains a 5-year review cycle for all defence activity.[146] Responsibility for delivering the defence strategy set out in the PSA resides with MoD's Defence Management Board (DMB), the membership of which is summarized in Figure 6.

Figure 6: MoD Defence Management Board

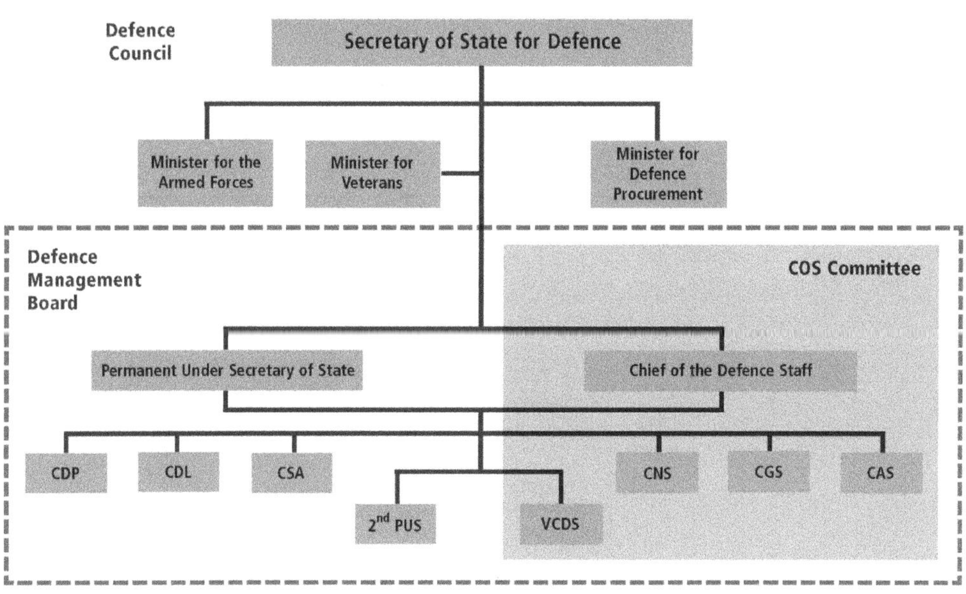

[145] M. Stewart, "Future Resource Management in Defence," *RUSI Journal*, April 1993, p. 75.
[146] K. Tebbit, "Delivering a Coherent Defence Policy," *Defence Management Journal*, Vol. 2, No. 4, 1999, p. 10.

Second was DMB's adoption of output-based strategic management planning. In effect, DMB acts as "the main corporate board of MoD, providing senior level leadership and strategic management of defence," which is reflected in its responsibility for defining the role of UK defence by providing strategic direction, vision, and values; setting objectives and targets that establish the key priorities and defence capabilities necessary to deliver MoD's departmental objectives; resource allocation and strategic balance of investment to match defence priorities and objectives; and, performance management and "driving corporate performance."

Third was delegation of authority and accountability at all levels within MoD and the armed services. Delivery of the DMB's "Departmental Plan," and the financial resources intended to meet it is made to 11 "Top Level" budget holders (TLBs) (see Figure 7), who then delegate resources for the implementation of their output-based plans to subordinate budget holders. Budget holders at all levels in this hierarchy have become "cost-centre" managers with "individual accountability and responsibility, and the concomitant authority to take decisions within clearly-defined parameters without constant reference up the line management chain,"[147] in a system of vertical customer-supplier contracts between each tier of the budget chain.

Figure 7: MoD Top Level Budget System

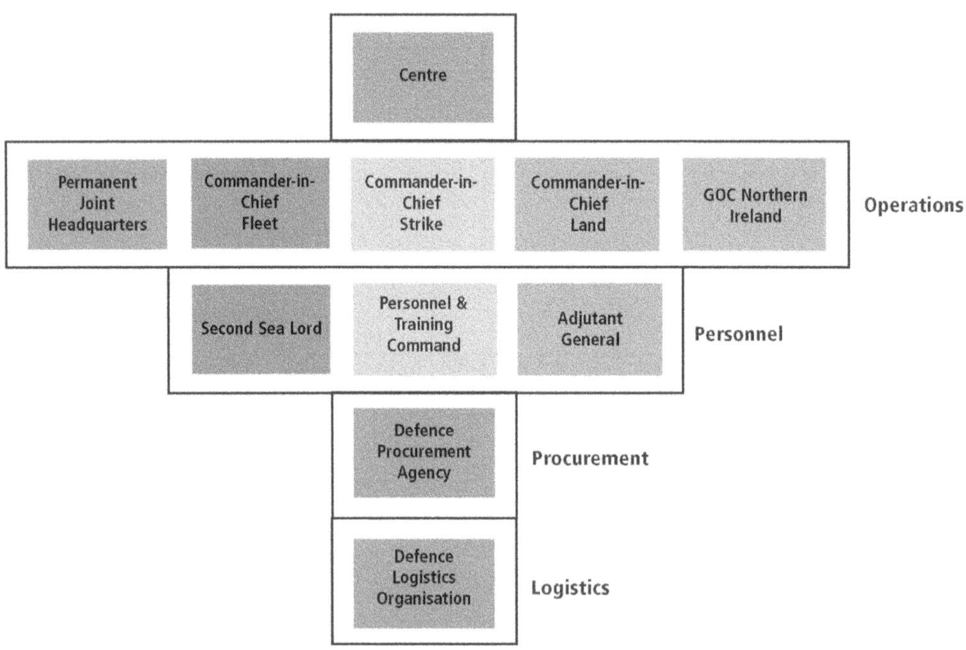

[147] Rifkind, p. 3. *See also* J. Williams and N. Holland "Developing Wider Market Opportunities Through Public Private Partnerships," *Defence Management Journal*, Issue 18, February 2002, pp. 62–63.

Evidence suggests this delegated management structure has generated incentives for all budget holders to pursue private sector partnering opportunities within their area of delegated responsibility. When delegation was first introduced in the early 1990s:

> lower levels of budget holders had the authority to look for value for money wherever it could be found. By so doing, they were therefore relieved of the requirement of having to go through "authorized" channels as in the past. The military were free to use the market place to purchase what they needed, and in essence the wider defence market began to be opened up to the private sector.[148]

In essence, the combination of vertical delegation and MoD's stated commitment to greater private sector provision seems to have created a framework where budget holders have been able to outsource functions in the knowledge they will gain higher-level endorsement. Moreover, outsourcing incentives seem to have been enhanced in 1998 when MoD policy became that certain receipts and efficiency savings from PPPs could be retained by budget holders and redirected to meet their management planning targets.[149]

Fourth was the creation of discrete "businesses" embedded within MoD and the armed services located either within the TLB structure, or operating as freestanding trading funds. This stemmed from the UK government's 1988 *The Next Steps* report, which recommended the establishment of semi-autonomous agencies to carry out the "executive" service delivery functions of government departments.[150] The MoDs operate under frameworks setting out their policy parameters, budgets, targets, and degree of delegated authority. Strategic control of agencies remains with Ministers, but once the policy and framework are set, agency chief executives have the authority to decide how agency objectives are met.[151]

The MoD's "Defence Agencies" currently employ 60 percent of MoD's civilian workforce and 11 percent of total uniformed personnel, and their operating costs account for approximately 35 percent of MoD's overall resource cost.[152] Each agency is mandated to provide defined services that are enshrined in quasi-contractual Customer Supplier Agreements (CSA) and Service Level Agreements (SLA) to "customers" elsewhere across or vertically within the TLB hierarchy. The MoD's stated rationale has been to ensure that "Throughout our business, there is an increasing emphasis on

---

148 M. Edmonds, "Defence Privatization: From State Enterprise to Commercialism, *Cambridge Review of International Affairs*, Autumn-Winter 1999, Vol. XIII, No. 1, p. 123.

149 Efficiency Unit, *Improving Management in Government: The Next Steps*, London: HMSO, 1988.

150 See P. Kemp, "Can the Civil Service Adapt to Managing by Contract?" *Public Money and Management*, Vol. 10, No. 3, Autumn 1990.

151 Ministry of Defence, Performance Report 2000/2001.

152 M. Stewart, "Future Resource Management in Defence," *RUSI Journal*, April 1993, p. 74.

defending the relationship between internal 'customers' and 'suppliers' and, in doing so, strengthening the hand of the customer."[153]

Like MoD budget holders, defence agency chief executives have incentives to meet their CSA and SLA delivery targets by identifying partnering opportunities with the private sector.[154] For example, the Defence Communication Services Agency (DCSA), responsible for providing satellite communications and information delivery to deployed headquarters, is attempting to meet its financial targets by retaining "only those military posts where military expertise is essential" and identifying functions "which can be done perfectly well and probably more cheaply by industry."[155] The Defence Aviation Repair Agency (DARA)—which is responsible for aircraft repair, maintenance, modification, and complementary logistic supply chain support services—has chosen to meet its financial targets by partnering with Agusta Westland and BAE systems.[156] The tri-Service Defence Transport and Movement Agency (DTMA), charged with the acquisition and allocation of freight and passenger movement capacity and movement plans and advice to the armed services, has extensively engaged contract-based capability and capacity.[157] Similarly, the Naval Recruitment and Training Agency (NRTA) has developed a comprehensive approach to meeting its performance targets that has included outsourcing noncore activities, partnership sourcing, and PFI arrangements for capital investment in its training estate.[158]

The fifth reform area has been in the weapons acquisition and logistics fields. Reflecting MoD's wider management reform philosophy, incentives exist for officials to look for private sector partnering in initial weapon procurement and the equipment's through-life support. Under the current "Smart Acquisition" procedures, responsibility for the acquisition and in-service support of individual items of equipment or platforms is delegated to "Integrated Project Teams" (IPTs). The IPTs are located in MoD's Defence Procurement Agency (DPA) until new equipment is brought into service, then they migrate to the Defence Logistics Organization (DLO) to oversee in-service support.[159] An outcome of "Smart Acquisition" is that individual

153 E. Mellon, "Executive Agencies: Leading Change from the Outside-in," *Public Money and Management*, Vol. 13, No. 2, April–June 1993.

154 Chief Executive Rear Admiral Rees Ward, quoted in M. Harte, "Information Anytime, Anywhere," *Defence Management Journal*, Issue 21, December 2002, p. 18.

155 Chief Executive S. Hill, "DARA Spearheads a Radical Change," *Defence Management Journal*, Vol. 4, Issue 2, Spring 2001, p. 6.

156 P. Cunliffe, "A Driving Force for Transport," *Defence Management Journal*, Vol. 3, Issue 2, Spring 2000, p. 27.

157 Chief Executive Rear Admiral J. Chadwick, "Pioneers of Partnering: NRTA Flagship," *Defence Management Journal*, Vol. 2, Issue 4, Autumn 1999, p. 92.

158 Following the 1998 Strategic Defence Review, single-service Land Maritime and Air acquisition and logistics organizations were amalgamated into the joint Defence Procurement Agency and Defence Logistic Organization.

159 Ministry of Defence, *The Smart Acquisition Handbook*, p. 16.

IPTs are tasked with producing cost-effective through-life solutions to capability requirements. Individual IPTs are required to "seek to harness innovation and industrial power to facilitate optimized and integrated commercial solutions" when considering in-service equipment support except in cases where this would "cause unacceptable risk to the front line."[160]

The sixth reform area has been MoD's adoption of a plethora of management tools and techniques originally developed in the private sector. The most significant has been the introduction of "Resource Accounting and Budgeting" (RAB), which measures the financial implications of vertical and horizontal "customer-supplier" transactions, and the cost to MoD of stocks and capital assets ownership.[161] The significance of RAB in the context of MoD outsourcing is two-fold. First, it has enabled MoD budget holders to compare the costs of its in-house activities on an equivalent basis to the private sector, and to identify where private sector provision is more cost-effective.[162] Second, depreciation charges imposed on MoD under RAB have created incentives for budget holders to consider greater reliance on leasing and other modes of PPP service delivery rather than retaining assets and facilities on the Defence Vote.

Consequently, at the strategic level, MoD's management approach since the early 1980s has been informed by a belief in the benefits of competition and contracting, whether internal or external. The overarching theme of MoD internal management reform has been to replace "traditional" bureaucratic structures and processes with a quasi-internal market of customers and suppliers. Here,

> The intended modus operandi of quasi markets is that central [MoD] decision makers determine the output they wish agencies to produce, and then "contract" with [its subordinate civilian and military] agencies to purchase those outputs for an agreed price. Fundamental to this has been the attempt to stimulate a purchaser/provider split, with formal "contracts" governing the terms upon which providers receive payment for the provision of defined outputs.[163]

At the same time, MoD's output-based management planning, delegated management structure, and adoption of new management tools have provided incentives for defense officials at all levels to harness private sector capability.

---

[160] See J. Oughton, "The Defence Logistics Organization—Transforming Logistic Support to the Armed Forces," *World Defence Systems*, Vol. 3, No. 2, July 2001, pp. 97–99.

[161] Hedley and Busby, p. 40.

[162] M. Robinson, "Contract Budgeting."

[163] Jackling, p. 93.

The available evidence suggests that MoD's NPM-style reform program has drawn contractors closer to the front line "in areas that—a few years ago—[were] thought to be the exclusive preserve of the Services."[164] However, more information is required before "too far" and "too little" concerns about the incentive structures surrounding deployed support outsourcing can be fully addressed. On the one hand, more data on the precise criteria employed by MoD officials in evaluating the relative costs and benefits of in-house and private sector alternatives are necessary to evaluate "too far" assertions that battlefield outsourcing reflects an ideological predisposition towards privatization. On the other hand, the release of information on, for example, the relative scale of deployed outsourcing between the various TLBs or the criteria employed to declare certain functions as "no go" areas for outsourcing is required, if "too little" concerns are to be allayed or confirmed.

The Financial Dimension

Have PPPs Reduced UK Defence Support Costs?

Reports by MoD spanning 2 decades all conclude that competitive tendering and contracting-out have generated cost savings across a range of *non-deployed* defence support functions. Audits of the "Competing for Quality" program and other initiatives suggest market testing and strategic outsourcing have produced 23 percent gross average savings on previous in-house delivery costs. According to MoD, when transaction costs "of the competitive process" are deducted, average net savings of approximately 18 percent have been achieved.[165] These results are similar to the average net 20 percent cost reductions the U.S. DoD has identified from the A-76 outsourcing program.[166] Evidence suggests that with "Competing for Quality" and similar programs, MoD has been able to define precise service requirements and contract management regimes prior to the competitive tendering process and attract the multiple private sector bidders necessary to make genuine "market testing" viable.[167]

Correspondingly, the financial outcomes where *deployed operational support functions* have been outsourced are less clear. In part, this reflects that more limited cost data have entered the public domain. It seems that MoD contracting procedures generally impose "value for money" mechanisms

164 Cabinet Office, *Competing for Quality Policy Review: An Efficiency Unit Scrutiny*, London: HMSO, 1996, p. 6.
165 Withers.
166 Cabinet Office, *Competing for Quality Policy Review*, p. 6.
167 Interview, SO1 J4 Contractor Logistics CONLOG. Open book accounting procedures allow MoD to scrutinize contractors' receipts for expenditures incurred in meeting additional MoD requirements not specified when the contract was originally awarded.

and reduce scope for contractor "ex post rent extraction." MoD procedures dictate that contracting authorities should select suppliers following a competition process, and that subsequent variations to service delivery requirements are dealt with through "open book accounting" and at pre-agreed profit rates.[168]

However, evidence indicates that *de facto* contracting processes for deployed support sometimes have been less robust. First, difficulties have been encountered in imposing rigid contract specifications and fixed price contracts for deployed functions where precise future deployed requirements are not known. Limited warning and preparation timescales for unforeseen operational deployments have also meant that MoD contracting authorities have approached "preferred suppliers" rather than employing open competitive tendering. Second, difficulties in predicting precise deployed support requirements have resulted in the award of "indefinite delivery, indefinite quantity" contracts, where MoD informs potential suppliers of the funds available for a particular deployed support function, and the latter submit bids with estimates of profit margins and risk. Under these conditions, questions remain about whether MoD has adopted the most cost-effective contractual framework and what the relative costs of military and civilian provision actually are.

Third, wider questions remain about the extent to which MoD can exploit competitive tendering to meet its deployed support needs. With large equipment-based PFI contracts, which currently include the Army's Heavy Equipment Transporter and the Royal Navy's Roll-On Roll-Off Ferries, the limited potential supplier base has forced MoD to estimate the relative costs of conventional procurement and private sector alternatives using a "Public Sector Comparator" (PSC) rather than market competition. The PSC is a hypothetical estimation of what the project will cost to design, build, and operate, normally based on historical data, and concludes that PFI deals offer a 10 percent saving against the cost of delivering services in-house. However, a concern remains that "calculation of the PSC is a contentious issue and some commentators claim that the difficult task of accurately compiling the PSC leads to [MoD claims of cost] savings that are not realistic."[169]

Consequently, no overwhelming evidence has entered the public domain to prove that the outsourcing of deployed support functions necessarily has been cheaper than direct military provision. Questions remain about whether MoD is engaging contractors in the most cost-effective contractual framework, and also what the relative costs of military and civilian alternatives

[168] S. W. Davies, *Private Finance Supporting the Trigger: An Examination of the Private Finance Initiative to Deliver Operational Capability*, unpublished Master of Defence Administration thesis, Cranfield University, 2003–04, p. 2–7.

[169] Interview, Defence Manufacturers Association CONDO Representative.

are. Until detailed information is released on the methods used by MoD to compare the costs of military and outsourced alternatives, including how transaction costs are factored into such calculations, then the true financial implications of outsourced deployed operational support are likely to remain contested. It may be the case, as MoD suggests, that deployed support contracting has generated economies and that information on the scale and scope of these savings will enter the public domain in due course. Until this occurs, however, then "too far" claims that MoD has an ideological predisposition towards privatization and "too little" concerns about "missed" outsourcing opportunities are likely to persist.

The Resource Redistribution Dimension

What are MoD assessments of the funding and military personnel that have been released/re-directed as a direct result of outsourcing? Whether outsourcing has provided additional resources that have enhanced the UK's overall defence capability remains contested. Despite MoD claims that resource reallocation has occurred, surprisingly little information has entered the public domain. No details have emerged on how or where the purported savings from contracting out have been reinvested across other defense priorities. Moreover, only anecdotal information is available on the redeployment of military personnel released from deployed support functions where activities have been transferred to the private sector.[170]

During Operation TELIC, for example, some 500 KBR personnel and its subcontractors were contracted to construct 10,000 units of temporary accommodation under a contract valued at £120m. However, in this case, it is not clear whether KBR's involvement reflected a calculated decision on MoD's part to release trained military manpower, or whether the UK armed services simply lacked any in-house capability to meet the requirement in the first place.

The resource redistribution dimension is clearly a central variable in the overall impact of military outsourcing. Consequently, until MoD quantifies these aspects of deployed contractor support, controversy is likely to remain. This suggests the need for detailed survey work within MoD to identify both the extend to which resources have been reallocated within defence, and the degree to which any savings have been clawed back by UK central government.

---

[170] See J. Oughton, "The Sinews of War," *Defence Review*, Spring 2002, p. 62.

The Operational Dimension

How Effective are MoD C² Arrangements to Manage Contractors on Deployed Operations?

By the late-1990s, MoD had some limited experience in using contractors on deployed operations. "Urgent Operational Requirement" contracts had been let for military vehicle upgrades in the 1991 Gulf War, camp construction and operation in Bosnia, and road transport from the UK to the Second Line in Theatre in Kosovo.[171] However, MoD officials recognized that the approach at that time had major deficiencies. In the absence of an overarching policy, operational support contracts were let on an unsystematic one-off basis, and issues including the status and security of contractors had not been resolved.[172] Moreover, officials recognized that:

> Short-term perspectives on contracting can restrict timely delivery of operational capability and can be wasteful of resources. This has entailed the drawing up of contracts from scratch, with optimistic timeframe and quality targets. Where these targets are not met (e.g., Bosnia) the effects on the deployed force, particularly on morale and confidence in the system of support, can be particularly detrimental.[173]

A further limitation was that contracts were generally "limited in scope and not buttressed by a solid foundation of policy and doctrine."[174] At the same time, industry's concern was that firms were involved in deployed operations on a "pretty *ad hoc* and frankly risky basis. Much of it was policy on the hoof. But worst of all, there [was] huge opportunity there for misunderstanding, misalignment, and hence failure of the support."[175]

In response, MoD began formulating what were intended to be coherent policy and doctrines to codify contractor battlefield support during 1997. From the outset, MoD sought to ensure partnership with contractors in policy formulation. The "Contractors on Deployed Operations" Partnering Support Steering Group (PSSG) was established which included MoD officials, senior industry representatives, and uniformed engineering and logistics staff. Policy was developed by three PSSG working groups: "Capability Definition and Development," responsible for identifying the scope for contractor involvement and devising mechanisms to measure the risks involved in using contractors in-theatre; the "Personnel Working Group," looking at the legal status of contractors and their position related to the military commander; and, "Contractual and Commercial," which

171 Brigadier T. Cross, "Logistic Support for UK Expeditionary Operations," *RUSI Journal*, February 2000, p. 74.
172 Joint Doctrine and Concepts Centre, Joint Doctrine Pamphlet 4/01, *Contractors on Deployed Operations*, December 2001, p. 1–4.
173 General Sir Sam Cowans, "Perspectives on Current MoD Policy," *RUSI Journal*, February 2000, p. 65.
174 Smart, p. 70.
175 Ministry of Defence, *JSP 567*.

focused on devising differentiation criteria between multifunctional logistic providers and specialized equipment maintainers.

Three major MoD initiatives have emerged. First is the "Contractors on Deployed Operations (CONDO)" policy, intended to harmonize procedures governing all contracts requiring contractors to "deploy in support of operations."[176] Second is MoD's "CONLOG Contract," a single-source enabling commercial support contract covering a range of Combat Support (CS) and Combat Service Support (CSS) capabilities. Third is the "Sponsored Reserve" (SR) Concept, whereby "services normally provided [to MoD] in peacetime by contractor staff are provided on operations by staff drawn from the contractor's workforce who are reservist members of the Armed Forces."[177] With these initiatives, MoD assumes it has measures in place to provide "an assured capability for the military commander" under arrangements that are "profitable for the contractor while demonstrating value for money for MoD," that ensure operational deployments are "as safe and secure as possible for the [contractor] workforce."[178] Evidence suggests that these MoD initiatives have identified and addressed many of the C^2 concerns raised by "too far" critics.

Before the CONDO policy, a limiting factor on UK military deployments arose from the dislocation between MoD arrangements for deployed support contracts and the actual control of contractor capability by military commanders in theatres of operation. The MoD management philosophy of delegation has "empowered" DPA IPTs and DLO Equipment Support Business Units (ESBUs) to contract for logistics functions or equipment support on behalf of the Army, RAF, and the RN, or the Single-Service Front Line Commands (FLCs). Before CONDO was developed, MoD's PJHQ had limited visibility or control over deployed commercial support arrangements entered into by the various contracting authorities. In theory, the PJHQ was the focal point at the "coupling bridge" into operational theatres for all commercial capabilities to support the FLCs. In reality, the PJHQ was bypassed because the FLCs, via the DPA and DLO, maintained direct control over "their" contractor support. The outcome was that PJHQ joint commanders lacked an overall picture of contractor capability available in theatre, or information on the scope of contracts with individual suppliers. Consequently, before CONDO, "too little" concerns about operational constraints arising from "management by contract" seemed valid.

The CONDO policy has introduced various measures to rectify these C^2 deficiencies that increase the oversight that commanders have over contractor

---

[176] *http://www.mod.uk/business/ppp/reserves.htm*, October 1, 2003. The Sponsored Reserve concept originated from the 1992 "Regular/Reserve Forces Mix Study," and legislation was put in place in the 1996 Reserve Forces Act, Part V.

[177] Ministry of Defence, *JSP 567*, p. 6.

[178] *Ibid.*, p. 12.

capacity at their disposal. In procedural terms, the FLCs, DPA, and DLO now pass their in-theatre contractor support requirements to the PJHQ Chief of Joint Operations for authority to deploy. This now ensures full PJHQ visibility of all contractor personnel and assets within the Joint Operating Area (JOA) at any one time, and the opportunity to exploit "best value for money by avoiding duplication of contracts and personnel within the JOA."[179] The CONDO policy also succeeds in integrating contractor support into the PJHQ operational planning process, thereby reducing "too far" concerns about measuring contractor readiness and capability. The PJHQ's Logistics Division[180] has an embedded and permanent "CONLOG Plans" unit that continually identifies and manages actual or potential future requirements for all contractor support, and a "CONLOG Operations Team" responsible for specific planning and implementation of commercial support to particular operations.

In addition, CONDO includes mechanisms to standardize the treatment of contractors and their personnel that apply to all categories of deployed support contracts (Figure 8) to ensure they are "adequately prepared for operational deployments."[181] These measures include training and briefings for contractor personnel on safety and security, discipline arrangements, insurance and indemnity, and detailed guidance intended to educate commanders on the legal aspects of employing contractor capability on deployments. Finally, CONDO includes detailed decisionmaking algorithms for PJHQ and FLC commanders considering the use of contractor support, providing criteria for identifying circumstances when commercial contractor support is optimal, and evaluating the potential operational impacts of contractor withdrawal.

The MoD claims its "CONLOG Contract" has further enhanced operational C^2 by providing "an efficient and cohesive contracting process for elements of support on operations."[182] The CONLOG is a nonexclusive 7-year contract with KBR to provide advice on the employment of contractor capability and to act as a potential single source for a broad range of deployed commercial support traditionally contracted through ad hoc UORs. Unlike other deployed support contracts, the CONLOG is "owned" by the PJHQ,[183] and the PJHQ "CONLOG Plans" organization includes embedded KBR personnel who provide continuous advice on commercial support potential and availability.

---

[179] The J1/J4 Logistics and Personnel staff are responsible for all logistic aspects of the planning, deployment, and sustainment of UK-led operations.
[180] Ministry of Defence, *JSP 567*, p. 14.
[181] *Ibid.*, p. 21.
[182] The PJHQ "contract owner" is the Assistant Chief of Staff ACOS J1/J4.
[183] Ministry of Defence, *JSP 567*, p. 21.

Figure 8: Scope of the CONDO Concept

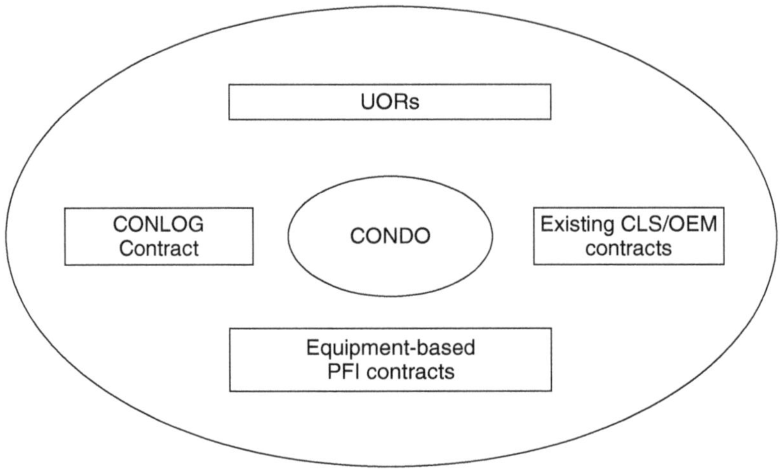

According to MoD, the PJHQ's embedded partnership and "mutual understanding" with KBR enhances deployed C^2 arrangements in several ways.[184] The CONLOG Plans organization and its "CONLOG Operations Team" are involved in each stage of deployed operations from initial "Logistic Estimate" production to the direction, deployment, sustainment, and recovery phases. Consequently, embedded KBR's expertise and capabilities can be exploited at the earliest possible opportunity to prepare detailed schedules of contractor support requirements, to rapidly mobilize a coherent package of commercial capability, and to deconflict similar military and CONLOG capabilities throughout an operation.[185] The terms of the CONLOG Contract, which required KBR to provide detailed deployed commercial package costings within 90 hours of a PJHQ request, ensure operational tempo can be maintained. Moreover, according to MoD, the enabling nature of the CONLOG contract provides joint commanders with flexibility, as private sector support taskings can be added or subtracted at short notice, and the "partnership" enables the PJHQ's to focus on defining its requirement and KBR to use its commercial expertise to focus on meeting the military needs.[186] This close cooperation also extends to the theatre of operation. When circumstances require it, the PJHQ can form a "Deployed CONLOG Operations Team" to support the deployed Force Commander, who manages KBR and subcontractor personnel in the theatre of operation.

[184] Ministry of Defence, Defence Council Instructions Joint Service, Contractors on Deployed Operations, *DCI JS 62 2003*, April 11, 2003, p. 41.
[185] Interview, SO1 J4 Contractor Logistics CONLOG.
[186] Interview, Directorate of Broadening and Deepening Smart Acquisition—Sponsored Reserves, Joint Services Command and Staff College, December 19, 2003.

Consequently, the CONDO and CONLOG initiatives do identify and address a range of C^2 concerns highlighted by "too far" critics. Measures are now in place to provide military commanders with enhanced visibility of contractor assets that should increase flexibility in planning and deployment. Procedures have been established that ensure both commanders and contractors understand the legal scope and limitations of private sector involvement. Indications are that MoD's decision to engage contractors in the formulation of CONDO/CONLOG policy, and to embed contractors in PJHQ operational planning and execution, have paid C^2 dividends.

However, evidence suggests important residual C^2 constraints remain to be addressed. First, though CONDO and CONLOG have introduced more robust protocols, MoD has a complex matrix of some 7,000 stand-alone "legacy" deployed support contracts entered into by the DPA, DLO, and FLCs.[187] Moreover, MoD's management philosophy of delegation means that the plethora of DPA and DLO IPTs can continue unilaterally to sign deployed support contracts on the basis of their individual "value for money" calculations. Though CONLOG does introduce a prime contractor to facilitate and integrate packages of deployed logistics support, this contract currently accounts for just 10 percent of MoD deployed support expenditure. Indications are that MoD intends to rationalize these fragmented contracts over the next 5 years by clustering together under a smaller number of large new prime contracts, but until the contractor supply chain is rationalized in this way, it is likely that C^2 arrangements will remain suboptimal.

Second, analyses into the UK's 2003 intervention in Iraq suggest that "although some positive steps have been taken over recent years to define MoD CONDO policy," there are still areas for improvement. One residual area of concern is that CONDO does not fully identify and reduce the key contractor risks on deployed operations in the areas of personnel security and safety, insurance cover, and corporate reputation. Other concerns are that CONDO fails to establish systems for addressing the impact of operational unknowns on contracts with industry, and that measures to assess the contractor's surge capabilities, availability and readiness for deployed operations could be strengthened.[188]

Has MoD outsourcing "augmented" or "replaced" in-house military capabilities, and how effective are MoD measures to manage the operational risks of potential contractor withdrawal? The MoD's stated policy is that contractor support "is not intended to replace core military manpower in the Order of Battle, but to augment that established when circumstances permit and thus

[187] Higginson Associates, *CONDO Risk Assessment: Final Report*, March 2004.

[188] Ministry of Defence, "The Current MoD Policy for Using Contractors on Deployed Operations," *http://www.ams.mod.uk/ams/contents/docs/condo.htm*, October 1, 2003.

reduce the pressure on deployable, organic logistic support for all three Services."[189] The MoD's objective is to take contractors "as close to the front-line as possible," but not "in circumstances where the operational effectiveness of the Armed Forces would be put at risk."

In response to "too little" concerns, MoD claims that mechanisms are in place to ensure contractor support is only used to "augment" military capability and adequate safeguards to militate against the risk of potential contractor withdrawal. The MoD's first assumption is that its CONDO deployment algorithms provide the necessary criteria and guidance to ensure that commanders only employ commercial capability in circumstances where military alternatives are available, as a safeguard, throughout deployments. The second assumption is that the risk of potential contractor withdrawal is minimized through its SR policy, which is intended to provide "value for money without an unacceptable diminution of capability [by making use of] skills found in the civilian sector to provide support to operations in nonbenign areas."[190]

The SR initiative stems from MoD's 1992 "Regular/Reserve Forces Mix Study," which recommended exploration of the feasibility of using civilians with Reserve status for operational support functions, and was legislated for in the 1996 Reserve Forces Act (Part V).[191] The SR concept enables MoD to contract with private suppliers for support functions provided by staff working as civilians in peacetime or in nonbenign deployed areas, but where the contractors' employees continue to provide services as an integral part of the deployed force in nonbenign areas as trained reservists. According to MoD, the SR model guarantees an assured and integrated contractor service beyond the "benign edge" that is more cost-effective than in-house military provision. In C^2 terms, the fact that contractor personnel become members of the Reserve forces on operational deployments means they are fully integrated into the military chain of command. In conceptual terms, MoD views as such, SRs as "the manning bridge between the service that a contractor may readily provide routinely using civilians, but could not provide routinely using civilians during certain operational deployment." (See Figure 9 and compare with Figure 4.)[192]

Despite these measures, evidence suggests that MoD has used contractors to "replace" military capability, and that "too far" concerns about potential

---

[189] Interview, Directorate of Broadening and Deepening Smart Acquisition—Sponsored Reserves.

[190] MoD, Public Private Partnerships, *Changing the Way We Do Business: Sponsored Reserves, http://www.mod.uk/business/ppp/reserves.htm.*

[191] ACDSRP, *Defence Policy on Contracting for Sponsored Reserves*, July 27, 2000, p. 2. According to MoD, the SR model provides the additional benefits of enabling commanders to focus regular Service manpower resources on tasks or skills that can only be undertaken or maintained by regular servicemen and women both in peace and on operations, and the ability to transfer of the risks of equipment ownership to the civilian sector.

[192] House of Commons Defence Select Committee, Fourth Report, Session 2001–02, July 3, 2002, Para. 58.

Figure 9: Sponsored Reserve Capability

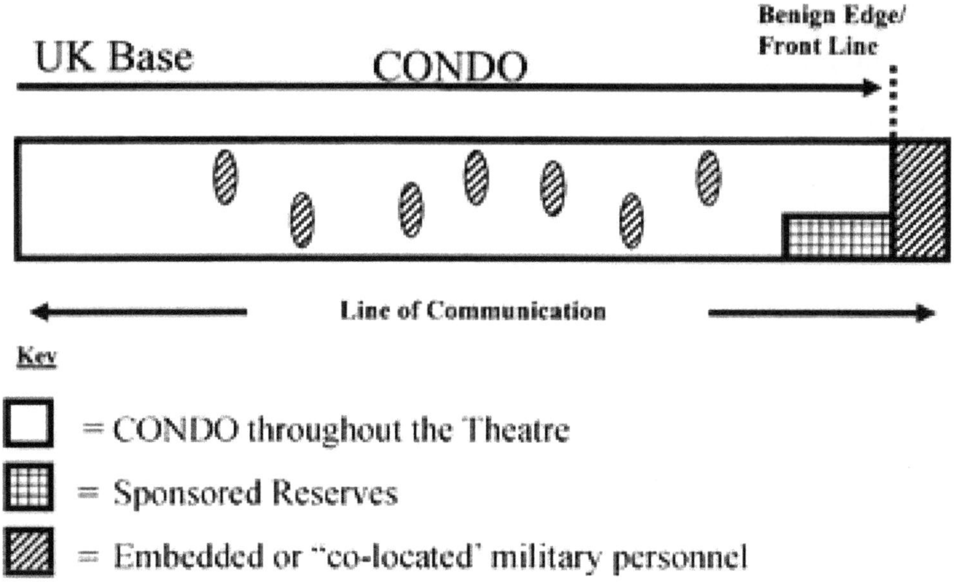

contractor withdrawal have not been fully addressed. As the House of Commons Defence Select Committee has pointed out, MoD has not produced "a clear set of criteria to define what constitutes the 'front-line' for the purposes of assessing the potential for using PFI" and CONDO.[193] When pressed on the issue of criteria MoD officials have made it clear that:

> we do not believe that such an approach would be possible . . . we do not believe that such a definition, even if one could be produced, would lead to different or better quality decisions on the use of PFI [and CONDO]. Decisions on projects need to be taken *case-by-case*, so that any impact on operational capability can be considered on its merits.[194]

When asked what potential "no-go" areas might be, MoD officials have defined the "front-line" as "fighting,"[195] and the only areas explicitly excluded from private sector provision to date are armed security, provost, secure couriers, and marine hydrography.

Evidence suggests that this remaining ambiguity about what constitutes "front-line" military capability and MoD's commitment to case-by-case contracting for deployed support does risk a situation where military capability

[193] House of Commons Defence Select Committee, Ministry of Defence Memorandum in Response to the House of Commons Defence Committee's Report on Major Procurement Projects, Sixth Special Report, October 16, 2002, Para. 29.

[194] House of Commons Defence Select Committee, Fourth Report, Para. 55.

[195] Interview, SO1 J4 Contractor Logistics CONLOG.

may be replaced rather than augmented. Under MoD's delegated contracting regime, the DPA, DLO, and other contracting authorities are still required to make "value-formoney" calculations when acquiring new equipment or support capabilities. A danger remains that these contracting authorities might look for value for money by cutting in-service support costs, with little thought about actual deployment implications, leading to "real replacement [of military capability with contractor capability]."[196] Similarly, studies suggest that industry is being used to bridge military capability gaps to the extent that "augmentation has gone out of the window."[197] In short:

> . . . there is clear evidence that CONDO is not only being used for military requirements as a "force multiplier," such as in the case of the CONLOG contract, but it is also being used by many of the Equipment Support Business Units to fill military capability gaps, and especially by Equipment Support, Contractor Logistic Support contracts within the Joint Operational Area, and furthermore, on occasions during armed conflict. The extensive use of CONDO has resulted in the creation of additional risk for MoD and of a concern to them that the contractor will deliver the service on time and that he will remain on contract, irrespective of the operational situation, and, above all, that he will provide an assured service to the military commander.[198]

Despite the operational flexibility and assured capability that the SR concept provides, practical developments to date have been limited. There are currently just 335 SRs available to the UK armed services linked to contracts with the Meteorological Office (Mobile Met Unit), crewing for six PFI-procured Strategic Sea-lift RO-RO vessels, ground support personnel for 32 Squadron BAe 125 communications aircraft with SERCo Aerospace, drivers/maintainers for the Army's new generation PFI-acquired heavy equipment transporters (HET), and hydrographic systems engineers for new generation survey vessels with Vosper Thorneycroft (UK) Ltd. Though MoD intends to increase the number of SRs in response to lessons from the UK's deployment in Iraq, indications are that the future scope will be limited to marine salvage support, MoD Fire Services, and the Royal Fleet Auxiliary.

This reflects various barriers to the more widespread application of the SR concepts. One factor has been cost: MoD contracts employing the SR models are funded out of the Defence Budget, whereas contractor provision through the UOR process is funded by the Treasury Contingency Fund at no cost to MoD, creating disincentives for MoD to invest in capability that

---

196 Interview, Defence Manufacturers Association CONDO Representative.
197 *Ibid.*
198 Higginson Associates.

otherwise would be paid for by the Treasury.[199] Moreover, it has been suggested that DPA and DLO IPTs have been reluctant to look for SR-based commercial support on new contracts because "there is still a general feeling that the SR concept is new and untried,"[200] and because there are legal difficulties in retrospectively incorporating SR provision into the array of existing CLS and OEM contracts. Finally, the armed services have been reluctant to replace organic military manpower with SRs because of concerns that the latter are less flexible and reliable on deployments.[201] Consequently, despite the assured capability that the SR model offers, the bulk of MoD deployed support is provided through potentially less reliable CONDO and CONLOG arrangements.

The MoD has responded to these concerns by claiming that the risk that contractors might fail to support deployed operations is remote, citing that of the 180 firms employed to support the UK armed services in Iraq during 2003, just two refused to deploy.[202] However, ongoing concern is that MoD currently lacks mechanisms to evaluate the "cumulative effects of the risks" involved in using contractors to fill capability gaps and "the impact this will have on military operational capability,"[203] the limited number of SR contracts and evidence that contractors are being used to support gaps in military capability, suggests that the ability of commanders to rely on an assured contractor service remains questionable.

It has been suggested that MoD has various potential courses of action to allay the residual "too far" concerns about contractor reliability.[204] One is the appointment of a high-level "champion" for CONDO policy within MoD who is able to identify all the operational capability gaps currently met by contractors, and thereby manage the cumulative effects of the risks associated with deploying CONDO capability. Another is a detailed assessment of which battle-winning capabilities should be provided through the less risky SR model, rather than CONDO arrangements. Finally, there is a requirement for commercial capability to be integrated with ongoing work by the DLO into its longer-term logistic architecture and design, "in order to maximise the potential of CONDO and thereby reduce the risks to MoD and the contractor."[205]

How effective are MoD procedures to evaluate the impact of defence PPPs on the morale, cohesion, ethos, and professionalism of the armed services? The MoD has addressed aspects of the debate concerning the impact of outsourcing on

[199] 199. Interview, Directorate of Broadening and Deepening Smart Acquisition—Sponsored Reserves.
[200] *Ibid.*
[201] Interview, SO1 J4 Contractor Logistics CONLOG.
[202] Higginson Associates.
[203] *Ibid.*
[204] *Ibid.*
[205] ACDSRP, *Defence Policy on Contracting for Sponsored Reserves,* July 27, 2000, p. 3.

the professionalism, ethos, and morale of the armed services. Current MoD policy dictates that the DPA, DLO, and FLCs should evaluate the potential effects on military personnel when the introduction of commercial support or SRs is under consideration. Moreover, acquisition officials are advised that military trade structures, promotion prospects, and intervals between roulement tours for military personnel should be "taken into account when putting together the detail of the [deployed support] proposal and in making the value for money decision."[206]

However, information on the extent to which these "impact on personnel issues" are factored into individual outsourcing assessments and how MoD actually monitors the cumulative effects of outsourcing on the armed services have not entered the public domain. The ongoing controversy surrounding the cultural impact of contractors on deployed operations suggests a need for MoD to conduct more extensive analysis. This should include officer attitude surveys addressing perceptions about the cultural impact on the three armed services and specific branches and trades within them. Data also might be collected on the effects of outsourcing, if any, on the outflow of trained military personnel. Finally, given MoD's "partnering" philosophy, further research needs to be conducted into the perceptions of contractors and their personnel working with "military partners" on deployed operations. Studies into these aspects of civilianization would enable firmer conclusions to be drawn on whether battlefield outsourcing has beneficial or detrimental effects on military morale, ethos and professionalism.

The Relevance of MoD Outsourcing Strategy for the U.S. Armed Services

There is close similarity between UK and U.S. military outsourcing philosophy. In contextual terms, both countries have transformed their post-Cold War defense policies, military doctrines, and force postures along similar lines. Moreover, MoD and DoD have both adopted NPM-style defense management reform trajectories. The MoD's "Executive Agency" program, for example, shares similarities with the DoD's development of "performance based organizations," of which the Defense Commissary Agency is representative. The DoD's "government-owned contractor-operated" approach affecting the U.S. Navy Military Sealift Command closely resembles MoD contracting for commercial management of UK government-owned dockyards. Similarly, DoD "public/private partnerships" and "joint ventures"

[206] For detailed discussion of these initiatives, see M. Hynes, S. N. Kirby, and J. Sloan, *A Casebook of Alternative Governance Structures and Organizational Forms*, Santa Monica CA: RAND, 2000, pp. 1–10.

for functions that include the Norfolk Port Facilities are a variant of MoD's PFI initiative.[207]

Outsourcing has become a core defense management tool in both countries, and the trend has been for MoD and the DoD to pursue closely aligned policies and copy "best practice" from each other.[208] The 1966 Office of Management and Budget Circular A-76 required the U.S. armed services to subject support activity to private sector competition. In the 1980s and 1990s, MoD vigorously applied this approach in its "market testing," CFQ and BQS initiatives during a period where the "Nichols Amendment" meant that few U.S. competitions were completed. Since the 1997 *Quadrennial Defense Review*—which recommended that the U.S. armed services compete, outsource, or privatize functions—the U.S. Army "has outlined an aggressive program of public-private competition" that closely resembles MoD's post-1980 agenda.[209] Policies on contractor support for deployed operations have followed a similar pattern, reflected in MoD's decision to formulate its CONLOG contract with principles laid down in the early 1990s by the U.S. Army for its Logistics Civil Augmentation Program (LOGCAP).[210]

Consequently, there are no fundamental differences in overarching MoD and DoD outsourcing philosophy. Both defense establishments share core assumptions about why contractor support is necessary in basic policy parameters. To the extent that variations do exist, this reflects different levels of practical experience in employing contractors on the battlefield, and the differing national military structures, contractual practices, and legal frameworks within which deployed contractor support has been engaged. It is at this level that DoD and MoD policymakers have scope to learn from each other.

On the one hand, MoD has practical lessons to learn from the DoD and U.S. armed services' accrued experience with deployed support contracting. The MoD decided to formalize its policy for the employment of contractors on deployed operations in 2000. In contrast, the U.S. armed services have routinely employed both deployed service and equipment contracts since the 1960s. The U.S. Army has relied heavily on its LOGCAP contract and many "original equipment manufacturers" during all phases of operations, and the LOGCAP program alone is worth between $3–10 billion per year.[211] Moreover, DoD officials and contractors have stated that "it has taken a

---

[207] For recent surveys of U.S. defense outsourcing initiatives, see, for example, A. Markusen, *The Case Against Privatizing National Security*, paper presented at the 2001 Meeting of the International Political Science Association, University of Oklahoma, Norman, OK, March 2001; and Spearing.

[208] See Pint and Hart, pp. 2–3.

[209] Interview, SO1 J4 Contractor Logistics CONLOG.

[210] Data derived from Higginson Associates.

[211] *Ibid.*

decade or more to establish their relationship and the ability to deliver the precise capability with availability that guarantees the service while demonstrating value for money and significant savings."[212] This, coupled with the extensive array of operational risk analysis tools, contingent pricing regimes, contractor management techniques, and doctrine innovations developed by the DoD and U.S. armed services,[213] suggests that MoD has much to learn from detailed monitoring and analysis of U.S. procedures and experiences.

On the other hand, MoD has made a series of conceptual, organizational, and procedural innovations that offer potentially useful lessons for the DoD and U.S. armed services. According to MoD officials, strengths of the UK's approach are that ownership and control of the CONLOG Contract resides with joint operational commanders at the PJHQ, and that this "reduces the supply chain and duplication of activity by contract."[214] Correspondingly, the U.S. approach is to maintain three single-service equivalents: the Army's LOGCAP, the Navy's Construction Capabilities Contract (CONCAP), and, the Air Forces' Air Force Contractor Augmentation Program (AFCAP) contract. In 1997, the U.S. General Accounting Office (GAO) concluded that "it might be more 'effective and efficient' if one service acted as the lead executive agent" or that "a joint civil augmentation program (JCAP) contract be established that will meet the needs of [each service] while eliminating duplication of effort."[215] Similarly, the GAO reiterated its concerns in June 2003 that:

> there are no DoD-wide policies on the use of contractors to support deployed forces. As a result, there is little understanding among the services as to the government's responsibility to contractors and contractor personnel in the event of hostilities. This lack of understanding can cause confusion at the deployed location and makes managing contractors more difficult because commanders often have contractors from several services at their location with different requirements, understandings, and obligations.[216]

These observations suggest that the DoD should analyse the C^2 and other benefits the U.S. armed services might obtain from a single joint overarching contractor support policy based on MoD's CONLOG model.

---

[212] The detailed content of the DoD's current approach under these headings is covered in R. King, DCS G-4 DSN, *Sustaining the Transforming Army*, presentation at the DMA MoD Contractors' Support to Deployed Operations Seminar, London, March 15, 2005.

[213] Interview, SO1 J4 Contractor Logistics CONLOG.

[214] M. J. Dowling and V. J. Fleck, *Feasibility of a Joint Engineering and Logistics Contract*, Wright Flyer Paper No. 7, Maxwell Air Force Base, AL: Air Command and Staff College, September 1999, pp. v–vi. *See also* D. M. Devens, *A Jointness Concept for the Future: Civilians, Contractors and Soldiers in SYNC*, Carlisle Barracks: U.S. Army War College, 1998.

[215] U.S. General Accountability Office, Military Operations: Contractors Provide Vital Services to Deployed Forces but Are Not Adequately Addressed in DOD Plans, GAO-03-695, June 2003, p. 35.

[216] *Ibid.*, p. 3.

Like MoD's DPA and DLO, the U.S. armed service program offices and material commands have delegated authority to write battlefield support contracts independently. However, MoD is unique in having an overarching CONDO policy that codifies and standardizes C^2 and other contractor-related procedures for all deployed commercial support. The GAO has recently expressed its concern that:

> Broader oversight is lacking in key areas, making it difficult for commanders to manage contractors effectively . . . Guidance at the DOD, combatant-command, and service levels regarding the use of contractors to support deployed forces varies widely, and mechanisms for managing these contractors are inconsistent, creating challenges that may hinder the efficient use of contractors.[217]

This suggests the DoD should consider adopting a CONDO-type policy to enhance U.S. commanders' awareness of contractor assets at their disposal and to codify contractor support arrangements.

A key element in MoD's approach to CONDO and CONLOG has been its emphasis on "partnership" as a mechanism to align military and private sector expertise and aspirations in policy formulation. This philosophy also has extended to policy implementation, reflected in the embedded KBR team located at the PJHQ. British officials have suggested that a key difference between U.S. and UK approaches is that implementation of "LOGCAP is left very much to the [U.S.] deployed commander, whereas in the UK, the PJHQ has control and the ability to plan and go for reach-back because KBR is embedded in the planning process."[218] Consequently, analysis of MoD's approach to establishing "partnerships" could offer valuable insights to DoD policymakers.

Finally, an innovative aspect of MoD policy is the SR concept, which is intended to bridge contractor provision and organic military capability. Indications are that the U.S. Air Force became interested in the SR concept during the mid-1990s, and the U.S. armed services continue to monitor MoD policy through the British Defence Mission in Washington.[219] Though the U.S. armed services currently lack dedicated legislation to develop this category of reserve forces, the SR concept may provide a useful template for the DoD to extend its relationships with the private sector in the future.

Conclusions and Recommendations

The author identifies three major conclusions and associated recommendations for consideration by MoD and DoD officials. The first is that the use

[217] Interview, SO1 J4 Contractor Logistics CONLOG.
[218] Interview, Directorate of Broadening and Deepening Smart Acquisition—Sponsored Reserves.
[219] MoD Director of Logistic Operations, *CONDO Policy and Implementation.*

of contractors on deployed operations is likely to remain a controversial aspect of UK and U.S. defense transformation unless steps are taken to address a range of unanswered questions. On the one hand, MoD and DoD officials claim that contractor support reduces defense costs and provides a crucial "force multiplier" to meet contemporary operational needs. They assert that the policy agenda has become one of refining procedures to engage private firms in the most cost-effective and operationally advantageous manner rather than any further questioning of the utility of contractors *per se*. On the other, "too far" critics continue to argue that MoD and DoD have a flawed ideological preference for outsourcing, and "too little" critics raise concerns about bureaucratic barriers to more extensive private sector solutions. This analysis suggests that controversies, myths, and emotions will remain unresolved until MoD and DoD release more data on the performance and impact of deployed operational outsourcing into the public domain. On this basis, the first recommendation is that MoD and DoD provide greater clarification by releasing more information, with accompanying assumptions, on:

- The detailed mechanisms employed to evaluate the relative financial and operational implications of in-house and outsourced provision of deployed operational support, including the treatment of transaction costs.
- The internal MoD and DoD policy guidance, organizational arrangements and institutional incentive structures under which officials evaluate the merits of in-house and private sector delivery.
- The precise mechanism employed to ensure that private contractors are precluded from extracting "excessive" profits on defense support contracts.
- The financial and personnel resource redistribution and reinvestment implications of deployed support outsourcing.
- The detailed methodology adopted by MoD and DoD in differentiating between force "augmentation" and "replacement" resulting from outsourcing on a contract-by-contract basis, and in terms of cumulative force posture impacts.
- The mechanisms in place to measure and evaluate the impact of defence outsourcing on the morale, cohesion, ethos, and professionalism of the armed services and the contractors' personnel supporting them.

Greater transparency on these issues will enable independent appraisal of the full range of benefits, limitations, and trade-offs associated with contractor support and a better-informed public policy debate.

The survey of MoD policies and doctrines indicates that sophisticated mechanisms are in place to manage contracting for UK deployed operations. The CONDO policy codifies contractor support and deployed C^2 arrangements, the CONLOG Contract has rationalized contractor supply chain management, and the SR Concept provides commanders with an interim option between regular military and civilian contractor personnel. Despite these innovations, the second conclusion is that there are still implementation issues that MoD needs to address and that "much needs to be done to better exploit commercial capability."[220] These implementation issues are equally relevant to future DoD reviews of the coherence and effectiveness of U.S. policies and doctrines towards deployed contractor support. The recommendations that emerge are that MoD and DoD should:

- Review the coherence of current guidance provided to individual contracting authorities when entering into commercial deployed support arrangements to ensure consistent contractor support arrangements are in place for military commanders. This should include analysis of the robustness of frameworks intended to regulate the approaches adopted by individual contracting authorities and the "endto-end" effectiveness of existing contracts.[221]
- Review the states of "availability and readiness" for existing contractors and their sub-contractors to deploy, the extent of "planned and unplanned" contractor surge capacity, and the measures that contractors can expect MoD and DoD to provide to prepare them for deployed operations.
- Review key MoD/DoD and contractor risks on deployed operations in the areas of personnel security and safety and insurance and corporate reputation.
- Identify and review all operational capability gaps currently met by contractors as a basis for understanding and managing the cumulative risks associated with relying on commercial capability.
- Review the current and longer-term ability of MoD and DoD contracting authorities to act as "intelligent customers" when contracting for deployed support. At issue is whether commercial officers are receiving appropriate training for deployed support contracting, whether

---

[220] Indications are that MoD's Defence Logistics Organization has recently recognized that reform in this area is required, and potential mechanisms to ensure greater regulation in contracting for the "Support Solutions Envelope" are now being evaluated. MoD Chief of Defence Logistics, *The DLO Mission: To Deliver Logistics for Operations*, Presentation at the DMA MoD Contractors' Support to Deployed Operations Seminar, London, March 15, 2005.

[221] A. Higginson, *MoD Contractors' Support to Deployed Operations (CONDO) Post Seminar Summary*, unpublished, March 18, 2005.

contracting authorities have the ability to determine where and how best to use contractors, and whether they understand the operational environment and have the skills to develop "imagination and flexibility in determining an appropriate contracting solution."

- Review the current and potential longer-term ability of the U.S. and UK armed services to remain "intelligent managers" of contracted deployed support. This should include analysis, for example, of the extent to which current and future commanders are educated in contractor management issues during their command and staff courses and precommand training.
- Review the scope for joint risk assessments and greater "habitualization" with industry when planning long-term commercial support arrangements.
- Review and clarify the distinction between benign and nonbenign operational conditions where contractor support options are under consideration.
- Identify the relative strengths and weaknesses of CONDO and SR-type arrangements for foreseeable deployed operational contingencies through the use of cost-benefit analysis.
- Review and quantify the likelihood and risk of contractor withdrawal on the armed services' ability to meet mission objectives.

The third conclusion is that the DoD and MoD have developed innovative mechanisms to harness private sector capability for contemporary operations, and that both organizations have scope to learn from each other. On the one hand, the U.S. armed services' tried-and-tested approaches to contracting for deployed operations over a number of decades suggest that MoD policymakers and practitioners have much to learn from DoD processes and procedures. On the other hand, though MoD's practical experience in employing contractors on deployed operations is more limited, it has developed coherent concepts that potentially have applicability with U.S. armed services. A final recommendation is that U.S. officials evaluate the content and performance of MoD's CONDO policy, CONLOG Contract, and SR Concept in terms of their potential utility for the U.S. armed services.

Officials at the DoD and MoD claim it is inevitable that all future UK and U.S. military operations will rely on a degree of contractor support. From their perspectives, the debate is no longer about whether there will be private firms on deployed operations; rather, the issue is when and where contractor support offers the most cost-effective solution in financial and operational terms. As this analysis shows, complex economic, operational, and policy implementation considerations are likely to dictate the future scale and scope of contractor involvement. This suggests the need for ongoing policy and doctrine refinement by defense officials, as well as greater independent scrutiny of developments, not least because the use of contractors on deployed operations has an important impact on government expenditure choices, public accountability, the efficiency and effectiveness of the military establishment, and the conduct and outcome of armed conflict.

USE OF CONTRACTORS IN IRAQ

Commentary

By
Douglas C. Lovelace, Jr.

The next section of *Use of Contractors in the War Against Terrorists,* presents comprehensive coverage of the most important case study for the increased use of contractors in what many believe is the central front of the war. The use of contractors in Iraq is significant for several reasons. First contractor use in Iraq is approximately two and a half times higher than for previous conflicts, with the exception of U.S. military operations in the Balkans in the 1990s. Funding for contractors in Iraq was a staggering $85 billion from 2003 through 2007, or approximately twenty percent of total funding for the war. Contractors provide much of the logistics support in Iraq across almost all classes of supply, services, and equipment. Additionally, private security companies contract to provide services that traditionally have been provided by uniformed military.

The use of private security contractors arguably has generated the most controversy concerning contractor use in the war against terrorists. Presently, there are roughly 6,000 private security contractors in Iraq, a very significant number. Unfortunate incidents involving those contractors, the most notable of which resulted in contractors killing seventeen Iraqis in September 2007, have caused the Department of Defense (DoD) to adjust rules for the use of force for private security contractors. Some, including many outspoken and influential Iraqis, believe private security contractors lack the training and discipline of uniformed military personnel and, therefore, allow situations to escalate into violent confrontations when they need not.

Military commanders warn of negative consequences of precipitate or reckless action by security contractors, not the least of which is its potential for creating future enemies. Consequently, military commanders, reportedly, have issued orders requiring private security contractors to accept more risk in dealing with potential belligerents before resorting to deadly force. According the Wall Street Journal, the orders urged security contractors to not view Iraqis as threats, until there is reason to do so and that "A mindset shift must occur in which armed contractors view every contact with Iraqi civilians as friendly until actions clearly prove otherwise." DoD's orders, obviously, apply only to private security contractors employed by DoD, and not to those who provide services to the Department of State or other U.S. agencies. Nonetheless, the impact such orders will have on the ability of private security contractors to recruit and retain qualified personnel at affordable cost could present additional challenges.

Another factor at work in Iraq that could actually reduce the controversy over the use of private security contractors is the continually improving security situation, especially for the missions performed by the contractors. For example, the Government Accountability Office reports a 60% drop in shooting incidents involving armed contractors used to protect U.S. diplomats, military convoys and facilities since the 2007 Blackwater incident. Additionally, the Private Security Company Association of Iraq reported that attacks on supply convoys have dropped considerably from over 10% a year ago to less than one percent presently. This is a welcome trend for security contractors for at least two reasons. First, the security environment appears to be changing in ways that make it more commensurate with security contractor capabilities. Second, it dampens somewhat the great concern Iraqi authorities have on their ability to hold such contractors accountable for improper actions.

As suggested above and by the documents presented in this section, the U.S. Congress has taken interest in the use of contractors in the war against terrorists. Some members, such as Sen. Kent Conrad (D-N.D.), believe the Bush administration's increased reliance on military contractors has set a dangerous precedence, by limiting oversight and accountability, enabling fraud and corruption, and perhaps even costing taxpayers more instead of less money. Consequently, in October 2006, The House of Representatives passed HR 2740, the MEJA Expansion and Enforcement act of 2007, to empower the U.S. government to hold private security contractors accountable through criminal prosecutions, for wrongdoing in Iraq and other war zones. It would add to the provisions of the Military Extraterritorial Jurisdiction Act signed into law on November 22, 2000. In the next section of this volume, we present both of these important initiatives to hold private security contractors more accountable in a theater of operations. Clearly, Congress it is concerned with ensuring proper accountability, albeit by U.S. authorities. Nonetheless, contractor accountability looms large as an issue in the status of forces agreement for the continued presence of U.S. forces in Iraq when the United Nations mandate expires at the end of this year.

The documents presented in this section of the volume include *REBUILDING IRAQ: Actions Needed to Improve Use of Private Security Providers; Private Security Contractors in Iraq: Background, Legal Status, and Other Issues; Defense Contracting in Iraq: Issues and Options for Congress; REBUILDING IRAQ: DOD and State Department Have Improved Oversight and Coordination of*

Private Security Contractors in Iraq, but Further Actions Are Needed to Sustain Improvements; and *Contractors' Support of U.S. Operations in Iraq*. Together, these documents cover the majority of contentious issues associated with the use of contractors in the war against terrorists.

REBUILDING IRAQ: Actions Needed to Improve Use of Private Security Providers is a 2005 Government Accountability Office (GAO) Report for Congress prepared to evaluate the extent to which U.S. agencies used contracted services in Iraq, the working relationships developed between the U.S. military and private security providers, and the relative costs of using the contractors. Although the report is somewhat dated, it still provides useful background as well as insights into how security for non-military personnel in Iraq is provided by a combination of military forces, Department of State security personnel, and private security providers. The report also addresses how the relationship between private security firms and the armed forces has improved and what actions should be taken to improve the effectiveness the contractors. The report also notes that at the time of its preparation, U.S. government agencies had little capability to assess the cost and impact of using private security contractors. Interestingly and counter-intuitively, this report found little evidence to support the belief that the increased use of private security contractors has contributed to attrition of uniformed service members.

The other findings presented in the report include the conclusion that U.S. government agencies and reconstruction contractors in Iraq employed private security contractors for tasks, such as personal and convoy security, because providing such security is not part of the U.S. armed forces stated mission, and U.S. military forces provide security only for DOD civilians and contractors who directly support the combat mission. That is an interesting finding, since providing overall security in areas of operations throughout a theater of war has traditionally been a valid military mission. One can reasonably conclude that it is a matter of choice rather than capability or mission that a large chunk of the responsibility for security in Iraq has been carved out for private security contractors. However, that observation must be qualified by recognizing that Department of State and other federal agencies' security requirements in Iraq, due to the simultaneous and interrelated reconstruction and security functions that must be performed in the midst of a virulent insurgency are much larger than they would be in other circumstances.

The GAO found that private security contractor efforts achieved only mixed results. That is particularly troubling, given that the agencies and reconstruction contractors GAO included in its review paid over $766 million to private security contractors. The lackluster performance of the private security contractors led to frequent contractor replacement upon contract expiration. The fact that change in contractors occurred in over half of the contract renewals draws into to question the claim that use of private security contractors is more cost-effective than using military personnel.

The report states that although contractor officers and military commanders developed cooperative working relationships, actions should be taken to improve the effectiveness of such relationships. According to other credible sources, the GAO report may underemphasize the working relationship difficulties encountered. Nevertheless, the GAO report accurately describes serious problems. As of the writing of the report, private security contractors still had not established a system for sharing intelligence on enemy forces and, perhaps more important, not even on their own respective locations and activities. Military units deploying to Iraq were not always fully aware of the organizations operating in the area of operations and the activities in which they were engaged. As a result, "blue-on-blue" confrontations were not as infrequent as one would prefer.

The report's recommendations follow logically from its findings. The report makes the requirements for better intelligence, knowledge of friendly organization location and activities, and training on the respective roles of the various organizations in the area of operations very apparent. The GAO also makes the very valid and important recommendation that all agencies and reconstruction contractors who use private security contractors should develop methodologies for accurately assessing the costs of the security services provided. Additionally, the costing tools must provide for measuring, assessing, and predicting costs.

The next document presented in this volume is a July 2007 Congressional Research Service (CRS) report entitled, *Private Security Contractors in Iraq: Background, Legal Status, and Other Issues*. The report correctly notes that the use of private security contractors in Iraq significantly enables reconstruction and stabilization efforts and contributes much to U.S., Iraqi, and international efforts to bring peace and security to the war-torn country. The report also notes, however, that such use of private security contractors raises many thorny issues ranging from transparency, oversight and accountability, legal status of such contractors, their appropriateness for the missions assigned them, and the suitability of their personnel. The report does an excellent job of presenting the most important issues to Congress, even if it is somewhat light on recommendations for legislative initiatives.

The first observation that the report makes is that the need for and suitability of private contractors to perform duties that do not require military expertise such as feeding, housing, and otherwise caring for soldiers' basic needs, is accepted by the majority of national security analysts as necessary to compensate for a "downsized" post-Cold War military. The report raises the related issue of what effect the use of contractors will have on the

U.S. military force structure. It cites the 1995 Commission on Roles and Mission's (CORM) finding that reliance on contractors could prove detrimental to military capabilities in a number of ways. The reader should note, however, that the CORM's authors did not contemplate the contemporary military operating environment and the demand it creates for contracting support services.

The next issue the report raises is the effects the extensive use of contractors could have on the successful accomplishment of U.S. military missions in Iraq. Specifically, it identifies possible complications for military commanders concerning the use of private security contractors who are not under their command. Commanders who approach their missions holistically and see the establishment and maintenance of good relations with the local populace as essential to success, often see their local efforts thwarted by the sometimes heavy-handed actions of security contractors. The report raises associated concerns regarding the relative flexibility of military members vice security contractors. Although contractors often can be introduced into the theater of operations faster than some military units, once there, military personnel, due to their extensive training and expert leadership, are able to respond with agility and adroitness security contractors generally lack.

The report correctly describes reliability and quality of contractor personnel concerns, when compared to dedication, skill and motivation of uniformed military. Many make the argument that since the private security firms recruit heavily from the military, they offer similar quality of service since personnel quality is comparable. Others make the counterargument that individuals motivated by economics, as opposed to selfless service, can reasonably be expected to render lower quality and less reliable service. Additionally, some argue that military personnel undergo sustained training over the span of a career, whereas contractor training is less robust and enduring, and the skills acquired by former military personnel when they were in the service atrophy over time when under the employ of a contractor.

The report raises the issue of oversight, control and coordination of contractors in general—a concern that is especially acute for security contractors. The U.S. government's contracting regulations provide that Contracting Officers and Contracting Officer Representatives (CORs) oversee, control, and coordinate contractor actions, to the extent that contracts even permit control and coordination. Military operations are overseen, controlled, and coordinated by highly trained and experienced commanders who rely on unity of command and unity of effort principles to accomplish missions. Contracting Officers and CORs are technicians who are not trained nor expected to exercise agile and decisive command. They adhere to the Federal Acquisition Regulations and technical contracting principles that are unsuitable for organizing and directing security operations. Furthermore, a

Contracting Officer typically is responsible for overseeing far more contractors and missions than could be effectively commanded and controlled, without the benefit of a military staff.

A related concern addressed in the report is the perceived lack of transparency in contract administration and the resulting insufficient congressional oversight. Members of Congress, as well as government officials, believe U.S. agencies do not adequately oversee contractors on the battlefield, fail to provide adequate information to Congress and, as mentioned above, do not provide adequate field oversight. This apparent breakdown in the process leads to the cost and accountability concerns suggested above and discussed further in the next section. The human rights concerns the report identifies feeds off and into the accountability concerns. All of these concerns combine to create, or at least exacerbate, the perception of ineffective national authority exercised over contractors and insufficient commitment to the responsible use of force to accomplish national security objectives.

The remaining three documents presented in this section provide updates and add texture to the myriad dimensions of using contractors to help wage the war against terrorists. *Defense Contracting in Iraq: Issues and Options for Congress* is a June 18, 2008 CRS Report. It addresses logistical support contracts administered through the U.S. Army's Logistics Civil Augmentation Program (LOGCAP), the relatively new process for managing civilian contracts for services during large-scale military operations. It reflects previously described congressional concerns regarding government oversight and management of DoD contracting in Iraq. Congressional concerns are well founded, given that the U.S. government was unable to substantiate the disbursement of at least $7.8 billion believed to be spent for goods and services in Iraq. The report also discusses legislation aimed at establishing better oversight and financial accountability. The report is an excellent update and complement to the documents previously provided in this volume.

REBUILDING IRAQ: DoD and State Department Have Improved Oversight and Coordination of Private Security Contractors in Iraq, but Further Actions Are Needed to Sustain Improvements is a July 2008 GAO Report on its examination of the extent to which the Department of Defense (DOD) and Department of State have improved oversight and coordination of private security contractors in Iraq. The report also provides some information on the legal basis for holding private security contractors accountable. It concludes that DoD and the Department of State have made improvements in their oversight of private security contractors in the past year, but several areas requiring improvement remain. Additionally, some of the measures taken to strengthen oversight appear temporary in nature, and the departments need to develop enduring solutions. The report offers two reasonable but general recommendations. It recommends that DoD develop a strategy to sustain the increase in the contractor oversight personnel it is now providing in Iraq. It also recommends that DoD update and expand on the training it provides deploying forces on oversight of private security contractor responsibilities and authorities.

The final document in this section is an August 2008 Congressional Budget Office (CBO) paper on *Contractors' Support of U.S. Operations in Iraq*. Responding to a Senate Committee on the Budget request, CBO examined the use of contractors in Iraq during the 2003–2007 periods. The paper provides a useful overview of contractor use that covers several major topics. They include costs of employing contractors, what they provide, personnel numbers, historical comparisons, and the use of private security contractors. The paper presents the previously mentioned astonishing datum: from 2003 through 2007, the United States spent $85 billion for contractor work in the Iraq theater, which accounted for almost 20 percent of the total cost of operations in Iraq. Furthermore, the paper estimates that as of early 2008 there were at least 190,000 contractor personnel employed in the theater.

Due to the controversy they have generated, it is no surprise that the paper focuses on private security contractors. For the period under study, the paper notes that $6-$10 billion was spent on private security contractors who employed approximately 25,000 to 30,000 personnel. The paper states, without complete analysis, that private security contractors cost about as much as U.S. military units performing similar functions. On the other hand, the paper states that private security contractors offer an advantage in that the contractors' cost disappears in peacetime, while the cost of maintaining military units remains. That is a very superficial and misleading claim. The paper reinforces many of the concerns raised in the other documents presented in this section, from a distinctly CBO perspective and, therefore, nicely rounds-out the presentation of the use of contractors in the central front of the war against terrorists.

DOCUMENT NO. 2

REBUILDING IRAQ: ACTIONS NEEDED TO IMPROVE USE OF PRIVATE SECURITY PROVIDERS

GAO Report
GAO-05-737

July 2005

What GAO Found

The civilian U.S. government agencies and reconstruction contractors in Iraq that GAO evaluated have obtained security services, such as personal and convoy security, from private security providers because providing security to them is not the U.S. military's stated mission. U.S. military forces provide security for those Department of Defense (DOD) civilians and contractors who directly support the combat mission. In Iraq, the Department of State and other federal agencies contract with several private security providers to protect their employees. Under their contracts, contractors rebuilding Iraq are responsible for providing their own security and have done so by awarding subcontracts to private security providers. As of December 2004, the agencies and contractors we reviewed had obligated more than $766 million for private security providers. The contractors' efforts to obtain suitable security providers met with mixed results, as they often found that their security provider could not meet their needs. Overall, GAO found that contractors replaced their initial security providers on more than half the 2003 contracts it reviewed. Contractor officials attributed this turnover to various factors, including the absence of useful agency guidance.

While the U.S. military and private security providers have developed a cooperative working relationship, actions should be taken to improve its effectiveness. The relationship between the military and private security providers is one of coordination, not control. Prior to October 2004 coordination was informal, based on personal contacts, and was inconsistent. In October 2004 a Reconstruction Operations Center was opened to share intelligence and coordinate military-contractor interactions. While military and security providers agreed that coordination has improved, two problems remain. First, private security providers continue to report incidents between themselves and the military when approaching military convoys and checkpoints. Second, military units deploying to Iraq are not fully aware of the parties operating on the complex battle space in Iraq and what responsibility they have to those parties.

Despite the significant role played by private security providers in enabling reconstruction efforts, neither the Department of State, nor DOD nor the U.S. Agency for International Development (USAID) have complete data on the costs of using private security providers. Even at the contract level, the agencies generally had only limited information readily available, even though agency and contractor officials acknowledged that these costs had diverted a considerable amount of reconstruction resources and led to canceling or reducing the scope of some projects. For example, in March 2005, two task orders for reconstruction worth nearly $15 million were cancelled to help pay for security at a power plant. GAO found that the cost to obtain private security providers and security-related equipment accounted for more than 15 percent of contract costs on 8 of the 15 reconstruction contracts it reviewed.

Abbreviations

CENTCOM	U.S. Central Command
CPA	Coalitional Provisional Authority
DFARS	Defense Federal Acquisition Regulation Supplement
DMDC	Defense Manpower Data Center
DOD	Department of Defense
GAO	Government Accountability Office
MNC-I	Multi-National Corps-Iraq
MNF-I	Multi-National Force-Iraq
PCO	Project and Contracting Office
ROC	Reconstruction Operations Center
USAID	U.S. Agency for International Development

United States Government Accountability Office
Washington, D.C 20548

July 28, 2005

Congressional Committees

The United States is spending billions of dollars to reconstruct Iraq while at the same time is engaged in combating an insurgency that has targeted military personnel, contractors, and the Iraqi people. According to the Department of Defense (DOD) and other sources, as of June 1, 2005, more than 1,600 U.S. and coalition military forces and 200 contractor personnel have been killed since major combat operations ended in May 2003. This uncertain security environment created a need for U.S. government agencies and contractors involved in rebuilding Iraq to obtain substantially more security services than is normally the case when operating in other countries. Creating a democratic Iraq and rebuilding its infrastructure is a U.S. national security and foreign policy priority, and, even without the need for enhanced security, is a challenging and complex effort.

Prior to the conflict, DOD and the U.S. government agencies responsible for the reconstruction of Iraq believed that reconstruction would take place in an environment with little threat from insurgents or terrorists. By June 2003 the security situation in Iraq began to worsen and it became clear in August 2003, with the bombing of the United Nations complex, that insurgents were targeting nonmilitary targets. The killings of four U.S. citizens working for a U.S. security provider in Iraq in March 2004 and the allegations of prisoner abuse at Abu Ghraib prison[1] resulted in significant congressional concern[2] over the use of private security providers in Iraq and raised a number of operational, legal, and contracting questions.

Because of the broad level of interest by Congress in issues dealing with Iraq, the Comptroller General initiated this review under his statutory authority. Specifically, we evaluated the extent to which (1) U.S. government agencies and contractors working in Iraq have acquired security services from private providers; (2) the U.S. military and private security providers in Iraq have developed a cooperative working relationship; and (3) U.S. government agencies assessed the costs associated with using private security providers on reconstruction contracts. Additionally, we assessed the impact of the increased use of private security providers on attrition in key military skills.

To identify the rules and regulations governing and assigning responsibility for protecting government and contractor personnel working in Iraq, we reviewed policies, regulations, instructions, guidance, and orders issued by DOD, the U.S. Central Command (CENTCOM),[3] and other DOD components relating to the use of contractors during wartime; orders and policies issued by the Coalition Provisional Authority (CPA) regarding

[1] We recently discussed breakdowns in the procurement process when contracting for interrogators and other services in Iraq. See GAO, *Interagency Contracting: Problems with DOD's and Interior's Orders to Support Military Operations*, GAO-05-201 (Washington, D.C.: Apr. 29, 2005).

[2] These concerns have been expressed in requests from numerous members of Congress that the Comptroller General review the operational, legal, and contracting issues involving the use of private security providers in Iraq. Congress has subsequently included several provisions in legislation designed to improve the management of and support and protection provided to contractor personnel who support deployed forces or who are in a combatant commander's area of responsibility. See Ronald W. Reagan National Defense Authorization Act for Fiscal Year 2005, Pub. L. No. 108-375, section 1205 and 1206 (Oct. 28, 2004) and H.R. 1815, 109th Cong. title XVI (2005).

[3] CENTCOM is the U.S. military command responsible for prosecuting the war in Iraq.

contractor operations in Iraq; and Department of State policies regarding the protection of U.S. government employees working abroad, including the Foreign Affairs Manual. We also interviewed military officials who had been stationed in Iraq as well as selected private security providers to understand their responsibilities and collaborative working relationship in Iraq. To understand the process by which contractors obtained private security providers, we selected 16 reconstruction contracts using a non-probabilistic methodology that considered such factors as the awarding agency; the year awarded; the contract's expected dollar value; and the type, nature and location of the reconstruction activity. These 16 contracts were awarded by various DOD components, including the U.S. Army Corps of Engineers; the Department of State; and the U.S. Agency for International Development (USAID). Nine of these contracts were awarded in 2003 and 7 were awarded in 2004. As of December 2004, the agencies had obligated about $8.6 billion on these contracts. We also obtained and reviewed six contracts that had been awarded the U.S. Army Corps of Engineers, the Department of State, USAID, and by Army activities on behalf of the CPA for the protection of their personnel and facilities in Iraq. We then compared the type of security-related requirements incorporated within U.S. government contracts with those incorporated into contracts awarded to prime reconstruction contractors and, in turn, to subcontracts with security providers. We interviewed agency and contractor officials, reviewed agency guidance provided to the contractors, reviewed the reconstruction contracts and security subcontracts, and analyzed the vouchers and other billing information submitted by the reconstruction contractors and security providers. To assess the impact on military attrition caused by the use of private security providers we obtained and analyzed DOD attrition data and spoke with private security providers and representatives of the U.S. Special Operations Command and the military services. We determined that the information and data discussed in this report were sufficiently reliable for the purposes of the report. Appendix I contains more detail on our scope and methodology. We conducted our review from May 2004 to June 2005 in accordance with generally accepted government auditing standards.

Results in Brief

All but one of the civilian U.S. government agencies and reconstruction contractors we evaluated that are operating in Iraq have obtained security services from private security providers. As of December 2004, the agencies and contractors we reviewed had obligated more than $766 million for private security providers. The use of private security providers reflects the uncertain security environment that was, and is still being encountered in Iraq, as well as the fact that providing security for agencies and contractors is not part of the U.S. military's stated mission. U.S. military forces in Iraq provide security only for those DOD civilians and contractors who directly support the military's mission. In Iraq, as elsewhere, the U.S. Ambassador, as Chief of Mission, has overall responsibility for the security of U.S. government executive branch employees, except for those under the force protection of the combatant commander. However, individual U.S. government agencies have had to arrange for their own security services. As neither DOD nor the Department of State is responsible for providing security to reconstruction contractors, the terms of their contracts require reconstruction contractors to provide for their own security; and, they typically have done so by awarding subcontracts to private security providers. The contractors' efforts to obtain suitable security providers met with mixed results, as many subsequently found that their initial security providers could not meet their needs. Overall, we found that contractors replaced their security providers on five of the eight reconstruction contracts awarded in 2003 that we reviewed.[4] Contractor officials attributed this turnover to various factors, including their lack of knowledge of the security market and of the potential security providers, and the absence of useful agency guidance.

Although the U.S. military and private security providers generally have developed a cooperative working relationship, actions can be taken to further improve its effectiveness. The relationship between the military in Iraq and employees of private security providers is one of coordination and cooperation, not control. Both U.S. Central Command officials and military personnel previously stationed in Iraq told us that there is no command and control relationship between the military and private security provider employees. At the same time, military and private security provider employees recognize the need to coordinate their actions. Prior to October 2004, coordination was informal, based on personal contacts often initiated by the contractors, and it was inconsistent. In October 2004, the Project and Contracting Office opened the Reconstruction Operations Center to share intelligence and coordinate military contractor interactions. While providers and the military agree that coordination has improved since the advent of the operations center, some problems remain. First, private security providers continue to report incidents occurring between themselves and the military when they approach military convoys and checkpoints. Second, the military may not have a clear understanding of the role of contractors, including private security providers, in Iraq and of the implications of having private security providers on the battle space.

Despite the significant role played by private security providers in enabling reconstruction efforts to proceed, neither the Department of State, nor DOD, nor USAID—the principal agencies responsible for Iraq reconstruction

[4] On one additional 2003 contract, the contractor provided its own security.

efforts—have complete data on the costs associated with using private security providers. In turn, the Department of State's quarterly report to Congress, which describes the status of projects, initiatives, and funding dedicated to Iraq reconstruction, does not provide information on the costs associated with using private security providers. Our discussions with agency officials found that the financial management and information systems used to prepare the reports are not set up to track security costs that are incurred under reconstruction contracts. Even at the contract level, the agencies generally had only limited information readily available on the costs associated with private security providers. While agencies do not specifically track such costs, both agency and contractor officials acknowledged that security costs had diverted a considerable amount of reconstruction resources and led to canceling or reducing the scope of certain reconstruction projects. For example, in March 2005, USAID cancelled two electrical power generation-related task orders totaling nearly $15 million to help pay for increased security costs being incurred at another power generation project in southern Baghdad.

Our review of 16 reconstruction contracts found that the cost to obtain private security providers and security-related equipment can be considerable. Overall, these costs accounted for more than 15 percent on 8 of the 15 reconstruction contracts for which data were available. On only 4 of those 8 contracts, however, did the agencies receive security cost information. Agency officials noted that increased costs or delays in reconstruction projects also reflect non-security-related factors, such as changes in planned funding levels or higher material costs.

While both Special Forces and military police officials believe that attrition is increasing in their military specialties, partially because of increased employment opportunities with private security providers, our review of DOD data shows that the attrition levels in fiscal year 2004 increased compared to fiscal years 2002 and 2003, but are similar to the levels seen in fiscal years 2000 and 2001, prior to the establishment of stop loss.[5] This similarity indicates that former military members in the Special Forces and military police communities are leaving in the same proportions as before the attacks of September 11, 2001 but, according to Army officials, have a wider range of employment opportunities today. However, given that stop loss policies depress attrition rates, we are unable to determine whether the increase in attrition rates in fiscal year 2004 compared to fiscal years 2002 and 2003 was due to the end of stop loss or to actual increases in attrition. Moreover, DOD data does not indicate why personnel are leaving the military—only the fact that they are doing so.

[5] Stop loss prevents servicemembers from leaving the service even though they may have reached the end of their enlistment or service obligation.

We are making recommendations to the Secretary of Defense to enhance military procedures to reduce incidences of the military firing on private security providers and provide training to U.S. military forces on the role of private security providers in Iraq. Additionally, we are making recommendations to the Secretary of Defense, the Secretary of State and the Administrator, USAID, which would enable contractors to obtain adequate security services, as well as enable government agencies to more efficiently plan for security costs in future reconstruction efforts.

DOD agreed with each of the recommendations, noting that it welcomed our assistance in improving how DOD and its contractors can plan for and effectively execute contracts in a complex and changeable security environment. DOD's comments appear in appendix II.

The Department of State disagreed with our recommendation to explore options to assist contractors in obtaining private security services, citing concerns that the government could be held liable for performance failures and noting it was unclear that a government-managed security contractor program would result in enhanced contractor security. While our work found that contractors had difficulty in obtaining security providers that met their needs and that they would have benefited from the agencies' assistance, we did not recommend a particular course of action nor recommend a government-managed security program. Rather, we recommended that the Department, working jointly with DOD and USAID, explore options to assist contractors that are unfamiliar with obtaining the type of security services needed in Iraq. Such an effort would necessarily entail a thorough assessment of the advantages, disadvantages and risk mitigation strategies of the potential options. The Department did not indicate whether it agreed with our recommendation to establish a means to account and plan for security costs. The Department's comments appear in appendix III.

USAID found the report factually correct, but did not comment on the recommendations. USAID's letter appears in appendix IV.

Background

The United States, along with its coalition partners and various international organizations and donors, has continued to support efforts to rebuild Iraq in the aftermath of the war that replaced Iraq's previous regime. From April 2003 to June 28, 2004, the CPA served as Iraq's interim government and was responsible for overseeing, directing, coordinating, and approving rebuilding efforts. With the establishment of Iraq's interim government, the CPA ceased to exist and its responsibilities were transferred to the Iraqi government or to other U.S. agencies. The Department of State is now responsible for overseeing U.S. efforts to rebuild Iraq. DOD's Project and Contracting

Office (PCO)[6] and the U.S. Army Corps of Engineers have played a significant role in awarding and managing reconstruction contracts. USAID has been responsible for various reconstruction and developmental assistance efforts, including those related to capital construction projects, local governance, economic development, education, and public health.

As Figure 1 demonstrates, the battle space in Iraq can best be described as complex. A complex battle space is one where military forces, civilian U.S. government agencies, international organizations, contractors, nongovernmental organizations, and the local population share the same geographical area.

Included on the complex battle space are private security providers. While there is no mechanism in place to track the number of private security providers doing business in Iraq or the number of people working as private security employees, DOD estimates that there are at least 60 private security providers working in Iraq with perhaps as many as 25,000 employees. The providers may be U.S. or foreign companies and their staffs are likely to be drawn from various countries, including the United States, the United Kingdom, South Africa, Nepal, Sri Lanka, or Fiji, and may include Kurds and Arabs from Iraq. Generally, private security providers provide the following services:

- Static security—security for housing areas and work sites.
- Personal security details—security for high-ranking U.S. officials.
- Security escorts—security for government employees, contractor employees, or others as they move through Iraq.
- Convoy security—security for vehicles and their occupants as they make their way into Iraq or within Iraq.
- Security advice and planning.

The CPA issued a number of orders or memoranda to regulate private security providers and their employees working in Iraq. Among these are CPA Order number 3, (Revised)(Amended) which described the types of weapons that can be used by private security providers; CPA Order number 17 (Revised), which stated that contractors (including private security providers) will generally be immune from the Iraqi legal process for acts performed in accordance with the terms and conditions of their contracts; and CPA memorandum number 17, which stated that private security

[6] In May 2004, the President signed National Security Presidential Directive 36, which established the PCO as a temporary organization within DOD. The PCO provides acquisition and project management support for the reconstruction effort in Iraq. PCO personnel in Iraq are permanently or temporarily assigned under the Chief of Mission authority.

Figure 1: The Complex Battle Space in Iraq

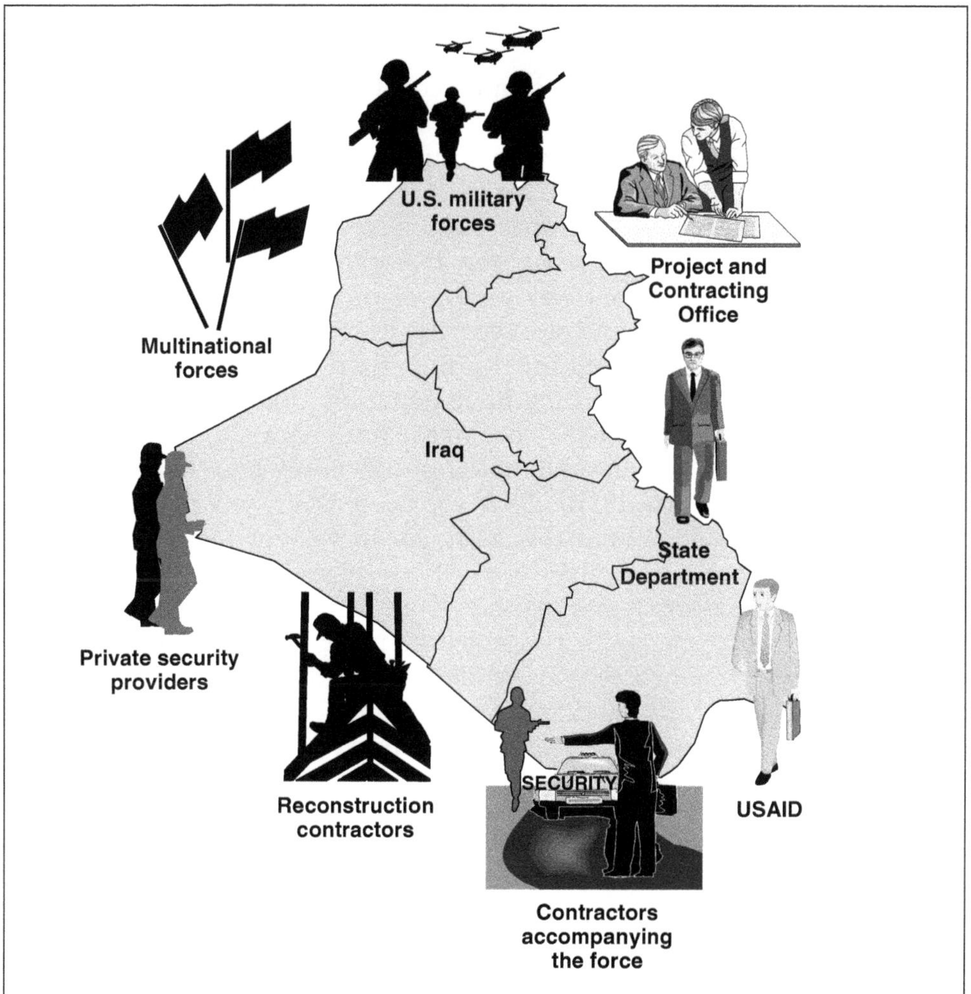

Source: GAO.

providers and their employees must be registered and licensed by the government of Iraq.

According to security industry representatives we contacted, there are no established U.S. or international standards that identify security provider qualifications in such areas as training and experience requirements, weapons qualifications, and similar skills that are applicable for the type of security needed in Iraq. Some security industry associations and companies have discussed the need for and desirability of establishing standards, but as of March 2005 such efforts are only in the preliminary stages of development.

Security for Civilians and Contractors in Iraq Is Provided by a Mix of Military Forces, State Department Security Personnel, and Private Security Providers

U.S. civilian government agencies and reconstruction contractors have had to contract with private security providers because it is not part of the U.S. military's stated mission to provide security to these organizations. U.S. forces in Iraq provide security to contractors and DOD civilians who support military operations. The Ambassador is charged with generally ensuring the security of most executive branch employees in Iraq. Government agencies have contracted with a number of private security providers to provide personnel, escort, and site security. Reconstruction contractors are generally responsible for providing for their own security according to the terms of their contracts, and they have generally done so by contracting with private security providers. The contractors' efforts to obtain suitable security providers have met with mixed results. More than half of the contractors awarded contracts in 2003 replaced their security providers. Contractor officials attributed this turnover to various factors, including the contractors' need to acquire security services quickly, their lack of knowledge of the security market and potential security providers available to provide the type of security services required in Iraq, and the absence of useful agency guidance. Finally, while the U.S. military is not responsible for providing security for civilian agencies and reconstruction contractors, it does provide some services, such as emergency medical support, to U.S. government-funded contractors.

The U.S. Military Provides Security for Civilians and Contractors Who Deploy with the Force

The stated mission of U.S. military forces in Iraq is to establish and maintain a secure environment, allow the continuance of relief and reconstruction efforts, and improve the training and capabilities of the Iraq Security Forces. As part of this mission, U.S. forces in Iraq provide security for DOD civilians who deploy with the force, non-DOD U.S. government employees who are embedded with the combat forces and contractors who deploy with the combat force. Among the contractors who deploy with the force are those that provide maintenance for weapon systems, those who provide linguistic and intelligence support to combat forces, and those who provide logistics support. Contractors who deploy with the force generally live with and directly support U.S. military forces and receive government-furnished support similar to that provided to DOD civilians.

According to CENTCOM officials, the military uses soldiers rather than private security providers to provide security to contractors, civilians, facilities, or convoys which support combat operations because of concerns regarding the status of security personnel under the law of international armed conflict.

This body of law considers contractors who deploy with the force generally to be noncombatant civilians accompanying the force who may not take a direct part in hostilities. CENTCOM is concerned that using armed private security employees to protect clearly military activities would risk a change in status for these contractors from noncombatants to illegal combatants. Thus, the private security employees could lose the protections otherwise granted contractors accompanying the force under international law.

At the time we published our report, DOD was in the process of establishing its first departmentwide policy on the military's security responsibilities for contractor personnel. The draft directive and instruction specify that the military shall develop a security plan for protection of contractor personnel and the contracting officer shall include in the contract the level of protection to be provided to contractor personnel. In appropriate cases, the combatant commander shall provide security through military means, commensurate with security provided DOD civilians. In May 2005, DOD also issued a new standard contract clause in the Defense Federal Acquisition Regulation Supplement (DFARS), to be included in all DOD contracts involving support to deployed forces stating that the Combatant Commander (for example, the CENTCOM Commander) will develop a security plan to provide protection, through military means, of contractor personnel engaged in the theater of operations unless the terms of the contract place the responsibility with another party.[7] Prior to the issuance of the new contract clause, the Army's policy expressly required Army commanders to provide security for deployed contractors, while the Air Force's policy gave the Air Force the option of whether or not to provide force protection to Air Force contractors. It is important to note, however, that the proposed DOD departmentwide policy, procedures and standard contract clause do not cover non-DOD government contractors who may be in a military theater of operations. As discussed in the following, these contractors are responsible for providing their own security.[8]

Civilian U.S. Government Agencies Provide for Their Own Security in Iraq

The State Department is responsible for the security of most of the executive-branch U.S. Government employees located in Iraq.[9] According to the President's Letter of Instruction, the U.S. Ambassador, as Chief of Mission, is tasked by the President with full responsibility for the safety

[7] DFARS Subpart 225.74.

[8] In response to public comments on the proposed new DFARS clause for contractor personnel supporting a force outside the United States, DOD stated that the new clause does not apply to nation building efforts such as the reconstruction of Iraq. See 70 *Fed. Reg.* 23791.

[9] We recently discussed the Department's efforts to protect U.S. officials working abroad. See GAO, *Overseas Security: State Department Has Not Fully Implemented Key Measures to Protect U.S. Officials from Terrorist Attacks Outside of Embassies*, GAO-05-642 (Washington, D.C.: May 9, 2005).

of all United States government personnel on official duty abroad except those under the security protection of a combatant commander or on the staff of an international organization. The embassy's Regional Security Officer is the Chief of Mission's focal point for security issues and as such establishes specific security policies and procedures for all executive branch personnel who fall under the Chief of Mission's security responsibility.

In June 2004, representatives[10] from the Department of State and DOD signed two memoranda of agreement to clarify each department's security responsibilities in Iraq. Among other things the agreements specify that

- In general, the Chief of Mission is responsible for the physical security, equipment, and personnel protective services for U.S. Mission Iraq;[11]
- The Commander, CENTCOM is responsible for providing for the security of the International Zone as well as regional embassy branch offices throughout Iraq;
- Military capabilities may be requested by the Chief of Mission to provide physical security, equipment, and personal protective services only when security requirements exceed available Marine Security Guard Detachment, Department of State Diplomatic Security Service, and Department of State contracted security support capabilities;
- U.S. forces will provide force protection and Quick Reaction Force support outside the International Zone, to the extent possible, for Embassy personnel and activities; and
- The Ambassador has security responsibility for DOD personnel under the authority of the Chief of Mission. This includes the Marine Security Detachment and personnel working for the PCO.

In Iraq, the State Department, USAID, the U.S. Army Corps of Engineers, and the CPA[12] contracted with commercial firms to provide security. Our review of six agency-awarded security contracts, awarded between August 2003 and May 2004, showed that as of December 31, 2004, the agencies had obligated nearly $456 million on these contracts. In turn, the private security providers had billed the agencies about $315 million by that date for providing various services, including personal security details; security guards; communications; and security management. The companies providing security for U.S. government agencies may be U.S. or foreign. For example, while USAID contracted with a U.S. firm, the U.S. Army Corps of

[10] One memorandum was signed by the Deputy Secretary of Defense and the Deputy Secretary of State, the second was signed by the Ambassador to Iraq and the Combatant Commander, U.S. Central Command. The first memorandum deals with security assistance, the second with security responsibilities.

[11] All executive branch agencies in Iraq are part of U.S. Mission Iraq except those which fall under the command of the CENTCOM commander.

[12] A U.S. Army contracting activity awarded several security contracts on behalf of the CPA.

Engineers and the PCO are using British companies to meet their security requirements. Security for the Ambassador is provided by a U.S. company, and only U.S. citizens are used to provide protection.

Security providers who provide security for executive branch employees follow the procedures and policies established by the Regional Security Officer. For example, one security provider told us that the Regional Security Officer recently increased the number of cars required for moving people within Iraq. The provider's representative told us that they were obligated to comply with the Regional Security Officer's instructions even though the contract was not awarded by the State Department and the company does not provide security for State Department personnel.

Contractors Rebuilding Iraq Obtained Their Own Security with Little Assistance from the Agencies

Contractors engaged in reconstruction efforts were generally required to provide for their own security, and they have done so by awarding subcontracts to private security providers. Contractors did not anticipate the level of violence eventually encountered in Iraq and found themselves needing to quickly obtain security for their personnel, lodgings, and work sites. As of December 31, 2004, our review of 15 reconstruction contracts for which we had data found that the contractors had obligated more than $310 million on security subcontracts, and in turn, the security providers had billed the contractors more than $287 million. The contractors' efforts to obtain suitable security providers met with mixed results, as many subsequently found that their security provider could not meet their needs. Overall, we found that contractors replaced their security providers on five of the eight reconstruction contracts awarded in 2003 that we reviewed.[13] This was attributable, in part, to the contractors' need to acquire security services quickly, their lack of knowledge of the security market and potential security providers available for the type of security services required for Iraq, and the absence of useful agency guidance. Information reflected in the agencies' own contracts for security, such as training and weapons qualifications requirements, could have assisted the contractors in identifying potential criteria for evaluating security providers and in structuring their subcontracts.

Agency officials expected that the post-conflict environment in Iraq would be relatively benign and would allow for the almost immediate beginning of reconstruction efforts. During a discussion with DOD we were told that this expectation was based on determinations made at the most senior levels of the executive branch and the contracting officials were bound to reflect that expectation in their requests for proposals. Consequently, they made few or no plans for any other condition. Reconstruction contractors

[13] On one additional 2003 contract, the contractor provided its own security.

shared this perspective, relying upon the language in the agency requests for proposals and the comments of agency representatives at pre-proposal and other meetings. Our discussions with contractor officials found that they anticipated providing for only a minimal level of security under their contracts, such as hiring guards to prevent theft and looting at residential and work sites. In one case, the contractor expected that the military would provide security for its personnel.

Our review of the agencies' request for proposals and other documents found that they were consistent with this expectation. For example, our review of five contracts awarded by late July 2003, including four awarded by USAID and one awarded by the U.S. Army Corps of Engineers, found that

- USAID's requests for proposals instructed the contractors that work was to begin only when a permissive environment existed. Contractors were given little guidance concerning security for their personnel and facilities and were not asked to estimate security costs as part of their proposals.
- The U.S. Army Corps of Engineers' request for proposal noted that the military was expected to provide security for the contractor and, thus, the contractor was not required to propose any security costs.

According to agency and contractor officials, the Iraqi security environment began to deteriorate by June 2003, although two contractors noted that the bombing of the United Nations compound in August 2003 made it apparent that the insurgency was beginning to target nonmilitary targets (see Figure 2).

Figure 2: Incidence of Attacks against Civilians and Infrastructure Targets between June 2003 and April 2005

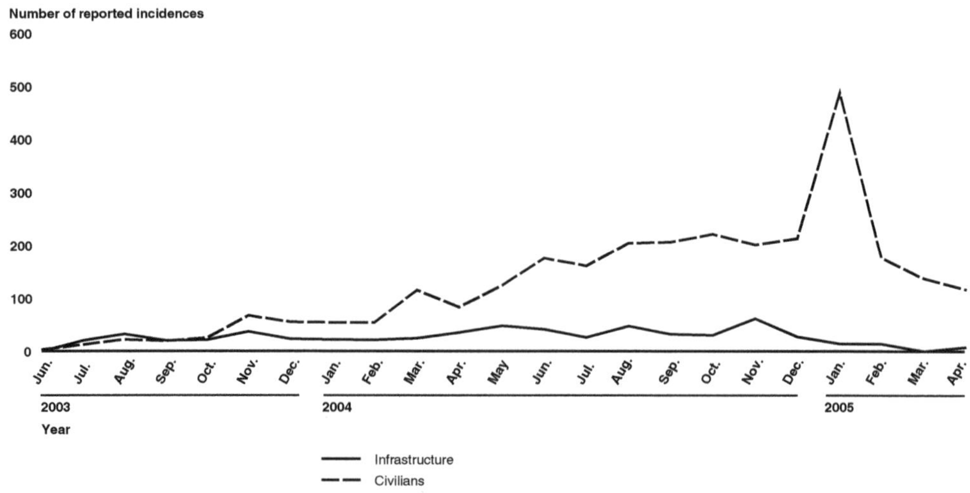

Source: GAO Analysis of data supplied by DOD.

Contractor officials told us that as the security environment worsened they unexpectedly found themselves in immediate need of enhanced security services. These officials told us that they received little guidance from the agencies relative to possible security providers. We found that the contractors' efforts to obtain security providers often met with mixed results. For example:

- One contractor, awarded a contract by the U.S. Army Corps of Engineers, expected that the U.S. military would provide security for its personnel. That contractor expressed concern, however, that the military protection being provided was insufficient to ensure its employees' safety and to allow for the performance of its mission and subsequently stopped work at one of its locations. In June 2003, the Army finally told the contractor that it did not have adequate forces to continue to provide security as promised, and advised the contractor to acquire its own security. Following a limited competition,[14] the contractor awarded a subcontract to a security provider in June 2003. In this case, the contractor has been satisfied with the services provided and retained the security provider when the contractor was subsequently awarded another reconstruction contract in June 2004.
- One USAID reconstruction contractor told us it quickly awarded a noncompetitive subcontract to a security provider in July 2003. Within three months, the security company notified the reconstruction contractor that it was pulling its employees out of the country. As a former prisoner-transport service firm trying to expand into the protective services area, it discovered it lacked sufficient capacity to fulfill its contract requirements in Iraq. The reconstruction contractor subsequently conducted a competition among security providers already operating in Iraq to meet its needs.
- Another reconstruction contractor initially hired a security service provider in October 2003. A contractor official stated that it soon became apparent that the security provider did not have the capacity to meet its security needs. As a result, the contractor awarded another subcontract, on a sole-source basis, to a security provider to augment the security services provided to its personnel.
- Three of the reconstruction contractors we reviewed hired a newly established security provider company that was marketing itself in Iraq in mid- to late 2003. Officials representing one contractor told us that the provider was the only known provider capable of meeting their needs; officials for another contractor told us that they selected the

[14] Pursuant to FAR Part 44, subcontracts are generally required to be awarded competitively, to the maximum practicable extent. The contractor prepared a justification, which was, in turn, approved by the contracting office.

provider based, in part, on its reputation. Each of the contractors, however, for various reasons, replaced the security provider. Subsequently, this security provider has been suspended from receiving further government contracts due to allegations of fraudulent billing practices.

Overall, we found that five of the eight reconstruction contractors that were awarded contracts in 2003 that we reviewed replaced their initial or second security provider with another company, while in other cases, the contractors needed to augment the security services provided by their initial provider. As shown in Figure 3, two contractors have awarded up to four contracts for security services.

Contractor officials attributed this turnover to various factors, including the urgent need to obtain security, the increasing threat level, their lack of knowledge of potential sources and the security market, and the absence of useful agency guidance. In this latter regard, the detailed standards and requirements in their own agency security contracts may have provided useful assistance to reconstruction contractors in identifying potential

Figure 3: Number of Security Providers Employed on Reconstruction Contracts Awarded in 2003 and Reviewed by GAO

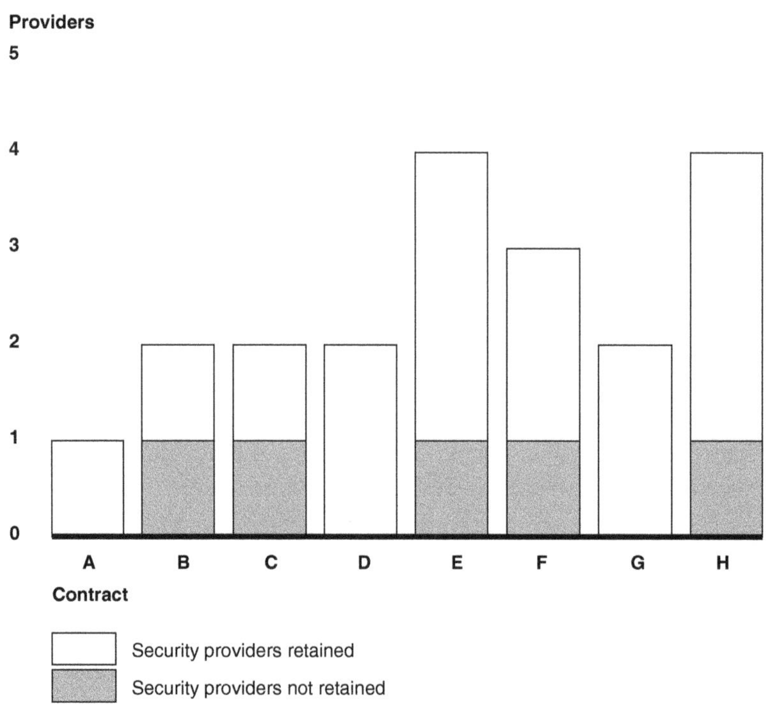

Source: GAO analysis of security provider subcontracts provided by reconstruction contractors.

criteria for evaluating security providers and in structuring their subcontracts. For example, the USAID security services contract, awarded in August 2003, contained

- a detailed and required organization structure to be used by the contractor, with titles, duties and responsibilities of various levels of security providers specified;
- requirements for background checks on potential employees and provisions for agency approval and acceptance of those employees;
- detailed standards of conduct for contractor employees;
- language, health, and training requirements;
- weapons capability requirements; and
- instructions regarding providing armored vehicles.[15]

Our review of five other agency security contracts awarded directly to private security providers from December 2003 through May 2004 for the protection of agency personnel in Iraq found that, to varying degrees, most of the cited areas were addressed. Conversely, our review of the subcontracts awarded by the reconstruction contractors to their security providers generally contained far less information.

According to most contractor officials with whom we spoke, information similar to that included in the agency's contracts would have assisted them in defining their security needs and structuring their security subcontracts.

Some contractor officials also noted that agency assistance with identifying and vetting potential security provider companies would have been very useful or would be useful in future similar situations. They discussed the possibility of a qualified vendors list, or, if time permitted, the establishment of a multiple award schedule of qualified security providers, which contractors could use to quickly contract for their security needs through competitive task orders.[16]

Agency officials believed that information regarding personnel qualifications and competent providers could be made available to contractor personnel in future efforts, especially if the information was provided for the contractor's consideration, rather than being a contract requirement.

---

[15] USAID awarded its security contract on a sole-source basis citing an urgent and compelling need. In January 2005, the USAID Inspector General found, however, that in its efforts to award the contract quickly, USAID failed to adequately document the selection of the security provider and the purchase of armored vehicles that did not meet U.S. government standards. USAID generally agreed with the Inspector General's findings and is taking corrective actions.

[16] For example, the General Services Administration currently maintains a multiple award schedule that federal agencies can use to obtain various types of security services within the United States.

For example, one agency official noted that his agency's requests for proposals for security services are publicly available. Some officials believed that making information a contractual requirement would infringe upon the contractor's privity of contract with its subcontractors and might pose a potential government liability should such requirements later prove inadequate. Other officials believed that it should be the contractor's responsibility to research and decide for itself its own needs and sources of security services without assistance from the government.

DOD Provides Emergency Quick Reaction Forces and Other Services to Contractors in Iraq

According to U.S. officials and contractor personnel we interviewed, U.S. military forces in Iraq will provide, when assets are available, emergency quick reaction forces to assist contractors who are engaged in hostile fire situations. The military is also providing other support services to U.S. government-funded contractors, to include private security providers. For example, U.S. military forces will assist with the recovery and return of contractor personnel who have been kidnapped or held hostage. Additionally, the U.S. military also provides medical services above the primary care level to contractors. These services include hospitalization, as well as laboratory and pharmaceutical services, dental services, and evacuation services, should the patient require them. In addition, the military is providing medical support to private citizens, third country nationals, and foreign nationals when necessary to save life, limb, or eyesight. Finally, contractors are entitled to receive mortuary affairs services. DOD is providing these services pursuant to authorities under Title 10, United States Code, as well as a variety of DOD Directives, a June 2004 support agreement between DOD and the Department of State, National Security Presidential Directive 36 (which governs the operations of the U.S. government in Iraq) and specific contract provisions.

While the Relationship between Security Providers and the Military Has Improved, Actions Should Be Taken to Further Improve Effectiveness

The military and the private security providers in Iraq have an evolving relationship based on cooperation and coordination of activities and the desire to work from a common operating picture. However, U.S. forces in Iraq do not have a command and control relationship with private security providers or their employees. Initially, coordination between the military and private security providers was informal. However, since the advent of the Reconstruction Operations Center in October 2004, coordination has evolved into a structured and formalized process. While contractors and the military agree that coordination has improved, some problems remain. First, private security providers continue to report incidents between themselves and the military when approaching military convoys and checkpoints. Second, military units may not have a clear understanding of the role of contractors, including private security providers, in Iraq or of the implications of having private security providers in the battle space.

U.S. Forces Do Not Have Command and Control over Private Security Providers Working In Iraq

According to CENTCOM officials and military personnel who have been stationed in Iraq, U.S. military forces in Iraq do not have a command and control relationship with private security providers or their employees. According to a DOD report[17] on private security providers working in Iraq, U.S. military forces in Iraq have no command and control over private security providers because neither the combatant commander nor his forces have a contractual relationship with the security providers.[18] Instead, military and security provider personnel who served in Iraq described a relationship of informal coordination, where the military and private security providers meet periodically to share information and coordinate and resolve conflicts in operations.

Despite a lack of command and control over private security providers and their employees, commanders always have authority over contractor personnel, including private security provider personnel, when they enter a U.S. military installation. Commanders are considered to have inherent authority to protect the health and safety, welfare, and discipline of their troops and installation.[19] This authority allows the commander to establish the rules and regulations in effect at each installation. For example, an installation commander may determine traffic regulations, weapons policies, force protection procedures, and visitor escort policies. Contractors, including private security providers, who fail to follow the military's rules and regulations while they are on the installation can be prohibited from entering the installation and using its facilities. As an example, one Army official told us that his unit had barred some private security employees from using the unit's dining facilities because the private security employees

---

17 DOD report to Congressional Defense Committees as required by the Ronald W. Reagan National Defense Authorization Act for fiscal year 2005, Pub. L. No. 108-375, section 1206 (Oct. 28, 2004).

18 Although DOD does not have an explicit command and control relationship with private security providers, there are sanctions that can be imposed in response to acts of misconduct. DOD points out in its report to Congress that private security providers, in the absence of a formal declaration of war by Congress, are generally not subject to prosecution under the Uniform Code of Military Justice, but they remain subject to prosecution by the Department of Justice under applicable U.S. federal laws, to include the Military Extraterritorial Jurisdiction Act (18 U.S.C. 3261), the special maritime and territorial jurisdiction provisions of 18 U.S.C. 7(9), and the War Crimes Act (18 U.S.C. 2441). To date, DOD reports that there have been no disciplinary actions brought against private security providers for acts of criminal misconduct.

19 See Department of Defense Directive 5200.8, Security of DOD Installations and Resources (Apr. 25, 1991).

insisted on carrying loaded weapons into the dining facility. The unit did not allow loaded weapons in the dining facility for safety reasons.

Coordination Between the Military and Private Security Providers in Iraq Has Evolved Since the Beginning of Reconstruction

Coordination between the military and the private security providers has evolved from an informal coordination based on personal relationships to a more structured, although voluntary, mechanism established by the Project and Contracting Office (PCO). According to military officials, contractors, and security providers coordination between the military and security providers was initially done informally. When a private security provider arrived in a unit's area of operation, the security provider would try to meet with key officials of the unit and establish a relationship. A private security provider we spoke with told us that the results of this informal coordination varied based on the individual personalities of the military and provider personnel. According to some security providers, although many military commanders were very interested in establishing a relationship with the security providers, others were not. Additionally, coordination was inconsistent. For example, one officer who had served with the 4th Infantry Division in Iraq told us that coordination in his area was mixed. According to the officer, some security providers, such as the one providing security for the Iraqi currency exchange program, would always coordinate with the division before moving through the division's area of operations but another contractor rarely coordinated with the division. This is similar to information we obtained from officials of the 2nd Armored Cavalry Regiment. One officer from one of the regiment's squadrons told us that contractors that worked within the unit's area of operation generally coordinated with the regiment while those who were traveling in or through his unit's area of operation generally did not coordinate with the regiment. He also told us that on one occasion security providers escorted the CPA administrator into their area of operation without the squadron's knowledge and while the squadron was conducting an operation in Najaf. According to the officer, a fire fight broke out at the CPA administrator's location and the squadron had to send troops to rescue the CPA administrator and his party. This had a significant impact on its operation, according to the officer. Another officer, who served on the Combined Joint Task Force-7[20] staff, told of instances when contractors died and the division commander did not know that the contractors were operating in his area of operations until he was instructed to recover the bodies. Finally, according to a military officer serving with the PCO at the time of our review, the

[20] Combined Joint Task Force-7 was a subordinate command of CENTCOM and was responsible for the daily prosecution of the war. It was succeeded by Multi National Force-Iraq (MNF-I) in May 2004.

genesis of the Reconstruction Operations Center (ROC) (discussed next) was the need to improve coordination between contractors and the major subordinate commanders.

The ROC serves as the interface between the military and the contractors in Iraq and is located within the PCO. In May 2004, the Army awarded a contract to a private security provider to provide security for PCO personnel and to operate the ROC, shown in Figure 4. The goal of the ROC, which became operational in October 2004, is to provide situational awareness, develop a common operating picture for contractors and the military, and facilitate coordination between the military and contractors.

The national ROC is located in Baghdad and six regional centers are colocated with the military's major subordinate commands, to enhance coordination between the military and the private security providers. Figure 5 shows the locations of the regional centers.

Participation in the ROC is voluntary (although some DOD officials told us that participation should be mandatory) and is open (at no cost) to all U.S. government agencies, contractors, and nongovernmental organizations

Figure 4: National Reconstruction Operations Center, Baghdad, Iraq

Source: Used with permission of the ROC contractor and the PCO.

Figure 5: Locations of the Regional Reconstruction Operations Centers in Iraq

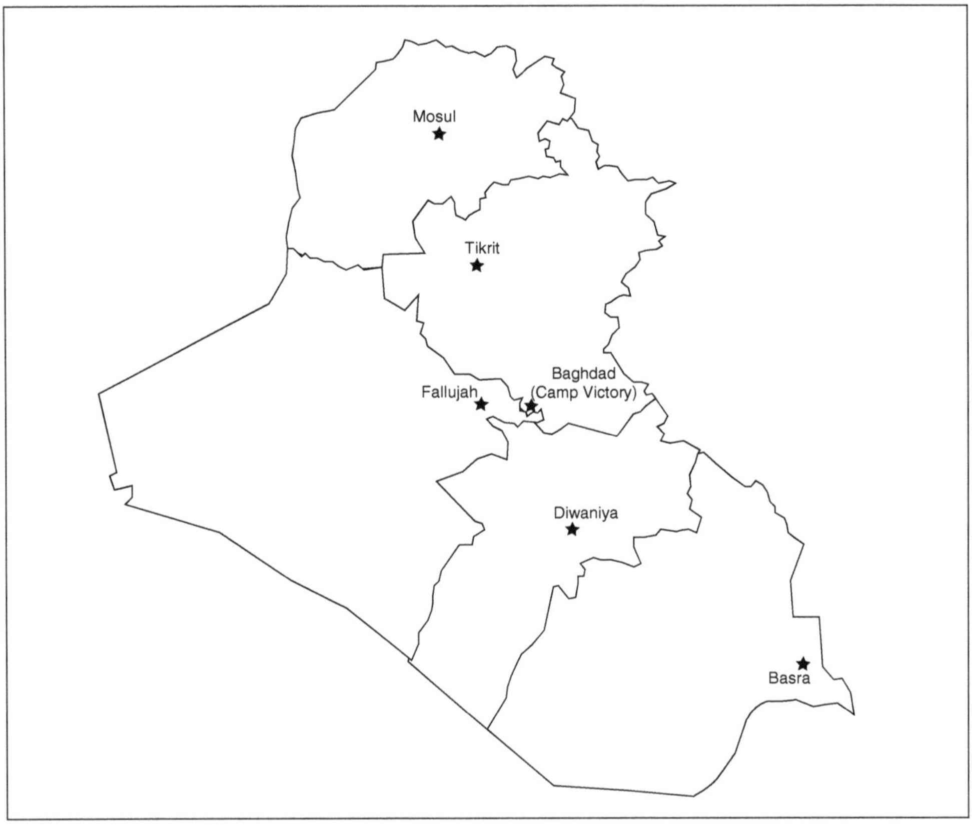

Source: DOD.

operating in Iraq. The ROC and the regional centers are staffed with a combination of military, U.S. government civilian, and contractor personnel who provide a number of services for private security providers and others. Among the services the ROC provides are:

- Intelligence information. The military provides unclassified intelligence information to the ROC for dissemination to contractors. Intelligence information is updated daily and information is available on a password-protected Web site and through daily intelligence briefings. In addition, contractors can request specific threat assessments on future building sites and planned vehicle routes. Contractors use the ROC to pass on information about incidents and threats to coalition forces as well.
- Military assistance. The ROC serves as the 911 for contractors who need military assistance. Contractors who need assistance contact

Figure 6: Process for Requesting Assistance through the ROC

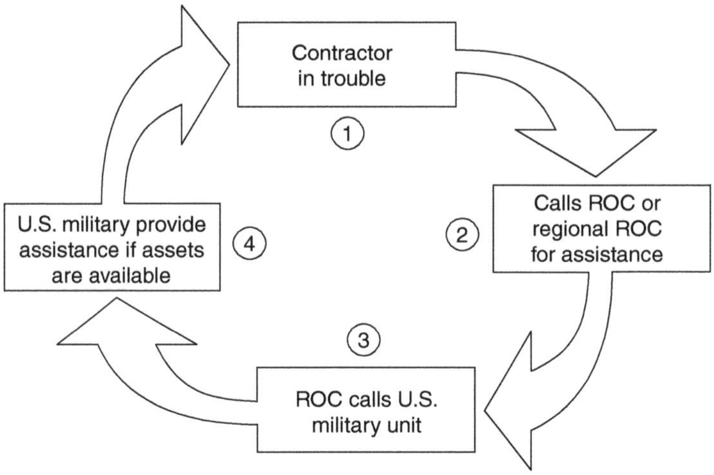

Source: GAO from data provided by ROC contractor.

either the national ROC or the regional ROCs and ROC personnel contact the closest military unit and ask it to provide assistance. Assistance, such as a quick reaction force or medical assistance, is provided if military assets are available. Security providers we spoke with said that they rarely call for a quick reaction force because incidents with insurgents are usually over within a matter of minutes but on some occasions the quick reaction forces have proved to be very helpful. For example, one after action report described an incident in February 2005 in which a private security team was ambushed by 20 insurgents and attacked by small arms fire and three rocket-propelled grenades. The contractors contacted both the regional ROC in Mosul and the national ROC in Baghdad. The military responded with fixed wing assets within 15 minutes and a rotary wing quick reaction force escorted the team safely back to Mosul. Contractors more frequently receive medical assistance from the military and described the assistance they received as excellent. Figure 6 depicts the process used to request assistance through the ROC or the regional ROCs.

- Improved communications. Communications with the military can be difficult in Iraq because of a lack of radio interoperability between the military and contractors. The ROC facilitates communications between the military and contractors. First, the ROC provides contact numbers for the military to private security providers to use when they are moving around in Iraq. Second, the ROC will ensure that the military is aware of contractor movements. Security providers who so choose can provide the ROC with information on convoy movements, which the ROC will forward to the appropriate military commands. Third, the ROC can contact the military to provide assistance to contractors, and finally, the ROC can track convoys through a real-time tracking system that uses the global positioning system and includes a communications link with the ROC if assistance is needed.

Some Coordination Problems Remain between Private Security Providers and the U.S. Military

While security providers, reconstruction contractors, and military representatives of the PCO believe that the ROC has improved coordination on the complex battle space in Iraq, both the private security providers and the military believe that several coordination issues remain to be resolved. Security providers and military officials expressed continuing concern about incidents between security providers and the military when approaching military convoys and checkpoints and the need for a better understanding of the complex battle space by both private security providers and the military.

Blue on While Incidents Are of Major Concern to the Military and Private Security Providers

One of the coordination issues that contractors and the military continued to be concerned about is blue on white violence. Blue on white violence is the term used by contractors and the military to describe situations when the military fires at friendly forces (such as contractors) or, as happens less frequently, when private security employees fire at military forces. An analysis of incident reports completed by the ROC indicates that these incidents happen most frequently when contractors encounter a military checkpoint or a military convoy. Private security providers have told us that they are fired upon by U.S. forces so frequently that incident reports are not always filed with the ROC. According to some incident reports filed with the ROC, some contractors believe that U.S. forces have fired on private security provider vehicles without provocation. For example, one security company official reported that his convoy was traveling on a route in Iraq when a U.S. military convoy approached. According to the report, the security convoy identified itself using generally recognized identification procedures and pulled off the road to allow the military convoy to pass. After about half of the 20-vehicle convoy had passed, a gunner in the military convoy began firing at the security convoy. According to the after incident report filed with the ROC, no injuries or damage resulted from this incident. A similar incident happened on the road from the International Zone to the Baghdad airport. As in the previous incident, part of a U.S. military convoy passed the private security convoy without incident when a gunner in the fourth vehicle of the convoy began to fire at the lead vehicle in the private security convoy. After this incident, the private security team leader received an apology from the servicemember who had fired on the security company vehicle. As a result of this incident, the company's vehicle was rendered unserviceable.

In another incident report, a private security provider documented an incident at a U.S. military checkpoint. According to the report, a security convoy had slowed to approach the checkpoint, and was then fired on by a U.S. soldier. The report went on to say that no verbal or hand warnings were given and no reason was given for the shooting. According to representatives of the security providers and the former director of security for the PCO, many of these incidents happen because of the military's concerns over insurgents using vehicle-borne improvised explosive devices, as well as the inexperience of some U.S. troops. Reducing the number of blue on white incidents is a high priority for the U.S. military, the PCO, private security providers, and the Private Security Company Association of Iraq, a Baghdad—based association that works with both the U.S. government and the Iraqi government to resolve issues related to private security providers. In late December 2004, in an effort to reduce the number of blue on white incidents, the Multi National Corps-Iraq (MNC-I) issued an order to major subordinate commands in Iraq establishing procedures for private security providers to use when approaching military convoys and military checkpoints. MNC-I directed the subordinate commanders to implement the procedures detailed in the order and to educate all private security providers and military on the procedures. Among the procedures were (1) a prohibition on nontactical vehicles (such as the vehicles used by private security providers) passing moving military convoys; (2) a requirement that warning shots, when fired, be aimed away from a vehicle and demonstrate a clear intention to do harm if directions are not obeyed; and (3) a requirement that vehicles should maintain a distance of a least 200 meters from a military convoy.

In early 2005, MNC-I completed an analysis of friendly-fire incidents that occurred between November 1, 2004 and January 25, 2005 to determine the top 10 lessons learned from such incidents. Among the top 10 lessons was the need for U.S. forces to comply with the rules of engagement, which require that U.S. troops determine that a person's intent is hostile before the military uses deadly force. The other lessons learned were similar to the procedures included in the order. According to a PCO official, the top 10 list was provided to the private security providers.

Despite the MNC-I order, blue on white incidents continue to occur and security providers remain concerned about the frequency of the attacks. In the 5 months (January to May 2005) since the order was issued, the ROC has received reports on 20 blue on white incidents and the number of actual incidents is likely to be higher since, as we noted previously, some providers no longer report these types of incidents. Data on the number of incidents for the 5 months before the order was issued was not available because the ROC did not start collecting information on blue on white incidents until November 2004. A ROC official noted that blue on white incidents had decreased in April 2005. He believed that the reduction was due, in part, to the adoption of the procedures outlined in the order. However, he also noted that the number of incidents could increase again as troops rotate in and out of Iraq or if terrorist attacks increase.

Units Do Not Receive Specific Training or Guidance about Working with Private Security Providers before Deploying

Military units that deployed to Iraq received no guidance or training regarding the relationship between private security providers and the military prior to deploying. Representatives from the 2nd Armored Cavalry Regiment, the 82nd Airborne Division, and the 1st Marine Expeditionary Force all told us that they received no guidance from either CENTCOM or Combined Joint Task Force-7 and that their units had not developed any written procedures for dealing with private security providers. Furthermore, a representative of a unit that is preparing to deploy, the 101st Airborne Division, told us that it had not received any guidance on how to work with private security providers nor had it been directed to include information on private security providers, the PCO, or the ROC in its pre-deployment training, even though the 101st will be co-located with a regional ROC. To highlight the lack of training and guidance, representatives from one unit told us that they did not know there were private security providers in their battle space until the providers began calling for assistance. They also noted that any information about who would be in the battle space and the support the military should be providing would be useful.

Several private security providers we spoke with told us that they believed it would be helpful if U.S. forces who deployed to Iraq received information on private security providers in Iraq. For example, the providers believed that U.S. troops needed more information on why private security providers are in Iraq, the impact of having private security providers there, and the operational styles of the private security providers. Army officials we spoke with believed that this type of information would be helpful and suggested that private security providers could use additional information about working with the U.S. military as well.

Agencies Have Limited Capabilities to Assess the Cost Impact of Using Private Security Providers

Despite the significant role played by private security providers in enabling reconstruction efforts to proceed, neither the Department of State, DOD, nor USAID has complete data on the cost associated with using private security providers. For example, the quarterly report submitted by the Department of State to Congress on the status of reconstruction projects and funding does not provide information on security costs that are incurred under reconstruction contracts. Even at the contract level, the agencies generally had varying degrees of information on the costs associated with private security providers. On 15 reconstruction contracts we found that the cost to obtain private security providers and security-related equipment at the reconstruction contract level can be considerable, as it accounted for 15 percent or more on 8 of the 15 contracts we reviewed; on only 4 of those 8 contracts, however, did the agencies formally track security costs under a separate task order or contract line item. Agency and contractor officials acknowledged that security costs had diverted planned reconstruction resources and led to canceling or reducing the scope of certain reconstruction projects, though they also noted that other factors have affected reconstruction projects.

Agencies Do Not Comprehensively Track Costs Associated with Private Security Providers

The Secretary of State is responsible for submitting a quarterly report to Congress that outlines the current status of programs, initiatives, and funds dedicated to the Iraq reconstruction efforts.[21] These quarterly reports provide information at the project and sector level—such as oil or electricity—and acknowledge the challenges and costs associated with the security environment in Iraq. For example, in its April 2005 report, the State Department noted that nearly $1.3 billion in funding has been, or will be, used in part to (1) cover unanticipated post-battle reconstruction costs, (2) cover indirect cost increases of contractors operating on cost-plus contracts that allow them to continue billing even during delays, and (3) account for increased security costs. The reports, however, do not identify the magnitude or impact of the costs associated with security providers on reconstruction efforts or available funding. Discussions with DOD and USAID personnel found that the financial and management information systems used to help prepare the report are not able to track costs incurred by reconstruction contractors for security services. Agency officials noted that to obtain such information would currently require the agencies to request such information from the contractors and manually prepare the information. Agency officials noted they have made inquiries on an ad hoc basis in the past, but cautioned that such requests can be burdensome for both the contractors and agency officials.

[21] Emergency Supplemental Appropriations Act for Defense and for the Reconstruction of Iraq and Afghanistan for FY 2004, Pub. L. No. 108-106, section 2207 (Nov. 6, 2004) as amended by Pub. L. No. 108-309, section 135 (Sep. 30, 2004).

Contractor officials acknowledge that the cost of private security services and security-related equipment, such as armored vehicles, has exceeded what they originally envisioned. In some cases, increased security costs resulted in reducing or canceling the scope of some reconstruction projects. For example:

- Contractor officials noted they were originally tasked to rehabilitate 23 electrical substations and had conducted site surveys and procured equipment for all 23 substations. According to contractor officials, however, the U.S. Army Corps of Engineers concluded that securing 14 of the substations would not be cost effective, and therefore reduced the scope to 9 substations. Contractor officials indicated that the equipment and materials procured for the 14 substations have been or will be turned over to the Iraqi Ministry of Electricity.
- In February 2004, USAID obligated an additional $33 million on one of its contracts to pay for unanticipated increases in security costs that left it short of funds to pay for construction oversight and quality assurance, as well as fund administrative costs.
- In March 2005, USAID cancelled two electrical power generation-related task orders totaling nearly $15 million to help pay for increased security costs being incurred at another power generation project in southern Baghdad.

Contractor officials noted, however, that other factors also affected reconstruction progress, such as changes in priorities or higher material costs. For example, officials at one contractor noted that security had not been a significant factor delaying their work; rather, they pointed to delays in reviewing and approving projects and slower than anticipated release of funding. Similarly, USAID officials noted that, among other materials, the cost of concrete is significantly higher than anticipated, driving up the cost of many reconstruction projects.

We found that at the contract level, agency personnel did not have consistent insight into security costs and their impact on reconstruction efforts. For example, agencies often did not require prospective bidders to propose meaningful security costs as part of their contract cost proposal nor require contractors to prepare a baseline security cost estimate at the time of contract award. Many of the contracts, including those awarded after the security environment began to deteriorate, were indefinite delivery contracts, in which the work to be accomplished was often described in general terms, with the specific work to be accomplished determined as task orders are issued. In several cases, agency personnel provided prospective contractors a sample task order to use in preparing their proposals. While the contractors' cost and technical proposals described how they would approach security issues and provided an associated cost estimate, such estimates were only for evaluation purposes and did not reflect meaningful security costs. Overall, in only 3 of the 16 contracts we reviewed did contractors prepare an initial security cost estimate for the entire contract.

Further, we found that in only 7 of the 16 contracts did the contractors regularly provide security-related cost information in either monthly progress reports or in separate contract line items or task orders. The level of information and insight provided varied greatly depending on the approach taken. For example, on three contracts, the contractor provided security cost-related information for each of its projects, but did not provide information at the total contract level. In one contract, security costs were reported on both the task order and contract level. In one contract, the security cost information was reported under a separate contract line item with other expenses, and visibility was more limited. In the remaining two contracts, the agency established separate task orders specifically to track security-related expenses at the contract level.

In 15 of the 16 reconstruction contracts that we reviewed, we were able to obtain data on the costs of acquiring private security services and related security equipment[22] by reviewing invoices that private security providers and security equipment providers submitted to contractors. Our analysis of this data found that at the reconstruction contract level there was considerable variation in estimated security costs as a percentage of total contract billings (see Figure 7).[23] Eight of the 15 contracts had security costs that exceeded 15 percent of total contract billings as of December 31, 2004; on 4 contracts, the percentage of contract billings accounted for by the cost of security subcontractors was more than 25 percent.[24] On only 2 of those 8 contracts in which security costs exceeded 15 percent did agency personnel require the contractors to formally track and report security costs under a separate task order or contract line item. Though not required, one contractor reported incurred security costs on two contracts on its own initiative.

While our analysis indicates that at the reconstruction contract level the cost of obtaining private security services can account for a significant percentage of the contract's total cost, it does not reflect total private security costs. For example, reconstruction contractors did not always specifically track security-related costs incurred by their subcontractors or lower tier suppliers. According to contractor officials, in seven of the sixteen reconstruction

[22] One contractor did not specifically track or report the security costs it incurred under the contract.

[23] Overall, the costs to obtain private security services and related security equipment for the 15 reconstruction contracts that we were able to obtain and review were about $334 million, or about 7 percent of total contract billings as of December 31, 2004.

[24] Several contractor officials noted the cost of security relative to total contract costs can vary over time. For example, they noted that initial security costs, such as for mobilizing and equipping security personnel and purchasing armored vehicles, can be considerable in relation to the amount of reconstruction work authorized. As additional work is authorized, the relative percentage accounted for by security costs could decrease considerably.

Figure 7: Percentage of Total Contract Billings Accounted for by Security Subcontractor Expenses as of December 31, 2004

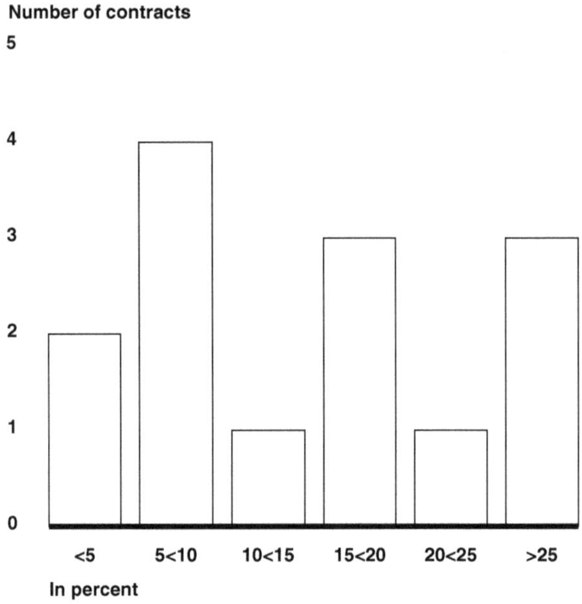

Source: GAO analysis of contractor supplied information.

contracts that we reviewed, at least one of their subcontractors provided for their own private security; in five of those seven contracts, all of the subcontractors were required to provide for their own security.[25] The cost for a subcontractor to obtain private security services can be considerable. For example, in one case, the costs incurred by a major subcontractor amounted to almost $10 million, or nearly one-third of what the reconstruction contractor was paying for security. In another case, the costs incurred by a major subcontractor exceeded $3.5 million, or about 8 percent of what the reconstruction contractor was paying for security.

Our analysis and discussions with agency and contractor officials identified several factors that influenced security costs, including (1) the nature and location of the work; (2) the type of security required and the security approach taken; and (3) the degree to which the military provided the contractor security services. For example, projects that took place in a fixed, static location were generally less expensive to secure than a project that extended over a large geographic location, such as electrical transmission lines. In other cases, contractors relied on former military personnel or

[25] In three other contracts, the contractors indicated that they provided security for their subcontractors; one contractor did not hire subcontractors; and in the five remaining contracts, the contractor did not know about or did not provide information on subcontractor security needs.

other highly-trained professionals to provide security to their employees. Conversely, some contractors made more extensive use of local Iraqi labor and employed less costly Iraqi security guards. Lastly, some contractors were able to make use of security provided by the U.S. military or coalition forces. For example, several contractors had facilities within or near U.S.-controlled locations, such as Baghdad's International Zone or on military bases, which reduced their need to obtain private security services. In another case, the contractor was provided a limited degree of protection by the U.S. Army.

Agency and contractor officials had mixed opinions on the value of establishing separate reporting or tracking mechanisms. For example, some agency officials believed that having visibility into security-related costs enabled them to provide more effective contract oversight, and identify security cost trends and their impact on the project. Other officials noted that many factors affect the cost and progress of reconstruction efforts, including changes in planned funding or projects, material costs, and the inability to find qualified workers willing to work in Iraq. Consequently, they indicated that they generally try to manage the projects at a total project level, rather than by individual elements, such as security. For example, they noted that when reviewing project status reports with the contractors, they will question the contractors on the factors causing delays or cost increases. They were not certain that having specific insight into security costs would help them better manage or oversee their projects. Agency program and financial management officials noted that from a budgeting perspective, tracking security cost information could enable staff to provide better estimates of future funding requirements.

Contractor officials generally indicated that establishing a separate task order or contract line item for security enabled them to more efficiently account for and bill security costs and to more accurately report reconstruction progress. For example, officials at one contractor noted that they often had several projects under way which required security. Prior to establishing a separate task order, the security provider would be required to allocate costs to each of the projects even though the security was provided for a given location, often resulting in lengthy and complex vouchers, higher potential for error, and increased administrative expenses. Once a separate task order was established, its security provider charged the costs incurred for providing security to the location, rather than each project, simplifying the billing and review process. Other contractor officials noted that the need to obtain security providers and security-related equipment often occurred during the early stages of the contract when the agencies had issued only a few task orders for specific reconstruction projects. Consequently, contractor officials told us they found themselves incurring considerable security-related expenses during the mobilization phase that had to be allocated to subsequent task orders, thereby increasing costs. These officials noted that allocating security costs to existing task orders would have resulted in the task's cost exceeding the government's estimate. Contractor officials indicated that a separate task order for security would have enabled them to better explain to agency personnel the cost of the reconstruction effort and the impact of security costs and enable them to account for and bill security costs more efficiently.

Expanded Use of Private Security Providers Does Not Appear to Be Increasing Attrition among Military Personnel

Data from the Defense Manpower Data Center (DMDC) [26]show that in fiscal year 2004, the attrition rates for the occupational specialties preferred by private security providers returned to the same or slightly lower levels than those seen prior to the institution of occupational stop losses[27] in September 2001 despite the increased use of private security providers. Private security providers working in Iraq are hiring former servicemembers with a variety of skills, including servicemembers with military police or Special Operations experience. Military officials told us that they believe that servicemembers with these skills are separating from the military earlier than in prior years. We are unable to determine from this data whether servicemembers are leaving the military for positions with private security providers as the data can only demonstrate trends in attrition, not explain why people are leaving the military or what they intend to do after leaving the military.

Private security providers prefer to hire former military members, particularly Special Operations forces, for their unique skills and experience. Servicemembers with Special Operations background are often hired to fill key positions, such as security advisors and project managers, and to provide personal security to high ranking government officials. These positions may pay as much as $33,000 a month. Other servicemembers may be hired to provide security to civilians in vehicle convoys with salaries between $12,000 and $13,000 per month, while some may be hired to provide site security for buildings and construction projects at somewhat lower salaries. For the most part, employees only receive these salaries when they are working in Iraq, typically 2 to 3 months at a time. All of the U.S.-based private security providers we spoke with told us that they do not actively recruit current servicemembers; however, they do recruit at military-sponsored transition job fairs, through the Internet, and with advertisements in military magazines and newspapers.

[26] DMDC collects and maintains an archive of DOD's automated manpower, training, and financial databases.

[27] Stop losses are short-term measures that increase force availability by retaining active or reserve component members on active duty beyond the end of their obligated service.

Officials from the Special Operations Command and Army Military Police Believe Attrition Is Increasing Due, in Part, to Security-Related Job Opportunities

Both Special Forces and military police personnel officials believe that attrition is increasing in their military specialties. For example, during a July 2004 hearing before the House Armed Services Committee, Subcommittee on Terrorism, Unconventional Threats and Capabilities, representatives from the U.S. Special Operations Command and the military services' Special Operations commands noted that the number of Special Forces enlisted personnel retiring at 20 years (the first time they are eligible) has been increasing due, in part, to the increased opportunities available in civilian government and with contractors. In addition, representatives of the Naval Special Operations Command and the Air Force Special Operations Command also noted that they were seeing increased attrition rates among those servicemembers with 8 to 12 years of service. According to these representatives, servicemembers leaving at this point in their careers are also leaving for opportunities with contractors.

Army officials have also expressed concerns about attrition in the military police force. For example, officials from the military police personnel office at the Army's Human Resources Command told us that they have seen a significant number of senior noncommissioned officers leave the military police for positions with private security providers. These officials also told us they have seen the average length of service for colonels in the military police branch decrease from 28 to 25 years. Furthermore, in an e-mail provided by the Army's Human Resources Command, a senior noncommissioned officer at the 16th Military Police Brigade noted that the brigade did not meet its reenlistment targets in fiscal year 2004. Finally, the Army Central Command's Provost Marshall in July 2004 told us that he had lost four of his eight senior noncommissioned officers to higher paying private security providers within the last year and was expecting to lose two more senior noncommissioned officers. He also noted that he had lost more than half of his company grade officers as well.

Efforts are being taken by both the military police and Special Forces communities to address retention concerns. For example, the Army plans to double the size of its military police force from 15,500 to 30,000 by 2006 and the Special Operations Command plans to increase its force size from 13,200 to 15,900 over the next 5 to 6 years. Increasing the size of the Army military police and Special Operations will decrease the high operational tempo[28] and relieve some of the stress on military personnel, which these communities believe contributed to higher attrition. In addition, DOD recently began to

[28] In this report, operational tempo refers to the total days military personnel spend participating in normal drills, training, and exercises, as well as domestic and overseas operational missions.

offer reenlistment bonuses to Special Operations personnel with 19 or more years of experience which range from $8,000 to those who reenlist for one year to as much as $150,000 for those who reenlist for an additional 6 years.

Attrition Rates for 2004 Returned to Level Seen Prior to Stop Loss Issuance

While data from several sources indicate increased attrition in fiscal year 2004 compared to fiscal years 2002 and 2003 in the military skills sought by private security providers, these data also showed that attrition rates in fiscal year 2004 had returned to the levels seen in fiscal years 2000 and 2001, prior to the majority of the stop loss policies that have been instituted by the services at various times since September 2001. Table 1 shows the dates of occupational stop losses for each of the services.

Each of the services added and released occupations from stop loss as the needs of the service dictated. For example, the Air Force placed all occupational specialties under a stop loss in September 2001 and then released a number of occupations from the stop loss in January and June 2002. As we noted, the Air Force ended all stop loss activities in June 2003. In the Army, Special Operations forces were placed under stop loss in December 2001 and were released from the stop loss in June 2003, while enlisted servicemembers who served as military police were placed under stop loss in February 2002 and were released from the stop loss in July 2003. Army officers serving as military police were placed under the stop loss in February 2002 and were released from the stop loss in June 2003.

Data obtained from DMDC on the military occupational specialties preferred by private security providers revealed that several of these specialties

Table 1. Occupational Stop Loss Dates for the Military Services

Service	Stop Loss Began	Stop Loss Ended
Army	December 2001	November 2003[a]
Navy	September 2001	August 2002
Air Force	September 2001	June 2003
Marine Corps	January 2002	May 2003

Source: GAO from DOD data.

[a]Although the Army terminated its occupational stop loss program, at the time we issued this report the Army had a unit stop loss program in effect. The Army's unit stop loss policy applies to soldiers in units preparing to deploy. It applies to all soldiers in a unit and prevents soldiers from leaving the Army within 90 days of their unit's deployment, during the unit's deployment, and 90 days after the unit has returned from its deployment.

show increased attrition in fiscal year 2004 over the attrition rates in fiscal year 2003. These specialties include:

- Air Force: Officer military police
- Army: Enlisted and Officer Infantry, military police, and Special Forces
- Marine Corps: Enlisted and Officer Infantry and military police
- Navy: Enlisted military police, Officer Special Forces, and Enlisted SEALs.

For the specialties listed, the average attrition rates for each fiscal year are shown in Figure 8. As seen in Figure 8, the attrition rates for these specialties decreased in fiscal year 2002 and 2003 from their 2000 and 2001 levels and showed an increase in attrition in fiscal year 2004. These data also show that the levels of attrition seen in fiscal year 2004 were actually lower than those seen in fiscal years 2000 and 2001.

The decrease in attrition rates seen in fiscal years 2002 and 2003 as compared to the rates seen in fiscal years 2000 and 2001 reflect attrition patterns that

Figure 8: Average Attrition Rates for Military Occupational Specialties Preferred by Private Security Providers which Experienced Increased Attrition in Fiscal Year 2004

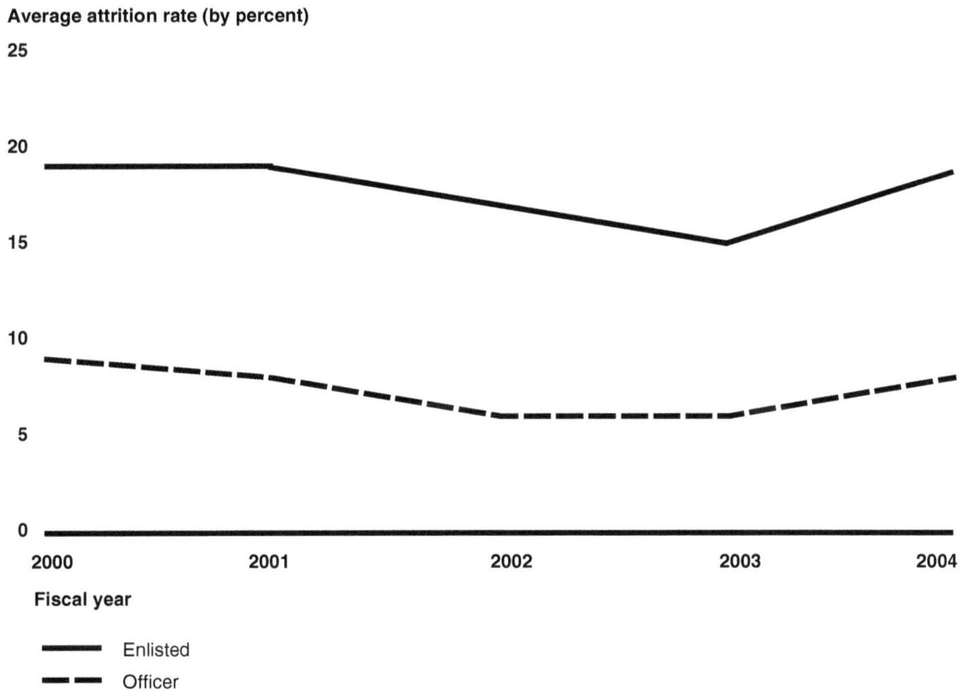

Source: GAO analysis of DOD data.

are seen during stop losses. Service officials told us that stop loss policies affect attrition rates; they can temporarily delay separations and artificially decrease attrition rates for the year of the stop loss. Officials at the Army Human Resources Command also found that stop loss policies can also increase attrition rates for the year preceding the stop loss. For example, the Army saw increased separations in 2002 for military police colonels in anticipation of their occupation-specific stop loss. Given the impact of stop loss policies on attrition, data may not accurately convey the typical personnel losses that would have occurred had the stop loss not been in effect as people left the military both in anticipation of stop loss and after stop loss was lifted. Thus, we are unable to determine whether the increase in attrition rates in fiscal year 2004 was due to the lifting of the stop loss policy or true increases in military attrition.

Figure 9 shows a pattern of decline in attrition rates during the stop loss period followed by a rebound for Army Special Forces in fiscal year 2004. Attrition rates for enlisted Army Special Forces were almost identical in fiscal years 2000 and 2001, and declined through 2003 during the Army Special Forces specific stop loss, which was in effect from December 2001 to June 2003. However, after the stop loss was lifted, attrition rates for the

Figure 9: Army Special Forces Attrition Rates

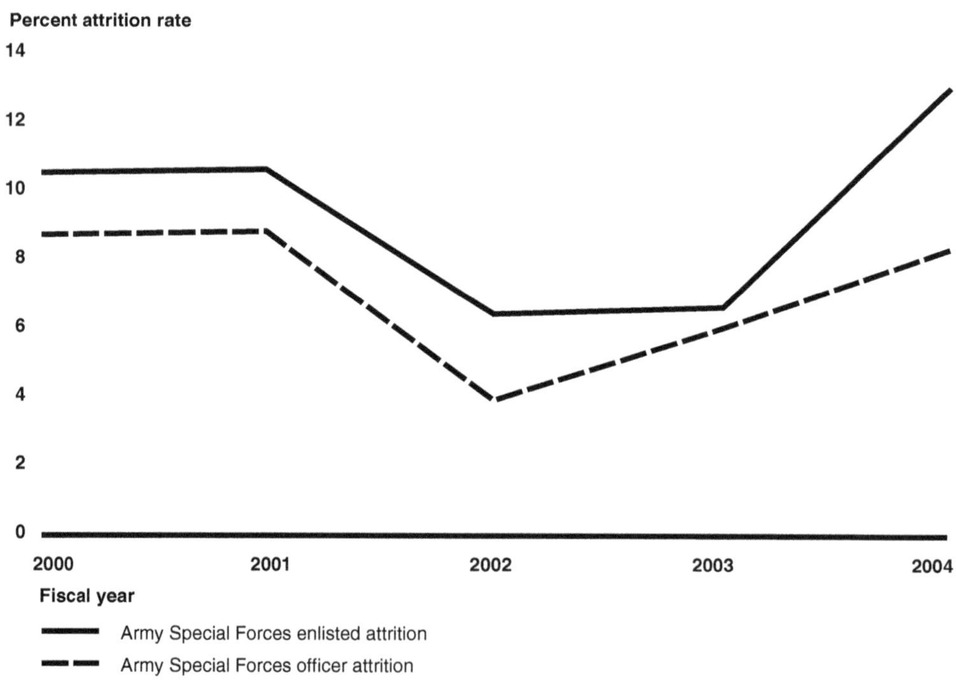

Source: GAO analysis of DOD data.

enlisted Army Special Forces almost doubled from 6.5 percent in fiscal year 2003 to 12.9 percent in fiscal year 2004, a level which was about 25 percent higher than the fiscal year 2000 rate. Attrition rates for Army Special Forces officers also declined during the stop loss period and returned to just below the fiscal years 2000 and 2001 levels in fiscal year 2004.

The Special Operations Command also provided us with continuation rates calculated by DMDC for the Army, Navy, and Air Force Special Operations Commands. Continuation rates were calculated by determining which personnel remained on active duty from one year to the next and are an alternative method used to demonstrate retention and attrition. The continuation rates showed an increase in losses in 2004 for the Army Special Operations and Navy Special Warfare Commands senior noncommissioned officers, as well as Army Special Operations warrant officers. Similar to the DMDC data provided to us, these commands also saw a decrease in losses (or a decrease in attrition rates) in 2002 after a stop loss was issued and, with the exception of the Navy Special Warfare warrant officers, an increase in losses (or an increase in attrition rates) after the stop loss was lifted.

Additionally, as shown in Figure 10, the continuation data for Army Enlisted Special Operations personnel with 14 through 19 years of service separated at only a slightly higher rate in 2004 than in the pre-stop loss years—fiscal years 2000 and 2001. In the July 2004 hearing before the House Armed Services Committee, Subcommittee on Terrorism, Unconventional Threats and Capabilities, the Senior Enlisted Advisor for the United States Special Operations Command stated that the loss of these mature, operationally experienced personnel creates critical operational risk for the Special Forces. According to the Special Operations Command officials with whom we spoke, because the command is losing some of its most experienced personnel, younger less experienced servicemembers are being promoted to leadership positions more quickly than in the past. This need to rely on less experienced personnel has created some concerns for the command.

Many Factors Influence the Decision to Separate from the Military

While available data indicate that attrition, in almost all of the military specialties favored by private security providers, has returned to pre-September 11, 2001 levels, the data do not indicate why personnel are leaving the military and what they are doing after they leave. Exit surveys conducted with service members leaving the military do not include questions on the service members' future employment plans. Officials at the Army Human Resources Command told us that after September 11, 2001, the opportunities for employment in the security field became more widespread as government agencies as well as private companies and organizations recognized the need to improve their security. These officials as well as officials from the Special Operations Command noted that they

Figure 10: Continuation Rates for Army Enlisted Special Operations Personnel with 14 through 19 Years of Service for Fiscal Years 2000 through 2004

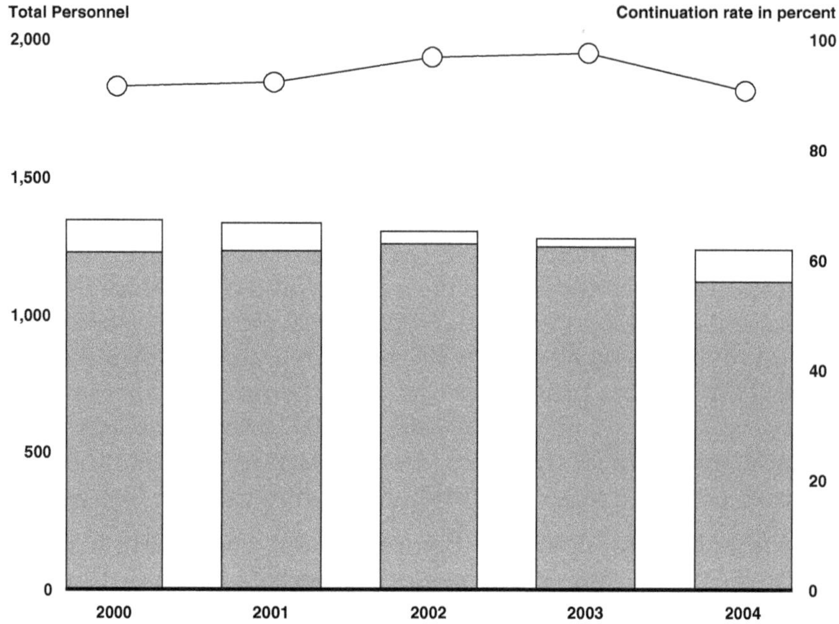

		2000	2001	2002	2003	2004
□	Loss	116	104	43	31	116
■	Con't	1,225	1,229	1,257	1,245	1,121
—○—	Con't	91.4	92.2	96.7	97.6	90.6

Source: Special Operations Command.
Note: Con't =continuation.

are losing personnel not only to private security firms operating in Iraq but also to security management companies operating in the United States, and security operations in other government agencies. Service officials at these commands also attributed the attrition rates to other factors, such as the attraction of a strong civilian economy, high operational tempo, and concerns about various quality of life conditions.

Conclusions

The reconstruction effort in Iraq is complex, costly, and challenging, in part, due to an urgent need to begin and execute reconstruction projects in an uncertain security environment. The extensive use of private security providers has raised a number of issues, particularly regarding how to facilitate methods contractors use to obtain capable providers. And, once security providers are actively working in an area, they must determine how best to establish effective coordination mechanisms with nearby military forces.

While the experience in Iraq was certainly unique relative to historical reconstruction and assistance efforts, it is far less certain whether or not the future will find the United States engaged in reconstruction and assistance efforts in other hostile environments with costs that are likely to be significant. Much has been learned in Iraq over the past two years on this subject that can serve the United States and its contractors well in planning for and executing future reconstruction or assistance efforts.

Recommendations for Executive Action

We are making four recommendations to address a number of immediate and long term issues:

- To assist contractors operating in hostile environments in obtaining security services required to ensure successful contract execution, we recommend that the Secretary of State, the Secretary of Defense, and the Administrator, U.S. Agency for International Development, explore options that would enable contractors to obtain such services quickly and efficiently. Such options may include, for example, identifying minimum standards for private security personnel qualifications, training requirements and other key performance characteristics that private security personnel should possess; establishing qualified vendor lists; and/or establishing contracting vehicles which contractors could be authorized to use.
- To ensure that MNF-I has a clear understanding of the reasons for blue on white violence, we recommend that the Secretary of Defense direct the Combatant Commander, U.S. Central Command, to direct the Commander, MNF-I, to further assess all of the blue on white incidents to determine if the procedures outlined in the December 2004 order are sufficient. Furthermore, if the procedures have not proven to be effective, we recommend that the Commander, MNF-I, develop additional procedures to protect both U.S. military forces and private security providers.
- To ensure that commanders deploying to Iraq have a clear understanding of the role of private security providers in Iraq and the support the military provides to them, we recommend that the Secretary of Defense develop a training package for units deploying to Iraq which provides information on the Reconstruction Operations Center, typical private security provider operating procedures, any guidance or procedures developed by MNF-I or MNC-I applicable to private security providers (such as procedures outlined in the December 2004 order to reduce blue on white incidents), and DOD support to private security provider employees. The training package should be re-evaluated periodically and updated as necessary to reflect the dynamic nature of the situation in Iraq.

- To improve agencies' ability to assess the impact of and manage security costs in future reconstruction efforts, we recommend that the Secretary of State, the Secretary of Defense, and the Administrator, U.S. Agency for International Development, establish a means to track and account for security costs to develop more accurate budget estimates.

Agency Comments and Our Evaluation

DOD, the Department of State and USAID provided written comments on a draft of this report. Their comments are discussed below and are reprinted in appendixes II, III, and IV, respectively.

DOD concurred with each of our recommendations, noting that it welcomed our assistance in improving how DOD and its contractors can plan for and effectively execute contracts in a complex and changeable security environment. Moreover, DOD described the steps it would take to implement some of our recommendations.

The Department of State disagreed with our recommendation to explore options to assist contractors in obtaining private security services, citing concerns that the government could be held liable for performance failures. For example, while the Department noted that it could provide the criteria it utilizes to select its contractors on a non-mandatory basis, it expressed concern that contractors relying on government minimum standards could assert that performance failures were the result of the government establishing poor standards. The Department also noted it was unclear that a government-managed security contractor program would result in enhanced contractor security, compared to a contractor-managed security program. While our work found that contractors had difficulty in obtaining security providers that met their needs and that they would have benefited from the agencies' assistance, we did not recommend a particular course of action nor recommend a government-managed security program. Rather, we recommended that the Department, working jointly with DOD and USAID, explore options to assist contractors that are unfamiliar with obtaining the type of security services needed in Iraq. Such an effort would necessarily entail a thorough assessment of the advantages, disadvantages and risk mitigation strategies of the potential options. Given the significance of contractors in accomplishing reconstruction objectives and the mixed results that they encountered when selecting their security providers, we continue to believe that thoroughly exploring potential options would be prudent.

The Department of State did not indicate whether it agreed with our recommendation to establish a means to track and account for security costs in order to develop more accurate budget estimates. It noted that it can capture costs associated with direct security providers and work with prime reconstruction contractors to determine the feasibility of providing subcontract security costs. It is not clear to us from the Department's comments how it intends to work with DOD and USAID to establish a uniform means to track and account for private security costs, which is essential given that DOD and USAID are the principal agencies responsible for awarding and managing the majority of reconstruction contracts.

In written comments on a draft of this report, USAID found the report factually correct, but did not comment on the recommendations.

We are sending copies of this report to the Chairman and Ranking Minority Member, House Committee on Government Reform; the Chairman and Ranking Minority Member, House Committee on Energy and Commerce; the Chairman and Ranking Minority Member, Senate Committee on Governmental Affairs; and other interested congressional committees. We are also sending a copy to the Secretary of Defense; the Secretary of State; the Administrator, U.S. Agency for International Development; and the Director, Office of Management and Budget, and will make copies available to others upon request. In addition, the report will be available at no charge on the GAO Web site at http://www.gao.gov.

If you or your staff have any questions, please contact Bill Solis at 202-512-8365 or by e-mail at solisw@gao.gov. Contact points for our Offices of Congressional Relations and Public Affairs are found on the last page of this report. GAO staff who made major contributions to this report are included in appendix V.

William Solis
Director,
Defense Capabilities and Management

David Cooper
Director,
Acquisition and Sourcing Management

List of Congressional Committees

The Honorable Richard G. Lugar
Chairman
Joseph R. Biden, Jr.
Ranking Minority Member
Committee on Foreign Relations
United States Senate

The Honorable John Warner
Chairman
The Honorable Carl Levin
Ranking Minority Member
Committee on Armed Services
United States Senate

The Honorable Henry Hyde
Chairman
The Honorable Tom Lantos
Ranking Minority Member
Committee on International Relations
House of Representatives

The Honorable Duncan L. Hunter
Chairman
The Honorable Ike Skelton
Ranking Minority Member
Committee on Armed Services
House of Representatives

Appendix I

Scope and Methodology

To determine the extent to which U.S. government agencies and contractors working in Iraq at the behest of the U.S. government have acquired security services from private security providers, we reviewed a wide array of documents to determine who was responsible for providing security to those types of organizations, including

- warning orders and fragmentary orders issued by the U.S. Central Command (CENTCOM), Combined Joint Task Force-7, Multi National Forces–Iraq, and Multi National Corps-Iraq to determine if any orders had been issued regarding providing security to U.S. government employees or contractors rebuilding Iraq;
- contracting documents such as statements of work, requests for proposals and contracts and contact modifications;
- Department of Defense (DoD) regulations and instructions that relate to the management of contractors during contingency operations;
- Departments of State and Defense memoranda of understanding regarding security and support;
- proposed guidance between the Department of State and the Department of Defense regarding contractor support;
- guidance to contractors prepared by the Coalition Provisional Authority (CPA) regarding contractor operations in Iraq; and
- Department of State rules and regulations, including the Foreign Affairs Manual.

We also met with officials from CENTCOM to obtain the command's position on the extent of the military's responsibility to provide security to civilian government employees and contractors, including both contractors supporting military forces and those engaged in rebuilding Iraq. In addition, we met with or obtained information from Army and Marine Corps units that served in Iraq to discuss their understanding of the military's responsibility to provide security to contractors and civilian government employees and interviewed representatives of the State Department's Office of Diplomatic Security to discuss the State Department's use of private security providers in Iraq as well as representatives of other government agencies working in Iraq who have contracted with private security providers to provide security to employees and facilities.

To determine how agencies addressed security needs when planning for and awarding Iraq reconstruction contracts, we interviewed officials at the

CPA; DOD, including the U.S. Army Corps of Engineers and the Project and Contracting Office (PCO); the Department of State; and the U.S. Agency for International Development (USAID). We discussed the guidance and direction they received prior to awarding contracts and how such information was provided to the contractors. We reviewed various acquisition documents, including agency acquisition plans, requests for proposals, price negotiation memoranda, correspondence between contractors, and other relevant documents. We met with agency and contractor officials to discuss the nature and type of guidance provided relative to the expected security environment, the need for obtaining security services, and requirements and standards for security personnel or security-related equipment.

We identified how security-related requirements were reflected in reconstruction contracts by selecting 16 contracts that were awarded to 10 reconstruction contractors. We selected these contracts using a nonprobabilistic methodology that considered such factors as the awarding agency; the year awarded; the contract's expected dollar value; and the type, nature and location of the reconstruction activity. Nine of these contracts were awarded in 2003 and 7 were awarded in 2004. For each of these contracts, we obtained the contract and contract modifications issued as of December 31, 2004, totaling about $8.6 billion; relevant sections of the contractor's cost and technical proposal; security plans; security-related subcontracts; and other pertinent documents. We also obtained and reviewed 6 contracts that had been awarded by the U.S. Army Corps of Engineers, the Department of State, USAID and by an Army contracting agency for the CPA, for the protection of their personnel and facilities in Iraq to compare the type of security-related requirements incorporated within U.S. government contracts with those incorporated into contracts awarded to reconstruction contractors and, in turn, to subcontracts with security providers.

We identified whether there are existing government or international standards relative to security providers that were applicable to the Iraqi security environment. We also spoke with agency security personnel, including the Department of State's Office of Diplomatic Security and the Overseas Security Advisory Council. We also contacted representatives from relevant industry associations, including the International Peace Operations Association, International Security Management Association, and the American Society for Industrial Security. We also researched European security-provider standards and conducted a literature review of articles relating to the security provider industry.

To assess the military's relationship with private security providers, we met with or spoke to representatives of CENTCOM, Army Central Command, and the PCO (at the Pentagon and in Baghdad) to discuss issues related to the military's authority over private security providers and reviewed a Department of Defense report to Congress addresses the use of private security providers in Iraq. We also met with or contacted representatives of Army and Marine Corps units that had been stationed in Iraq to determine if they had been provided guidance on working with private security providers and discussed issues related to command and control of private security providers.

To assess the level of cooperation and coordination between the military and private security providers both before and after the advent of the Reconstruction Operations Center (ROC), we spoke with 9 private security providers working in Iraq as well as representatives of military units which had served in Iraq to determine the state of coordination prior to and after the ROC became operational. We spoke with representatives of the PCO to discuss the ROC's role in coordinating the interactions between the military and private security providers and any actions the PCO was taking to improve coordination between private security providers and U.S. military forces. We also discussed coordination issues with the executive director of the Private Security Company Association of Iraq and several reconstruction contractors. We also reviewed information posted on the ROC Web site related to security and reviewed documents developed by the ROC to explain its operations and functions.

To determine the extent to which government agencies assessed the costs associated with using private security providers and security-related costs, we reviewed various contractual documents, including the 16 reconstruction contracts and subsequent modifications, consent to subcontract requests, and monthly cost and progress reports submitted by the contractors we reviewed. We also met with agency and contractor officials to determine the means by which they maintained visibility over security providers and security-related expenses, as well as their general experiences in Iraq, the impact of security on reconstruction efforts, and the process by which they obtained security providers.

We collected data on the costs associated with acquiring and using private security providers or in-house security teams; and the cost associated with acquiring security-related equipment, such as armored vehicles, body armor, communication equipment, and other security-related costs. We did not attempt to quantify the impact of the security environment on increased transportation or administrative expenses, on the pace of reconstruction efforts caused by security-related work stoppages or delays, or the cost associated with repairing the damage caused by the insurgency on work previously completed. We also excluded the cost associated with the training and equipping of Iraqi security forces, or the costs borne by DOD in maintaining, equipping, and supporting U.S. troops in Iraq.

For the 16 contracts we reviewed, we identified whether the agencies or the contractors had initially projected the cost of obtaining private security services. We reviewed various documents, including agency acquisition strategy plans and price negotiation memoranda; the contractor's cost proposals and security plans; and interviewed agency and contractor officials. We identified the actual costs incurred for security services and equipment by reviewing various cost documentation, including invoices, vouchers, and billing logs submitted by the contractors and their security provider(s) through the period ending December 31, 2004. We analyzed this information to determine

- the total amount billed by the contractor to the government;
- the amount billed by security subcontractors to the contractor; and
- the amount billed for other security-related expenses, such as armored vehicles, body armor, communication, transportation costs, lodging, and other security-related equipment.

We estimated the percentage of costs accounted for by private security providers and for security-related equipment by comparing the combined amount billed for these activities to the total amount billed by the reconstruction contractor to the government. We did not attempt to comprehensively identify costs that may have been incurred by subcontractors or lower tier contractors. We did, however, request information from the contractors as to whether their subcontractors required security above that which would typically be required, and if so, whether the subcontractor arranged for its own security or relied on security provided by the reconstruction contractor. We obtained examples and cost information on selected cases in which subcontractors provided their own security.

As part of our efforts, we reviewed pertinent sections of the Federal Acquisition Regulation, and in particular, the subcontractor competition and notification requirements provided for under Part 44; and relevant CPA, DOD, State Department, and USAID acquisition regulations, policy memoranda and guidance. We coordinated our work with and reviewed reports prepared by the Inspectors General for DOD, State, and USAID; the Special Inspector General for Iraq Reconstruction; and the Defense Contract Audit Agency.

To determine whether private security providers were hiring former military service members, we interviewed three private security providers from the United States that are working in Iraq and discussed the skill sets they hire. Additionally, we spoke with officials at the Marine Corps and Navy human resources commands; the Air Force's Deputy Chief of Staff, Personnel; the Army's Human Resources Command Military Police Branch and the Special Operations Command Personnel Division to ascertain whether certain military occupational specialties and ranks were seeing increased attrition and if private security providers were affecting military attrition.

We also reviewed a transcript of a congressional hearing on Special Operations Forces personnel issues held in July 2004.

To assess the extent to which military occupational specialties utilized by private security providers in Iraq are seeing increased attrition we obtained attrition information from the Defense Manpower Data Center's Active Duty Military Officer and Enlisted Master Files, which is an inventory of all individuals on active duty in the services. Our analysis was limited to active duty personnel and did not include reservists. The Center provided information on personnel numbers and losses for fiscal years 2000, 2001, 2002, 2003, and 2004. Attrition for the purposes of this report is an active duty member who is on active duty at the start of a given fiscal year and is no longer on active duty in the same service in the same pay category at the end of that fiscal year. An enlisted member who becomes a warrant or commissioned officer (or vice versa) or a member who changes services is considered to be a loss. The fiscal year lasts from October 1st of the previous year to September 30th of the named year. For example, fiscal year 2000 lasted from October 1, 1999 to September 30, 2000. Personnel numbers were calculated as the total number of members at the start of the fiscal year (for example, October 1, 1999 for fiscal year 2000). Losses are the endforce members who have attrited during the fiscal year (For example, for fiscal year 2000, losses would be the number of personnel attrited from October 1, 1999 to September 30, 2000.).

We received data from the Defense Manpower Data Center on active duty attrition rates for five military occupational specialties: special forces, military police, infantry, para-rescue, and combat controller. These military occupational groupings were selected because they represented military occupational skills most sought after by private security providers working in Iraq, as determined through interviews with officials at the human resources commands and private security companies. These data were then analyzed to determine whether attrition rates had increased in the past five years and whether servicemembers were separating from the military at increasing rates in certain ranks or number of years of service.

We assessed the reliability of the Defense Manpower Data Center's Active Duty Military Personnel Master file by (1) reviewing existing information about the data and the system that produced them, and (2) interviewing agency officials knowledgeable about the data. We determined that the data were sufficiently reliable for the purpose of this report.

We visited or interviewed officials from the following organizations during our review:

Department of State

- Bureau of Diplomatic Security, Washington, D.C.;

- U.S. Embassy, Amman, Jordan;
- The U.S. Agency for International Development, Washington, D.C., Baghdad, Iraq; and Amman, Jordan.

Department of Defense

- Office of the Under Secretary of Defense, Personnel and Readiness, Military Personnel Policy, the Pentagon;
- The Defense Contract Audit Agency, Fort Belvoir, Virginia.

Department of the Air Force

- Office of the Deputy Chief of Staff, Personnel, Force Management Division.

Department of the Army

- United States Army Human Resources Command Military Police Branch, Alexandria, Virginia;
- United States Army Central Command (Rear), Fort McPherson, Georgia;
- Project and Contracting Office (Rear), the Pentagon;
- U.S. Army Corps of Engineers, Washington, D.C.;
  - Southwestern Division, Dallas, Texas;
  - Transatlantic Program Center, Winchester, Virginia;
  - Gulf Regional Division, Baghdad, Iraq;
- The Army Contracting Agency, Fort Eustis, Virginia;
- 1st Armored Division, Wiesbaden, Germany;
- 82nd Airborne Division, Fort Bragg, North Carolina;
- 2nd Armored Cavalry Regiment, Fort Polk, Louisiana;
- 1st Cavalry Division, Fort Hood, Texas.

Department of the Navy

- Naval Personnel Command, Millington, Tennessee;
- Marine Corps Manpower Plans and Policy Division, Washington, D.C.;
- 1st Marine Corps Expeditionary Force, Camp Pendleton, California.

Unified Combatant Commanders

- United States Central Command, MacDill Air Force Base, Florida;
- United States Special Operations Command Personnel Division, MacDill Air Force Base, Florida.

Contractors

- Aegis Defence Services, Ltd., London, United Kingdom;
- ArmorGroup, London, United Kingdom;
- BearingPoint Inc., McLean, Virginia;
- Bechtel National, Inc., San Francisco, California;
- Blackwater USA, Moyock, North Carolina;
- CONTRACK International, Inc., Arlington, Virginia;
- Control Risk Group, London, United Kingdom;
- Creative Associates International, Inc., Washington, D.C.;
- DynCorp International, Irving, Texas;
- Fluor Intercontinental, Inc., Greenville, South Carolina;
- General Electric, Atlanta, Georgia;
- Global Risk Strategies, London, United Kingdom;
- Kellogg Brown and Root Services, Inc., Houston, Texas;
- Olive Security, London, United Kingdom;
- Parsons Corporation, Pasadena, California;
- Perini Corporation, Framingham, Massachusetts;
- Research Triangle Institute, Research Triangle Park, North Carolina;
- Triple Canopy, Lincolnshire, Illinois;
- The Hart Group, London, United Kingdom; and
- Washington Group International, Inc., Boise, Idaho; and Princeton, New Jersey.

Industry Associations

- American Society for Industrial Security International, Alexandria, Virginia;
- International Peace Operations Association, Washington, D.C.;
- International Security Management Association, Buffalo, Iowa;
- Private Security Company Association of Iraq, Baghdad, Iraq;
- Professional Services Council, Arlington, Virginia.

We conducted our review from May 2004 through June 2005 in accordance with generally accepted government auditing standards.

Appendix II
Comments from the Department of Defense

OFFICE OF THE UNDER SECRETARY OF DEFENSE
3000 DEFENSE PENTAGON
WASHINGTON, DC 20301-3000

ACQUISITION, TECHNOLOGY AND LOGISTICS

JUL 19 2005

Mr. William M. Solis
Director, Defense Capabilities and Management
U.S. General Accountability Office
441 G Street, N.W.
Washington, D.C. 20548

Dear Mr. Solis:

This is the Department of Defense (DoD) response to the GAO draft report, "REBUILDING IRAQ: Actions Needed To Improve Use Of Private Security Providers," dated June 15, 2005 (GAO Code 350554/GAO-05-737). We welcome your assistance in improving how the DoD and its contractors can plan for and effectively execute contracts for reconstruction or assistance efforts in a complex and changeable security environment. Enclosed are DoD's detailed comments regarding the recommendations on pages 45 and 46 of your draft report.

We appreciate the opportunity to review and comment on your findings.

Sincerely,

Deidre A. Lee
Director, Defense Procurement
and Acquisition Policy

Enclosure:
As stated

GAO DRAFT REPORT - DATED JUNE 15, 2005
GAO CODE 350554/GAO-05-737

"REBUILDING IRAQ: ACTIONS NEEDED TO IMPROVE USE OF PRIVATE SECURITY PROVIDERS"

DEPARTMENT OF DEFENSE COMMENTS TO THE RECOMMENDATIONS

RECOMMENDATION 1: The GAO recommended that the Secretary of State, the Secretary of Defense, and the Administrator, Agency for International Development, explore options that would enable contractors to obtain security services quickly and efficiently. Such options might include identifying minimum standards for security personnel qualifications, training requirements and other key performance characteristics that security personnel should possess. (pages 45 & 46/GAO Draft Report)

DOD RESPONSE: Concur.

RECOMMENDATION 2: The GAO recommended that the Secretary of Defense direct the Combatant Commander, U.S. Central Command, to direct the Commander, Multi-National Force-Iraq (MNF-1), to further assess all of the blue on white incidents to determine if the procedures outlined in the December 2004 order are sufficient. If the procedures have not proven to be effective, the GAO recommends that the Commander, MNF-I, develop additional procedures to protect both U.S. military forces and private security providers. (p. 46/GAO Draft Report)

DOD RESPONSE: Concur. DoD's current approach, which leverages the Reconstruction Operations Center (ROC) to improve coordination between military forces and Private Security Companies (PSC), is proving effective. There is value in re-evaluating its effectiveness in reducing blue-on-white engagements after a period of time. The Joint staff will develop an approach for assessing and improving procedures for coordination between military forces and PSCs.

RECOMMENDATION 3: The GAO recommended that the Secretary of Defense develop a training package for units deploying to Iraq which provides information on the Reconstruction Operations Center, typical private security provider operating procedures, any guidance or procedures developed by MNF-I or MNF-C applicable to private security providers, and DoD support to private security provider employees. (p. 46/GAO Draft Report)

DOD RESPONSE: Concur. Training materials would benefit both operational military forces and PSCs. The Joint Staff will develop an appropriate training strategy.

RECOMMENDATION 4: The GAO recommended that the Secretary of State, the Secretary of Defense, and the Administrator, U.S. Agency for International Development, establish a means to track and account for security costs in order to develop more accurate budget estimates. (p. 46/GAO Draft Report)

DOD RESPONSE: Concur. The Secretary of State is responsible for submitting a quarterly report to Congress that outlines the current status of programs, initiatives and funds dedicated to the Iraq reconstruction efforts. As such, the Department of Defense will support the Department of State's efforts to collect security cost data, since the Department of State is the lead organization responsible for directing and reporting on U.S. reconstruction efforts in Iraq. The Department of Defense will collect readily available data on incurred security costs under existing contracts and will establish procedures on accounting for security costs under future reconstruction contracts. Additionally, the Under Secretary of Defense (Comptroller) will work collaboratively with the Department of State and the Administrator, U.S. Agency for International Development to establish a uniformed means to track and account for costs incurred by reconstruction contractors for private security costs in order to develop more accurate budget estimates in the future.

Appendix III
Comments from the Department of State

United States Department of State

Assistant Secretary and Chief Financial Officer

Washington, D.C. 20520

JUL 1 5 2005

Ms. Jacquelyn Williams-Bridgers
Managing Director
International Affairs and Trade
Government Accountability Office
441 G Street, N.W.
Washington, D.C. 20548-0001

Dear Ms. Williams-Bridgers:

We appreciate the opportunity to review your draft report, "REBUILDING IRAQ: Actions Needed to Improve Use of Private Security Providers," GAO Job Code 120354 and 350544.

The enclosed Department of State comments are provided for incorporation with this letter as an appendix to the final report.

If you have any questions concerning this response, please contact Corey Rindner, Procurement Executive, Bureau of Administration, at (703) 516-1689.

Sincerely,

S. Kaplan

Sid Kaplan (Acting)

cc: GAO – Tim DiNapoli
A – Frank Coulter
State/OIG – Mark Duda

Department of State Comments on GAO Draft Report
REBUILDING IRAQ: Actions Needed to Improve
Use of Private Security Providers
(GAO-05-737, GAO Code 120354)

Thank you for the opportunity to comment on your draft report entitled *Rebuilding Iraq: Actions Needed to Improve Use of Private Security Providers*. Where the Department of State has additional comments they are outlined after the recommendation as noted below.

GAO Draft Recommendation 1: To assist contractors operating in hostile environments in obtaining security services required to ensure successful contract execution, we recommend that the Secretary of State, the Secretary of Defense, and the Administrator, U.S. Agency for International Development, explore options that would enable contractors to obtain such services quickly and efficiently. Such options might include, for example, identifying minimum standards for ***[Recommend GAO insert*** "private"] security personnel qualifications, training requirements and other key performance characteristics that ***[Recommend GAO insert*** "private"] security personnel should possess, establishing qualified vendor lists, and/or establishing contracting vehicles which contractors could be authorized to use.

Department of State Comment: State disagrees with the recommendation. The Department can make available to contractors the criteria it utilizes to select its contractors, but would be reluctant to mandate the use by contractors selecting their own security providers. Contractors relying on government minimum standards could assert that performance failures are the result of poor standards established by the government.

Government established contracts and qualified vendor lists also subject the government to claims in the event of poor performance. The government would have to determine that all vendors are responsible and capable of performance. Failure to perform could be alleged to be the result of poor government selection.

Furthermore, the Department of State is unclear from GAO's report what evidence exists that a Government-managed security contractor program for private contractors would result in enhanced contractor security, compared to a contractor-managed security program. Yet, the Department of State does recognize that the additional administrative costs and potential liability from a Government-managed security contractor program could be substantial.

GAO Recommendation 4: To improve agencies' ability to assess the impact of and manage security costs in future reconstruction efforts, we recommend that the Secretary of State, the Secretary of Defense, and the Administrator, U.S. Agency for International Development, establish a means to track and account for security costs in order to develop more accurate budget estimates.

Department of State Comment: For those contracts that are direct security providers, State can capture those contract costs. For contracts that would require a prime contractor to subcontract for security services, State can work with prime contractors to determine the feasibility of providing the subcontracting costs for security services.

Appendix IV
Comments from U.S. Agency for International Development

USAID
FROM THE AMERICAN PEOPLE

July 8, 2005

Mr. William S. Solis
Director
Defense Capabilities and Management
U.S. Government Accountability Office
441 G Street, N.W.
Washington, D.C. 20548

Dear Mr. Solis:

I am pleased to provide the U.S. Agency for International Development's (USAID) formal response on the draft GAO report entitled Rebuilding Iraq: Actions Needed to Improve Use of Private Security Providers [GAO-05-737].

USAID has reviewed the report and finds it to be factually correct. We have no further comments on the report.

Thank you for the opportunity to respond to the GAO draft report and for the courtesies extended by your staff in the conduct of this review.

Sincerely,

Steven G. Wisecarver
Acting Assistant Administrator
Bureau for Management

U.S. Agency for International Development
Office of Iraq Reconstruction
1300 Pennsylvannia Ave. N.W.
Washington DC 20523

Tel: 202-712-0448
Fax 202-216-3872

Appendix V

GAO Contacts and Staff Acknowledgements

GAO Contacts

William Solis (202) 51-8365

David Cooper (617) 788-0555

Acknowledgments

In addition to the contacts named above, Steve Sternlieb, Timothy DiNapoli, Carole Coffey, Gary Delaney, John Heere, William Petrick, Timothy Wilson, Moshe Schwartz, Kate Walker, Robert Ackley, David Mayfield, and Sylvia Schatz made key contributions to this report.

GAO's Mission

The Government Accountability Office, the audit, evaluation and investigative arm of Congress, exists to support Congress in meeting its constitutional responsibilities and to help improve the performance and accountability of the federal government for the American people. GAO examines the use of public funds; evaluates federal programs and policies; and provides analyses, recommendations, and other assistance to help Congress make informed oversight, policy, and funding decisions. GAO's commitment to good government is reflected in its core values of accountability, integrity, and reliability.

Obtaining Copies of GAO Reports and Testimony

The fastest and easiest way to obtain copies of GAO documents at no cost is through GAO's Web site (www.gao.gov). Each weekday, GAO posts newly released reports, testimony, and correspondence on its Web site. To have GAO e-mail you a list of newly posted products every afternoon, go to www.gao.gov and select "Subscribe to Updates."

Order by Mail or Phone

The first copy of each printed report is free. Additional copies are $2 each. A check or money order should be made out to the Superintendent of Documents. GAO also accepts VISA and Mastercard. Orders for 100 or more copies mailed to a single address are discounted 25 percent. Orders should be sent to:

U.S. Government Accountability Office
441 G Street NW, Room LM
Washington, D.C. 20548

To order by Phone: Voice: (202)512-6000
TDD: (202)512-2537
Fax: (202)512-6061

To Report Fraud, Waste, and Abuse in Federal Programs

Contact:

Web site: www.gao.gov/fraudnet/fraudnet.htm
E-mail: fraudnet@gao.gov
Automated answering system: (800) 424-5454 or (202) 512-7470

Congressional Relations

Gloria Jarmon, Managing Director, JarmonG@gao.gov (202) 512-4400 U.S. Government Accountability Office, 441 G Street NW, Room 7125 Relations Washington, D.C. 20548

Public Affairs

Paul Anderson, Managing Director, AndersonP1@gao.gov (202) 512-4800 U.S. Government Accountability Office, 441 G Street NW, Room 7149 Washington, D.C. 20548

DOCUMENT NO. 3

PRIVATE SECURITY CONTRACTORS IN IRAQ: BACKGROUND, LEGAL STATUS, AND OTHER ISSUES

CRS Report
RL32419

July 11, 2007

Jennifer K. Elsea
Legislative Attorney
American Law Division

Nina M. Serafino
Specialist in International Security Affairs
Foreign Affairs, Defense, and Trade Division

Summary

The United States is relying heavily on private firms to supply a wide variety of services in Iraq, including security. From the information available in published sources, this apparently is the first time that the United States has depended on contractors to provide such extensive security in a hostile environment, although it has previously contracted for more limited security services in Afghanistan, Bosnia, and elsewhere. In Iraq, private firms known as Private Security Companies (PSC) are currently providing security services such as the protection of individuals, non-military transport convoys, buildings and other economic infrastructure, as well as the training of Iraqi police and military personnel.

By providing security for reconstruction and stabilization efforts, private contractors contribute an essential service to U.S. and international efforts to bring peace to Iraq, according to many analysts and policymakers. Nonetheless, the use of armed contractors raises several concerns, including transparency and accountability. Transparency issues include the lack of public information on the terms of their contracts, including their costs and the standards governing their hiring and performance, as well as the background and training of those hired under contract. The apparent lack of a practical means to hold contractors accountable under U.S. law for abuses and other transgressions, and the possibility that they could be prosecuted by foreign courts, is also a source of concern.

Contractors working with the U.S. military (or with any of the coalition forces) in Iraq are non-combatants who have no combat immunity under international law if they engage in hostilities, and whose conduct may be attributable to the United States. Section 522 of the John Warner National Defense Authorization Act for FY2007 (P.L. 109-364) makes military contractors supporting the Armed Forces in Iraq subject to court-martial, but until the Department of Defense publishes implementing regulations, it is more likely that contractors who commit crimes in Iraq would be prosecuted under criminal statutes that apply extraterritorially or within the special maritime and territorial jurisdiction of the United States, or by means of the Military Extraterritorial Jurisdiction Act (MEJA). Iraqi courts do not have jurisdiction to prosecute contractors without the permission of the relevant member country of the Multi-National Forces in Iraq. It is possible that some contractors may remain outside the jurisdiction of U.S. courts, civil or military, for improper conduct in Iraq.

This report summarizes what is currently known publically about companies that provide personnel for security missions in Iraq and some sources of controversy surrounding them. A treatment of legal status and authorities follows, including an overview of relevant international law as well as Iraqi law, which currently consists primarily of Coalition Provisional Authority (CPA) orders that remain in effect until superceded. The various possible means for prosecuting contractors under U.S. law in civilian or military courts are detailed, followed by a discussion of possible issues for Congress. This report will be updated as events warrant.

Introduction

The 110th Congress is grappling with a broad range of issues regarding the use of private contractors to provide security for people and property in Iraq and elsewhere. For over a decade, the United States has gradually increased the types of tasks and roles for which it contracts private companies in military operations. Congress has generally accepted the concept of using unarmed private contractors to carry out support functions in military operations, such as providing food and laundry services, although not without concerns regarding the costs of contracts and alleged favoritism in issuing them. But Iraq is in some ways an atypical situation. There, the United States is relying heavily, apparently for the first time in an unstable environment, on private firms to supply a wide variety of security services.[1] Especially given a shortage of U.S. troops, private security contractors are widely viewed as vital to U.S. efforts to stabilize and reconstruct Iraq. Nevertheless, many Members are concerned about transparency, accountability, and legal and symbolic issues raised by the use of armed civilians to perform security tasks formerly performed by the military, as well as possible long-term effects on the military.

This report first summarizes available information on the private contractors providing security services under U.S. government contracts in Iraq.[2] It then provides information on relevant U.S., international, and Iraqi law, and legal issues involved in the use of armed contractors. It concludes with a discussion of issues involving the need for and suitability of private contractors, costs, and oversight and control, as well as potential foreign policy implications.

Background

The U.S. government is just one of many entities—including other governments, international organizations, and nongovernmental organizations—that employ private security contractors in Iraq. The U.S. use of private security contractors in Iraq represents a continuation of a trend that has seen the increasing growth—by many nations and organizations, including the United Nations—of the use of private contractors to provide security, as well as a variety of other functions in support of stabilization and reconstruction efforts.[3]

[1] Iraq appears to be the first case where the U.S. government has used private contractors extensively for protecting persons and property in potentially hostile or hostile situations where host country security forces are absent or deficient, but it is not the first time private contractors have been used for such purposes. In Afghanistan, there appears to be some contracting for protecting Afghani government officials, but so far reports on its extent suggest it is more limited than in Iraq. The U.S. General Accounting Office (GAO) reported that contractors have provided security guards in the Balkans and Southwest Asia, noting that in Bosnia "the Army replaced soldiers at the gate and base perimeter with contracted security guards." *Military Operations: Contractors Provide Vital Services to Deployed Forces but Are Not Adequately Addressed in DOD Plans.* GAO-03-695, June 2003, p 8. The United States also uses private contractors (U.S. and foreign citizens) for guard duty at U.S. military installations and U.S. embassies and consulates in a number of countries where stability generally is not an issue.

[2] This report does not deal with private contractors whose function is to gather intelligence from prisoners, even though reports indicate that they may be armed. For information on such contractors, see CRS Report RL32395, *U.S. Treatment of Prisoners in Iraq: Selected Legal Issues*, by Jennifer K. Elsea.

[3] According to one publication, "Not since the 17th century has there been such a reliance on private military actors to accomplish tasks directly affecting the success of military engagements. Private contractors are now so firmly embedded in intervention, peacekeeping, and occupation that this trend has arguably reached the point of no return." Fred Schreier and Marina Caparini. *Privatising Security: Law, Practice and Governance of Private Military and Security Companies.* Geneva, Switzerland: Geneva Centre for the Democratic Control of Armed Forces, March 2005. p. 1. For discussions on the growth of private companies providing security and other support to military efforts worldwide, see, for example: Deborah D. Avant. *The Market for Force: The Consequences of Privatizing Security.* Cambridge, UK; New York: Cambridge University Press, 2005; Simon Chesterman and Chia Lehnardt. *From Mercenaries to Market: The Rise and Regulation of Private Military Companies.* Oxford, UK; New York: Oxford University Press, 2007; and Singer, Peter W. *Corporate Warriors: The Rise of the Privatized Military*

Private security contractors (PSCs) protect individuals, buildings and other infrastructure, and transport convoys.[4] Currently, U.S. contracts for these services in Iraq are issued by agencies of the Department of Defense (DOD) and the Department of State (DOS). There are many companies providing private security services in Iraq, but only a handful appear to be contracted directly by the U.S. government. (A State Department website lists some 28 such companies operating there,[5] but this list appears to be incomplete as it does not include at least one company with a U.S. government contract.) An unknown number are, however, providing security services indirectly under subcontracts with U.S. contractors. There is no count of the total number of contractors or subcontractors who carry weapons while performing services contracted for by the United States.

The numbers employed under U.S. government contracts in Iraq for functions once carried out by the U.S. military are but estimates. An estimated 20,000 to 30,000 individuals perform protective security functions for private firms under U.S. government contracts.[6] Of these, a little over 2,500 were serving under Department of State contracts as of May 2007 (see **Table 1** below). The great majority of the remainder are most likely under DOD contracts, although at least one other U.S. agency has contracted for private security personnel at some point.

Private security contractors constitute a small but significant portion of the many thousands of individuals employed under U.S. government contracts to perform the spectrum of functions once carried out by U.S. military personnel. According to a July 2007 news report, some 182,000 are employed

Industry. Ithaca, NY: Cornell University Press, 2003. For a discussion of United Nations use of such contractors, see William J. Durch and Tobias C. Berkman. Who Should Keep the Peace? Providing Security for the Twenty-First-Century Peace Operations. Washington, D.C.: The Henry L. Stimson Center, September 2006. pp. 83–84.

[4] The term "security" can encompass a wider variety of functions. This report uses the narrowest definition, that is, the provision of protective services. In its work, GAO adds the provision of security advice and planning. In other works, the term can also include military and police training, repair and maintenance for weapons systems, prison administration, interrogation, and intelligence. A few works use the term to refer to the entire spectrum of military functions performed by private contractors, including logistics and base maintenance.

[5] Security Companies Doing Business in Iraq, available at [http://travel.state.gov/travel/cis_pa_tw/cis/cis_1763.html].

[6] A *Washington Post* article of May 27, 2007, attributes estimates of 20,000 to 30,000 armed security contractors working in Iraq to the "Pentagon and company representatives." Steve Fainaru and Saad Al-Izzi. U.S. Security Contractors Open Fire in Baghdad. *Washington Post*. May 27, 2007. p. A21. The Government Accountability Office (GAO) reported in 2006 that the Director of the Private Security Companies Association of Iraq estimated that as of March 2006, there were a total of 181 private security companies with just over 48,000 employees working in Iraq. (U.S. Government Accountability Office. *Rebuilding Iraq: Actions Still Needed to Improve the Use of Private Security Providers*. Testimony of William Solis, Director, Defense Capabilities and Management, before the Subcommittee on National Security, Emerging Threats, and International Relations, Committee on Government Reform. GAO-06-865T. June 13, 2006.)

under U.S. government contracts.[7] Of these, some 127,000 are under DOD contracts, according to testimony at April 2007 congressional hearings.[8]

In recent congressional hearings, Representative Patrick T. McHenry, a member of the House Oversight and Government Reform Committee, stated that approximately 60 private security companies are currently working for the U.S. government in Iraq, "according to the research we've done."[9] DOD has not released figures on the number of private contractors providing protective services under DOD contracts. In May, the Department of State listed 2,522 private security contractors working under its two security contracts, but did not know how many such contractors were working on subcontracts under Department of State and USAID reconstruction contracts. (See below for details on the Department of State contract).

Most individuals hired by the companies providing security services under U.S. government contracts or subcontracts are Iraqis, and a good number are third-country nationals. Of the 182,000 total contractors cited above, some 118,000 (i.e., about two-thirds) are Iraqis, and some 43,000 (about one-quarter) are third-country nationals. Only some 21,000 (a little over one-eighth) are Americans, according to the same news article.[10] According to a DOD official, just 17% of the total 127,000 individuals working under DOD contracts or subcontracts in Iraq (i.e., somewhat over 21,000) are U.S. citizens, although the proportion may be different for private security contractors.[11] Citizens of Chile, Fiji, Nepal, South Africa, the United Kingdom, and other countries reportedly carry arms under private security contracts. Peter Singer of the Brookings Institution estimates that citizens of some 30 countries are employed by private security companies in Iraq.[12] Nonetheless, most of those working in Iraq as private security contractors are Iraqi, according to Doug Brooks of the International Peace Operations Association

---

7 T. Christian Miller. "Private Contractors Outnumber U.S. Troops in Iraq." *Los Angeles Times*. July 4, 2007. Sources cited are State Department and Defense Department figures.

8 CQ Transcriptions. *Opening remarks of Rep. Martin T. Meehan. Chairman*. House Armed Services Subcommittee on Oversight and Investigations Holds Hearing on Iraqi Security Forces Contracting. April 25, 2007. The *New York Times* attributes to the Pentagon a figure of about "126,000 men and women" as serving as contractors alongside U.S. troops in Iraq. John M. Broder and James Risen. Death Toll for Contractors Reaches New High in Iraq. *New York Times*. May 19, 2007.

9 CQ Transcriptions. House Oversight and Government Reform Committee Holds Hearings on Waste, Fraud and Abuse in Iraq Reconstruction, Part 2. February 7, 2007. (Part 1 of these hearings was held on February 6; Part 3 on February 8.)

10 Private Contractors Outnumber U.S. Troops in Iraq. *op.cit*. There appears to be some disconnect between the numbers report in this article and the earlier testimony on DOD contractors, unless it can be assumed that virtually all Americans working as contractors in Iraq, except for the approximately 2,500 working under Department of State security contracts, are working under DOD contracts or subcontracts.

11 CQ Transcriptions. *Remarks of Gary Motsek, Assistant Deputy Undersecretary of Defense for Program Support, Office of the Undersecretary of Defense for Acquisition, Technology and Logistics*. House Armed Services Subcommittee on Oversight and Investigations Holds Hearing on Iraqi Security Forces Contracting. April 25, 2007. The percentage of U.S. citizens may have changed somewhat, as Mr. Mostek indicated that new figures were due in May 2007.

12 Conversation with Peter Singer, Brookings Institution, June 13, 2007.

(IPOA), an industry group.[13] U.S. citizens also work for foreign companies providing security for foreign employers.

Pay scales for these contractors reportedly vary depending on their experience and perceptions of risk, as well as their nationality. When the hiring of such contractors first became controversial, the news media reported (in April 2004) a pay range of $500 to $1,500 per day.[14] Now, however, some analysts state that pay is on the average lower globally as the supply of those desiring such work has risen,[15] even as risk may be perceived as increasing. The highest amounts are paid to highly experienced former military personnel, such as former U.S. and British special forces, with lower amounts paid to personnel from Third World countries such as Chile and Nepal, and the lowest amounts going to locally hired Iraqis.

Like soldiers, private security contractors incur the risk of death and injury from insurgents in Iraq. U.S. Army Corps of Engineers data reportedly show that an increasing proportion of registered supply convoys has been attacked, rising from 5.5% in 2005 to 14.7% for 2007 through May 10 (i.e., about the first 18 weeks of 2007).[16] Of those involved in the 12,860 Corps-registered convoys that transported supplies in Iraq from August 2004 through May 10, 2007, some 132 "security employees and drivers" were killed and 416 were wounded, according to a report on that data.[17] (The cause of death and injury was not reported, however, and may include accidents and well as shooting deaths. The totals for all convey may well be substantially higher as there are likely deaths and injuries associated with convoys that are not registered with the Corps' Reconstruction Logistics Directorate.) Convoy-related deaths appear to be a significant portion of total private contractor deaths. An earlier news report cited Department of Labor statistics showing 917 private contractors have died and more than 12,000 have been wounded in battle or in job-related accidents in the four years since the war (i.e., March 2003 through March 2007); of these, some 146 died and another 3,430 were wounded or injured in the first three months of 2007.[18] During that same period, some 244 U.S. soldiers died, according to the news report.

The total cost to the U.S. government of such security services in Iraq is not known. Estimates of the portion of reconstruction project costs consumed by security have varied. A 2006 SIGIR report surveying nine major U.S. contractors found their costs to range from a low of 7.6% to a high of 16.7%,

[13] E-mail correspondence from Doug Brooks, President, International Peace Operations Association, July 2, 2007.

[14] David Barstow. Security Companies: Shadow Soldiers in Iraq. *New York Times*, April 19, 2004.

[15] Interview with Doug Brooks, December 13, 2006.

[16] Steve Fainaru. Iraq Contractors Face Growing Parallel War. *Washington Post*. June 16, 2007. p. A12.

[17] *Ibid.*

[18] *New York Times*. May 19, 2007. *op.cit.* The article states that the New York Times obtained the data through a Freedom of Information Act request it filed with the Department of Labor.

whereas the State Department estimated it in 2005 as 16%–22%.[19] This year, House Oversight and Government Reform Committee Chairman Henry Waxman stated at the committee's February hearings on Iraq reconstruction that almost $4 billion "has been paid for private security services in the reconstruction effort alone."[20]

Whether the use of private contracts for such services is cost effective is another question that cannot be answered definitively with current information. The Government Accountability Office (GAO), in a recent report on costs of operations and maintenance support services notes that appropriate information is lacking to make such a calculation for such services and that the analyses needed to make such a determination "can be expensive and time-consuming."[21]

State Department and DOD Private Security Contracts[22]

Little information is publically available on State Department and DOD contracts for private security services in Iraq. The State Department has recently made available the names of the companies holding its primary contracts for such protective services and the numbers of security personnel serving directly and indirectly under those contracts. The State Department has not made public the names of the subcontractors who perform security services for those carrying out reconstruction activities under State Department contracts. The DOD has not publically released information on its contractors and subcontractors; information on these subjects must be compiled from secondary sources.

State Department Private Security Contracts. The State Department has three prime security contractors hired under a Worldwide Personal Protective Services (WPPS) umbrella contract, dating from July 2005, according to information provided by the department: *Blackwater U.S.A.*; *DynCorp International, LLC,* and *Triple Canopy, Inc.*[23] WPPS contracts are used to provide bodyguards and "static" guards (i.e., guards for buildings and other infrastructure) in Baghdad and other areas throughout Iraq. Triple Canopy also holds another State Department contract to provide local guard services for the U.S. Embassy and other sites in the Baghdad "Green Zone," which are under Chief of Mission control.

---

[19] As cited in CRS Report RL31833, *Iraq Reconstruction Assistance,* by Curt Tarnoff. April 6, 2007. p. 25.

[20] CQ Transcriptions. House Oversight and Government Reform Committee Holds Hearings on Waste, Fraud and Abuse in Iraq Reconstruction, Part 2. February 7, 2007. This is about a fifth of the $20 billion in spending through FY2007 from the Iraq Relief and Reconstruction Fund and over a tenth of the $35 billion in total U.S. Reconstruction Assistance, as computed in CRS Report RL31833, *op. cit.*, p. 3.

[21] U.S. Government Accountability Office. *Trends in Operation and Maintenance Costs and Support Services Contracting*. GAO-07-631. May 2007.

[22] Information on the Department of State in this paragraph from the author's interview with State Department officials on May 24, 2007.

[23] The WPPS contracts are also used to provide security services not only in Iraq, but also in Afghanistan, Bosnia, and Israel.

Blackwater USA, founded in 1997 and headquartered in Moyock, North Carolina, has provided a variety of protective services in Iraq. It was one of the original companies providing such services to the Coalition Provisional Authority (CPA), including protection for CPA chief Paul Bremer as well as other CPA employees and visiting dignitaries. Its staff includes former military, intelligence, and law enforcement personnel. According to news reports and its website, Blackwater was founded by three former Navy SEALs.

DynCorp International LLC evolved, according to its website, from a company formed in 1946 that provided support and services to U.S. military aircraft and weapons systems under Air Force contracts. Named DynCorp since 1987, it was acquired in 2003 by Computer Sciences Corporation (CSC) and now has nearly 14,000 employees in 30 countries.[24] Besides the WPPS contract, DynCorp also holds another State Department contract, under the Bureau of International Narcotics and Law Enforcement, to provide police training and related services in Iraq.

Triple Canopy, Inc., founded in September 2003, bills its operational leadership as "comprised of former operators from tier-one special operations units. . . ." Its two founders and co-chairman both served with the U.S. Army Special Forces, one with Special Forces "Delta Force" unit.[25]

The State Department provided information on the number of people performing under contracts with these companies, as well as related subcontracts, and identified them by nationality group (i.e., U.S. citizen, Iraqi citizen, and other foreign nationals). The numbers of those serving are only the DOS's prime contractors and their subcontracts. It does not include private security personnel who have been hired by DOS contractors providing other services, for instance, guards hired by a company that has a contract to provide engineers.

The U.S. Agency for International Development initially contracted Knoll, Inc. to provide security for its personnel, but now they receive protection under the State Department contracts. USAID contractors hire their own security; a USAID official stated that the organization has no accounting of the number of security companies for personnel providing security to USAID contractors.[26]

---

[24] Information on the company's history and size from its website at [http://www.dyncorpinternational.com]. DynCorp's performance under the INL contract was reviewed by the OSIGIR. Review of DynCorp International, LLC, Contract Number S-LMAQM-04-C-0030, Task Order 0338, for the Iraqi Police Training Program Support. SIGIR-06-029. DoS-OIG-AUD/IQO-07-20, January 30, 2007. According to this report, the contract was awarded in February 2004, for a base year and four renewable one-year options. Its potential value was $1.8 billion.

[25] From the company's history posted on the Triple Canopy website at [http://www.triplecanopy.com].

[26] Telephone conversation of June 26, 2006.

Table 1. Department of State Security Contractors in Iraq

Company	Number of Americans	Number of Iraqis	Number of Third-Country Nationals	Total
Worldwide Personal Protective Services Contracts				
Blackwater, USA	744	12	231	987
DynCorp International, LLC	100	15	36	151
Triple Canopy	101	2	154	257
Total WPPS	**945**	**29**	**421**	**1,395**
Local Guard Service Contract				
Triple Canopy	**113**	**122**	**992**	**1, 227**

Source: Department of State.

Notes: The information was provided in May 2007, from data collected May 9, 2007. It comes with the warning that the actual numbers of employees working in Iraq vary widely on a daily basis due to personnel rotations, medical evacuations, and R&R travel.

DOD PSC Contract Information from Secondary Sources. There is little public information at this point on DOD contracts for security services; it is not even clear how many companies provide such services directly or indirectly under DOD contracts. In 2004, CRS prepared a list of nine companies that public source information, primarily press reports and websites, described as providing security services to the Coalition Provisional Authority in Iraq,[27] which may have indicated the existence of a DOD contract.[28] A scan of the same sources this year yields much less information, with only four companies linked to recent and current DOD security contracts or subcontracts.

There is authoritative secondary information on only one company, *Aegis Defense Services Limited,* that directly provides security services under a DOD contract. On May 25, 2004, DOD contracted *Aegis Defence Services Limited,* a British firm, to provide a variety of security-related services, including intelligence and protective services. According to an audit

[27] These companies were identified and discussed in the May 28, 2004 edition of this report. They varied greatly in size and several offered a wide variety of security-related and other services. Some were founded decades ago, some within the last few years. The companies were: ArmorGroup, Blackwater Security Consulting (now Blackwater USA), Custer Battles, Diligence LLC, Erinys Iraq, Global Risk Strategies, ISI Iraq, Special Operations Consulting-Security Management Group (SOC-SMG), and The Steele Foundation. Sources consulted for these profiles include company websites, where available, news articles, and government sources cited in that edition of the report.

[28] The U.S. Department of the Army was named the CPA's "executive agent" with the responsibility of executing contracts on behalf of the CPA, but it appeared that not all of those contracts were issued by the Army.

report prepared by the Office of the Special Inspector General for Iraq Reconstruction, Aegis was contracted "to provide a comprehensive security management team that provides anti-terrorism support and analysis, close personal protection, movement and escort security, and security program management"[29] throughout Iraq. Under the contract, Aegis is to "continuously gather, interpret, and expeditiously disseminate information on the security situation throughout Iraq . . ." and to provide "guidance and coordination for the security planning and protection of the ten major prime reconstruction contractors and their subcontractors." The contract also calls for Aegis to provide a range of guard services to DOD Project and Contracting Office (PCO) personnel and offices, as well as to PCO reconstruction contractor personnel. Such services include security escort teams for travel to reconstruction sites, around-the-clock personal security details for senior PCO management, and static guards for PCO facilities.[30]

The Aegis contract extended over a base year and two optional renewable years: the first year was valued at approximately $92 million, the second at $97 million, and the third at $103 million,[31] for a potential total value of $292 million. The contract was to expire at the end of May 2007, but reportedly has been extended for up to six months because of challenges to the process for a new contract to provide the same intelligence and protective services. Aegis reportedly is bidding on the new contract, valued up to $475 million, as are several other companies, including the two challengers, Blackwater Security Consulting and Erinys Iraq.[32]

FedSpending.org, a website operated by a nongovernmental organization[33] indicates that a third company, *Erinys International, Iraq*, held a DOD contract to provide security services in Iraq during FY2006. A recent news article reports that Erinys works "side-by-side" with Aegis "in Baghdad's Green Zone on similar but separate contracts."[34] Erinys was one of the nine contractors CRS identified in 2004.[35]

---

[29] Office of the Special Inspector General for Iraq Reconstruction (SIGIR). Audit Report: Compliance with Contract No. W911S0-C-0003 Awarded to Aegis Defense Services Limited. Report Number 05-005. April 20, 2005. p. 1. The audit found several deficiencies in the areas of personal security detail qualifications, regional operations centers, and security escorts and movement control (p. 3), which the Aegis website states had been corrected by the time the audit was issued [http://www.aegisworld.com/aegis-faq.html].

[30] SIGIR, op.cit., p. 3.

[31] *Ibid.*

[32] Alec Klein and Steve Fainaru. Firms Protest Exclusion From Iraq Security Bid. *Washington Post.* May 5, 2007.

[33] FedSpending.org [http://www.fedspending.org] is a project of OMB Watch. It provides data in readily retrievable form that it obtains from the Federal Procurement Data System (FPDS)—Next Generation and other federal government sources through Eagle Eye Publishers, Inc.

[34] *Washington Post.* May 5, 2007. *op. cit.*

[35] Erinys Iraq held a major contract to protect Iraq's oil fields, and trained Iraqis for that task. The contract reportedly was worth $39 million over two years. Also, according to its website in 2004, Erinys Iraq had a contract with the U.S. Army Corps of Engineers to provide "nationwide personal security details and protective services." According to one news account at the time, the company was a joint

Triple Canopy, Inc. has been identified in the press as providing security services to a DOD contractor, KBR. This identification surfaced as a result of the court case brought by two former Triple Canopy employees.

ArmorGroup International, a British company founded some 25 years ago, was also identified in a recent news article as a U.S. government contractor. According that article, ArmorGroup, with some 1,200 employees in Iraq, "protects 32 percent of all nonmilitary supply convoys" and has lost some 26 employees in Iraq.[36] It is not clear from the article whether ArmorGroup operates as a contractor or subcontractor for all of its work, but other information indicates it works as a subcontractor. ArmorGroup is reportedly a leading contender for the Aegis contract now up for bids. ArmorGroup was one of the nine contractors CRS identified in 2004.[37]

The U.S. military plans to let three large security contracts valued at about $1.4 billion this year, according to a recent news report. One is the U.S. Army Corps of Engineers contract for up to $475 million in intelligence and protective services that is currently under challenge, as discussed above. The others are (1) a contract to protect U.S. bases in Iraq valued up to $480 million, and (2) a contract to protect reconstruction convoys valued up to $450 million.[38] The news report also states that the Army has "tested a plan to use private security on military convoys for the first time, a shift that would significantly increase the presence of armed contractors on Iraq's dangerous roads."[39]

Sources of Controversy

Public awareness of the extent to which private contractors were being used for security purposes was highlighted by the deaths on March 31, 2004, of four Blackwater guards in Fallujah. The guards were three former Army Rangers and a former Navy SEAL. They were killed while escorting

venture between Erinys International, (founded in 2001 and cited by some sources as a South African company, by another as British) and associates of Ahmad Calaba. (*Financial Times*, December 12, 2003. *op.cit.*) At that time, the company employed a small number of former British special operations personnel as managers and trainers, according to one source (telephone interview with Patrick Culled, April 16, 2004), and some 14,000 Iraqis to guard the wells, according to a variety of reports.

36 *Washington Post*. June 16, 2007. *op.cit.*

37 ArmorGroup provided security services to the CPA. According to its website, ArmorGroup provides "defensive, protective security services to national governments, multinational corporations and international peace and security organisations operating in hazardous environments." It currently has some 9,000 employees and "long term" operations in 38 countries, [http://www.armorgroup.com]. A 2005 publication provides a list of ArmorGroup clients, apparently for security guarding supply convoys and humanitarian aid deliveries, at that time: "UN agencies, the governments of the UK [United Kingdom], US, Switzerland, Sweden, Japan, and Canada, the EU [European Union], ECHO [the European Commission's humanitarian aid department], USAID, the ICRC [International Committee of the Red Cross], as well as a number of NGO's including the International Rescue Committee, CARE, and Caritas."

38 *Washington Post*. June 16, 2007. *op.cit.*

39 *Ibid.*

trucks carrying supplies for a private company that provided food services to U.S. military dining facilities in Iraq, and their bodies were then dragged through the streets and hung for display. Days later, Blackwater personnel again hit the news as they reportedly fought a prolonged gun battle in Najaf on April 4, 2004, defending the U.S. government headquarters there. These events sparked congressional debate over the role of private contractors in U.S. military operations, the desirability of using such contractors, and the appropriate legal and contractual framework to control them.

Concerns over the quality of security personnel being hired under U.S. government contracts were triggered by news reports that possible human rights violators were being hired. According to one source, in February 2004, Blackwater started training former Chilean commandos—some of whom served during the Pinochet years in Chile—for duty in Iraq.[40] Another news report at the time indicated that four guards killed in January while working for an Erinys subcontractor had served in South Africa's security forces during the apartheid era, and one of them had applied for amnesty for crimes that he had committed.[41]

More recently, Congress has taken a renewed interest in questions about accountability and transparency. In November 2006, news reports about a lawsuit filed in Fairfax [VA]County Circuit Court brought to light allegations that a Triple Canopy employee in Iraq twice had fired want only at Iraqi civilians in the summer of 2005 and possibly killed one person. The two Triple Canopy employees filing the lawsuit state that they were fired for reporting that their supervisor had committed the act. According to a news report, the Triple Canopy employee was operating at the time under a KBR subcontract when the alleged shootings occurred.[42] Most recently, a news article discussing an incident in which a Blackwater guard shot dead an Iraqi driver in May 2007 quoted an Iraqi official's statement that the Iraqi Interior Ministry had received four previous complaints of shootings involving Blackwater employees.[43]

The House hearings also revealed that the U.S. government has not been aware of the extent to which contractors and subcontractors employ private security personnel, and of the broad network of subcontracts over which the U.S. government, according to some, has exercised little oversight.

[40] Barry Yeoman, "Need an Army? Just Pick Up the Phone" [Op-Ed], *New York Times*, April 2, 2004.
[41] *New York Times*, April 19, 2004. *op.cit.*
[42] Tom Jackman. U.S. Contractor Fired on Iraqi Vehicles for Sport, Suit Alleges. *Washington Post*. November 17, 2006.
[43] *Washington Post*. May 27, 2007, *op.cit.*

Legal Status and Authorities

Contractors to the coalition forces in Iraq operate under three levels of legal authority: (1) the international order of the laws and usages of war and resolutions of the United Nations Security Council; (2) U.S. law; and (3) Iraqi law, including orders of the CPA that have not been superceded. Under the authority of international law, contractors working with the military are civilian non-combatants whose conduct may be attributable to the United States.[44] Iraqi courts do not have jurisdiction to prosecute them for conduct related to their contractual responsibilities without the permission of the Sending State.[45] Some contractors, particularly U.S. nationals, may be prosecuted in U.S. federal courts or military courts under certain circumstances.

International Law

The international law of armed conflict, particularly those parts relating to belligerent occupation (at least for conduct that occurred prior to the handover of sovereignty on June 28, 2004) and non-international armed conflict, appear to be relevant in Iraq.[46] The status of armed contract personnel in such circumstances falls into a grey area.[47] While civilians accompanying the Armed Forces in the field are generally entitled to treatment as

[44] Conduct that violates international obligations is attributable to a State if it is committed by the government of the State or any of its political subdivisions, or by any official, employee, or agent operating within the scope of authority of any of these governments, or under color of such authority. American Law Institute, Restatement (Third) of the Foreign Relations Law of the United States, Vol II (1987), § 207. Principles of State responsibility require a State in breach of an obligation to another State or international organization, without justification or excuse under international law, to terminate the violation and provide redress. *Id.* at § 901, comment a.

[45] CPA Order 17, Status of the CPA, MNFI, Certain Missions and Personnel in Iraq, June 27, 2004, § 4 (Contractors) *available at* [http://www.cpa-iraq.org/regulations/20040627_CPAORD_17_Status_of_Coalition__Rev__with_Annex_A.pdf] (last visited May 4, 2007). A "Sending State" is defined in § 1(5) of CPA Order 17 to mean "a State providing personnel, International Consultants, services, equipment, provisions, supplies, material, other goods or construction work to: (a) the CPA, (b) the MNF [Multi-National Forces], (c) international humanitarian or reconstruction efforts, [and] (d) Diplomatic or Consular Missions. . . ."

[46] The relevance of various sources of international law may have fluctuated as the status of the Iraqi government has transformed from an interim government to a permanent government with a permanent Constitution. For a description of law applicable in Iraq after June 28, 2004, see CRS Report RL31339, *Iraq: Post-Saddam Governance and Security*, by Kenneth Katzman. The Multi-National Forces in Iraq (MFN-I)are currently fulfilling a UN mandate established by United Nations Security Council (UNSC) Resolution 1511 (October 16, 2003) and continued by UNSC Resolution 1546 (June 8, 2004), UNSC Resolution 1637 (November 8, 2005), and UNSC Resolution 1723 (November 28, 2006). The resolutions affirm the importance for MFN-I to "act in accordance with international law, including obligations under international humanitarian law . . .," but do not clarify what those obligations entail. UNSC resolutions are accessible at [http://www.un.org/Docs/sc/ unsc_resolutions.html].

[47] *See* Rebecca Rafferty Vernon, *Battlefield Contractors: Facing the Tough Issues*, 33 Pub. Cont. L.J. 369, 401 (2004); P.W. Singer, *War, Profits, and the Vacuum of Law: Privatized Military Firms and International Law*, 42 Colum. J. Transnat'l L. 521, 525-26 (2004) (arguing that international law applicable to privatized military firms is nonexistent or outdated).

prisoners of war (POW)[48] if captured by an enemy State during an international armed conflict, they are considered civilians (non-combatants) who are not authorized to take part in hostilities.[49]

Can Contractors Be "Combatants"? A critical question appears to be whether the duties of contractors amount to "taking an active part in hostilities." In an international armed conflict or occupation,[50] only members of regular armed forces and paramilitary groups that come under military command and meet certain criteria (carry their weapons openly, distinguish themselves from civilians, and generally obey the laws of war) qualify as combatants.[51] Because contract employees fall outside the military chain of command,[52] even those who appear to meet the criteria as combatants could be at risk of losing their right to be treated as POWs if captured by the enemy.

The Geneva Conventions and other laws of war do not appear to forbid the use of civilian contractors in a civil police role in occupied territory, in which case they might be authorized to use force when absolutely necessary to defend persons or property.[53] Given the fluid nature of the current security situation in Iraq, it may sometimes be difficult to discern whether civilian security guards are performing law-enforcement duties or are engaged in combat. If their activity amounts to combat, they would become

---

[48] Geneva Convention Relative to the Treatment of Prisoners of War, 6 U.S.T. 3316 (entered into force October 21, 1950) [hereinafter "GPW"]. GPW art. 4(A)(4) extends POW status to

> Persons who accompany the armed forces without actually being members thereof, such as civilian members of military aircraft crews, war correspondents, supply contractors, members of labour units or of services responsible for the welfare of the armed forces, provided that they have received authorization from the armed forces which they accompany, who shall provide them for that purpose with an identity card. . . .

[49] Convention Respecting the Laws and Customs of War on Land, with Annex of Regulations, October 18, 1907, Annex art. 3, 36 Stat. 2277, 2296 (entered into force January 26, 1910) [hereinafter "Hague Regulations"].

[50] The 1949 Geneva Conventions share several types of common provisions. The first three articles of each Convention are identical. Common Article 2 defines the scope of application of the Geneva Conventions in international armed conflicts as "all cases of declared war or of any other armed conflict which may arise between two or more of the High Contracting Parties . . . [and] all cases of partial or total occupation of the territory of a High Contracting Party. . . ."

[51] *Id.* at 4; Department of the Army Field Manual (FM) No. 3-100.21, Contractors on the Battlefield ¶ 2-33, January 3, 2003.

[52] *See* FM 3-100.21, *supra* note 34, ¶ 1-22:

> Management of contractor activities is accomplished through the responsible contracting *organization*, not the chain of command. Commanders do not have direct control over contractors or their employees (contractor employees are not the same as government employees); only contractors manage, supervise, and give directions to their employees.

[53] Army doctrine does not allow civilians to be used in a "force protection" role. *See id.* ¶ 6-3 ("Contractor employees cannot be required to perform force protection functions described [in ¶ 6-2] and cannot take an active role in hostilities but retain the inherent right to self-defense."). Force protection is defined as "actions taken to prevent or mitigate hostile actions against DOD personnel, resources, facilities and critical information." *Id.* ¶ 6-1. An Army combatant commander may issue military-specification sidearms to contractor employees for self-defense purposes, if the contractor's company policy permits employees to use weapons and the employee agrees to carry the weapon. *Id.* ¶ 6-29.

lawful targets for enemy forces during the fighting, and, if captured by an enemy government (if one should emerge), could potentially be prosecuted as criminals for their hostile acts.[54]

On the other hand, if the conflict in Iraq is a non-international armed conflict within the meaning of Common Article 3 of the Geneva Conventions (CA3),[55] customary international law would no longer distinguish between "unlawful" and "lawful combatants."[56] Contractors captured by enemy forces who had engaged in hostilities would be entitled to the minimum set of standards set forth in CA3, but their right to engage in hostilities in the first place would likely be determined in accordance with the prevailing local law. In this case, Iraqi law, including CPA orders that have not been rescinded, apply.[57]

Are They "Mercenaries"? Mercenaries are persons who are not members of the armed forces of a party to the conflict but participate in combat for personal gain. They may be authorized to fight by a party to the conflict, but their allegiance to that party is conditioned on monetary payment rather than obedience and loyalty.[58] For this reason, mercenaries are sometimes treated as "unlawful combatants" or "unprivileged belligerents," even though their employment is not strictly prohibited by international law.[59] As discussed above, they may not qualify for POW treatment under GPW, and those meeting the definition of "mercenary" under the 1977 Protocol I to the Geneva Conventions[60] are explicitly denied combatant status.[61] Because mercenaries are not entitled to combat immunity, they may be tried, and if found guilty, punished for their hostile actions (including by the death penalty), even if such actions would be lawful under the law of war if committed by a soldier. Soldiers with a nationality other than that

---

[54] The Army discourages the use of contractors in roles that could involve them in actual combat. Major Brian H. Brady, *Notice Provisions for United States Citizen Contractor Employees Serving With the Armed Forces of the United States in the Field: Time to Reflect Their Assimilated Status in Government Contracts?*, 147 MIL. L. REV. 1, 62 (1995) (citing Department of the Army, AR 700-137, Army's Logistics Civil Augmentation Program (LOGCAP) ¶ 3-2d(5)(1985) "Contractors can be used only in selected combat support and combat service support activities. They may not be used in any role that would jeopardize their role as noncombatants.")

[55] Common Article 3, expressly applicable only to conflicts "not of an international nature," has been described as "a convention within a convention" to provide a general formula covering respect for intrinsic human values that would always be in force, without regard to the characterization the parties to a conflict might give it. *See* JEAN PICTET, HUMANITARIAN LAW AND THE PROTECTION OF WAR VICTIMS 32 (1975).

[56] Common Article 3 does not provide for POW status. Its protections extend to all persons who are not or are no longer participating in combat. FM 3-100.21, *supra* note 34, does not distinguish between international and non-international armed conflicts.

[57] *See infra.*

[58] *See* Gregory P. Noone, *The History and Evolution of the Law of War Prior to World War* II, 47 NAVAL L. REV. 176, 187 (2000) (recounting origin of prohibition on mercenaries after the Middle Ages).

[59] *See* Singer, *supra* note 30, at 534.

[60] Protocol Additional to the Geneva Conventions of 12 August 1949, and Relating to the Protection of Victims of International Armed Conflicts (Protocol I) art. 47, June 8, 1977, *reprinted in* 16 I.L.M. 1391.

[61] *Id.* art. 43.

of the party on whose side they fight are not automatically considered mercenaries.[62] Article 47 of Protocol I defines a mercenary as follows:

> 2. A mercenary is any person who:
>
> (a) Is specially recruited locally or abroad in order to fight in an armed conflict;
>
> (b) Does, in fact, take a direct part in the hostilities;
>
> (c) Is motivated to take part in the hostilities essentially by the desire for private gain and, in fact, is promised, by or on behalf of a Party to the conflict, material compensation substantially in excess of that promised or paid to combatants of similar ranks and functions in the armed forces of that Party;
>
> (d) Is neither a national of a Party to the conflict nor a resident of territory controlled by a Party to the conflict;
>
> (e) Is not a member of the armed forces of a Party to the conflict; and
>
> (f) Has not been sent by a State which is not a Party to the conflict on official duty as a member of its armed forces.[63]

Under this definition, it appears that contractor personnel who are not U.S. nationals, the nationals of other coalition allies or Iraqi nationals, and who were hired to—and in fact do—take part in hostilities might be considered to be mercenaries, assuming the definition in Protocol I applies as customary international law in the context of the current hostilities in Iraq. On the other hand, it is not altogether clear what constitutes "direct participation in an armed conflict," and some of the other requirements are inherently difficult to prove, particularly the element of motivation.[64]

Iraqi Law (Including Coalition Provisional Authority Orders)

Contractors to U.S. agencies or any of the multinational forces or diplomatic entities in Iraq operate under the law of the government of Iraq, which includes orders issued by the CPA prior to the hand-over of sovereignty to the Iraqi Interim Government that have not been rescinded

---

[62] *See* Hilaire McCoubrey, 2 International Humanitarian Law 145 (1998) (noting that not all foreigners in service of armed forces of other countries should be treated as "mercenaries," as some may serve with the approval of their home governments or for moral or ideological reasons); Howard S. Levie, Prisoners of War in International Armed Conflict 75 (1979) (describing entitlement to POW status of nationals of neutral states or states allied with enemy state as well-settled, while status of an individual who is a national of a capturing state or its allies is subject to dispute).

[63] The United States has not ratified Protocol I; however, some of its provisions may be considered binding as customary international law. *See* Michael J. Matheson, *The United States Position on the Relation of Customary International Law to the 1977 Protocol Additional to the 1949 Geneva Convention*, 2 Am. U. J. Int'l L. & Pol'y 419 (1987).

[64] *See* Singer, *supra* note 30, at 532 (commenting on similar definition found in the International Convention against the Recruitment, Use, Financing, and Training of Mercenaries, to which the United States is not a party).

or superceded.[65] Under CPA Order Number 17, as revised June 27, 2004, contractors are exempt from Iraqi laws for acts related to their contracts.[66] That order provides that "[c]ontractors shall not be subject to Iraqi laws or regulations in matters relating to the terms and conditions of their Contracts . . .," but that they are subject to all relevant regulations with respect to any other business they conduct in Iraq (section 4(2)). Contractors are also immune from Iraqi legal processes for acts performed under the contracts (section 4(3)). Iraqi legal processes could commence against contract personnel without the written permission of the Sending State, but that State's certification as to whether conduct at issue in a legal proceeding was related to the terms and conditions of the relevant contract serves as conclusive evidence of that fact in Iraqi courts (section 4(7)).

CPA Order Number 3, as revised on December 31, 2003,[67] governs the use of weapons. It restricts the authority to carry weapons to members of Iraqi security forces and Coalition forces, and "groups and individuals who have been authorized to carry weapons in the course of their duties by the CPA or Commander, Coalition Forces or their duly authorized delegates," (section 3). It further provides that "private security firms may be licensed by the Ministry of the Interior to possess and use licensed Firearms and Military Weapons, excluding Special Category Weapons, in the course of their duties, including in public places." *Id.* All others must apply to the Iraqi Ministry of the Interior for a license in order to possess a weapon. The unauthorized use or possession of weapons is subject to penalty.

CPA Memorandum Number 17[68] provides for the registration and regulation of private security companies (PSC) operating in Iraq. Two annexes to the Memorandum provide for binding Rules for the Use of Force (Annex A) and is a Code of Conduct (Annex B) that all PSC employees must follow. Section 9 prohibits PSC employees from conducting law enforcement activities; however, section 5 of Annex A permits PSC employees to stop, detain, search, and disarm civilians where the employees' safety requires it or if such functions are specified in the contract. Section 6 prohibits PSC employees

[65] The Coalition Provisional Authority dissolved at the end of June, 2004, but certain orders issued by the CPA, as modified by CPA Order 100, were to remain in place unless modified or rescinded by the Iraqi Government. *See* CRS Report RS21820, *Iraq: June 30, 2004, Transition to Sovereignty*, by Kenneth Katzman and Jennifer K. Elsea.

[66] Under CPA Order 17, Status of the Coalition, Foreign Liaison Missions, Their Personnel and Contractors, June 23, 2003, Coalition forces were immune from Iraqi legal processes for their conduct during the period the CPA is in power. CPA Order 100 modified CPA Order 17 to substitute the MNF-I for the CPA and otherwise reflect the new political situation. *See* CPA Order 17, as amended June 17, 2004, *available at* [http://www.cpa-iraq.org/regulations/20040627_CPAORD_17_Status_of_Coalition__Re v__with_Annex_A.pdf].

[67] CPA Order 3, Weapons Control December 31, 2003, *available at* [http://www.iraqcoalition.org/regulations/20031231_CPAORD3_REV__AMD_.pdf].

[68] CPA Memorandum Number 17, Registration Requirements for Private Security Companies (PSC), June 26, 2004, *available at* [http://www.iraqcoalition.org/regulations/20040626_CPAMEMO_17_Registration_Requirements_for_Private_Security_Compani es_with_Annexes.pdf].

from joining Coalition or Multi-national Forces in "combat operations except in self-defense or in defense of persons as specified in [their] contracts." Section 9 makes PSC subject to all "applicable criminal, administrative, commercial and civil laws and regulations," and provides that their "officers and employees may be held liable under applicable criminal and civil legal codes," except as otherwise provided by law.

U.S. Law

U.S. contractor personnel and other U.S. civilian employees in Iraq may be subject to prosecution in U.S. courts. Additionally, persons who are "employed by or accompanying the armed forces" overseas may be prosecuted under the Military Extraterritorial Jurisdiction Act of 2000 (MEJA)[69] or, in some cases, the Uniform Code of Military Justice (UCMJ).[70] However, some contractor personnel who commit crimes might not fall within the statutory definitions described below, and thus might fall outside the jurisdiction of U.S. criminal law, even though the United States is responsible for their conduct as a matter of state responsibility under international law.[71]

Prosecution in U.S. Federal Court. U.S. contractor personnel and other U.S. civilian employees in Iraq are subject to prosecution in U.S. courts under a number of circumstances. Jurisdiction of certain federal statutes extends to U.S. nationals at U.S. facilities overseas that qualify as part of the special maritime and territorial jurisdiction (SMTJ) of the United States.[72] For crimes involving a U.S. citizen as a perpetrator or a victim, the SMTJ includes

> (A) the premises of United States diplomatic, consular, military or other United States Government missions or entities in foreign States, including the buildings, parts of buildings, and land appurtenant or ancillary thereto or used for purposes of those missions or entities, irrespective of ownership; and
>
> (B) residences in foreign States and the land appurtenant or ancillary thereto, irrespective of ownership, used for purposes of those missions or entities or used by United States personnel assigned to those missions or entities.

[69] P.L. 106-523, 114 Stat. 2488 (2000), *codified at* 18 U.S.C. §§ 3261–67.
[70] Chapter 47 of title 10, U.S. Code.
[71] *See supra* note 27.
[72] 18 U.S.C. § 7(9) (as amended by the § 804 of the USA PATRIOT Act, P.L. 107-56, title VIII, October 26, 2001, 115 Stat. 377) (excluding persons covered by the Military Extraterritorial Jurisdiction Act, 18 U.S.C. § 3261).

Criminal statutes that apply within the SMTJ include maiming,[73] assault,[74] kidnapping,[75] murder[76] and manslaughter.[77] The Department of Justice (DOJ) is responsible for prosecuting crimes in this category. A CIA contractor was convicted under this provision for the assault of a detainee in Afghanistan.[78]

Extraterritorial Jurisdiction. In addition, many federal statutes prescribe criminal sanctions for offenses committed by or against U.S. nationals overseas,[79] including the War Crimes Act of 1996.[80] The federal prohibition on torture applies to acts outside the United States regardless of the nationality of the perpetrator (non- U.S. nationals need only be "found" in the United States to be prosecuted).[81]

The War Crimes Act, as amended by the Military Commissions Act of 2006,[82] prohibits "grave breaches" of Common Article 3,[83] which are defined to include torture, cruel or inhuman treatment, performing biological experiments, murder of an individual not taking part in hostilities, mutilation or maiming, intentionally causing serious bodily injury, rape, sexual assault or abuse, and taking hostages. Federal jurisdiction is established for these crimes when they are committed by or against U.S. nationals or U.S. servicemembers. Other criminal proscriptions with extraterritorial reach include assaulting, killing or kidnapping an internationally protected person, or threatening to do so.[84] Jurisdiction exists over these offenses if the victim or offender was a U.S. national, or if the offender is afterwards found in the United States.

Military Extraterritorial Jurisdiction Act (MEJA). Persons who are "employed by or accompanying the armed forces" overseas may be prosecuted under the Military Extraterritorial Jurisdiction Act (MEJA) of 2000[85]

---

[73] 18 U.S.C. § 114 punishes any individual who, within the SMTJ and with the intent to torture, maim, or disfigure, "cuts, bites, or slits the nose, ear, or lip, or cuts out or disables the tongue, or puts out or destroys an eye, or cuts off or disables a limb or any member of another person; or . . . throws or pours upon another person, any scalding water, corrosive acid, or caustic substance. . . ."

[74] 18 U.S.C. § 113 (prohibiting assault with intent to commit murder or a felony, assault with a dangerous weapon, assault "by striking, beating, or wounding," simple assault, and assault resulting in serious or substantial bodily injury).

[75] 18 U.S.C. § 1201 (punishing "whoever seizes, confines, inveigles, decoys, kidnaps, abducts, or carries away and holds for ransom or reward or otherwise any person, except in the case of a minor by the parent thereof . . .").

[76] 18 U.S.C. § 1111 (unlawful killing of a human being with malice).

[77] 18 U.S.C. § 1112 (voluntary or involuntary unlawful killing of a human being without malice).

[78] Department of Justice Press Release, *David Passaro Sentenced to 100 months imprisonment: First American Civilian Convicted of Detainee Abuse During the Wars in Iraq and Afghanistan*, February 13, 2007, available at [http://charlotte.fbi.gov/dojpressrel/2007/ce021307.htm].

[79] See CRS Report 94-166, *Extraterritorial Application of American Criminal Law* by Charles Doyle.

[80] P.L. 104-192, § 2(a), 110 Stat. 2104 (August 21, 1996)(codified as amended at 18 U.S.C. § 2441.

[81] 18 U.S.C. § 2340–40B.

[82] P.L. 109-366 § 6, 120 Stat. 2632 (Oct. 17, 2006).

[83] 18 U.S.C. § 2441(d).

[84] 18 U.S.C. § 112 (assault); 18 U.S.C. § 1116 (killing);18 U.S.C. § 1201 (kidnapping); 18 U.S.C. § 1203 (hostage-taking); 18 U.S.C. § 878 (threats).

[85] P.L. 106-523, 114 Stat. 2488 (2000), *codified at* 18 U.S.C. § 3261–67.

for any offense that would be punishable by imprisonment for more than one year if committed within the special maritime and territorial jurisdiction of the United States.[86] Persons "[e]mployed by the armed forces" is defined to include civilian employees of the Department of Defense (DOD) as well as DOD contractors and their employees (including subcontractors at any tier), and civilian contractors and employees from other federal agencies and "any provisional authority" (e.g., the CPA), to the extent that their employment is related to the support of the DOD mission overseas.[87] It does not appear to cover civilian and contract employees of agencies engaged in their own operations overseas. It also does not cover nationals of or persons ordinarily residing in the host nation.

In December 2005, DOD issued proposed regulations for implementing MEJA, but the rules have not yet gone into effect.[88] DOD Instruction 5525.11, *Criminal Jurisdiction Over Civilians Employed By or Accompanying the Armed Forces Outside the United States, Certain Service Members, and Former Service Members*, March 3, 2005, implements policies and procedures pursuant to MEJA. Under the Instruction, the DOD Inspector General (IG) has the responsibility to inform the Attorney General whenever he or she has reasonable suspicion that a federal crime has been committed.[89] The DOD IG is also responsible for "implementing investigative policies" to carry MEJA into effect. The Instruction notes that the Domestic Security Section of the DOJ Criminal Division has agreed to "provide preliminary liaison" with DOD and other federal entities and to designate the appropriate U.S. Attorney's Office to handle a case.

It appears that only one successful prosecution of a DOD contractor has occurred under MEJA. A contractor working in Baghdad pleaded guilty to possession of child pornography in February 2007.[90]

Uniform Code of Military Justice (UCMJ). Contract personnel may be subject to military prosecution under the Uniform Code of Military Justice (UCMJ) for conduct that takes place during hostilities in Iraq in some circumstances, although any trial of a civilian contractor by court-martial is likely to be challenged on constitutional grounds. Article 2(a)(10), UCMJ,[91] as amended by § 552 of the John Warner National Defense Authorization

---

86 18 U.S.C. § 3261.

87 18 U.S.C. § 3267(1)(A), as amended by The Ronald W. Reagan National Defense Authorization Act for FY2005, P.L. 108-375 § 1088, 118 Stat. 2066 (October 28, 2004).

88 70 *Fed. Reg.* 75,999 (December 22, 2005).

89 DoD Instruction 5525.11 § 5.

90 Press Release, United States Attorney for the Eastern District of Virginia, Military Contractor Sentenced for Possession of Child Pornography in Baghdad (May 25, 2007), *available at* [http://www.usdoj.gov/].

91 10 U.S.C. § 802(a)(10). For summaries of legislative history and application of the provision (and its predecessors) prior to amendment, see David A. Melson, *Military Jurisdiction over Civilian Contractors: a Historical Overview*, 52 Naval L. Rev. 277 (2005); Wm. C. Peters, *On Law, Wars, and Mercenaries: The Case for Courts-martial Jurisdiction over Civilian Contractor Misconduct in Iraq*, 2006 B.Y.U. L. Rev. 367 (2006).

Act for Fiscal Year 2007 (P.L. 109-364)("FY07 NDAA"), extends military jurisdiction in "time of declared war or a contingency operation,"[92] to "persons serving with or accompanying an armed force in the field." Additionally, if offenses by contract personnel can be characterized as violations of the law of war, the UCMJ may extend jurisdiction to try suspects by court-martial[93] or by military commission.[94]

Prior to the FY2007 NDAA, the UCMJ covered civilians serving with the Armed Forces in the field only in "time of war." As a reflection of the constitutional issues that arise whenever civilians are tried in military tribunals,[95] as recognized by a series of Supreme Court cases beginning in 1957 with *Reid v. Covert*,[96] courts have interpreted the phrase "in time of war" to mean only wars declared by Congress.[97] In *Covert*, a plurality of the Supreme Court rejected the proposition that Congress's power to regulate the land and naval forces justifies the trial of civilians without according the full panoply of due process standards guaranteed by the Bill of Rights. The Supreme Court has also found that former servicemembers who have severed all ties to the military cannot be tried by court-martial for crimes they committed while on active duty.[98]

The trial of civilian contractors by courts-martial will likely be subject to challenge on constitutional grounds. Congress's authority to "make Rules

---

[92] "Contingency operation" is defined under 10 U.S.C. § 101(a)(13) to mean a military operation that—

> (A) is designated by the Secretary of Defense as an operation in which members of the armed forces are or may become involved in military actions, operations, or hostilities against an enemy of the United States or against an opposing military force; or
>
> (B) results in the call or order to, or retention on, active duty of members of the uniformed services under section 688, 12301 (a), 12302, 12304, 12305, or 12406 of [title 10], chapter 15 of [title 10], or any other provision of law during a war or during a national emergency declared by the President or Congress.

[93] 10 U.S.C. § 818 (providing jurisdiction over "any person who by the law of war is subject to trial by military tribunal").

[94] 10 U.S.C. § 821 (preserving "concurrent jurisdiction with respect to offenders or offenses that by statute or by the law of war may be tried by military commissions, provost courts, or other military tribunals"); *cf. Ex Parte* Quirin, 317 U.S. 1 (1942).

[95] *See, e.g., Ex Parte* Milligan, 71 U.S. (4 Wall.) 2 (1866); Duncan v. Kahanamoku, 327 U.S. 304 (1945).

[96] Reid v. Covert, 354 U.S. 1 (1957) (plurality opinion overturning two cases involving civilian spouses convicted of capital crimes by courts-martial, pursuant UCMJ Art. 2(11) as "persons accompanying the armed forces," for the murders of their military spouses at overseas bases); Kinsella v. United States *ex rel.* Singleton, 361 U.S. 234 (1960)(applying *Reid* to non-capital case involving civilian dependent); Grisham v. Hagan, 361 U.S. 278 (1960)(extending *Covert* to prohibit court-martial of civilian employee of the Army for a capital offense); McElroy v.Guagliardo, 361 U.S. 281 (1960) (same, with respect to non-capital offense). UCMJ art. 2(11) defines as persons subject to the UCMJ those who, "[s]ubject to any treaty or agreement to which the United States is or may be a party or to any accepted rule of international law, [are] serving with, employed by, or accompanying the armed forces outside the United States and outside the Commonwealth of Puerto Rico, Guam, and the Virgin Islands."

[97] See Robb v. U. S., 456 F.2d 768 (Ct. Cl. 1972); U.S. v. Averette, 41 C.M.R. 363 (1970); *see also* Latney v. Ignatious, 416 F.2d 821 (D.C. Cir. 1969)(finding that even if the Vietnam conflict constituted a "war" within the meaning of the UCMJ, conduct must be intimately connected to military in order for jurisdiction under Art. 2(10) to apply).

[98] United States *ex rel.* Toth v. Quarles, 350 U.S. 11 (1955).

for the Government and Regulation of the land and naval Forces"[99] empowers it to prescribe rules for courts-martial that vary from civilian trials and are not restricted by all of the constitutional requirements applicable to Article III courts. In addition to the express exception in the Fifth Amendment regarding the right to presentment and indictment in "cases arising in the land or naval forces, or in the Militia, when in actual service in time of War or public danger," the Supreme Court has found implicit exceptions to other fundamental rights as they pertain to servicemembers.[100] Statutes relating to courts-martial have withstood objections based on due process.[101] While the UCMJ offers soldiers procedural protections similar to and sometimes arguably superior to those in civilian courts,[102] courts have been reluctant to extend military jurisdiction to civilians.[103]

On the other hand, the *Covert* Court distinguished the peacetime court-martials of civilian spouses at issue from *Madsen v. Kinsella*,[104] in which a military spouse was tried by military commission in occupied Europe, on the basis that

> [that case] concerned trials in enemy territory which had been conquered and held by force of arms and which was being governed at the time by our military forces. In such areas the Army commander can establish military or civilian commissions as an arm of the occupation to try everyone in the occupied area, whether they are connected with Army or not.[105]

If *Madsen* remains valid, if and for so long as the United States is considered an "occupying power" in Iraq, it may be acceptable under the Constitution to subject DOD contractors there to military jurisdiction.

Further, the *Covert* plurality held open the possibility that civilians who were part of the armed services could be tried by court-martial during wartime.[106]

---

99 U.S. CONST., art. I, § 8, cl. 14.

100 *See, e.g.*, Kahn v Anderson, 255 US 1 (1921)(Sixth Amendment does not require jury in cases subject to military jurisdiction); Weiss v. United States, 510 U.S. 163 (1994) (rejecting challenge to the military justice system based on the fact that military judges are not "appointed" by the President within the meaning of Article II of the Constitution, and the judges are not appointed to fixed terms of office); Parker v. Levy, 417 U.S. 742, 758 (1974) (stating, in the context of First Amendment protections, that "[t]he fundamental necessity for obedience, and the consequent necessity for imposition of discipline may render permissible within the military that which would be constitutionally impermissible outside it").

101 *See* AM. JUR. 2D Military and Civil Defense § 221.

102 For a comparison of due process rights, see CRS Report RL31262, *Selected Procedural Safeguards in Federal, Military, and International Courts*, by Jennifer K. Elsea.

103 Reid v. Covert, 354 U.S. 1, 21 (1957)("Every extension of military jurisdiction is an encroachment on the jurisdiction of the civil courts, and, more important, acts as a deprivation of the right to jury trial and of other treasured constitutional protections."); O'Callahan v. Parker, 395 U.S. 258, 267 (1969)("[C]ourts-martial have no jurisdiction to try those who are not members of the Armed Forces, no matter how intimate the connection between their offense and the concerns of military discipline."), *overruled on other grounds by* Solorio v. United States, 483 U.S. 435 (1987)(overturning "service-connection rule" in favor of a rule based strictly on military status).

104 343 U.S. 341 (1952).

105 354 U.S. at 35, & n.10.

106 Reid v. Covert, 354 U.S. 1, 33–36 (1957).

While the Court has suggested in dicta that courts-martial are never proper for the trial of civilians,[107] it has never expressly stated that the Constitution forbids military jurisdiction over civilians who might properly be said to be "in" the Armed Forces during war.[108] Lower courts addressed the issue during World War II, and upheld courts-martial of civilian employees of the U.S. Army in Eritrea.[109] Merchant seamen were sometimes tried by court-martial by the Navy. One such conviction was overturned by a federal court on habeas corpus review because the offense charged, striking a superior officer, was essentially a military charge.[110] However, another court upheld the conviction of a merchant seaman for desertion.[111]

Assuming the Constitution permits the trial of civilians accompanying the Armed Forces in wartime, a particular case will also have to satisfy the statutory requirements of the UCMJ. To determine whether a civilian contractor who is suspected of having committed an offense is subject to prosecution under the UCMJ, it will be necessary to determine whether he is "serving with or accompanying an armed force" that is operating "in the field." The phrase "serving with or accompanying" the forces was historically construed to require that the civilian's "presence [must be] not merely incidental to, but directly connected with or dependent upon, the activities of the armed forces or their personnel."[112] Courts have found that military jurisdiction over a civilian "cannot be claimed merely on the basis of convenience, necessity, or the non-availability of civil courts."[113]

The phrase "in the field" means serving "in an area of actual fighting" at or near the "battlefront" where "actual hostilities are under way."[114] Whether an armed force is "in the field" is "determined by the activity in which it may be engaged at any particular time, not the locality where it is found."[115]

---

[107] O'Callahan v. Parker, 395 U.S. 258 (1969).

[108] *Covert*, 354 U.S. at 23 (noting "there might be circumstances where a person could be 'in' the armed services for purposes of [Congress's authority to regulate the armed services] even though he had not formally been inducted into the military").

[109] Perlstein v. United States, 151 F.2d 167 (3d Cir. 1945)(concluding that accompanying an armed force under "stark war conditions" justified trial by court-martial of a civilian employee for a criminal offense); *In re* diBartolo, 50 F. Supp. 929, 930 (S.D.N.Y. 1943).

[110] Hammond v. Squire, 51 F. Supp. 227 (D. D.C. 1943).

[111] McCune v. Kilpatrick, 53 F. Supp. 80 (E.D. Va. 1943).

[112] United States v. Burney, 21 C.M.R. 98 (1956) (concluding that a contractor's connection with the military, despite his indirect employment through a private company, was sufficient to constitute "serving with or accompanying" an armed force). Some of the factors leading to the court's conclusion were that

> [T]he accused worked directly for the benefit of the Air Force, he was supervised by Air Force personnel, he was quartered and messed on a military installation by military personnel, and he was accorded privileges normally granted only to military personnel. The operational success of that military command depended upon civilians such as this accused, and each of the services has found it necessary to rely on civilian technicians to repair and maintain the highly specialized signal and radar equipment now being used.

[113] *In re* diBartolo, 50 F. Supp. 929, 930 (S.D.N.Y. 1943).

[114] Reid v. Covert, 354 U.S. 1, 35 (1957).

[115] Burney, 21 C.M.R. at 109.

Therefore, it appears that contractors will not be subject to military jurisdiction merely because of their employment in Iraq. They might, however, be subject to jurisdiction even if the conduct occurs outside of Iraq, so long as there is sufficient connection to military operations there.[116]

Other likely issues include whether civilian contractors may be prosecuted for military crimes, such as disrespect of an officer or failure to obey a lawful command. In addition, if misconduct by a contract employee results in his or her immediate dismissal by the contractor, military jurisdiction may also cease.[117] DOD has not yet published any guidance indicating how the new law is to be implemented.

Issues for Congress

The use of private contractors in military operations raises many questions regarding the appropriateness and practicality of entrusting private companies with duties that have been traditionally reserved for military personnel. Several issues are particularly sensitive when States hire private contractors for potentially hostile situations. Some are even more sensitive when State-hired contractors carry arms, even on a strictly defensive basis.[118] These issues, as related to contractors as a whole and to private security contractors in particular, are briefly discussed below.

Need for and Suitability of Private Contractors[119]

Many defense analysts and analysts have viewed private contractors as an indispensable "force multiplier," especially needed over the past decade to

[116] *Ex parte* Gerlach, 247 F. 616, 617 (S.D.N.Y. 1917)(stating that "the words 'in the field' do not refer to land only, but to any place, whether on land or water, apart from permanent cantonments or fortifications where military operations are being conducted"); Hines v. Mikell, 259 F. 28, 34 (4th Cir.), *cert. denied*, 250 U.S. 645 (1919)(upholding court-martial jurisdiction over a civilian at Camp Jackson, South Carolina, during the First World War by finding that "any portion of the army confined to field training in the United States should be treated as 'in the field'").

[117] At least one court has concluded otherwise. *See* Perlstein v. United States, 151 F.2d 167 (3d Cir. 1945)(military jurisdiction remained valid over fired contract employee so long as he remained in military garrison). However, this conclusion might not be followed today in light of *United States ex rel. Toth v. Quarles*, 350 U.S. 11 (1955), in which the Court held a serviceman who had been discharged was no longer amenable to court-martial.

[118] To some analysts, however, providers of armed protection are not the most worrisome of the gamut of providers of military services, at least as far as those contracted by non-governmental organizations (NGOs) are concerned. "While it is conceivable that some regulation might be useful, in fact, informal voluntary agreements between the NGO community and PSCs mean that such regulation is not critical and may in fact reduce the level of flexibility that makes these agreements possible." The companies these analysts find of most concern for regulation are the private military companies (PMCs) "that generally work for states and provide military services designed to significantly impact strategic situations. . . . *active* PMCs willing to carry weapons into combat, and *passive* PMCs that focus on training and organizational issues." *Privatising Security, op. cit.*, p. 36.

[119] This section and the following section draw on the section on commercial contractors in CRS Report 97-454 F, *Peacekeeping Options: Considerations for U.S. Policymakers and the Congress*, by Marjorie Ann Browne, Ellen Collier (Consultant), and Nina Serafino.

ease the strain on a downsized military.[120] By supplementing overstretched active duty personnel, beginning in the early 1990s, with contractors for jobs that do not require military expertise such as feeding, housing, and otherwise caring for soldiers' basic needs, policymakers hoped to meet the demands on the force while minimizing an increase in the number of military personnel and repeated call-ups of reserve units. The U.S. government's subsequent turn to private contractors for a assistance with a wide variety of security needs served the same purposes. In Iraq, particularly, the use of private contractors may serve a variety of other interests. As Iraqis may well constitute a sizable majority of private security contractors, the use of private contractors provides a cultural and linguistic advantage over the use of U.S. soldiers and ameliorates much potential friction with the local populations, according to one expert. They may also as forestall possible criticism from U.S. taxpayers for using U.S. soldiers to protect the profit-making companies that carry out U.S. reconstruction efforts.[121]

Without private contractors, the U.S. military would not have sufficient capabilities to carry out an operation of the scale of Iraq, according to many analysts. If the United States wishes to engage in and contribute to sizable stabilization and reconstruction operations without contractor support to the U.S. military, policymakers would probably need to contemplate an increase in the number of U.S. troops, perhaps increasing incentives to attract volunteers or re-instituting the draft. On the other hand, some analysts question whether the use of private security providers in Iraq and elsewhere is beneficial to the U.S. military in the long run. Although contracting private sector firms for guard duties may help alleviate the current shortage of military personnel, analysts point to potential downsides to the "force multiplier argument." One important area of concern is whether their use is detrimental to military force structure; other areas are their potential effect on the military mission, their flexibility, and their quality of the personnel hired.

Effects on the U.S. Military Force Structure. In arguments on the general use of military contractors that could also apply to the security sector, analysts for the 1995 Commission on Roles and Missions (CORM) found that reliance on contractors could prove detrimental to military capabilities in a number of ways, the first of which was that it could keep the United States "from building and maintaining capacity needed for strategic or other

[120] For instance, in a 2005 study, the Defense Science Board referred to the private sector as the "fifth force provider" in stability operations, i.e., in addition to the four branches of the armed services, and recommended that a new institution be established to "effectively exploit" the private sector. Office of the Under Secretary of Defense for Acquisition, Technology, and Logistics. *Institutionalizing Stability Operations Within DoD*. September 2005. p. 38.

[121] E-mail correspondence from Doug Brooks, July 9, 2007.

important missions."[122] Anecdotal reports that private security firms have been hiring away military personnel, particularly special forces personnel, with high salaries seem to illustrate the possibility that a competing private sector could deplete the military of highly trained personnel in needed specialties.

Proponents of the use of private sector security providers discount such concerns, stating that the numbers employed by private security companies are too low to have a significant effect on U.S. capabilities. Quantifiable evidence of a detrimental effect is lacking. A 2005 GAO analysis shows that the *average* attrition rates for military occupational specialities preferred by private security providers were lower in FY2004 (when demand for such providers in Iraq was high) than in fiscal years 2000 and 2001. (These specialities were Army and Navy enlisted and officer special operations forces, Army infantry, and military police from all four services.) In the *particular* case of Army Special Forces enlisted personnel, however, attrition was somewhat higher in 2004 than in 2000 and 2001. The GAO pointed out that a variety of factors could play into an individual's decision to leave the services.[123]

Effects on the U.S. Military Mission in Iraq. Recent reports also point to possible complications for military commanders with the use of private security guards. Many analysts point out that the primary mission of private security personnel is to ensure the security of the individuals, the transport convoys, and the property they were hired to protect. News reports from Iraq indicate that this may have led in some cases to a disregard of the sensitivities of and consequences for the Iraqi public.[124] For a U.S. commander in Iraq, whose mission may well entail the winning of

[122] The other two ways in which they judged the use of contractors could adversely affect military capabilities were by limiting training opportunities in some military specialties (which has occurred in some cases with non-security contractors: see GAO Report GAO-03-695, *op.cit.* p. 9) and result in inadequate stocks of equipment needed to perform certain tasks. Christine Cervenak and George T. Raach. "Contracting and Privatization in Peace Operations," in *Peace Operations: Developing An American Strategy*, edited by Antonia Handler Chayes and George T. Raach. Washington, D.C.: National Defense University Press, 1995, pp. 137–151. Although possible equipment needs have not been raised as an issue, it is conceivable that if the U.S. military were to deploy to an operation where it was providing more security, it might find itself with a shortage of the types of armored vehicles now brought to Iraq by private security firms.

[123] U.S. Government Accountability Office. *Rebuilding Iraq: Actions Needed to Improve Use of Private Security Providers*. GAO-05-737. July 2005. p. 43. "While available data indicate that attrition, in almost all of the military specialties favored by private security providers, has returned to pre-September 11, 2001 levels, the data do not indicate why personnel are leaving the military and what they are doing after they leave. . . . Officials at the Army Human Resources Command told us that after September 11, 2001, the opportunities for employment in the security field became more widespread as government agencies as well as private companies and organizations recognized the need to improve their security. These officials as well as officials from the Special Operations Command noted that they are losing personnel not only to private security firms operating in Iraq but also to security management companies operating in the United States, and security operations in other government agencies. Service officials at these commands also attributed the attrition rates to other factors, such as the attraction of a strong civilian economy, high operational tempo, and concerns about various quality of life conditions."

[124] For example, see *Washington Post*, November 17, 2006, *op.cit.*

"hearts and minds," such a disregard is problematic, some analysts argue. These reports, however, discuss incidents involving contractors who are American, not Iraqi or other foreign nationals; as noted above, proponents argue that a sizable presence of Iraqis among those providing security under U.S. contracts overall reduces the possible friction that the use of U.S. soldiers in these positions would entail.

Concerns Regarding Flexibility. Some also argue that military forces have additional benefits in hostile situations. Although some have argued that private contractors can be deployed more quickly than military forces, others have argued that military commanders can respond more quickly to changing situations when military forces rather than contractors are used. Commanders do not exercise "command and control" over private contractors, nor do they have the authority to amend contracts in the midst of an operation to reallocate contract employees to perform necessary tasks that fall outside the terms of the contract.[125] Proponents of the use of private security contractors discount such concerns, however, arguing that they are not employed on the battlefield, where such flexibility is a needed.

Concerns About Reliability and Quality. Questions are also raised regarding the reliability and quality of service provided by private contractors compared to military personnel, particularly in risky situations. Proponents of the use of private security contractors argue that they are as responsible as serving military personnel because many are former soldiers or individuals equally dedicated to the national mission. Skeptics voice concerns that individual contractors may be less reliable in some situations as they probably bear lesser costs than military personnel if they refuse to perform a particular task. According to a 2003 GAO report, DOD recognized the risk that contractors might not be available in crisis or hostile situations.[126] Nevertheless, proponents argue that private security contractors, as well as other contractors, have been "remarkably robust in terms of reliability."[127] There is little evidence to the contrary.[128]

[125] GAO-05-737, *op.cit.*, p. 20, and DOD Report to Congressional Defense Committees, as required by Section 1206 of the Ronald W. Reagan National Defense Authorization Act for Fiscal Year 2005 (P.L. 108-375), October 28, 2004. p. 6, hereafter referred to as the Section 1206 Report.

[126] See GAO Report GAO-03-695, *op.cit.* The GAO noted that despite this determination, it "found little in the way of backup plans to replace mission essential contractor services during crises if necessary." p. 16.

[127] E-mail correspondence from Doug Brooks, July 9, 2007.

[128] A recent news report from a Santiago, Chile newspaper reported that in 2005 "the Your Solutions security firm sent 147 Chileans into conflict zones in Iraq; 28 of the recruits broke their contracts and returned home early, claiming they received inadequate training and poor equipment." The article implies that these Chileans were contracted on behalf of a U.S. company, but does not state that directly nor name a U.S. firm. Mike Hager. *The Santiago Times.* "Chile's Iraq Mercenaries Under Investigation by U.N. Group." July 9, 2007, as posted online by Worldpress.org at [http://www.worldpress.org/Americas/2853.cfm]. A report

The quality of private security providers is also a matter of concern. The larger companies particularly have reputations for supplying high-quality personnel. Some wonder, however, if they can maintain that standard as demand increases, and in the face of possible pressures to decrease costs. Although U.S. companies have generally hired U.S. professional military personnel with established careers, who may still possess the discipline, professionalism, and *esprit de corps* that the U.S. Armed Forces seeks to instill in its soldiers, the increasing use of private personnel may reduce the quality of contractor recruits, some fear. On the other hand, some analysts point out that private companies can maintain top quality people in the field indefinitely, whereas the military is required to rotate soldiers regularly. Those who favor the use of such contractors also argue that private companies can maintain standards because they can draw from a larger and more competitive pool of personnel than the U.S. military does, including former military personnel from elite forces of other countries and former police personnel.

Some critics are also concerned about the high number of non-U.S. citizens hired under U.S. government contracts, especially third-country nationals from lesser-developed countries who are difficult to screen. A GAO official noted in June 2006 testimony that (1) private security companies and DOD "have difficulty completing comprehensive criminal background screenings for U.S. and foreign nationals when data are missing or inaccessible," and (2) "[n]o U.S. or international standards exist for establishing private security provider and employee qualifications."[129] A year later, this situation does not appear to have changed significantly.

Nevertheless, the companies have incentives and opportunities to control quality, proponents argue. Companies employing individual contractors have opportunities to observe their behavior and performance during training sessions and, according to analysts, can screen out potential misfits at that stage. U.S. government agencies establish some baseline standards in contracts, by specifying either performance standards and/or precise qualifications to be met. U.S. government agencies have mandated changes—under threat of penalties—when contracted personnel are perceived as not up to standard, according to Doug Brooks, of the IPOA. In addition, according to Brooks, there are many examples of companies that act proactively to address client complaints.[130] The IPOA, an industry association, has instituted a system to review complaints concerning its member and to sanction those found to have violated the associations code of conduct. (Information on the code of conduct and enforcement mechanism can be accessed through the organizations website at [http://www.ipoaonline.org]). IPOA members include four of the six companies listed above

[129] GAO Report GAO-06-865T. *op.cit.*
[130] E-mail correspondence from Doug Brooks, July 9, 2007.

(i.e., ArmorGroup, Blackwater USA, DynCorp International, and Erinys International).

Oversight and Control/Coordination Issues

Many analysts claim that the U.S. government is unable to adequately oversee and control or coordinate the performance of military contractors in general and private security contractors in particular. Members are concerned with transparency issues that impede oversight by Congress, as well as control and coordination in the field.

Transparency and Congressional Oversight. Some Members have been concerned with the dearth of information made available to Congress by the Administration and to the public on U.S. government contracts with contractors in general and private security contractors in particular. As oversight hearings held by several committees in 2006 and 2007 demonstrate,[131] the executive branch either has not kept sufficient records to produce or has been unwilling to present basic, accurate information on the companies employed under U.S. government contracts and subcontracts in Iraq. The lack of contracting personnel, discussed below, may be responsible at least in part for this problem.

Oversight in the Field. One industry professional has described the oversight situation as "a nightmare" and stated that "the better" companies would prefer closer oversight.[132] Some U.S. government officials also believe that U.S. agencies do not adequately supervise contracts. At the field level, this problem is attributed by many, including U.S. government personnel, to a lack of contracting officer's representatives (CORs),[133] who are responsible for supervising the contracted work. Arguing for an increase in such personnel, they state that over the years, the number of such representatives has been cut sharply in the Departments of Defense and State, while the number of contractors has escalated.

Control and Coordination in the Field. The GAO has issued several reports regarding DOD contracting in Iraq that address or touch on issues regarding the use of private security contractors, several of which mention control and coordination issues. As pointed out above, military commanders do not have a "command and control" relationship with contractors, and thus must know how to secure cooperation from contractors to promote

[131] For hearing citations, see footnotes 8, 9, and 20.

[132] Interview with Doug Brooks, *op.cit.*

[133] A COR "is an individual appointed in writing by a contracting officer to act as the eyes and ears of the contracting officer," according to Army doctrine. "This individual is not normally a member of the Army's contracting organizations . . . but most often comes from the requiring unit or activity." U.S. Army. Headquarters. *Contractors on the Battlefield*. Field Manual No. 3-100.21. January 2003. p. 4. According to the same source, a contracting officer is "the official with the legal authority to enter into, administer and/or terminate contracts."

order in the theater of operations.[134] In June 2006 testimony before Congress, a GAO official cited two major related problems: (1) that private security providers did not coordinate with the U.S. military when they entered the "battle space" in Iraq, and (2) that military units were not trained prior to deployment on (a) private security provider operating procedures and (b) the role of the Reconstruction Operations Center (ROC).[135] (The ROC is charged with coordinating interaction between military and private security personnel.) In March 2007, DOD set forth a new requirement that companies enter data on their personnel, before deployment, into a new "Synchronized Predeployment and Operational Tracker" (SPOT).[136] In April 2007 testimony, the Comptroller General stated that the GAO continued "to find little evidence that DOD has improved training for military personnel on the use of contractors prior to deployment."[137]

Cost Issues

Proponents of the use of private security contractors argue that they are less expensive than using U.S. military forces because private companies can employ locals and third-country nationals, whose earnings are a fraction of U.S. servicemembers. Private contractors can incur much lower costs by using local hires extensively, as they do not have to transport them, house or feed them, and can pay them wages that are relatively low compared to those of U.S. servicemembers. Private security contractors in Iraq keep costs low by employing many Iraqis, according to proponents.

The relative direct cost advantage of contractors can vary, and may diminish or disappear altogether, depending on the circumstances and contract conditions. Apart from the direct cost of salaries, which will vary according to the mix of countries of origin of employed personnel offered, the costs to

[134] According to the Section 1206 Report, *op.cit*, however, the terms and conditions of contracts with private security (and other) companies largely set the parameters for the military-contractor relationships. "The interaction between U.S. military forces and security contractors in Iraq is one of coordination rather than control because private security contractors have no direct contractual relationship with the commander. If a Federal agency or a reconstruction contractor issued a contract that required the private security firm to coordinate with military units . . . such a contract would need to contain clauses . . . giving the Commander coordination authority over private security contractors." Nevertheless, according to the document, Commanders can, to a certain extent, "influence the discipline of contractor employees [by] working with the contracting officer to pursue contract remedies. Commanders can also limit or revoke any benefits or special status of a contractor employee accompanying the force, if the contractor employee violates the Commander's instructions or directives." p. 6.

[135] GAO Report GAO-06-865T. *op.cit.*

[136] Office of the Under Secretary of Defense, Acquisition, Technology, and Logistics. Memorandum for Directors of Defense Agencies, et al. *Class Deviation—Synchronized Predeployment and Operational Tracker*. March 19, 2007. Accessed July 11, 2007, through [http://www.acq.osd.mil/dpap/policy/policyvault/2007-0605-DPAP.pdf].

[137] U.S. Government Accountability Office. *Stabilizing and Rebuilding Iraq: Conditions in Iraq are Conducive to Fraud, Waste, and Abuse*. Statement of David M. Walker, Comptroller General of the United States, before the Subcommittee on Defense, House Committee on Appropriations, GAO-07-525T. April 23, 2007.

the U.S. government of private security contracts can depend on any benefits provided and the terms negotiated in a contract or a subcontract. Thus, one recent congressional analysis found that in the case of personnel provided by one company (i.e., Blackwater USA), the total cost of private security personnel was "significantly higher than the direct costs that would be incurred by the [U.S.] military" because of markups and other costs charged the U.S. government.[138]

Calculations of the relative advantage or disadvantage of private security contractors also vary depending on whether indirect costs are taken into account. For instance, the U.S. government does not pay for benefits such as health insurance or incur long-term liabilities such as disability compensation and pensions when private security contractors are employed. Nor does it (as far as is known) pay to purchase and maintain their equipment. On the other hand, some analysts have argued that the total costs of private security contracts have been underestimated because they do not include the subsidy that the U.S. government in effect provides contracting companies when former U.S. soldiers, trained at taxpayer expense, are employed.

Implications for U.S. Foreign Policy

The use of private security contractors who are hired to carry weapons, albeit just for defensive purposes, is problematic in ways that the use of contractors for routine tasks might not be, some policymakers fear.

Accountability. U.S. and foreign constituencies may well expect personnel who are legally permitted to use deadly force to be highly trustworthy. Thus, accountability issues, such as the U.S. government's practical inability to discipline errant contract employees and the perceived difficulties of holding U.S. and third-country national employees legally accountable for abuses or criminal acts may become more salient when contractors are armed. A lack of strict accountability in case of an abuse by a contractor could severely undermine goodwill toward the United States or incur liability on the part of the United States for a breach of its international obligations.

[138] A February 7, 2007, Memorandum to Members of the Committee on Oversight and Government Reform, written by the Committee's Majority Staff and posted on the Committee's website, states that the "security services provided by Blackwater would typically be performed by an Army Sergeant, whose salary, housing, and subsistence pay range from approximately $140 to $190 per day, depending on rank and years of service. These equate to an annual salary ranging from approximately $51,100 to $69,350 per year." According to the memo, Blackwater was providing those services in conjunction with a Kuwaiti company, Regency Hotel & Hospital Company, to ESS Support Services Worldwide "which in turn was providing dining services and construction for other contractors such as KBR and Fluor Corporation." Taking markups and other costs into account, the memo concluded that the "Blackwater costs are four to tens time higher" than the costs of a U.S. soldier. (Memo last accessed June 19, 2007, through [http://oversight.house.gov], pp. 4–5.)

Human Rights Concerns: Possible Employment of Human Rights Violators. One of the earliest concerns regarding the use of private security contractors was whether the United States' commitment to observe and promote human rights and humanitarian law is undermined by the types of personnel hired by some contractors. For some policymakers, the reported employment of South Africans who served in the military during the years of apartheid, one of whom reportedly has confessed to human rights abuse, and of Chileans, who reportedly served during the period of military rule, is problematic.[139] Employment of such personnel indicates not only a lack of transparency in the U.S. contracting system, as the names of those contracted is kept confidential, but also a lack of adherence by contractors to U.S. foreign policy interests and goals, they argue. At best, some argue, it sends dubious signals about U.S. seriousness about human rights and, at worst, raises the possibility that such contractors may commit abuses in Iraq, for which the United States may be responsible under international law.

As of 2007, concerns about the affiliations of foreign providers have diminished, especially, as some proponents point out, the most prominent human rights abuses that have occurred in Iraq to date, most notably Abu Graib, were committed by U.S. military personnel and American contractors. Contracting companies, one proponent argues, have strong legal and financial incentives to ensure such human rights abuses do not occur, as they would be a clear breach of contract and could lead to catastrophe.[140] Some analysts also argue that the most important consideration in hiring security personnel is their degree of military professionalism and training in the disciplined use of weapons, as former soldiers with good records are much less likely to commit abuses and fire their weapons without good cause than less qualified personnel.

Human Rights Concerns: Alleged Mistreatment of Third-Country Private Security Contractors. A developing area of concern in international human rights circles is the alleged mistreatment of third-country nationals employed as private security contractors. Over the past year, the United Nations Working Group on the Use of Mercenaries has collected complaints related to such abuse in five countries from which private security personnel are recruited (i.e., Chile, Ecuador, Fiji, Honduras, and Peru) and urged the government of those countries to adopt national legislation and adhere to international treaties in order to provide a legal framework to protect against mistreatment. Complaints include contractual irregularities, poor working conditions, partial or non-payment of salaries, and neglect of basic

[139] See, for example, Jonathan Franklin, "Chile: US Contractor Recruits Guards for Iraq in South Africa," *Guardian* [London], March 5, 2004, (the contractor referred to is Blackwater) and Julian Rademeyer, "Iraq Victim Was Top-Secret Apartheid Killer," *Sunday Times* [South Africa], April 18, 2004.

[140] E-mail correspondence from Doug Brooks. July 9, 2007.

needs such as access to medical services. No companies are named in statements issued by the Working Group, but the statements on Fiji and Peru mention Iraq as a place of employment of nationals of those countries.[141] While there is no indication that U.S. companies (or the United Nations, for that matter) have employed the complainants in Iraq or elsewhere, to the extent that mistreatment is believed to be the result of U.S. employment of such contractors, such allegations can damage perceptions of the United States.

Perception of State Authority and Commitment. A third issue with foreign policy implications is the desirability of entrusting the capability to legally use force on behalf of the United States to private, including non-U.S. citizens. Although many analysts perceive the officially-sanctioned private use of force as significantly eroding the modern state's monopoly on the use of force, whether this erosion is beneficial or detrimental to U.S. foreign policy and to the international order is a matter of dispute.[142] To the extent that private companies are perceived as participating in combat operations, it may be difficult for the United States to persuade other states to recognize contractors' rights to protection under the Geneva Conventions. On a symbolic level, the use of private companies instead of national military forces may be perceived by some observers as signaling a lesser U.S. commitment.

Selected Legislation

S. 674 (Obama)—Transparency and Accountability in Military and Security Contracting Act of 2007

S. 674 would require the Secretaries of Defense, State, and the Interior; the Administrator of the U.S. Agency for International Development (USAID); and the Director of National Intelligence to provide information within 90 days of enactment on U.S. government contractors and subcontractors working in Afghanistan and Iraq, with particularly detailed requirements for information on private security contractors. Also contains provisions intended to improve coordination between the U.S. Armed Forces and contractors performing private security functions, and to clarify the legal status of contract personnel.

[141] United Nations Press Release. *UN Working Group on the Use of Mercenaries Concludes Visit to Fiji*, May 18, 2007, and United Nations Press Release. *UN Working Group on Use of Mercenaries Concludes Visit to Peru*, February 5, 2007.

[142] For an examination of a variety of related issues and perspectives, see, among others: Deborah Avant, *The Privatization of Security and Change in the Control of Force*, International Studies Perspectives, Vol. 5, Issue 2, May 2004; David Shearer, *Outsourcing War*, Foreign Policy Magazine, Fall 1998; and P.W. Singer, *Corporate Warriors: The Rise of the Privatized Military Industry*, Ithaca and London: Cornell University Press, 2003.

Introduced February 16, 2007. (Similar to H.R. 369.) Referred to the Senate Armed Services Committee.

S. 1547 (Levin)—National Defense Authorization Act for FY2008

Section 871 of S. 1547 would require the Secretary of Defense to prescribe, within 120 days of enactment, regulations on the selection, training, equipping, and conduct of personnel performing private security functions under a covered contract or covered subcontract in a combat area. These would include processes for (1) registering, processing, and accounting for such personnel; (2) authorizing and accounting for their weapons, and (3) investigating the death and injury of such personnel and their discharge of weapons, as well as incidents of alleged misconduct. The regulations would also provide guidance to commanders of combatant commands on orders, directives, and instructions to contractors and subcontractors performing private security functions relating to force protection, security, health, safety, relations and interaction with locals, and rules of engagement. Would revise the relevant Federal Acquisition Regulation to require all contracts and subcontracts for such personnel to conform with these regulations. Section 872 would allow the Secretary of Defense to procure products and services, including security services, in Iraq and Afghanistan under special conditions.

Introduced June 5, 2007. Senate Armed Services Committee reported an original measure the same day (S.Rept. 110-77). Referred to the Senate Select Committee on Intelligence June 13, 2007; reported (amended) by the committee on June 29, 2007 (S.Rept. 110-125). Placed on the Senate Legislative Calendar under General Orders, Calendar No. 260, June 29, 2007.

H.R. 369 (Price)—Transparency and Accountability in Military and Security Contracting Act of 2007

H.R. 369 would require the Secretaries of Defense and State and the Administrator of the U.S. Agency for International Development to prescribe minimum hiring standards and issue equipment guidance for contracts regarding private security contractors and would require contractors to provide specified information on costs and personnel and update it during the period of contract performance. Also contains provisions intended to improve coordination between the U.S. Armed Forces and contractors performing private security functions, and to clarify and extend the Military Extraterritorial Jurisdiction Act (MEJA). Would extend MEJA to cover contractors "while employed under a contract (or subcontract at any tier) awarded by any department or agency of the United States, where the work under such contract is carried out in a region outside the United Sates in which the Armed Forces are conducting a contingency operation." MEJA covers contractors only if employed by "the Armed Forces outside the United States," or if employed by other federal agencies or provisional authority, to the extent their employment is related to the support of the DOD mission overseas. (This last provision is also included in H.R. 2740, below.)

Introduced January 10, 2007. (Similar to S. 674.) Referred to the House Armed Services Committee (HAS) and the Judiciary Committee. Referred to the HAS Subcommittee on Readiness, February 1, 2007. Referred to the Judiciary Committee's Subcommittee on Crime, Terrorism, and Homeland Security, February 2, 2007.

H.R. 528 (Lynch)—Iraq Contracting Fraud Review Act of 2007

H.R. 528 would require the Secretary of Defense, acting through the Defense Contract Audit Agency, to review all defense contracts relating to reconstruction or troop support in Iraq involving any contractors, subcontractors, or federal officers or employees that have been indicted or convicted for contracting improprieties.

Introduced January 17, 2007. Referred to the House Armed Services Committee.

H.R. 663 (Blumenauer)—New Direction for Iraq Act of 2007

H.R. 663 contains provisions regarding Iraq contracts on war profiteering, the recovery of funds from terminated contracts, and congressional oversight.

Introduced January 24, 2007. Referred to the House Committees on Armed Services and Foreign Affairs. House Foreign Affairs Committee hearing held, March 20, 2007.

H.R. 897 (Schakowsky)—Iraq and Afghanistan Contractor Sunshine Act

H.R. 897 would require the Secretary of Defense, Secretary of State, Secretary of the Interior, and the Administrator of the U.S. Agency for International Development to provide Congress with copies and descriptions of contracts and task orders over $5 million.

Introduced February 7, 2007. Referred to the House Armed Services and Foreign Affairs Committees. House Foreign Affairs Committee hearing held March 20, 2007.

H.R. 1581 (Lantos)—Iraq Reconstruction Improvement Act of 2007

H.R. 1581 would mandate a variety of measures to improve oversight and transparency regarding reconstruction contracts in Iraq.

Introduced March 20, 2007. Referred to the House Armed Services, Foreign Affairs, and Judiciary Committees. Referred on April 20, 2007, to the Judiciary Committee's Subcommittee on Immigration, Citizenship, Refugees, Border Security and International Law.

H.R. 1585 (Skelton)—National Defense Authorization Act for FY2008

As passed by the House, Section 831 of H.R. 1585 would prohibit (with waivers permitted on national security grounds) the Departments of Defense and State and the United States Agency for International Development from entering into contracts in Iraq and Afghanistan after January 1, 2008, unless the heads of those agencies have entered into a memorandum of understanding (MOU) regarding contracting in Iraq and Afghanistan, including matters related to authorizing the carrying of weapons, establishing minimum qualifications for personnel carrying weapons, and setting rules of engagement for the use of those weapons. The MOU is also to cover the identification of a common database for information on all contracts in Iraq and Afghanistan. Section 832 would require the Comptroller General to review contracts in Iraq and Afghanistan every six months and submit a report to Congress on that review. Section 833 covers definitions.

Introduced March 20, 2007. Referred to the House Armed Services Committee. Referred to HASC subcommittees April 10, 2007. Subcommittee mark-ups held May 2–8, 2007. Committee consideration and mark-up held May 9, 2007. Reported (amended) May 11, 2007 (H.Rept. 110-146). Supplemental report filed May 14, 2007 (H.Rept. 110-146, part 2). Substitute amendment passed House May 17, 2007. Placed on Senate calendar, June 5, 2007; laid before the Senate by unanimous consent, June 28, 2007.

H.R. 2740 (Price)—MEJA Expansion and Enforcement Act of 2007

H.R. 2740 would extend the coverage of the Military Extraterritorial Jurisdiction Act (MEJA) to include all persons "while employed under a contract (or subcontract at any tier) awarded by any department or agency of the United States, where the work under such contract is carried out in a region outside the United Sates in which the Armed Forces are conducting a contingency operation." Currently, MEJA covers contractors only if employed by "the Armed Forces outside the United States," or if employed by other federal agencies or "provisional authority," to the extent their employment is related to the support of the DOD mission overseas. The bill would mandate that the Federal Bureau of Investigation (FBI) establish a "Theater Investigative Unit" for each contingency operation in which covered contract personnel are working to investigate suspected misconduct. It would also require that the Department of Justice Inspector General report to Congress within 30 days of enactment on the investigation of abuses alleged to have been committed by contract personnel.

Introduced June 15, 2007. Referred to the House Judiciary Committee.

H.Res. 97 (Murphy, Patrick)—Providing for Operation Iraqi Freedom Cost Accountability

H.Res. 97 resolves that the Department of Defense Inspector General and the Special Inspector General for Iraq Reconstruction should report to Congress on the expenditure of military and reconstruction funds in Iraq and on the types and terms of U.S. contracts there. Resolves that Congress should create a "Truman Commission" to conduct an ongoing investigation of the award and implementation of U.S. contracts with regard to Operation Iraqi Freedom.

Introduced January 24, 2007. Referred to the House Armed Services and Foreign Affairs Committees. House Foreign Affairs Committee hearing held March 20, 2007.

DOCUMENT NO. 4

DEFENSE CONTRACTING IN IRAQ: ISSUES AND OPTIONS FOR CONGRESS

CRS Report
RL33834

June 18, 2008

Valerie Bailey Grasso
Specialist in Defense Acquisition Policy
Foreign Affairs, Defense, and Trade Division

Summary

This report examines logistical support contracts for troop support services in Iraq primarily administered through the U.S. Army's Logistics Civil Augmentation Program (LOGCAP). LOGCAP is an initiative designed to manage the use of civilian contractors that perform services during times of war and other military mobilizations. On April 18, 2008, DOD announced the Army's LOGCAP IV contract awards to three companies—DynCorp International LLC, Fort Worth, TX; Fluor Intercontinental, Inc, Greenville, SC; and KBR, Houston, TX, through a full and open competition. The LOGCAP IV contract calls for each company to compete for task orders. Each company may be awarded up to $5 billion annually for troop support services with a maximum annual value of $15 billion. Over the life of LOGCAP IV, the maximum contract value is $150 billion.

Congress is concerned about the Federal oversight and management of DOD contracting in Iraq. Recent assessments from the Government Accountability Office (GAO), DOD Office of the Inspector General (IG), and the Special Inspector General for Iraq Reconstruction (SIGIR) reveal a lack of accountability for large sums of money spent for Iraq contracts. For example, an audit conducted by the DOD IG revealed that the Federal government failed to substantiate the disbursement of at least $7.8 billion of $8.2 billion dollars believed to be spent for goods and services in Iraq.

The IG's investigation estimated that the Army disbursed $1.4 billion in commercial payments that lacked the minimum supporting justification and documentation required for valid payments—such as certified vouchers and invoices. In one instance, a $320 million cash payment was made without justification beyond a signature.[1] Many observers view these investigations as a call for new rules on contract oversight, management, and accountability.

The Fiscal Year (FY) 2008 Defense Authorization Act (P.L. 110-181) contains provisions that are intended to reduce instances of DOD contract waste, fraud, abuse, and mismanagement. Other provisions require the Secretary of Defense to provide a plan for addressing skill shortfalls in the DOD acquisition workforce; provide for a periodic and independent management review of DOD contracts; prohibit the awarding of sole source contracts and non-competitive grants; and establish a commission on wartime contracting to investigate contracts in Iraq and Afghanistan. The House and Senate proposed FY2009 Defense Authorization bills contain new provisions that extend these safeguards to all for all Federal contracting.

This report will be updated as warranted.

Introduction

Purpose and Scope

This report will examine logistical support contracts for troop support services (also known as service contracts[2]) in Iraq, primarily administered through a smaller program, the United States Air Force Contract Augmentation Program (AFCAP) and a larger program, the United States Army's Logistics Civil Augmentation Program (LOGCAP).[3] This report will focus primarily on contracts involving Department of Defense (DOD) appropriated funds, although some projects involve a blending of funds from other agencies.[4]

---

[1] U.S. Congress. Accountability Lapses in Multiple Funds for Iraq. Testimony of Mary L. Ugone, Deputy Inspector General for Auditing, U.S. Department of Defense, Office of the Inspector General. Hearing before the House Oversight and Government Reform Committee, May 22, 2008.

[2] Federal Acquisition Regulation (FAR) 37, Subpart 37.1 defines "service contracts" as contracts that directly engage the time and effort of a contractor whose primary purpose is to perform an identifiable task rather than to furnish an end item of supply.

[3] Department of the Army. Logistics Civil Augmentation Program (LOGCAP). Army Regulation (AR) 700-137, Introduction, 1-1. Purpose, p. 1.

[4] For a fact sheet on the application of federal procurement statutes to contracts for the reconstruction of Iraq, see CRS Report RS21555, *Iraq Reconstruction: Frequently Asked Questions Concerning the Application of Federal Procurement Statutes*, by John R. Luckey; for a discussion on Iraqi Relief and Reconstruction Fund (IRRF) contracting issues, see CRS Report RL31833, *Iraq: Recent Developments in Reconstruction Assistance*, by Curt Tarnoff. For a discussion on private security contracting see CRS Report RL32419, *Private Security Contractors in Iraq: Background, Legal Status*, and Other Issues, by Jennifer K. Elsea and Nina M. Serafino. For a discussion of war-related costs see CRS Report RL33110, *The Cost of Iraq, Afghanistan, and Other Global War on Terror Operations Since 9/11*, by Amy Belasco. For

Air Force Contract Augmentation Program

The U.S. Air Force has a smaller contingency contracting support program for services in Iraq. The Air Force Contract Augmentation Program (AFCAP) administers logistical support service contracts in Iraq. AFCAP is the largest contingency support contract awarded by the Air Force. AFCAP is an "umbrella" contract, similar to the U.S. Army's LOGCAP. It was designed to provide an on-call capability for troop sustainment and support. The program was established in 1997 for a wide-range of non-combatant, civil engineering services during wartime, contingency operation, and humanitarian efforts. AFCAP provides for contractor support to relieve active duty and air reserve personnel in the areas of food service, lodging, carpentry, plumbing, electrical, mechanical, air conditioning, laundry plant operations, fire protection emergency management, project and program management.

Initially, AFCAP began as a five-year, $475 million program; now it is a 10year, $10 billion program. AFCAP is managed by the Air Force Civil Engineer Support Agency at Tyndall Air Force Base and the Air Force Services Agency in San Antonio, Texas. The contract consists of administrative task orders awarded to six companies: Washington Group International, CH2M Hill Global Services, URS/Berger JV, Bechtel National, DynCorp International and Readiness Management Support. The AFCAP contractor maintains a core staff in theater to plan, organize, and acquire resources on an as-needed basis.[5]

Logistics Civil Augmentation Program

LOGCAP was established by the U.S. Army on December 6, 1985 with the publication of Army Regulation 700-137. LOGCAP is an initiative to manage the use of civilian contractors who perform services in support of DOD missions during times of war and other military mobilizations. The use of LOGCAP contracts augments combat support and combat service support to military forces.[6]

On October 1, 1996, LOGCAP management was transferred to the U.S. Army Material Command. In September 2006 the ASC was created to serve as the "logistics integrator" for the contingency contracting and sustainment

a discussion on the FY2008 DOD appropriations and authorization bills, refer to CRS Report RL33999, *Defense: FY2008 Authorization and Appropriations*, by Pat Towell, Stephen Daggett, and Amy Belasco.

[5] $10 Billion AFCAP III Award Provides Expeditionary Engineering. *Defense Industry Daily: Military Purchasing News for Defense Procurement Managers and Contractors*, at [http://www.defenseindustry-daily.com/10b-afcap-iii-program-contract-provides-expeditionary-engineering-01468/].

[6] LOGCAP contracts have been previously awarded for work in Rwanda, Haiti, Saudi Arabia, Kosovo, Ecuador, Q atar, Italy, southeastern Europe, Bosnia, South Korea, Iraq, and Kuwait. Under LOGCAP, private sector contractors are used to provide a broad range of logistical and other support services to U.S. and allied forces during combat, peacekeeping, humanitarian and training operations.

needs of the military worldwide. ASC oversees about 65,000 contractors and manages about $25 billion in contracts.[7]

LOGCAP Contracts (1992–2007)

The first LOGCAP contract (LOGCAP I) was awarded on August 3, 1992 to Brown and Root Services of Houston, Texas (also know as KBR). Reportedly, the contract was competitively awarded and consisted of a cost-plus-award-fee contract for one year followed by four option years. The Army Corp of Engineers reportedly held a competition to award the second LOGCAP contract (LOGCAP II). The contract, a cost-plus award fee contract for one base year followed by four option years was awarded to Dyncorp on January 1, 1997. The third LOGCAP contract (LOGCAP III) was awarded in 2001 to Halliburton/KBR.[8]

LOGCAP III, a ten-year contract (one base year followed by nine option years), was awarded to Halliburton/KBR to perform a variety of tasks. Initial press reports indicated that the 2001 LOGCAP III contract would be for the development of a contingency plan for extinguishing oil well fires in Iraq; however, subsequent press reports indicate that the contract included such tasks as providing housing for troops, preparing food, supplying water, and collecting trash. This contract was awarded under a cost-plus-award-fee, Indefinite-Delivery/Indefinite-Quantity (ID/IQ) contract.[9] The 2001 contract was based on specific task orders which are issued individually and only for those services that DOD felt were necessary to support the mission in the near term. During 2003, LOGCAP III contract rose to more than $3.5 billion. According to one press account, Halliburton/KBR reportedly earned a fixed 1% profit above costs on LOGCAP III, with the possibility of an additional 2% incentive bonus,[10] while another press account reported that the Halliburton/KBR LOGCAP III contract was a cost-plus, award fee contract that earned a 2% fixed fee with the potential for an extra 5% incentive fee.[11]

The fourth LOGCAP contract (LOGCAP IV) was executed with a different acquisition strategy. According to the Army, the LOGCAP IV contract award as based on a full and open competition. Instead of using a single contractor, the contract called for multiple contractors. Competitions were held and the contracts were awarded based on what represented the best value to the

---

[7] [http://www.aschq.army.mil/home/missionvision.htm].

[8] KBR was formerly known as Brown and Root Services. Brown & Root Services was the original LOGCAP contractor.

[9] Indefinite delivery/indefinite quantity contracts, also known as ID/IQ contracts, supply an indefinite quantity of supplies, goods, or materials for an indefinite period of time. See FAR, Part 16, Types of Contracts.

[10] Jaffe, Greg and King, Neil, Jr. U.S. General Criticizes Halliburton. *Wall Street Journal*, March 15, 2004.

[11] See the Center for Public Integrity's website at [http://www.publicintegrity.org/wow/] under the section for Windfalls of War, U.S. Contractors in Afghanistan and Iraq.

government.[12] In best value source selections, the government may make trade offs to make awards based on factors other than costs or technical superiority. The use of multiple LOGCAP contractors is reportedly intended to reduce the government's risk. Under the new strategy, the three performance contractors may compete for individual LOGCAP task orders, creating a competitive environment meant to control costs and enhance quality.

LOGCAP IV Contract Awards

The planning contract was awarded to Serco. In August 2006 the Army held a competition to select a logistical planning and program support contractor for LOGCAP IV. Two proposals were received and in February 2007 the ASC selected Serco, Inc., of Vienna, VA. This contract will have a minimum value of $613,677 with a contract period of one base year followed by up to four one-year options with a maximum annual contract value of $45 million and a maximum contract value of $225 million.[13]

The ASC news release announcing the initial award selection described the range of logistical and program services provided under the contract. They appear on ASC website.

- Augmenting the Army's capability to develop and update worldwide management and staffing plans for contingencies;
- working with LOGCAP IV performance contractors to assure that they understand these plans;
- helping theater planners integrate LOGCAP into their plans;
- assisting planners in incorporating a broad range of contracted logistics support;
- developing scopes of work officially referred to as procurement work statements;
- preparing independent government cost estimates which are compared against the contractor's bids to assure valid costs for task orders;
- conducting analysis of how performance contractors will do the work outlined in the task orders' scopes of work;
- analyzing performance contractors' costs;
- working with the Army to measure LOGCAP IV contractor performance; and
- recommending process improvements in the above actions.[14]

[12] FAR, Part 15. Contracting by Negotiation.

[13] U.S. Army Sustainment Command, February 16, 2007; News Release, U.S. Army Sustainment Command, June 27, 2007.

[14] *Ibid.*, p. 1.

ASC selected the performance contractors. The Army conducted a competition to select up to three performance contractors for services similar to those rendered under LOGCAP III.[15] Solicitations were issued in October 2006 and six proposals were received. In June 2007 the ASC selected three companies to serve as performance contractors—DynCorp International LLC, Fort Worth, TX; Fluor Intercontinental, Inc, Greenville, SC; and KBR, Houston, TX.

Protests. On June 27, 2007 the losing companies filed protests with GAO over the LOGCAP IV award decision.[16] GAO sustained the protests on October 5, 2007. The Army reopened the competition. Five companies submitted bids. On April 17, 2008, the Army announced that it would re-award the LOGCAP IV contract to the three companies previously awarded contracts under LOGCAP IV.

Contract Details. The LOGCAP IV contract will cover a range of services:

- supply operations, including food, water, fuel, spare parts, and other items
- field operations, including food, laundry, housing, sanitation, waste management, postal services, and morale, welfare and recreation activities; and
- other operations, including engineering and construction; support to the communication networks; transportation and cargo services; and facilities and repair.[17]

[15] From the Army's FY2008 Budget Estimates for the Global War on Terrorism: LOGCAP augments combat support and combat service support force structure by reinforcing military assets with civilian contract support. The program provides primarily base life support services to the forces in theater. Base life support services provide a full spectrum of services, including food service, power generation, electrical distribution, facilities management, dining facility operations, pest management, hazardous and non-hazardous waste management, latrines, water systems, billeting management, fire fighting and fire protection services, and laundry service operations. In Iraq, the program provides for the Multi-National Force—Iraq base logistics support, base camp reorganization, the International Zone, Camp Bucca Prisoner of War base operations support, and contractor support management in theater. In Afghanistan, the program manages base operations support for the Coalition Joint Operations Area—Afghanistan, and the Kabul, Bagram, Kandahar, and Salerno airfields. In Kuwait, the program manages Camps Spearhead, Udari, Arifjan; theater Retrograde operations; the theater-wide transportation mission; theater oil analysis and test facilities; management and diagnostic equipment, and bulk fuel operations. Army Operations and Maintenance, Volume 1, February 2007, p. 13, at [http://www.asafm.army.mil/budget/fybm/fybm.asp].

[16] Kelley, Matt. GAO Challenges $150B Contract Awarded By Army: Urges Review of 10year Deal to Support Troops. *USA Today*, October 31, 2007, p. 5A. According to the article, the ASC spokesperson identified was Daniel Carlson. According to Dan Gordon, a GAO official identified in the article, the ruling was issued under seal. Also, see GAO Upholds Protests to Army's Award of $50 Billion for LOGCAP 4. *Engineering News-Record*, November 5, 2007, Construction Week; pg. 9, Vol. 259, No. 16. An ASC spokesperson announced that the LOGCAP III contract would be extended while the Army made a final decision.

[17] Sheftick, Gary. Three Firms to Vie for LOGCAP Services in Theater. *Department of Defense, U.S. Army Release*. April 18, 2008.

LOGCAP IV contracts were awarded as ID/IQ contracts with one base year followed by nine option years. Each company will compete for task orders. Each of the three contracts will have a maximum value of $5 billion per year, with a collective annual maximum value of $15 billion and lifetime maximum value of $150 billion for LOGCAP IV.[18]

Congressional Interest

Legislation passed in the FY2008 National Defense Authorization Act (P.L.110181) requires increased oversight and accountability for DOD contracting during combat operations. The House passed H.R. 5658, their version of the Fiscal Year (FY) 2009 National Defense Authorization bill on May 22, 2008 and the bill was later placed on the Senate Legislative Calendar. Overall these provisions seek to enhance competition, reduce sole-source contracts, improve the acquisition workforce, address waste, fraud, and mismanagement, and provide mechanisms for greater oversight and transparency. A group of twenty-four provisions included in the bill are known as the Clean Contracting Act of 2008. A similar bill, H.R. 6069, was introduced in the second session of the 109th Congress.

The Senate introduced S. 3001, their version of the FY2009 Defense Authorization bill, on May 12, 2008, and placed it on the Legislative Calendar. One provision, Section 812, would establish a DOD Contingency Contracting Corps to ensure the capability to provide staff for deployment both within and outside of the United States.

Policymakers continue to express concern over the oversight of Iraq contracts for several reasons including the expense and difficulty of managing logistical support contracts; allegations and reported instances of contract waste, fraud, abuse, and financial mismanagement; and questions regarding DOD's ability and capacity to manage such contracts. Some policymakers have raised questions as to whether DOD has the right mix of acquisition workforce personnel trained and equipped to oversee these large-scale contracts. Due to such concerns, Congress has extended the tenure of the Office of the Special Inspector General for Iraq Reconstruction (SIGIR). From March 2004 through April 2008 SIGIR conducted audits and investigations and presented recommendations for improving the management of Iraq reconstruction and relief activities.[19]

---

[18] U.S. Army Sustainment Command. ASC Selects LOGCAP IV Contractors, June 27, 2007. Visited October 30, 2007 at [http://www.aschq.army.mil/commandnews/default.asp].

[19] See the Special Inspector General for Iraq Reconstruction, Quarterly Report to Congress, April 30, 2008, at [http://www.sigir.mil/reports/quarterlyreports/default.aspx]. The SIGIR replaced the Inspector General for the Coalition Provisional Authority (CPA-IG). As provided for in P.L. 108-106, the SIGIR provides an independent and objective audit, analysis, and investigation into the use of U.S.-appropriated resources for Iraq relief and reconstruction. The SIGIR, Stuart W. Bowen, Jr., was appointed as CPA-IG on January 20, 2004. He reports to both the Department of State and the Department of Defense, provides quarterly reports and semi-annual reports to Congress, and has

Recent assessments from GAO, DOD's IG, and the SIGIR reveal a lack of Federal oversight, management, and accountability for funds spent for Iraq contracting. An audit conducted by the DOD IG revealed that the Federal government failed to substantiate the disbursement of at least $7.8 billion of $8.2 billion dollars spent for goods and services in Iraq. In a May 22, 2008 congressional hearing before the House Oversight and Government Reform Committee, DOD officials revealed estimates that the Army disbursed $1.4 billion in commercial payments that lacked the minimum supporting justification and documentation for a valid payment—such as certified vouchers and invoices. In one reported instance, a $320 million payment in cash was made without justification beyond a signature.[20]

Background

Awarding of Defense Contracts

In most cases, federal government contracts are awarded under "full and open competition." However, there are exceptions, particularly during times of war.

Full and Open Competition. In general, authorities that govern the awarding of most federal government contracts can be found in the United States Code (U.S.C.) and the Federal Acquisition Regulation (FAR). The Competition in Contracting Act of 1984[21] explicitly states that the federal government "shall obtain full and open competition through use of the competitive procedures in accordance with the requirements of this title and the FAR."[22] The FAR and the Defense Federal Acquisition Regulation Supplement (DFARS) give DOD at least seven exceptions to the use of other than full and open competition in the awarding of contracts.[23]

---

offices in Baghad and Arlington, VA. For a summary of the history of U.S. reconstruction assistance in Iraq, see CRS Report RL31833, *Iraq: Recent Developments in Reconstruction Assistance*, by Curt Tarnoff.

[20] U.S. Congress. Accountability Lapses in Multiple Funds for Iraq. Testimony of Mary L. Ugone, Deputy Inspector General for Auditing, U.S. Department of Defense, Office of the Inspector General. Hearing before the House Oversight and Government Reform Committee, May 22, 2008.

[21] 41U.S.C. 253. CICA can also be found in Title 10 U.S.C., Chapter 137, and was included in Section 805 of the FY2004 National Defense Authorization Act (P.L. 108-136).

[22] 41 U.S.C. 253 (a)(1)(A).

[23] The Defense Federal Acquisition Regulation and AIDAR are supplements to the FAR. See DFARS, Subpart 206.3, and AIDAR, Subpart 706.3, Other Than Full and Open Competition. The exceptions are: (1) There is only one responsible source available to fulfill the contract requirements; (2) the federal agency's need for these goods or services is of such an unusual and compelling urgency that the federal government would be seriously injured if this contract were not awarded; (3) the federal government needs to ensure that suppliers are maintained in the event of a national emergency, or to achieve industrial mobilization, or to establish or achieve or maintain an engineering, development, or research capability; (4) The federal government has an international agreement to make this acquisition through means other than through full and open competition; (5) a statute specifically authorizes or requires that the contract be made through a specific source; (6) The use of full and open competition may compromise national security; (7) The public interest would be better served by use of other than full and open competition. The procedures for submitting written justifications to use other than full and

Two of the seven circumstances are (1) when the Secretary of Defense determines that DOD's need for a property or service is of such an "unusual and compelling urgency" that the United States would be seriously injured unless DOD is permitted to limit the number of sources from which it solicits bids or proposals; and (2) when the use of full and open competition would compromise national security.

Emergency Contracting Authorities. Title 41 USC Section 428a grants special emergency procurement authority to heads of executive agencies where it is determined that a procurement is to be used in support of a contingency operation, or to facilitate defense against or recovery from nuclear, biological, chemical, or radiological attack.

Contingency Contracting. Contingency contracting differs from emergency contracting—the first usually describes situations where urgent requirements are necessitated by disasters, while the second usually describes military, humanitarian, or peacekeeping operations.[24] DOD has developed initiatives to strengthen DOD contracting operations, particularly in contingency contracting situations.[25] Section 817 of the National Defense Authorization Act for Fiscal Year (FY) 2006[26] directs the Secretary of Defense, in consultation with the Chairman of the Joint Chiefs of Staff, to develop a joint policy for contingency contracting during combat operations and post-conflict operations no later than one year from the bill's enactment. Sections 815 and 854 of the John Warner National Defense Authorization Act for FY2007required DOD to report to Congress on contingency contracting requirements and program management, and to develop instructions to implement a contingency contracting program. The report was issued in October 2007.[27]

Rapid Acquisition Methods. Section 811 of the FY2005 National Defense Authorization Act[28] grants the Secretary of Defense limited rapid acquisition authority to acquire goods and services during combat emergencies.

---

open competition, including review requirements and delegation of authority, are outlined in DFARS, Subparts 206.303-1 and 206.304, and AIDAR 706.3. For a more detailed discussion on the seven exceptions to the use of full and open competition, refer to CRS Report RS21555, *Iraq Reconstruction: Frequently Asked Questions Concerning the Application of Federal Procurement Statutes*, by John R. Luckey.

24 Drabkin, David, and Thai, Khi V. Emergency Contracting in the US Federal Government. *Journal of Public Procurement 2007*, Vol. 7, No. 1, p. 84.

25 For further information on DOD Procurement and Acquisition Policy governing contingency contracting, refer to [http://www.acq.osd.mil/dpap/pacc/cc/about.html], visited November 7, 2007.

26 P.L. 109-16.

27 Report on DOD Program for Planning, Managing, and Accounting for Contractor Services and Contractor Personnel during Contingency Operations, accompanied by a memorandum to the Honorable Richard B. Cheney from the Honorable P. Jackson Bell, Deputy Under Secretary of Defense for Logistics and Materiel Readiness, October 15, 2007. Section 815 covers the implementation of DOD Instruction (DODI) 3020.41,Contractor Personnel Authorized to Accompany Armed Forces, October 3, 2005, at [http://www.dtic.mil/whs/directives/corres/html/302041.htm].

28 Section 806 of the Bob Stump National Defense Authorization Act for Fiscal Year 2003 (10 U.S.C. 2302 note) is amended through the passage of Section 811.

Also, Title 10, Section 2304 outlines the use of ID/IQ task orders, sealed bidding, certain contract actions, and set-aside procurement under section 8(a) of the Small Business Act[29] as examples of ways to expedite the delivery of goods and services during combat operations or post-conflict operations.

Audits, Investigations, and Reports

Role of Federal Agencies. No one federal agency has the sole mission to audit, investigate, or oversee DOD-appropriated funds for troop support services under LOGCAP. Multiple agencies share responsibility, among them the Defense Contract Audit Agency (DCAA), the Defense Contract Management Agency (DCMA), the Army Audit Agency (AAA), and the DOD Inspector General.

Special Inspector General for Iraq Reconstruction (SIGIR). Media reports suggests that a perceived lack of transparency in the earliest Iraq contracts led to the appointment of the Special Inspector General for the Coalition Provisional Authority (now SIGIR). SIGIR Stuart Bowen has audited and investigated contracts for Iraq reconstruction and relief funds, although some projects have involved a blending of IRRF funds with DOD appropriated funds.[30] The SIGIR's additional investigations into LOGCAP contracts have largely described LOGCAP contracts as lacking transparency, oversight, and financial accountability, and his investigations have documented some cases of waste, fraud, abuse, and financial mismanagement. According to the Congressional Budget Office, the SIGIR has produced more than 150 reports, audits, or investigations of reconstruction-related activities.[31] Estimates have been made that the SIGIR's work has resulted in significant benefits to the federal government.[32]

In June 2007 the SIGIR released a report based on its partial audit of Task Order 130, awarded to KBR on April 27, 2006 to provide support services to officials at the U.S. Embassy in Iraq as well as other Iraq sites. This report found substantial deficiencies in both KBR's ability to provide enough data for the SIGIR to perform an adequate audit and investigation of (what appeared to be) gross overcharges for fuel and food services. Additionally, the

---

[29] 15 U.S.C. 637(a).

[30] For a discussion of contract funds for Iraqi Relief and Reconstruction projects, see CRS Report RL31833, *Iraq: Recent Developments in Reconstruction Assistance,* by Curt Tarnoff. Also, for a discussion on federal procurement statutes as they affect Iraq reconstruction projects see CRS Report RS21555, *Iraq Reconstruction: Frequently Asked Questions Concerning the Application of Federal Procurement Statutes,* by John R. Luckey.

[31] Paying for Iraq Reconstruction. An Update of the January 2004 analysis. Congressional Budget Office, December 8, 2006.

[32] Senator Collins Works To Extend The Term of the Office that Oversees Billions in Iraqi Reconstruction Dollars. Press Release of the United States Senate Committee on Governmental Affairs, November 13, 2006. Also, see SIGIR website [http://www.sigir.mil/] for audits reports.

report found that the government's oversight and management of the contract was inadequate and contributed to the SIGIR's inability to completely audit and investigate the contract—including an evaluation of the government's ability to provide oversight and management.[33]

Overall, the SIGIR has recommended that the federal government "generally avoid the use of sole-source and limited-competition contracting actions."[34] The report concludes that the use of sole-source and limited competition contracting in Iraq should have ended sooner, and that contracts issued previously under limited or sole-source competition should have been subject to re-competition.

Latest SIGIR Review

The latest LOGCAP review is a continuation of a past review of LOGCAP Task Order 130 (awarded on April 27, 2006 with an estimated value of $283 million) and a new review of LOGCAP Task Order 151 (awarded on June 6, 2007 with an estimated value of $200 million). Both task orders were awarded to KBR for support services to the Chief of Mission and Multi-National Force-Iraq staffs (located at the U.S. Embassy-Iraq) and for services at other Chief of Mission sites within Iraq (located in Baghdad, Basra, Al Hillah and Kirkuk.) SIGIR conducted its review at KBR sites in Baghdad and involved interviews with personnel responsible for the administration and oversight from DCMA, DCAA, and DOS; personnel with the Joint Area Support Group-Central appointed as the Contracting Officer's Technical Representatives (COTRs); the LOGCAP Task Order 151 Support Officer; personnel at the Army's Logistic and Budget Offices, and KBR managers and operational personnel.[35] From the report, here is an excerpt which described the costs.

> Because these task orders provided support to both the Department of Defense (DOD) and Department of State (DOS) missions in Iraq, DOD and DOS agreed that the reimbursement of costs associated with these task orders would be shared 60% by DOS and 40% by DOD. The total cost of these four task orders is approximately $1.5 billion.[36]

[33] Logistics Civil Augmentation Program Task Order 130: Requirements Validation, Government Oversight, and Contractor Performance. SIGIR 07-001, June 22, 2007, at [http://www.sigir.mil/reports/pdf/audits/07-001.pdf]

[34] Lessons in Contracting from Iraq Reconstruction. Lessons Learned and Recommendations from the SIGIR, July 2006.

[35] Both Task Orders are a continuation of services previously awarded under Task Order 100 and Task Order 44. Logistics Civil Augmentation Program Task Orders 130 and 151: Program Management, Reimbursement, and Transition. SIGIR-08-002, October 30, 2007, Appendix A, Scope and Methodology p. 22, at [http://www.sigir.mil /reports/pdf/audits/08-002.pdf]

[36] Logistics Civil Augmentation Program Task Orders 130 and 151: Program Management, Reimbursement, and Transition. SIGIR-08-002, October 30, 2007, pages 1–2, at [http://www.sigir.mil/reports/pdf/audits/08-002.pdf]

Overall, the SIGIR's audit and investigation found that the federal government and KBR had improved its oversight and management of Task Orders 130 and 151. However, the report identified areas where the government should make specific improvements in both oversight and management.[37]

DOD Inspector General. Thomas F. Gimble, Principal Deputy Inspector General for the Department of Defense, testified at the September 20, 2007 hearing before the House Armed Services Committee on "Accountability During Contingency Operations: Preventing and Fighting Corruption in Contracting and Establishing and Maintaining Appropriate Controls on Materiel."[38] In his testimony he described DOD's past and present efforts to provide oversight for contracting during contingency operations.

> To date, over $550 billion has been appropriated to the Department of Defense in support of the men and women of our Armed Forces in Southwest Asia and the fight against terrorism. To provide oversight, we have over 225 personnel working on 29 audits and 90 investigations that address a wide variety of matters to include contracting, accountability, and required documentation. Additionally, we are working with other DoD organizations, such as the Army Audit Agency, the Army Criminal Investigation Command, and the Defense Finance and Accounting Service, to evaluate and provide recommendations for actions addressing these critical mission support areas.[39]

He also described the formation of a new partnership to combine the efforts of multiple federal agencies to combat both waste, fraud, abuse, and mismanagement of Iraq reconstruction contracts.

> More recently, as a result of the magnitude of alleged criminal activities within the Iraqi theater, a group of Federal agencies has formalized a partnership to combine resources to investigate and prosecute cases of contract fraud and public corruption related to U.S. Government spending for Iraq reconstruction. The participating agencies in the International Contract Corruption Task Force (ICCTF) are DCIS; Army CIDs Major Procurement Fraud Unit; the Office of the Inspector General, Department of State; the FBI; the Special Inspector General for Iraq Reconstruction; and the Office of the Inspector General, Agency for International Development.
>
> The ICCTF has established a Joint Operations Center which is a case coordination cell and criminal intelligence element aimed at achieving maximum interagency cooperation to successfully prosecute fraud and corruption cases in support of the war effort in Iraq. The mission and objectives of the ICCTF are a shared responsibility of the participating agencies. Case information and criminal intelligence are shared without reservation and statistical accomplishments will be reported jointly.

---

[37] *Ibid.*, pp. 4–20.

[38] Statement of Mr. Thomas F. Gimble, Principal Deputy Inspector General, Department of Defense, before the House Armed Services Committee, September 20, 2007.

[39] *Ibid.*, p. 1.

As a result of closed and ongoing investigations, five Federal criminal indictments and ten Federal criminal information have been issued, and two Article 32 hearings under the Uniform Code of Military Justice have been conducted. As a result of the investigations, nine U.S. persons and one foreign person have been convicted of felonies, resulting in a total of approximately fifteen years of confinement and eleven years of probation. Four individuals and one company were debarred from contracting with the U.S. Government; nineteen companies and persons were suspended from contracting; and two contractors signed settlement agreements with the U.S. Government. In all, $9.84 million was paid to the U.S. in restitution; $323,525 was levied in fines and penalties; $3,500 was forfeited; and $61,953 was seized.[40]

Government Accountability Office (GAO). GAO has identified DOD contract management as a high risk area and monitors DOD's performance with periodic progress updates.[41] GAO has conducted numerous studies of Iraq contracting including several studies of logistical support contracts.[42] Since 2003 GAO has issued a number of Iraq-related reports and testimonies to Congress.

The Comptroller General David Walker appeared in July 2007 before the Senate Homeland Security and Governmental Affairs Committee to discuss four specific challenges facing federal agencies in the oversight and management of contracts. There he made several important observations:

> Managing risks when requirements are in transition requires effective oversight. DOD lacked the capacity to provide sufficient numbers of contracting, logistics, and other personnel, thereby hindering oversight efforts. The challenges faced in Iraq are a symbol of systematic challenges facing DOD. DOD cannot develop a complete picture of the extent to which it relies on contractors to support its operations. Information on the number of contractor employees, and the services they provide, is not aggregated within DOD or its components. DOD recently established an office to address contractor support issues, but the office's specific roles and responsibilities are under study. DOD and its contractors need to clearly understand DOD's objectives and needs. To produce desired outcomes with available funding and within required time frames, they need to know the goods or services required, the level of performance or quality desired, the schedule, and the cost.[43]

---

[40] *Ibid.*, pp. 11–13.

[41] "High Risk Area: Defense Contract Management." GAO-05-207, February 2005.

[42] GAO-04-854, Military Operation. DOD's Extensive Use of Logistics Support Contracts Requires Strengthened Oversight. July 2004.

[43] GAO-07-358T, p. 13. Also see GAO-07-1098T. Federal Acquisitions and Contracting. Systemic Challenges Need Attention. Statement of David M. Walker, Comptroller General of the United States, July 17, 2007; GAO-07-145. Military Operations: High-Level DOD Action Needed to Address Long-standing Problems with Management and Oversight of Contractors Supporting Deployed Forces, December 2006, p. 53.; and GAO-04-854. Military Operations: DOD's Extensive Use of Logistics Support Contracts Requires Strengthened Oversight. July 2004, p. 67.

Potential Oversight Issues

Potential contract oversight issues that Congress may choose to examine include various aspects of contract administration such as contract costs, development of contract requirements, costs-reimbursement and sole-source contracts; transparency and the size, shape, and skill diversity of the acquisition workforce.

Contract Oversight. One rationale often cited for the outsourcing of program management to industry is that DOD no longer has the in-house expertise needed to manage such complicated acquisition programs. Some Members of Congress may want DOD to develop a long-term plan to restore in-house expertise to make the government a smarter customer. Because of several cases in which high profile weapons acquisition programs have been affected by escalating costs and technical shortcomings, Congress may choose to review the management of individual programs and the evolution of DOD's acquisition management processes with an eye toward using the FY2008 funding bills to strengthen the government's hand in dealing with industry. As an example, Secretary of the Navy Donald C. Winter and Chief of Naval Operations Adm. Michael G. Mullen have reported that the Navy intends to reclaim some of the authority over ship design it has ceded to industry. Congress may also choose to study the Army's Future Combat System (FCS) and may question the amount of managerial discretion the Army has vested in the Lead System Integrator (LSI).[44]

Contract Administration. Contract administration includes contract management and contract oversight. FAR Part 37 states that "agencies shall ensure that sufficiently trained and experienced professionals are available to manage contracts."[45] The burden rests with the federal government to ensure that enough appropriately-trained professionals are available to manage contracts. This is essential, particularly before the requirements generation process, when the government determines the scope of work to be completed. Contract management is also described in the Office of Federal Procurement Policy's (OFPP) "Guide To Best Practices for Contract Administration" where it states that "The technical administration of government contracts is an essential activity . . . absolutely essential that those entrusted with the duty ensure that the government gets all that it bargains for . . . and they must be competent in the practice of contractor administration."[46]

---

[44] For a discussion of the LSI concept, see CRS Report RS22631, *Defense Acquisition: Use of Lead System Integrators (LSIs)—Background, Oversight Issuers, and Options for Congress*, by Valerie Bailey Grasso; CRS Report RL33753, *Coast Guard Deepwater Program: Background, Oversight Issues, and Options for Congress*, by Ronald O'Rourke; and CRS Report RL32888, *The Army's Future Combat System* (FSC): *Background and Issues for Congress*, by Andrew Feickert.

[45] FAR Part 37.

[46] OFPP Guide at [http://www.acqnet.gov/comp/seven_steps/library/OFPPguide-bp.pdf].

Over the past few years the size, shape, and complexity of logistical support service contracts have grown with the technical requirements. However, the size of the federal contractor workforce has decreased. There is now an imbalance - there are fewer federal contracting officials to manage the large-scale contracts and in some cases the government has sought to hire contractors to do the job that federal employees use to perform. For example, GAO reported that military officials utilizing LOGCAP had little understanding of LOGCAP or their contract management responsibilities. Additionally, some logistical support units intended to assist military commanders had no prior LOGCAP or contracting experience.[47]

Two former OFPP administrators, Steven Kelman and Allan Burman, stated that the current contracting situation creates a crisis. Here they offer their assessment.

> Hiring contracting officials is hardly the way to dress for political success—who wants to bring in more "bureaucrats?"—but there can't be well-managed contracts without people to manage them. The current situation creates a vicious circle: Overstretched people make mistakes, producing demands for more rules, creating additional burdens, giving people even less time to plan effective procurement and manage performance.[48]

It is important that both civilian and military procurement sectors have qualified and experienced contract professionals. In the case of service contracts, having professionally trained contracting personnel could be even more critical than contracts for tangible goods. With tangible goods, there is an identifiable product. In the absence of a product, it becomes even more important that DOD and the contractor both exercise good stewardship of federally appropriated dollars.

DOD Contracting Officials. Contracting officials are expected to make tough decisions. As an example, Ms. Bunnatine Greenhouse, formerly the highest ranking civilian at the U.S. Army Corps of Engineers (USACE), raised important questions on the rationale for awarding KBR contracts without competition. She objected to the awarding of one contract award as well as the five-year contract term.[49] The basis for her refusal to approve the proposed five-year, sole-source contract between KBR and the U.S. Army [for the Restore Iraqi Oil (RIO) contract] was because: (1) KBR had been paid $1.9 million to draft a contingency plan to design the "guts" of the contract, including the process, budget, and other details; and (2) selecting

[47] Logistical support units write performance statements of work, prepare independent government cost estimates, and review contractor estimates on behalf of the government. See GAO-04-854. Military Operations: DOD's Extensive Use of Logistics Support Contracts Strengthen Oversight, July 21, 2004.

[48] Burman, Allan and Kelman, Steven. "Better Oversight of Contractors," *The Boston Globe*, January 16, 2007, p. A9.

[49] Schnayerson, Michael. "Oh, What a Lucrative War," *Vanity Fair*, April 2005, p. 9.

KBR for the five-year contract would violate procurement protocol, as (reportedly, Ms. Greenhouse stated) contractors who draw up a contingency plan cannot be allowed to bid on the job to *execute* the same plan.[50] She stated that bidding on the contract would give KBR an unfair advantage over any competitors. When pressured to sign the KBR contract, Ms. Greenhouse added the following contract language: "I caution that extending this sole source effort beyond a one-year period could convey an invalid perception that there is not strong intent for a limited competition."[51] The contract was later investigated by the SIGIR.[52] Various media reports suggested that in the case of Bunnatine Greenhouse, a trained and experienced senior DOD contract management official was eventually demoted and later fired for doing her job.[53]

Another senior DOD civilian testified that he made a decision to award KBR a task order under the LOGCAP contract without conducting any competition. Michael Mobbs, then-Special Assistant to the Undersecretary of Defense for Policy, testified that he made the decision to award KBR the contingency planning contract over the objections of an attorney with the Army Materiel Command. The attorney had determined that the oil-related task order was outside of the scope of the LOGCAP troop support contract. Later, GAO concluded that the lawyer's position was the correct one and that the work "should have been awarded using competitive procedures."[54]

Development of Contract Requirements. LOGCAP contracts have often by-passed the process to define realistic funding, appropriate time frames, and other important requirements through the use of "undefinitized" contract actions. Undefinitized contract actions[55] do not require that the DOD contracting official write a completed performance work statement before the work is performed. Some proponents of undefinitized task orders have stated that they give the contractor more flexibility in getting

50 For additional information, see CRS Report RL32229, *Iraq: Frequently Asked Questions About Contracting*, by Valerie Bailey Grasso (Coordinator).

51 Vanity Fair, p. 149.

52 It should be noted here that the KBR sole-source contract, according to the SIGIR, complied with applicable federal regulations for sole-source contracts, according to the SIGIR. The SIGIR concluded that "the justification used was that KBR had drafted the Contingency Support Plan (CSP), had complete familiarity with it, had the security clearances necessary to implement it, and the contract needed] to be immediately available to implement." Lessons In Contracting and Procurement. Iraq Reconstruction. Special Inspector General for Iraq Reconstruction. July 2006, p. 20.

53 Witte, Griff. Halliburton Contract Critic Loses Her Job. *Washington Post*, August 29, 200, p. A11. For additional information, see the following documents: Letter to Tom Davis, Chairman, Committee on Government Reform, House of Representatives, from Henry A. Waxman, Ranking Minority Member, House of Representatives, November 10, 2004; Testimony of Bunnatine Greenhouse before the Senate Democratic Policy Committee, June 27, 2005; and Letter to Donald Rumsfeld, Secretary of Defense, from Senators Byron L. Dorgan and Frank Lautenberg, and Representative Henry A. Waxman, August 29, 2005.

54 Briefing by Michael Mobbs, Special Assistant to the Undersecretary of Defense for Policy, for staff of the House Government Reform Committee, June 8, 2003. Also, see GAO-04-605. Rebuilding Iraq: Fiscal Year 2003 Contract Award Procedures and Management Challenges, June 2004.

55 Also referred to as undefinitized task orders.

work started sooner. However, recent DCAA audits have found that these undefinitized task orders have given KBR a significant cost advantage. Auditors have found that DOD contracting officials were more willing to rely on KBR's costs estimates, estimates later found to be greatly inflated. According to DCAA auditors, DOD contracting officials rarely challenged these cost estimates. The estimates became the baseline from which KBR established their costs upon which to bill the government, which later increased their overall profit.

In testimony before the Senate Armed Services Committee, the SIGIR stated that contracting personnel must be provided with an adequate description of a customer's needs. The inability to properly define and prepare requirements appeared to be a significant oversight challenge in the Iraq contracting process.[56]

Use of Indefinite-Delivery/Indefinite-Quantity Contracts. FAR Subpart 16.5 defines ID/IQ contracts.[57] In the case of ID/IQ contracts, task and delivery orders are issued; these orders do not define a firm quantity of goods or services.[58] Task orders are the "to do" portion of the contract, the contractor's action list. LOGCAP contracts allow task orders to be approved as needed without being subject to competition among multiple contractors. Each task and delivery order acts like a single contract, potentially allowing costly amounts of work to be performed on a non-competitive basis. Task Order 59 was one of the largest single task orders on the LOGCAP III contract. It was issued in May 2003 and includes various discrete functions, supporting up to 130,000 U.S. troops, and has reportedly resulted in estimates of charges to the government of about $5.2 billion dollars from June 2003 through June 2004.

Costs and the Use of No-Bid and Sole-Source Contracts. Much has been written in the media about the use of sole-source contracting in Iraq.[59] In general, most authorities believe that government contract costs are influenced significantly by the degree of competition; that having several competitors will reduce overall cost. However, questions have been raised as to whether contract costs in a war zone are inherently uncontrollable.

---

[56] Testimony of the Special Inspector General for Iraq Reconstruction, before the Senate Armed Services Committee, February 7, 2006.

[57] FAR Subpart 16.5 Indefinite delivery/indefinite quantity contracts, also known as IDIQ contracts, supply an indefinite quantity of supplies, goods, or materials, for an indefinite period of time. See FAR, Part 16, Types of Contracts. There are three types of indefinite-delivery contracts: definite-quantity contracts, requirements contracts, and indefinite-quantity contracts. The appropriate type of indefinite-delivery contract may be used to acquire supplies and/or services when the exact times and/or exact quantities of future deliveries are not known at the time of contract award. Pursuant to 10 U.S.C. 2304d and section 303K of the Federal Property and Administrative Services Act of 1949, requirements contracts and indefinite-quantity contracts are also known as delivery order contracts or task order contracts.

[58] Indefinite-quantity contracts are also known as delivery order contracts or task order contracts.

[59] Sole-source contracts are contracts which are not subject to competition.

DOD has argued that Iraq contracting costs are expensive because of the uncertainty of war-related requirements for goods and services. Government contingency contracting in times of war has often favored using programs such as LOGCAP because it enables contracting officials to move quickly to secure contractors, who in turn can be deployed quickly into the combat theater.

While full and open competition is the standard for government contracting, full and open competition has not been the standard for contracting for troop support services under LOGCAP. One report stated that of the $145 billion in noncompetitive contracts awarded by the federal government in 2005, $97.8 billion was awarded in "no-bid" contracts. Of that $97.8 billion in contracts, $63.4 billion was awarded under the rationale that only one contractor could supply the needed goods or services. The remaining $34.4 billion was awarded in no-bid contracts under a variety of other exceptions to full and open competition. $8.7 billion was awarded for emergency situations, and $2.9 billion was awarded for circumstances where a statute authorizes or requires restricted competition.[60] Finally, $47.2 billion in contracts was awarded in cases where the competitive range was limited to a small group of companies (referred to as a "limited" competition).

The Special Investigations Division of the House Government Reform Committee has issued a report titled "Dollars, not Sense: Government Contracting Under the Bush Administration." According to this report, in 2000 the federal government awarded $67.5 billion in non-competitive contracts; that figure rose to $145 billion in 2005, an increase of 115%. While the contracts awarded were larger, the value of contracts overseen by the average government procurement official rose by 83% (between 2000–2005).

Cost-reimbursement Contracts. Cost-reimbursement contracts can be: (1) cost-plus award fee; (2) cost-plus incentive fee; or (3) cost-plus fixed fee.[61] In 2000, the federal government spent $62 billion on cost-plus contracts; in 2005, that figure increased to $110 billion. Nearly half of all costs-plus contracts ($52 billion) were costs-plus award fee contracts. LOGCAP was the single largest cost-plus award fee contract, and at one time was valued at about $16.4 billion.[62] In costs-plus contracts, contractor's fees rise with contract costs. Increased costs means increased fees to the contractor. There is no incentive for the contractor to limit the government's costs.

[60] Dollars, Not Sense: Government Contracting Under the Bush Administration. United States House of Representatives, Committee on Government Reform—Minority Staff, Special Investigations Division, p. 7–9.

[61] Cost-reimbursement types of contracts provide for payment of allowable incurred costs, to the extent prescribed in the contract. These contracts establish an estimate of total cost for the purpose of obligating funds and establishing a ceiling that the contractor may not exceed (except at its own risk) without the approval of the contracting officer.

[62] Army Field Support Command, Media Obligation Spreadsheet, April 20, 2006.

Use of Overhead Fees. The SIGIR's past investigations into reconstruction contracts revealed that, in some contracts, overhead expenses accounted for more than half of the costs that Kellogg, Brown, and Root (KBR) billed the federal government. A recent audit report, "Review of Administrative Task Orders for Iraq Reconstruction Contracts," found that relatively high overhead costs were charged, and that these costs were significantly higher than work performed by other companies in Iraq. For these contracts, overhead costs ranged from 11% to 55% of projected contract budgets. For example, the SIGIR found that in five KBR projects, administrative costs outdistanced the costs of the projects alone. For example, the report cites a project where administrative costs totaled about $52.7 million, while the actual project costs were about $13.4 million. In another case, the combined administrative costs for five contractors totaled about $62 million, while the direct construction costs totaled $26.7 million.[63] The SIGIR found that overhead expenses accounted for more than half of the costs KBR billed the federal government.

Overhead fees can also result as a part of fees passed from one contractor to another. One such example is the case of Blackwater Security Firm's contract for private security services in Iraq. Blackwater's contract paid workers who guarded food trucks a salary of $600 a day. The company added overhead costs and a 36% markup to its bill, then forwarded the bill to a Kuwaiti company. The Kuwaiti company then added costs and profit, then sent the bill to the food company. The food company did the same, and finally sent the bill to KBR. KBR passed its cost to DOD. Yet the U.S. Army stated in a congressional committee hearing that it had never authorized KBR to enter into a subcontracting relationship with Blackwater. The matter remains pending.[64]

Transparency. Transparency allows the federal government to better administer contracts and oversee contractors. For example, the federal government has had difficulty getting certain contractors to provide important information on their invoices and billing statements. The SIGIR released a series of audit and investigative reports which drew attention to barriers that hampered the government's efforts. In one report, SIGIR Bowen reported that it was difficult to complete the investigation into the KBR contracts because KBR "routinely and inappropriately marked their data as proprietary."[65]

---

[63] Powers, Mary Buckner. Congress Moves To Reinstate Iraq Contracting Overseer. Engineering News-Record, Vol. 257, No. 19, p. 13. November 13, 2006.

[64] "Watching War Costs," *The News & Observer*, Raleigh, NC, December 9, 2006. Retrieved January 21, 2007, at [http://www.nexis.com/research/search/submitViewTagged].

[65] Powers, Mary Buckner. Congress Moves To Reinstate Iraq Contracting Overseer. Engineering News-Record, Vol. 257, No. 19, p. 13. November 13, 2006.

Another problem with a lack of transparency is the relationship between the federal government, the prime contractor, and the subcontractors. The federal government has a contractual relationship with the prime contractor, not with subcontractors. Thus the government may be somewhat limited in providing full accountability for tax-payer dollars. While the prime contractor-subcontractor relationship is between private sector companies, the monies are from public funds.[66]

Acquisition Workforce. According to DOD, its acquisition workforce has been reduced by more than 50 percent between 1994–2005.[67] Infuture years, between 2006–2010, half of the federal acquisition workforce will be eligible to retire.[68] It has been reported that DOD does not have sufficient numbers of contractor oversight personnel, particularly at deployed locations. This limits DOD's ability to assure that taxpayer dollars are being used in a judicious manner. For example, in recent testimony before Congress, a GAO official reported that if adequate staffing had been in place, the Army could have realized substantial savings on LOGCAP contracts in Iraq.[69] The GAO official also stated that one DCMA official, who is responsible for overseeing the LOGCAP contractor's performance at 27 locations, reported that he was "unable to visit all of those locations during his six-month tour to determine the extent to which the contractor was meeting the contract's requirements."[70]

Earlier mandates to reduce the size of the DOD acquisition workforce reflected Congress' view that the workforce had not been downsized enough—that reductions continued to lag in proportion to the decline in

[66] "Commentary: Watching War Costs," *The News & Observer*, Raleigh, NC, accessed on January 10, 2007 at [http://www.nexis.com/research/search/submitViewTagged].

[67] In 1998, the House National Security Committee asked GAO to review DOD's progress in achieving a 25-percent reduction in the acquisition organizations' workforce, examine the potential savings associated with such reductions, determine the status of DOD efforts to redefine the acquisition workforce, and examine DOD's efforts to restructure acquisition organizations. GAO concluded that "DOD has been reducing its acquisition workforce at a faster rate than its overall workforce and is on schedule to accomplish a 25-percent reduction by the fiscal year 2000. However, potential savings from these reductions cannot be precisely tracked in DOD's budget. In addition, some of the potential savings from acquisition workforce reductions may be offset by other anticipated costs. Such costs include those for contracting with private entities for some services previously performed by government personnel (i.e., substituting one workforce for another." U.S. Congress. General Accounting Office. Defense Acquisition Organizations: Status of Workforce Reductions. Report to the Chairman, Committee on National Security, House of Representatives. GAO/NSIAD-98-161. June 1998. 20 pages. For another source of data on the federal acquisition, see Report on the Federal Acquisition Workforce, FY 2003–2004, Federal Acquisition Institute Report, Executive Summary, p. vii.

[68] S. Assad, Director, Defense Procurement and Acquisition Policy, in testimony before the Acquisition Advisory Panel, June 13, 2006, p. 57–58 (excerpted from the Final Panel Working Draft, Report of the Acquisition Advisory Panel to the Office of Federal Procurement Policy and the U.S. Congress, December 2006.

[69] GAO-07-359T. Defense Acquisitions: DOD Needs to Exert Management and Oversight to Better Control Acquisition of Services. Statement of Katherine V. Schinasi, Managing Director, Acquisition and Sourcing Management, before the Subcommittee on Readiness and Management Support Committee on Armed Services, United States Senate, January 17, 2007.

[70] GAO-07-359T, p. 8.

the size of the overall defense budget, in general, and to the acquisition portion of the defense budget, in particular. At that time, Congress and DOD were at odds over the need for further reductions in the defense acquisition workforce. Reducing the defense acquisition workforce had been viewed by the Congress, in the past, as a necessary requirement for eliminating wasteful spending, and providing DOD with increased funding for other priorities.

Staffing shortages in the defense contracting personnel to oversee Iraq contracts have become part of a larger, systemic problem within DOD.[71] In reducing the size and shape of the federal acquisition workforce, an unanticipated result has been the increase in the growth of the private sector service contracts. With the growth in service contracting; the increase in the number of complex, billion dollar contracts; and the decline in the number of federal acquisition workforce employees, some officials have asserted that there are not enough DOD contracting officials, onsite in Iraq, who are available and experienced enough to manage the complexities of the new acquisition programs, or oversee private sector contractors.

It appears to some that DOD has downsized the federal acquisition workforce, particularly those that oversee large-scale contracts like LOGCAP, to dangerously low levels. They note that the past downsizing of the defense acquisition workforce has resulted in the loss of technical personnel and a talent drain on DOD's ability to meet its mission and objectives. There are concerns over potential deficits and imbalances in the skills and experience levels of personnel who manage large-scale weapon acquisition programs and defense contracts.

The Gansler Commission. The Secretary of the Army commissioned a study headed by former Deputy Secretary of Defense Jacques Gansler to analyze "structural weaknesses and organizational deficiencies in the Army's acquisition and contracting system used to support expeditionary operations." Dr. Gansler has recently presented the Commission's findings and recommendations before Congress.[72] Here is an excerpt of the Commission's analysis of the acquisition workforce.

> The expeditionary environment requires more trained and experienced military officers and non-commissioned officers (NCOs). Yet, only 3 percent

[71] The same observations were made about the U.S. Coast Guard's Deepwater contract. According to Admiral Thad Allen, Commandant, the issue concerns "the capacity of our acquisition staffs to deal with the myriad definitization of task orders, particular line items, the ability to interact with the extensive amount of nodes that you have in Integrated Coast Guard Systems . . . I'm not sure that we understood going how much we had to be prepared to handle the work load in terms of capacity and competency in human capital, and that's one of the main things I'm focusing on." Cavas, Christopher P. Millions for Deepwater, No One to Spend It. U.S. Coast Guard Adds Acquisition Experts for Modernization. *Defense News*, Vol. 22, No. 2, January 8, 2007, p. 1.

[72] Senate Armed Services Committee, Subcommittee on Readiness and Management Support on December 6, 2007. [http://armed-services.senate.gov/e_witnesslist.cfm?id=3048].

> of Army contracting personnel are active duty military and there are no longer any Army contracting career General Officer (GO) positions. The Army's acquisition workforce is not adequately staffed, trained, structured, or empowered to meet the Army needs of the 21st Century deployed warfighters. Only 56 percent of the military officers and 53 percent of the civilians in the contracting career field are certified for their current positions. Notwithstanding a seven-fold workload increase and greater complexity of contracting, the Institutional Army is not supporting this key capability. Notwithstanding there being almost as many contractor personnel in the Kuwait/Iraq/Afghanistan theater as there are U.S. military, the Operational Army does not yet recognize the impact of contracting and contractors in expeditionary operations and on mission success. What should be a core competence—contracting (from requirements definition, through contract management, to contract closeout)—is treated as an operational and institutional side issue.[73]

The Commission's report recommends that the Army makes systemic and fundamental changes in the way it conducts business, and has divided its recommendations into four major areas as described here.

- Increase the stature, quantity, and career development of military and civilian contracting personnel (especially for expeditionary operations);
- Restructure the organization and restore responsibility to facilitate contracting and contract management in expeditionary and CONUS operations;
- Provide training and tools for overall contracting activities in expeditionary operations; and
- Obtain legislative, regulatory, and policy assistance to enable contracting effectiveness in expeditionary operations.[74]

Potential Options for Congress

Congress may choose to consider the following options when examining DOD contracts for troop support: (1) implementing of the Gansler Commission's recommendations; (2) broadening of the jurisdiction of the SIGIR to include DOD contracts for troop support services (like LOGCAP contracts); (3) convening of a study of the federal employee and contractor workforce; (4) requiring more detail to give Congress better information to perform its oversight role; and (5) establishing a dedicated office to conduct audits and investigation of DOD contracts.

[73] U.S. Army. Urgent Attention Required: Army Expeditionary Contracting, Report of the Commission on Army Acquisition and Program Management, November 1, 2007, p. 10, at [http://www.army.mil/docs/Gansler_Commission_Report_Final_071031.pdf].

[74] *Ibid.*, p. 13.

Option 1: Implementing the Gansler Commission Recommendations

Perhaps the most significant recommendation of the Gansler Commission is that the Army address some institutional and cultural issues that may provide an obstacle to moving forward. The Commission interviewed a number of knowledgeable Army officials and concluded with the following observations about the challenges that the Army will face in making significant improvements in its business operations, as described here in the report:

> Those charged with getting the job done have provided valuable insight into the doctrine, policies, tools, and resources needed for success. Clearly, the Army must address the repeated and alarming testimony that detailed the failure of the institution (both the Institutional Army and the Department of Defense) to anticipate, plan for, adapt, and adjust acquisition and program management to the needs of the Operational Army as it has been transformed, since the end of the Cold War, into an expeditionary force. The Institutional Army has not adjusted to the challenges of providing timely, efficient, and effective contracting support to the force in Operation Iraqi Freedom (more than half of which is contractor personnel). Essentially, the Army sent a skeleton contracting force into theater without the tools or resources necessary to adequately support our warfighters. The personnel placed in that untenable position focused on getting the job done, as best they could under the circumstances—where support is needed in a matter of hours, or, at best, days. They used their knowledge, skill, limited resources, and extraordinary dedication to get contracts awarded. Alarmingly, most of the institutional deficiencies remain four-and-a-half-years after the world's best Army rolled triumphantly into Baghdad.[75]

Option 2: Expanding the SIGIR's Jurisdiction

Another option is to give the SIGIR the authority to audit and investigate DOD logistical support contracts in Iraq. The SIGIR has already established a presence in Iraq, and has issued more than 150 reports, including audits and investigations. His efforts have largely resulted in the arrest of five people, and the convictions of four of them, with more than $17 million in assets seized.[76] The SIGIR has made several recommendations related to his audit and investigation of contracts under his jurisdiction. His observations and insights may be relevant and appropriate for the contract administration and oversight of DOD contracts for troop support services.[77]

---

[75] *Ibid.*, p. 16.

[76] Senator Collins Works To Extend The Term of the Office that Oversees Billions in Iraqi Reconstruction Dollars. Press Release of the United States Senate Committee on Governmental Affairs, November 13, 2006.

[77] As an example, the SIGIR recommends the creation of an "enhanced contingency FAR" to simplify the rules governing contingency contracting. SIGIR, Lessons in Contracting and Procurement, July 2006, p. 97.

Option 3: Convening a Study of the Federal Employee and Contractor Workforce

Congress may want to convene a study of the federal employee and contractor workforce. The study could examine three important questions: (1) Is there an appropriate balance of federal employee and contractor roles? (2) Is there an appropriate federal role and presence in the oversight area? and (3) Is the federal government attracting the right types of acquisition professionals?

Congress could require a separate report, from each military service, on the size, scope, costs, and structure of its acquisition workforce (including military, civilian, and contractor personnel).

Option 4: Requiring More Detail for Better Oversight

Congress could require DOD to provide more details for better congressional oversight. There are five questions that Congress could consider: (1) Should DOD move to limit sole-source or limited competition for Iraq contracts? (2) Should DOD use more fixed-priced contracting in Iraq? (3) Should task and delivery orders have certain dollar constraints? (4) Should task orders be subject to public notice? and (5) Should larger contracts be divided into smaller contracts, with better-defined, discrete tasks?

To create more transparency and openness in defense acquisitions regarding contract administration, costs, and performance, Congress could require a separate report from each military service. Each report could include data on the size, scope, costs, and structure of all contracts, particularly no-bid, sole-source, and costs-reimbursement contracts.

Congress also could require that specific criteria be met before certain contract arrangements can be approved by DOD or by Congress. In addition, Congress could require a periodic re-competition of certain types of contracts, like LOGCAP, that have the potential of spanning for many years. Congress could also require, for example, that task orders beyond a certain size be treated as a separate contract, and thus subject to competition among multiple contractors.

And finally, Congress could require that large defense contracts be subject to competition and that a minimum of three contractors be selected for contracts beyond a certain size.[78] Some have suggested based on available press accounts that some contracts for services in Iraq might have been segregated (into smaller contracts) and opened for competitive bidding. Financial oversight might be more manageable in administering smaller

[78] On April 18, 2008, DOD announced that the Army had awarded contracts to three companies under LOGCAP IV. Each company will compete for task orders.

contracts. Small businesses may have more of an ability to compete for contracts.

Option 5: Establishing a Dedicated Office to Conduct Audits and Investigation of DOD Contracts

One of the recommendations of the SIGIR is to "designate a single, unified contracting entity to coordinate all contracting in theater."[79] One way to accomplish this is to establish a Contingency Contracting Corp (a DOD initiative currently underway is studying the issue) that will deploy to Iraq and establish a standing presence. However, what additional resources might be necessary in order to provide better contract management and oversight of DOD-appropriated funds?

Given that the mission of the DOD Inspector General's office is to promote "integrity, accountability, and improvement of Department of Defense personnel, programs and operations to support the Department's mission and to serve the public interest,"[80] should the DOD Inspector General have a stronger presence in Iraq? Given the many problems associated with LOGCAP contracts, oversight agencies like the DOD IG could have a pivotal role in preventing future contractor waste, fraud, or mismanagement.

Congress may want to consider creating a singularly dedicated office for the audit and investigation of DOD contracts for troop support services.

---

79 Lessons in Contracting and Procurement, SIGIR, July 2006, p. 95.
80 From the DOD Inspector General's website at [http://www.dodig.osd.mil/mission.htm].

Appendix A. Selected Reports

During the last four years, the Congressional Research Service, General Accounting Office, Department of Defense Inspector General, Army Audit Agency, Air Force Audit Agency, and the Special Inspector General for Iraq Reconstruction have issued numerous reports on Iraq contracting issues, including those listed below.

Congress

Dollars, Not Sense: Government Contracting Under the Bush Administration. Prepared by the Special Investigations Division, Committee on Government Reform-Minority Staff, U.S. House of Representatives, June 2006.

Congressional Research Service

CRS Report RL33110, *The Cost of Iraq, Afghanistan, and Other Global War on Terror Operations Since 9/11*, by Amy Belasco.

CRS Report RL32419, *Private Security Contractors in Iraq: Background, Legal Status, and Other Issues*, by Jennifer K. Elsea and Nina M. Serafino.

CRS Report RS21555, *Iraq Reconstruction: Frequently Asked Questions Concerning the Application of Federal Procurement Statutes*, by John R. Luckey.

CRS Report RL31833, *Iraq: Recent Developments in Reconstruction Assistance*, by Curt Tarnoff.

CRS Report RL32229, *Iraq: Frequently Asked Questions About Contracting*, by Valerie Bailey Grasso (Coordinator), Rhoda Margesson, Curt Tarnoff, Lawrence Kumins, Kyna Powers, Carolyn C. Smith, and Michael Waterhouse.

Government Accountability Office

GAO-07-1098T. Federal Acquisitions and Contracting. Systemic Challenges Need Attention. Statement of David M. Walker, Comptroller General of the United States, July 17, 2007.

GAO-07-359T. Defense Acquisitions: DOD Needs to Exert Management and Oversight to Better Control Acquisition of Services. Statement of Katherine V. Schinasi, Managing Director, Acquisition and Sourcing Management. Testimony Before the Subcommittee on Readiness and Management Support, Committee on Armed Services, U.S. Senate, January 17, 2007.

GAO-07-145. Military Operations: High-Level DOD Action Needed to Address Long-standing Problems with Management and Oversight of Contractors Supporting Deployed Forces, December 16, 2006.

GAO-06-800T. DOD Acquisitions: Contracting for Better Outcomes. September 7, 2006.

GAO-06-838R. Contract Management: DOD Vulnerabilities to Contracting Fraud, Waste, and Abuse, GAO-06-838R, July 7, 2006.

GAO-05-274. Contract Management: Opportunities to Improve Surveillance on Department of Defense Service Contracts, March 17, 2005.

GAO-05-207. GAO, High Risk Series: An Update, January 2005.

GAO-04-854. Military Operations: DOD's Extensive Use of Logistics Support Contracts Requires Strengthened Oversight, July 19, 2004.

Special Inspector General for Iraq Reconstruction

Quarterly Report to Congress, April 30, 2008.

Department of Defense Inspector General

Semi-Annual Report to Congress. October 1, 2006–March 31, 2007.

Semi-Annual Report to Congress. April 1, 2006–September 30, 2006.

Semi-Annual Report to Congress. October 1, 2005–March 31, 2006.

Semi-Annual Report to Congress. April 1, 2005–September 30, 2005.

Semi-Annual Report to Congress. October 1, 2004–March 31, 2005.

Army Audit Agency

(The website is restricted to military domains (.mil) and to the Government Accountability Office)

Report Number A-2005-0043-ALE Logistics Civil Augmentation Program in Kuwait, U.S. Army Field Support Command, November 24, 2004.

Gansler Commission

U.S. Army. Urgent Attention Required: Army Expeditionary Contracting, Report of the Commission on Army Acquisition and Program Management, November 1, 2007, at [http://www.army.mil/docs/Gansler_Commission_Report_Final_071031. pdf].

Appendix B. Selected Legislative Initiatives on Iraq Contracting

Selected Legislation Introduced in the 110th Congress

The House has approved four bills, as noted below.

H.R. 3033, Contractors and Federal Spending Accountability Act of 2008. This provision would require the Administrator of General Services to establish and maintain a database on defense contractors containing updated information on criminal, civil, or debarment and suspension proceedings as well as establish the Interagency Committee on Debarment and Suspension. Congress would require a report within 180 days of the act's enactment.

H.R. 5712, Close the Contractor Fraud Loophole Act. This provision would require federal contractors to report violations of federal criminal law and over-payments on contracts valued greater than $5 million.

H.R. 3928, Government Contractor Accountability Act of 2007. This provision would require "covered" government contractors to submit certification and other financial disclosure requirements in cases where the contractor receives 80 percent or less of their annual gross revenue from federal contracts. Contractors covered by this provision are those receiving more than $25 million in annual gross revenues from federal contracts, but are not publicly traded companies required to file reports with the Security and Exchange Commission.

H.R. 4881. Contracting and Tax Accountability Act of 2008. This provision would require tax compliance as a prerequisite fo r receiving federal contracts, and would prohibit contract awards to certain delinquent federal tax debtors.

Several other have been introduced during the 110th Congress. Each could potentially impact DOD contracting in Iraq, as described below.

H.R. 4102/S. 2398,Stop Outsourcing Security Act. This provision would require that only U.S. federal government personnel provide security to personnel at U.S. diplomatic or consular mission in Iraq by six months after enactment, and require the President to report to Congress s on "the status of planning for the transition away from the use of private contractors for mission critical or emergency essential functions by January 1, 2009, in all conflict zones in which Congress has authorized the use of force."

S. 2147, Security Contractor Accountability Act of 2007. This provision would expand the coverage of the Military Extraterritorial Jurisdiction Act (MEJA) to include all persons "while employed under a contract (or subcontract at any tier) awarded by any department or agency of the United States, where the work under such contract is carried out in a region outside the United States in which the Armed Forces are conducting a contingency operation."

H.R. 528, Iraq Contracting Fraud Review of 2007. This provision would require the Secretary of Defense, acting through the Defense Contract Audit Agency, to review all Iraq defense contracts for reconstruction or troop support involving any contractors, subcontractors, or federal officers or employees indicted or convicted for contracting improprieties.

H.R. 663, New Direction for Iraq Act of 2007. These bill contains provisions addressing war profiteering, the recovery of funds from terminated contracts, and other issues A select number of additional legislative initiatives, proposed during the 110th Congress, that may impact defense contracting will follow.

H.R. 4102, Stop Outsourcing Security Act. This provision would require that only U.S. federal government personnel provide security to personnel at U.S. diplomatic or consular mission in Iraq within six months after bill enactment, and would require that the President report to specified congressional committees on "the status of planning for the transition away from the use of private contractors for mission critical or emergency essential functions by January 1, 2009, in all conflict zones in which Congress has authorized the use of force."

S. 2147, Security Contractor Accountability Act of 2007. This provision would broaden the Military Extraterritorial Jurisdiction Act (MEJA) to include all persons "while employed under a contract (or subcontract at any tier) awarded by any department or agency of the United States, where the work under such contract is carried out in a region outside the United Sates in which the Armed Forces are conducting a contingency operation."

H.R. 897, Iraq and Afghanistan Contractor Sunshine Act. This provision would require the Secretaries of Defense, State, Interior, and the Administrator of the U.S. Agency for International Development to provide Congress with copies and descriptions of all contracts and task orders valued at over $5 million.

H.R. 3695, Freeze Private Contractors in Iraq Act. This provision would prohibit an increase in the number of private security contractors employed by DOD, State, and USAID that perform certain security functions in Iraq.

Selected Legislation Passed in the 110th Congress

P.L. 110-181, the FY2008 National Defense Authorization Act, H.R. 4986 (formerly H.R. 1585). Several provisions contained in H.R. 4986 focus on the management and oversight of DOD contracts.[81] Key provisions are listed below.

- Section 802 prohibits future contracts for the use of new Lead System Integrators;[82]
- Section 813 requires the Comptroller General to report to Congress on potential modifications to the organization and structure of DOD Major Defense Acquisition Programs;
- Section 816 directs the Under Secretary of Defense for Acquisition, Technology, and Logistics to conduct an annual review on the systematic deficiencies in Major Defense Acquisition Programs;
- Section 830 directs the Comptroller General to report to Congress on DOD's use of noncompetitive awards;
- Section 841 establishes a commission to study federal contracting in Iraq and Afghanistan, called the "Commission on Wartime Contracting;"
- Section 842 requires the DOD Inspector General, the SIGIR for Iraq Reconstruction, and the SIGIR for Afghanistan Reconstruction to collaborate on the development of comprehensive plans to perform a series of audits on DOD contracts, subcontracts, and task and delivery orders for the performance of logistical support activities of coalition forces in Iraq and Afghanistan, as well as audits for federal agency contracts, subcontracts, and task and delivery orders for the performance of security and reconstruction functions in Iraq and Afghanistan;
- Section 851, which would require that the Secretary of Defense (as part of the Strategic Human Capital Plan for 2008) include a separate section of the report focused on the military and civilian acquisition workforce;
- Section 852 establishes a Defense Acquisition Workforce Development Fund;
- Section 861 requires coordination between the DOD, the Department of State, and the United States Agency for International Development through the creation of a Memorandum of Understanding between

[81] Excerpts from H.R. 1585 discuss the rationale for legislative initiatives focused on the oversight and accountability for contracts in Iraq and Afghanistan: "The committee remains concerned about the level of oversight for contracting in Iraq and Afghanistan. These countries present uniquely complex challenges for contracting and contract oversight, but U.S. efforts in these countries will continue to require significant contractor support. The committee believes that government responsibilities for a range of issues involving contracting in Iraq and Afghanistan are unclear. The committee believes that clarification of roles and responsibilities for contracting in Iraq and Afghanistan and increased oversight will enhance the effectiveness of U.S. Government efforts in both countries

[82] For a brief discussion on the role of the Lead System Integrator, see CRS Report RS22631, *Defense Acquisition: Use of Lead System Integrators (LSIs)—Background, Oversight Issues, and Options for Congress*, by Valerie Bailey Grasso.

the three agency heads on matters relating to contracting in Iraq and Afghanistan;

- Section 862 requires that the Secretary of Defense prescribe, within 120 days of enactment, regulations on the selection, training, equipping, and conduct of personnel performing private security functions under a covered contract or covered subcontract in a combat area. These regulations would include processes for registering, processing, and accounting for such personnel; and authorizing and accounting for weapons, and investigating the death and injury of such personnel, their discharge of weapons, and incidents of alleged misconduct. The regulations would also provide guidance to combatant commanders on orders, directives, and instructions to contractors and subcontractors performing private security functions relating to force protection, security, health, safety, relations and interaction with locals, and rules of engagement;
- Section 863 requires the Comptroller General to review annually all contracts in Iraq and Afghanistan and report to Congress on the total number of contracts and task orders, total number of active contracts and task orders, total value of all contracts and task orders, the degree to which DOD has awarded noncompetitive contracts, the total number of contractor personnel (including the total number of contractor personnel performing security functions and the total number of contractor personnel killed or wounded); also, Section 863 would require the Secretaries of Defense and State to provide the Comptroller General full accesses to the database as described in Section 861;
- Section 871 establishes a Defense Materiel Readiness Board;
- Section 872 grants authorityto the Secretary of Defense to designate critical readiness shortfalls; and
- Section 941 requires the Secretary of Defense to conduct a comprehensive assessment of the roles and missions of the military forces, known as a quadrennial roles and missions review.

DOCUMENT NO. 5

REBUILDING IRAQ: DOD AND STATE DEPARTMENT HAVE IMPROVED OVERSIGHT AND COORDINATION OF PRIVATE SECURITY CONTRACTORS IN IRAQ, BUT FURTHER ACTIONS ARE NEEDED TO SUSTAIN IMPROVEMENTS

GAO Report
GAO-08-966

July 2008

This report was revised on August 1, 2008 to reflect a change to the text on page 2, in line 11 of the second paragraph, "provisions of the 2007 National Defense Authorization Act" is revised to "provisions of Section 862 of the 2008 National Defense Authorization Act."

What GAO Found

Both DOD and the State Department have taken steps to strengthen oversight of private security contractors in Iraq since September 2007. However, staffing and training challenges remain for DOD. DOD has increased the number of personnel in Iraq assigned to provide oversight for DOD's PSCs but has not developed plans or a strategy to sustain this increase. An Army-commissioned report has specifically raised concerns about the lack of personnel available to provide sufficient contracting support to either expeditionary or peacetime missions. In the short term, DOD has increased the number of oversight personnel in Iraq by shifting existing oversight personnel from other locations into Iraq. However, without developing and implementing a strategy for providing and sustaining an increased number of personnel dedicated to oversight of PSCs, it is not clear whether DOD can sustain this increase because of the limited number of oversight personnel in the workforce. Moreover, while DOD has provided some training on PSCs for units deploying, the training has not been updated to reflect the changes made by DOD since September 2007 to increase oversight. As a result, military units may be unaware of their expanded oversight and investigative responsibilities. The State Department has implemented

11 of 18 actions recommended in October 2007 by a panel tasked by the Secretary of State with reviewing that agency's use of private security contractors in Iraq. For example, the State Department has increased the number of diplomatic security personnel stationed in Iraq to provide oversight of contractor activities and has requested and received funding to hire and train 100 additional agents to replace those who were transferred from other State Department programs in the United States to Iraq. According to State Department officials, the additional personnel will help sustain the increased number of agents in Iraq. In addition, as of June 2008, the State Department has equipped 140 of its security vehicles with video recording equipment and plans to equip an additional 93 vehicles.

Coordination among DOD, the State Department, and the government of Iraq has significantly improved since September 2007. The State Department coordinates its PSC movements with DOD through liaison officers, and by providing a daily briefing to Multi-National Forces-Iraq (MNF-I) on upcoming PSC activities. MNF-I 's Armed Contractor Oversight Division facilitates coordination for PSC matters among DOD, State Department, the government of Iraq, and the PSC community. Further, DOD and the State Department signed a memorandum of agreement detailing coordination activities to be undertaken.

Various laws hold PSC employees accountable for their actions in Iraq, including U.S. criminal laws that may be applied extraterritorially, the Military Extraterritorial Jurisdiction Act, and the Uniform Code of Military Justice. The applicability of these laws depends on the circumstances—e.g., the nature and location of the alleged crime and the nationality of the accused—of any specific incident. The legal framework for holding PSCs accountable also includes Iraqi and international law and contract provisions.

Abbreviations

ACOD	Armed Contractor Oversight Division
CENTCOM	U.S. Central Command
COM	Chief of Mission
CONOC	Contractor Operations Cells
COR	Contracting Officer's Representative
CPA	Coalition Provisional Authority
DCMA	Defense Contract Management Agency
DOD	Department of Defense
DS	Diplomatic Security
JCC-I/A	Joint Contracting Command-Iraq/Afghanistan
MEJA	Military Extraterritorial Jurisdiction Act
MNC-I	Multi-National Corps-Iraq

MNF-I	Multi-National Force-Iraq
PSC	private security contractor
RSO	Regional Security Office
TOC	tactical operations center
UCMJ	Uniform Code of Military Justice
USAID	U.S. Agency for International Development
WPPS	Worldwide Personal Protective Services

United States Goverment Accountablity Office
Washington, DC 20548

July 31, 2008

Congressional Committees

Since military operations began in Iraq in 2003, the United States government has relied extensively upon the services of private security contractors (PSC). For the Department of Defense (DOD) these services include providing security for senior military officials such as the Commanding General of the Multi-National Force-Iraq and for personnel from the Army Corps of Engineers, protecting military facilities, and protecting more than 19,000 supply convoys traveling throughout Iraq.[1] For the Department of State, PSCs provide security for the ambassador, other U.S. government officials working in Iraq as well as visiting Members of Congress and visiting officials of the executive branch. PSCs also provide site security of the embassy and other State Department facilities in Iraq. The number of PSCs in Iraq is also substantial. DOD and the Department of State estimate that about 11,000 private security employees (9,952 with DOD, 1,400 with the State Department) are working in Iraq under direct contracts with the U.S. government. DOD has estimated that it would need to create nine new Army brigades to replace the current number of PSC employees working in Iraq.[2]

Because of incidents involving PSCs in Iraq, concern regarding the level of oversight and the legal accountability over these firms and their employees has increased. Incidents occurring between PSCs and Iraqis and between

[1] According to DOD officials from August 2004 to February 2008, the Department launched 19,268 supply convoys. These convoys moved reconstruction supplies as well as logistic supplies for the Iraq Security Forces and were protected by PSCs.

[2] DOD made this estimate based on the analytical framework of a CBO study, *Logistics Support for Deployed Forces*, 2005.

PSCs and U.S. forces have been reported since 2004. In July 2005, we issued a report that examined how the U.S. government and reconstruction contractors used PSCs.[3] In that report we made a number of recommendations including one addressed to DOD to develop a training package for military units deploying to Iraq that included information on (1) the role of PSCs in Iraq, (2) typical PSC operating procedures, (3) guidance related to PSCs, and (4) the military's responsibilities to PSCs. In 2006, we testified that coordination between the U.S. military and the PSCs needed improvement and that further action needed to be taken by DOD to implement the pre-deployment training recommendation from 2005.[4] According to the report of the Secretary of State's Panel on Personal Protective Services in Iraq, on September 16, 2007, an incident involving a PSC firm working for the Department of State resulted in the deaths of 17 Iraqi civilians in Baghdad. In the wake of this incident, which U.S. government officials describe as a watershed event, both DOD and the State Department began to examine their efforts to provide oversight, improve coordination between DOD, the State Department and the government of Iraq, and enhance accountability for the PSCs they employ in Iraq.

Because of continuing congressional interest in the use of PSCs in Iraq, we began in August 2007, under the authority of the Comptroller General to conduct evaluations on his own initiative, a review to update our work on the U.S. government's use of PSC. This report examines the extent to which DOD and the Department of State have strengthened (1) oversight and (2) coordination of private security contractors in Iraq. In addition, we are providing information on the legal framework in place to hold private security contractor employees legally accountable for their actions in Iraq. Later this year, we plan to issue a report on other PSC issues related to selection, training, and weapons accountability as well as DOD's implementation of provisions of Section 862 of the 2008 National Defense Authorization Act which requires DOD to prescribe regulations for the use of private security contractors in contingency operations.

To assess the U.S. government's efforts to improve oversight and coordination of PSCs it employs in Iraq, we reviewed recent DOD, United States Central Command (CENTCOM), Multi-National Force-Iraq (MNF-I), and State Department policies and guidance addressing the requirements, procedures, and responsibilities for the oversight and coordination of PSCs. These documents include new MNF-I PSC guidance and policies on incident reporting, investigation requirements, coordination, and contract

[3] GAO, *Rebuilding Iraq: Actions Needed to Improve the Use of Private Security Providers,* GAO-05-737 (Washington, D.C.: July 2005).

[4] GAO, *Rebuilding Iraq: Action Still Needed to Improve the Use of Private Security Providers,* GAO-06-865T (Washington, D.C.: June 13, 2006).

oversight. In addition, we reviewed the memorandum of agreement between DOD and the State Department on PSCs working for the U.S. government in Iraq. We reviewed these policies to determine the U.S. government's authority and responsibility for the oversight and coordination of PSCs in Iraq that have contracts with the U.S. government. In February 2008, we traveled to Iraq to examine what, if any, improvements had been made after the Nisour Square incident. In Iraq we met with officials from DOD, including officials from MNF-I, the Joint Contracting Command-Iraq/Afghanistan (JCC-I/A), and the Defense Contract Management Agency (DCMA), as well as officials from the State Department, including officials from the U.S. Embassy-Baghdad and its Regional Security Office, to discuss issues related to oversight, coordination, and accountability over PSCs in Iraq. While in Iraq, we observed operations at DOD's Contractor Operations Cell and at the State Department's Tactical Operations Center, witnessing the planning, oversight and coordination, and tracking of PSC movements throughout Iraq. We also met with the Executive Secretary of the Secretary of State's panel established to review the State Department's security practices in Iraq. We also interviewed officials from ten selected private security firms who currently provide or have recently provided private security functions in Iraq, as well as representatives from an Iraq-based private security association.

To describe the legal framework in place to hold PSC employees accountable we reviewed various laws including the Uniform Code of Military Justice and the Military Extraterritorial Jurisdiction Act. We also interviewed officials from DOD's Office of the General Counsel, the State Department's Office of the Legal Adviser and from the Department of Justice to gain an understanding of the process used to hold PSCs accountable. Moreover, we also reviewed applicable U.S. government PSC contract clauses that outline and regulate contractor behavior.

Our work focused on PSCs who have a direct contractual relationship with the United States government and we did not assess the use of PSCs by reconstruction contractors, non-governmental organizations or other coalition nations. We reviewed processes used to provide oversight and coordination over PSCs in Iraq but did not evaluate how effectively they were being implemented because the processes reviewed are new. We also did not evaluate how laws were being used to hold contractors accountable. Appendix I contains a more detailed presentation of our scope and methodology. We conducted this performance audit from February 2008 to June 2008, in accordance with generally accepted government auditing standards. Those standards require that we plan and perform the audit to obtain sufficient, appropriate evidence to provide a reasonable basis for our findings and conclusions based on audit objectives. We believe that the evidence obtained provides a reasonable basis for our findings and conclusions based on our audit objectives.

Results in Brief

Since the Nisour Square incident in September 2007, DOD and the State Department have taken action to improve oversight of PSCs in Iraq,. However staffing and training challenges remain for DOD. In November 2007 MNF-I established the Armed Contractor Oversight Division to provide oversight and serve as MNF-I's overall point of contact on policies that govern DOD's PSCs. MNF-I has also published comprehensive guidance related to the oversight of DOD PSCs and has made military units more responsible for providing oversight of PSCs in terms of incident reporting and investigating as well as contract management. However, while DOD has incorporated information on working with PSCs into senior military staff and unit training programs and exercises, this training does not reflect the increased PSC oversight responsibilities and organizational structures established since the September 2007 incident. Thus, military units may not be aware of and trained on how to carry out their expanded oversight responsibilities and the required incident investigations may not occur. Further, while DOD has increased the number of personnel in Iraq devoted to providing contract oversight and management over private security contracts it is not clear whether DOD can sustain this increase because limited number of oversight personnel in the workforce. In the short-term, DOD has increased the number of oversight personnel in Iraq by shifting existing oversight personnel from other locations into Iraq. However, if DOD is unable to sustain the increase in oversight personnel, the improvements in contract oversight gained by the current personnel increases may well be lost. The State Department has implemented 11of the 18 actions recommended by a panel that reviewed the Department's use of PSCs in Iraq and continues to implement others. Among the recommendations it has implemented or is in the process of implementing are recommendations to install video recording equipment in its security vehicles, place a diplomatic security agent in each PSC motorcade, and increase the number of Diplomatic Security agents stationed in Iraq to improve contract oversight and management. To provide these additional agents, the State Department moved personnel from other assignments both in the U.S. and abroad which negatively affected other Diplomatic Security missions. The State Department has requested and received funding for an additional 100 diplomatic security agents in its fiscal year 2008 supplemental appropriations request.

Coordination between DOD, the State Department, and the government of Iraq has improved since the Nisour Square incident. For example, the State

Department now coordinates its PSC movements with DOD through liaison officers, and by providing a daily briefing to MNF-I regarding upcoming PSC activities. Multi-National Corps-Iraq (MNC-I) has established several operations centers to track and coordinate the movement of DOD PSCs with U.S. military units throughout Iraq, as well as to coordinate the movements of PSCs working for the State Department. Prior to the establishment of these operations centers, PSC movements were not always coordinated with U.S. military units. Moreover, MNF-I 's Armed Contractor Oversight Division facilitates coordination for PSC matters in Iraq among DOD, the State Department, the government of Iraq, and the PSC community in Iraq. Prior to the establishment of the oversight division the U.S. government did not coordinate PSC issues with the Government of Iraq. Since the establishment of the division, representatives of the State Department and the oversight division meet regularly to listen to concerns, resolve issues, and generate joint solutions. In addition, the division notifies the Iraq Ministry of the Interior when an incident occurs involving PSCs and Iraqi civilians. Finally, in December 2007 DOD and the State Department signed a memorandum of agreement that details specific coordination activities to be undertaken by the departments.

Various laws exist to hold PSC employees accountable for criminal acts committed in a wartime environment beyond the borders of the United States. These laws include U.S. criminal laws that may be applied extraterritorially, the Military Extraterritorial Jurisdiction Act (MEJA), the Uniform Code of Military Justice (UCMJ), international law, as well as Iraqi laws. Whether a particular law provides extra-territorial jurisdiction over a criminal act by a PSC employee depends on the specific facts of the incident, such as the time, nature and location of the alleged crime, the nature of the contractor's employment, and the nationality of the accused. For example, an employee of a DOD contractor, whether a U.S. citizen or Third Country National, who commits a felony while accompanying the Armed Forces in Iraq during a contingency operation may be charged under the UCMJ or MEJA. With regard to other than DOD contractor employees, a panel of State Department representatives reporting on protective services in Iraq concluded in October 2007 that the legal framework for holding non-Department of Defense contractor employees accountable under U.S. law is inadequate. Congress is presently considering legislation that would clarify and extend U.S. criminal jurisdiction over individuals employed under a contract awarded by any U.S. department or agency where contract performance is located in the area of a contingency operation. In addition to U.S. law, the legal framework for holding PSCs accountable includes applicable international law and Iraqi law. Also, contract provisions serve to regulate contractor behavior.

We are making recommendations to the Secretary of Defense to (1) take the necessary steps to ensure that the Joint Contracting Command Iraq/Afghanistan has sufficient personnel to meet its contract oversight and management responsibilities; (2) update training materials to reflect the current guidance and oversight requirements; and (3) fully implement our 2005 recommendation by including information on PSC typical operating procedures and the military's responsibilities to PSCs.

The Department of Defense agreed with our recommendations and noted that it welcomed our assistance in improving how DOD and its contractors can plan for and effectively execute comments in a complex and changeable security environment. DOD's comments appear in appendix III.

In commenting on our report the State Department noted that in addition to the oversight improvements discussed in this report, the State Department and the Bureau of Diplomatic Security have increased and realigned staff to enhance oversight. In addition, the State Department expressed concern over our depiction of the status of implementation of the Secretary of State's Panel on Personal Protective Services in Iraq in appendix II. In its comments the State Department stated that it has implemented 16 of the 18 recommendations made by the panel. In our draft report we originally assessed 9 recommendations as complete. Based on additional information provided by the State Department we changed our assessment of the status of two recommendations (recommendation numbers 3 and 11 in appendix II) and now we are reporting that the State Department has completed 11 of the 18 recommendations. The State Department's comments and our detailed responses appear in appendix IV.

In addition, both Departments provided technical comments which we incorporated as appropriate.

Background

PSCs are defined as private companies, and/or personnel, that provide physical security for persons, places, buildings, facilities, supplies, or means of transportation. These contractors provide security services for a variety of U.S. government agencies in Iraq; however, they principally are hired by DOD and the State Department. Given the security concerns in Iraq, the U.S. government has relied upon PSCs to fulfill a variety of important security functions throughout the country in support of the DOD military mission and the State Department's diplomatic mission.[5]

[5] Additionally, PSCs are hired by many other non-U.S. government affiliated organizations operating in Iraq such as the government of Iraq, the United Nations, private companies, various non-governmental organizations, and the media.

The mission of PSCs hired by the U.S. government in Iraq is to protect government agency officials as they perform their duties in the unstable security environment currently present. These contractors may be U.S. or foreign-based and their employees are recruited and hired from a wide variety of countries, including the United States, the United Kingdom, South Africa, Nepal, Sri Lanka, and Fiji. They also include Kurds and Arabs from Iraq. These firms may provide a variety of security related services including:

- static security—security for housing areas and work sites, including U.S. military installations;
- personal security details—security for high-ranking U.S. officials and Chief of Mission personnel;
- security escorts—security for U.S. government employees, contractor employees, or others as they move through Iraq;
- convoy security—security for vehicles and their occupants as they make their way into Iraq or within Iraq; and
- security advice and planning.

In Iraq, two distinct authorities are responsible for the security of U.S. government employees and contractors. The U.S. military, under the authority of the Secretary of Defense and the Combatant Commander, is responsible for the security of all personnel who are under direct control of the Combatant Commander.[6] The State Department, under the authority of the Secretary of State, is responsible for the security of all other U.S. government personnel on official duty abroad.[7] In Iraq, that responsibility is delegated to the U.S. Ambassador as Chief of Mission and to the U.S. Embassy's Regional Security Officer who is the Chief of Mission's focal point for security issues and as such establishes specific security policies and procedures. While these two agencies also are responsible for providing oversight, coordination and accountability for U.S. government PSCs, the government of Iraq also plays a role. Figure 1 depicts the organizations that play a key role in the oversight and coordination of PSCs operating in Iraq.

DOD and the State Department Have Increased Oversight Efforts Regarding PSCs, but Staffing and Training Challenges Remain for DOD

DOD and the State Department have both taken action to increase their oversight efforts over PSCs in Iraq, however, staffing and training challenges remain for DOD. In Iraq, MNF-I has established an office to provide

[6] A Memorandum of Agreement between DOD and State Department signed December 5, 2007, identifies their authorities as derived from 10 U.S.C. §164 (2007) and 22 U.S.C. §4802(a)(1)(A)(2007).
[7] 22 U.S.C. §4802(a)(1)(A)(2007).

Figure 1: Key Organizations with Roles in Oversight and Coordination of Private Security Contractors in Iraq

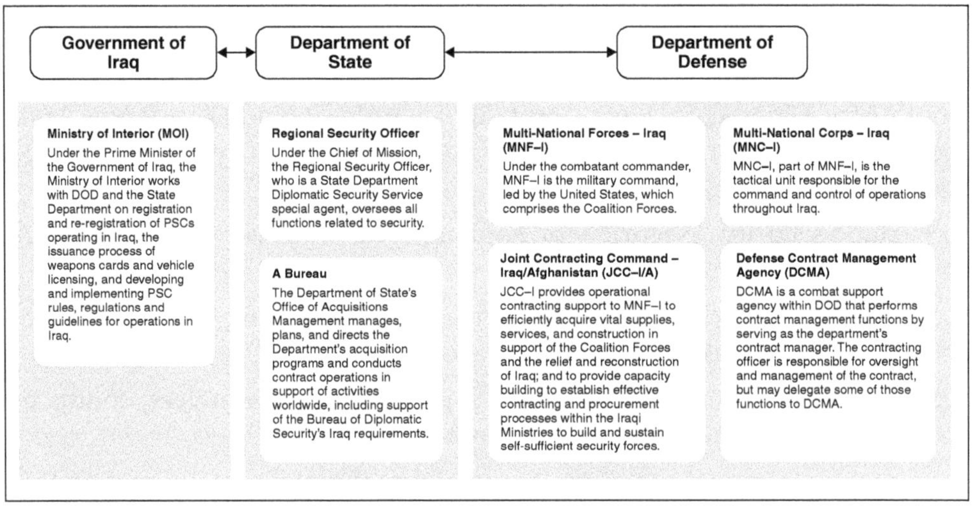

Source: DOD data; GAO presentation.

PSC oversight and MNF-I has published comprehensive mandatory guidance related to the oversight of DOD PSCs and has made military units more responsible for providing oversight to PSCs in terms of incident reporting and investigating. However, senior military staff as well as units may not be aware of their increased responsibilities because DOD has not incorporated information on the revised guidance and increased responsibilities in its training program. Further, while DOD has increased the number of personnel in Iraq devoted to providing contract oversight and management over private security contracts it is not clear based on our current and past work whether DOD can sustain the increased number of contract oversight and management personnel it has sent to Iraq since late 2007. In addition, the State Department has implemented 11 of the 18 recommendations made by a panel appointed by the Secretary of State to review the agency's oversight of PSCs in Iraq. Among the recommendations implemented or being implemented are recommendations to increase the number of agents in Iraq to provide oversight over its PSC contractors, install audio and video recording equipment in security vehicles, and a recommendation to place a diplomatic security agent in each PSC motorcade.

Multi-National Force-Iraq Has established an Office to Provide Oversight over DOD PSCs in Iraq

Prior to the incident in Baghdad in September 2007, the U.S. military lacked a single structure for managing its PSCs in Iraq. In November 2007,

Figure 2: Armed Contractor Oversight Division (ACOD) Organizational Structure

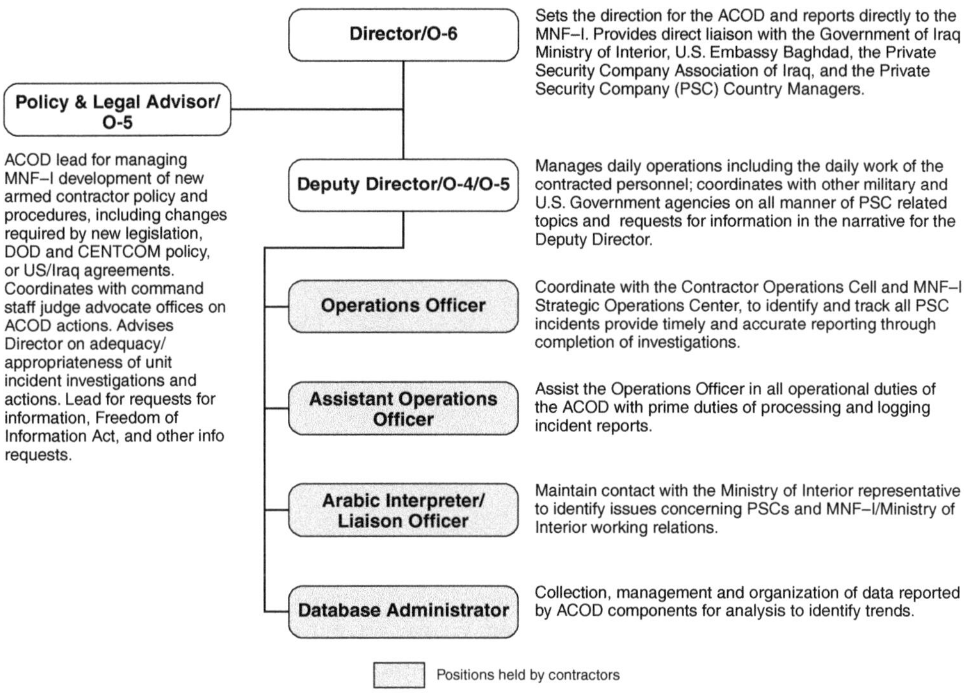

Source: DOD Presentation.

MNF-I, established a new organization, the Armed Contractor Oversight Division,[8] to serve as MNF-I's overall point of contact for policy issues relating to PSCs hired by DOD[9] as well as to provide broad oversight over these contractors. According to MNF-I officials, the office's goals include (1) working to reduce the number of incidents of PSCs discharging weapons or behaving in a manner that undermines the credibility of U.S. efforts; (2) developing a mechanism for holding PSCs accountable for their actions; (3) reducing the time that elapses between the occurrence of an incident and the reporting of that incident; and (4) minimizing the impact of an incident on the credibility of U.S. efforts in Iraq.[10] The office is currently staffed with 7 full time employees comprised of 3 military personnel and 4 contractors. Figure 2 depicts the Armed Contractor Oversight Division's organizational structure and the responsibilities of each staff member.

[8] The Armed Contractor Oversight Division was previously known as the Contractor Procedures Oversight Division.

[9] The Armed Contractor Oversight Division is only responsible for providing oversight to PSCs, and is not responsible for providing oversight over other DOD contractors.

[10] We were unable to determine if the Armed Contractor Oversight Division had met its goals because it was still in the process of standing up when we traveled to Iraq.

Figure 3: Description of the PSC Incident Reporting Process

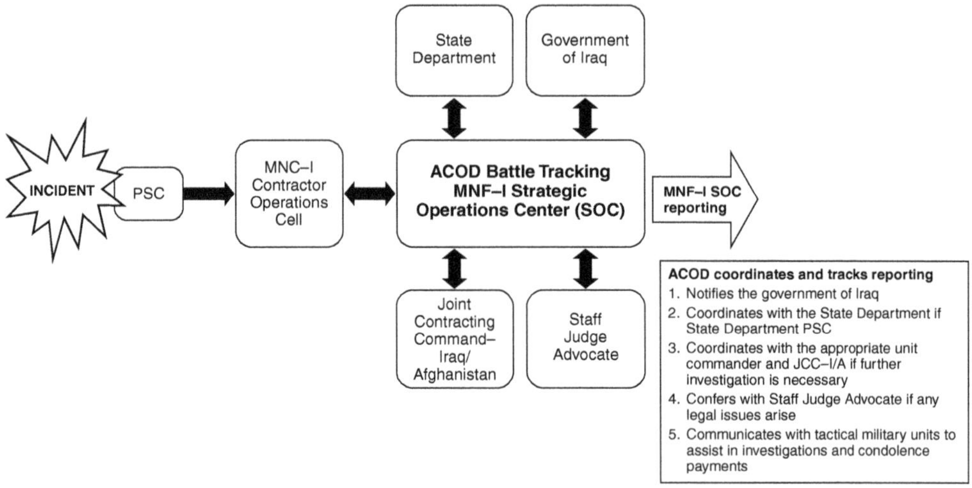

Source: DOD Presentation.

One of the key efforts of the Armed Contractor Oversight Division is to monitor, review, and report all PSC incidents. These incidents include those involving injuries; deaths; negative reports in the media; weapons discharges; complaints from U.S. military commanders, local Iraqi citizens or the government of Iraq; and other allegations of PSC misconduct. PSCs are required to report these incidents in writing to the MNC-I CONOC. The office then reviews each incident report to determine whether the incident requires additional investigation. After an investigation is completed by the appropriate unit commander, the Armed Contractor Oversight Division tracks corrective or disciplinary actions initiated by the commander or the PSC. The Armed Contractor Oversight Division also conducts a trend analysis of incident reporting data. According to officials, since the office began oversight over PSCs in October 2007, weapons discharges by PSCs have decreased approximately 60 percent.[11] Figure 3 depicts how the Armed Contractor Oversight Division monitors and reports PSC incidents.

DOD Has Consolidated and Strengthened Its PSC Oversight Guidance by Requiring Further Incident Investigation

According to MNF-I officials, prior to December 2007 there were between 40 and 50 separate fragmentary orders relating to regulations applicable to

[11] This information was provided by the Armed Contractor Oversight Division and GAO did not independently verify it. Additionally, other factors, such as the increase in the number of U.S. troops in Iraq may have led to the decrease in weapons discharges. As such, we cannot reasonably conclude that this decrease was solely caused by the office's strengthened oversight.

PSCs in Iraq. As such, contracting officers as well as military commanders rotating into Iraq may not have been aware of all of the regulations covering PSCs. In December 2007, MNF-I issued Fragmentary Order 07-428, to consolidate the previous fragmentary orders and establish authorities, responsibilities and coordination requirements for MNC-I to provide oversight for all armed DOD contractors and civilians in Iraq including PSCs. The establishment of the consolidating fragmentary order creates a single source for CENTCOM mandated orders, regulations and mandatory contract clauses relating to requirements, procedures, and responsibilities for control, coordination, management, and oversight of PSCs in Iraq. Specifically, the order addresses PSC requirements including arming procedures and responsibilities, rules for the use of force and mandates strengthened serious incident reporting procedures and responsibilities. For example, under the new order when a PSC observes, suspects, or participates in a serious incident such as a weapons discharge, PSCs are required to submit an immediate incident report at the earliest opportunity via the most secure means available to MNC-I and then submit an initial written report of the incident not later than 4 hours after the incident in contrast to the previous 48 hour reporting requirement.[12] The order requires the initial report to contain a highlighted version of the incident, including critical information such as who was involved and when and where the incident occurred. PSCs are required to file a final report with 96 hours of the incident.

Additionally, the fragmentary order increases the oversight responsibilities for military units by requiring the military to investigate serious incidents involving a DOD PSC. Previous orders only directed the military to investigate incidents related to contractors firing weapons. According to the December 2007 order, the military unit that receives the contracted security services is required to conduct a preliminary inquiry if contractors are involved in a serious incident. The order also stipulates that at a minimum, a commander's inquiry will be conducted and documented. Previously, there was no requirement that commanders' investigations be documented. Incidents that involve death, serious injury, or property damage in excess of $10,000 must be investigated by the appropriate level commander. Previous investigative requirements did not include this requirement. The order directs commanders to involve criminal investigative authorities if the preliminary investigations suggest either criminal misconduct, a violation of the rules for the use of force, or an inappropriate graduated force response. Finally, the order requires that any military unit observing or becoming aware of a serious incident provide an investigative

[12] The fragmentary order defines a serious incident as a weapons discharge including negligent discharges, traffic accidents, and criminal acts including but not limited to murder, kidnapping, theft, and assault.

report to the unit's operational chain of command and to include photographs and names if possible. In reviewing investigative reports to determine whether PSC misconduct was involved, commanders are to use the same standards as they would for their own units' actions. Investigations or inquiries completed by the military are forwarded to the Armed Contractor Oversight Division and the MNC-I Staff Judge Advocate for review. Moreover, according to an Armed Contractor Oversight Division official, if a military investigation is deemed to have been inadequate, MNF-I or MNC-I can direct another investigation. Prior to the establishment of the Armed Contractor Oversight Division there was no MNF-I level review of incident reports.

The fragmentary order also requires that PSCs report all weapons discharges on a monthly basis to the contracting officer's representative or sponsoring activity. The monthly report, which includes information on the type of discharge, is to be annotated to include information on the type and status of the investigation and who conducted it. In addition, if an action such as a fine or termination was taken against a contractor employee, this information also is to be included in the report. The reports are provided to the MNC-I office responsible for authorizing individual contractor employees to carry weapons and may be considered when MNC-I determines whether an individual will be allowed to carry a weapon. The monthly reports are also provided to the Armed Contractor Oversight Division, which analyzes the data for trends. Previous guidance did not require the monthly weapons discharge report.

The fragmentary order also addresses the contracting officer representative's (COR) critical role in contract support and provides information to properly designate, train, and support the COR in government oversight and administration of security contracts. A DOD guidance memo assigning contract administration functions lists oversight over a contractor's compliance with CENTCOM policies and directives among contract administration responsibilities. The order states that organizations supported by security services shall insure a COR is nominated to perform contract oversight. The order further states that contracting officers are responsible for monitoring PSC performance and ensuring PSC compliance with contractual requirements. According to the order, contracting officer representatives should be selected at a rank commensurate with the contract's oversight responsibilities and that contract oversight should be their primary function. The contracting officer's representative should also be at a location to allow sufficient direct oversight of contractor operations. Prior to the fragmentary order there was not a comprehensive document describing these responsibilities and how they relate to providing oversight over PSCs.

DOD Has Increased the Number of Personnel Devoted to Contract Management and Oversight, but It Is Unclear Whether the Increase Can Be Sustained

DOD contract oversight efforts in Iraq have also been strengthened through actions taken by the Undersecretary of Defense, Acquisition Technology and Logistics and the Defense Contract Management Agency (DCMA). However the Department may be challenged to continue to provide the increased number of personnel needed to sustain the additional oversight. In October 2007, the Undersecretary issued memoranda giving JCC-I/A new authorities and responsibilities for PSCs contracting in Iraq. Specifically, JCC-I/A is responsible for all contract administration for DOD's security contracts in Iraq.[13] In Iraq, JCC-I/A has delegated to DCMA the responsibility to provide contract administration over private security contracts. This newly delegated authority enables DCMA, with its presence in Iraq, to implement a systematic approach toward oversight of PSCs contracts. DCMA officials told us that this approach, which did not exist prior to DCMA receiving this authority, includes developing a quality assurance framework, a key component of which is the agency's development of a series of quality assurance checklists for PSCs. DCMA officials stated that the checklists have been developed by incorporating requirements from the statements of work in PSC contracts and current MNF-I guidance and fragmentary orders and translating these requirements into objective measurable standards intended to enable the agency to conduct regular and unbiased inspections of contracting personnel, known as surveillance audits. According to DCMA officials, these checklists are intended to ensure that PSCs are meeting contract requirements and that DOD is providing appropriate oversight over the contracts. The checklists translate security contract requirements into an audit document. According to DCMA officials, the agency coordinates with the Armed Contractor Oversight Division to ensure that the checklists reflect current MNF-I guidance and fragmentary orders related to PSCs.

To assist in its greater role in Iraq to provide contract award, administration and oversight, JCC-I/A plans to add additional personnel in Iraq while DCMA has increased its number of oversight personnel in Iraq and hopes to add additional personnel. DCMA has approximately doubled the number of oversight personnel in the CENTCOM area of responsibility by shifting personnel from other areas. Of the personnel in theater in March 2008, somewhat more than half were deployed to Iraq to provide

[13] The memo also implemented a process known as the Theater Business Clearance Process. Under this process JCC-I/A reviews all contracts being written by DOD contracting offices outside of Iraq to ensure that the contracts conform to CENTCOM and MNF-I policies, directives, and fragmentary orders.

greater oversight of contracts in Iraq including private security contracts.[14] Furthermore, DCMA plans to increase the number of staff deployed to the theater to 348 by the end of 2008. While the contracting command and DCMA both hope to be able to increase the number of personnel available in Iraq to provide additional oversight of DOD's PSC contracts, our current and past work suggests that the agencies may not be able to fill all of the positions or sustain this increase. For example, during our visit to Iraq officials from JCC-I/A stated that while they had a joint manning document that authorizes 39 additional staff, the positions would not be immediately filled and thus they continued to work with the individual services to fill the positions. As of June 2008, JCC-I/A officials reported that 32 of the 39 positions listed in the joint manning document had been created and should be filled by the services soon. DCMA also developed a joint manning document and is asking the services to provide the additional oversight and management personnel needed in part because DCMA lacks the personnel to meet the additional requirements. During our visit to Iraq, DCMA officials expressed concerns about maintaining the increase in the number of oversight personnel in Iraq over the long-term. In 2007 the report of the Commission on Army Acquisition and Program Management in Expeditionary Operations stated that the Army lacks the leadership and military and civilian personnel to provide sufficient contracting support to either expeditionary or peacetime missions.[15] According to the commission, Army contracting personnel experienced a 600 percent increase in their workload and are performing increasingly complex tasks, but the number of Army civilians and military in the contracting workforce has either remained static or declined because of congressional direction to DOD and the Army to make significant cuts in the acquisition workforce.[16] According to a May 2008 Congressional Research Service report, the earlier reductions in the contracting workforce reflected Congress' view that the workforce had not been reduced enough in proportion with the overall defense budget, particularly the acquisition portion of the defense budget.[17] However, concomitant to the workforce reduction was the department's decision to increase its reliance on contractors to provide services previously provided by DOD civilians or service members. As a result, the actual workload of contracting personnel (the people charged with writing, negotiating,

---

[14] The remaining DCMA personnel were deployed to Afghanistan, Kuwait, and Qatar. In addition to private security contracts, DCMA provides oversight for the Army and Air Force's logistics support contracts.

[15] Commission on Army Acquisition and Program Management in Expeditionary Operations, *Urgent Reform Required: Army Expeditionary Contracting* (October 31, 2007).

[16] Congress has taken steps to increase the quality and quantity of acquisition professionals in DOD's workforce. For example, the Congress recently provide additional funds to add 200 more contracting officers at DCMA to help with the added workload.

[17] Congressional Research Service, *Defense Contractors in Iraq: Issues and Options for Congress* (Washington, D.C.: May 21, 2008).

monitoring, and enforcing performance of the contracts) was substantially increasing in complexity and volume. Furthermore, in a June 2008 report to Congress, the Air Force commented that in the current conflict it was strained to cover its own contracting requirements and provide 67 percent of the contracting personnel to support joint contracting requirements. These comments cast doubt on the Air Force's ability as well as the Army's ability to fully support either JCC-I/A or DCMA. As we noted in our January 2008 testimony, without adequate contract oversight personnel in place to monitor DOD's many contracts in deployed locations such as Iraq, DOD may not be able to reasonably assure that contractors are meeting their contract requirements efficiently and effectively.[18]

Units Continue to Deploy to Iraq without Training on Increased PSC Oversight Responsibilities

In July 2005, we reported that units deploying to Iraq received no training on working with PSCs and were unclear as to their responsibilities towards PSCs.[19] At that time we recommended that DOD establish and incorporate a training program into the mission-rehearsal exercises and predeployment training for units deploying to Iraq. In response to the recommendation, DOD has incorporated training on PSCs into various predeployment training programs and exercises. For example, the Joint Forces Command has developed training on the role of PSCs in the battlespace for senior military staff in Iraq. The Army has a pilot program to incorporate PSC scenarios into its Battle Command Training Program, which trains Corps, division and brigade staff. The Army and the Marine Corps also incorporated scenarios on the rules of engagement and escalation of force involving PSCs into unit predeployment training. Additionally, according to DOD officials, PSC scenarios have been incorporated into two recent training exercises for senior staff. However, this training does not include all of the topics we recommended in 2005 such as information on PSC standard operating procedures nor does it reflect the increased PSC oversight responsibilities and organizational structures established since the September 2007 incident, such as training on the role of the Armed Contractor Oversight Division. When we made our recommendation, DOD's use of PSCs was limited to a few contracts that provided support to the Army Corps of Engineers and to static security for work areas within military installations. Since then DOD's use of PSCs has increased significantly and military units at all levels have been given more oversight responsibility for PSCs as well as more responsibilities for coordination as we discuss below.

[18] GAO, *Military Operations: Implementation of Existing Guidance and Other Actions Needed to Improve DOD's Oversight and Management of Contractors in Future Operations*, GAO-08-436T (Washington, D.C.: January 24, 2008).

[19] GAO, *Rebuilding Iraq: Actions Needed to Improve the Use of Private Security Providers*, GAO-05-737 (Washington, D.C.: July 2005).

Without training that reflects current policies, practices and procedures, military units deploying to Iraq may not conduct the independent incident investigations required to ensure contractor accountability.

The State Department Has Begun to Increase Its Oversight Efforts in Iraq

After the Nisour Square incident, the Secretary of State assembled a panel of experts to review the agency's security practices in Iraq and make recommendations to reduce the likelihood of future incidents that could adversely affect the overall U.S. mission in Iraq. The panel found that while the State Department's security operations had been highly effective in ensuring that mission personnel were safe, improvements were needed to address deficiencies in oversight and coordination. To address these deficiencies, the panel made 18 recommendations to improve oversight of PSCs contracted by the State Department in Iraq. The State Department has implemented 11of the recommendations and is in the process of implementing the remaining recommendations. Appendix II provides additional information on all of the panel's recommendations, their implementation status, and our comments on the implementation status.

When we met with State Department officials at the U.S. Embassy in Baghdad, officials told us that the department had made progress in implementing some of these recommendations. For example, one of the panel's principal recommendations was to increase the number of Diplomatic Security Special Agents in Iraq in order to expand oversight of the department's PSCs. State Department officials told us that the agency is increasing the number of agents in Iraq from 36 to 81 permanent and 7 temporary duty personnel to provide additional oversight of the department's PSCs, such as accompanying the PSC contractors on each personal protection mission. According to the State Department, these positions are expected to be filled by September 2008. The State Department has acknowledged that it does not have sufficient numbers of diplomatic security agents to meet the agency's security requirements and as a result relies on and will continue to rely on private security contractors to provide additional capacity. According to the State Department, in order to provide enough Diplomatic Security Special Agents in Iraq, the department had to move agents from other programs, and those moves have negatively affected the agency's ability to perform other missions including providing security for visiting dignitaries and visa, passport, and identity fraud investigations. For example, the official stated that the agency had to borrow personnel from another federal law enforcement agency in order to provide security at the Middle East Peace Summit held in Annapolis, Maryland. According to the State Department, 100 new agents are needed in order to sustain this increase and will continue to be needed after the hostilities in Iraq are over. The State

Department received funding for the new agents in the 2008 supplemental appropriations act signed by the President of the United States on June 30, 2008, which covers the 4th quarter of fiscal year 2008 and all of fiscal year 2009. According to the State Department, these positions will be included in the agency's fiscal year 2010 budget request.

Similar to DOD, the State Department has developed directives to consolidate and establish the agency's rules, regulations, and policies for PSCs in Iraq. As of May 2008, the State Department has issued four directives that provide guidance similar to the fragmentary order issued by MNF-I. The purpose of these policy directives is to provide PSCs with rules, regulations, and requirements for operating in Iraq. The topics covered in these directives cover rules for the use of force, escalation of force, serious incident reporting, and investigating as well as coordination with DOD. According to State Department officials, these directives consolidate previously issued guidance and ensure that all of the State Department's PSCs are aware of current department policies.

Coordination, Including Interagency Coordination, Related to PSCs in Iraq Has Improved

DOD and the State Department have improved coordination related to PSCs in Iraq. For example, since the Nisour Square incident in late 2007, the agencies have increased interagency coordination of their PSC movements in Iraq through liaison officers and other means. In addition, MNC-I has established several operation centers to track the movement of DOD PSCs as well as to coordinate the movements of PSCs working for the State Department. MNF-I's Armed Contractor Oversight Division has also been coordinating efforts related to PSC oversight and accountability among DOD, the State Department, the Government of Iraq, and the PSC community in Iraq. Moreover, in December 2007, DOD and the State Department entered a memorandum of agreement that covers a broad range of management and operational procedures intended to improve the U.S. government's management coordination over PSC operations in Iraq.

Interagency Coordination Has Improved between DOD and the Department of State and between the U.S. Government and the Government of Iraq

Prior to the Nisour Square incident, DOD and the State Department did not maintain regular communication or coordination on the departments' efforts related to PSCs in Iraq, and neither DOD nor the State Department coordinated on a regular basis with the Government of Iraq on issues related to PSCs. According to State Department officials, much of the prior coordination with MNF-I was ad hoc in part because MNF-I lacked a focal point to coordinate with. During our visit to Iraq, DOD and State Department officials told us that since the incident, both agencies have implemented several measures to improve communication and coordination between the two agencies. For example, the State Department has a liaison officer stationed at MNC-I's operations cell, and MNC-I continues to maintain a liaison officer in the RSO's operations center. In addition, representatives from the State Department participate in daily MNF-I briefings to coordinate with MNF-I regarding planned State Department personnel movements. Additionally, the agencies have increased their coordination on the reporting and investigation of serious incidents involving PSCs. For example, the State Department's Tactical Operations Center coordinates with and reports all serious incidents involving its PSCs to the Armed Contractor Oversight Division. Moreover, State Department officials in Iraq stated that they are now sharing additional information and have enhanced coordination on PSC movements with DOD, requesting route intelligence from DOD, and providing DOD feedback on route security. While the State Department provided MNF-I with route information and scheduled personnel movements prior to the Nisour Square incident, MNF-I did not know that the information was being provided by the State Department. The State Department uses a data tracking system to provide DOD tactical units with situational awareness of State Department PSC movements. According to DOD and State Department officials, these improvements were driven in part by recommendations made by the State Department panel reviewing PSC operations and by the signing of a memorandum of agreement between the two agencies stating that they agree to work together on PSC matters in Iraq.

Additionally, the director of the Armed Contractor Oversight Division coordinates with the State Department by co-chairing an incident review board with the Regional Security Officer. This board meets quarterly to examine incidents involving U.S. government PSCs in order to identify trends and make recommendations to improve U.S. Government oversight of PSCs in Iraq. The board also identifies best practices and communicates these practices with PSCs. Furthermore, Armed Contractor Oversight Division officials told us that the office has increased its coordination efforts with the government of Iraq. For example, the division and the State Department's Regional Security Officer regularly meet with the Ministry of the Interior to coordinate on managing PSCs, and listen to concerns, resolve issues, and generate joint solutions. This process did not occur prior to the establishment of the oversight division. Furthermore, the division ensures that the Ministry is immediately notified when incidents occur involving PSCs and Iraqi civilians.

Multi-National Corps-Iraq Has Created a Group of Operations Centers to Coordinate Movement of DOD and State PSCS

Prior to the issuance of the fragmentary order, DOD tracked the movement of its PSCs through the Reconstruction Operations Center, which was run by a U.S. Army Corps of Engineers contractor. As directed by the fragmentary order, MNC-I has established six Contractor Operations Cells to assume the responsibility to provide battlefield coordination, previously handled by the Reconstruction Operations Center, control of PSC movement throughout Iraq, and facilitate the expedient reporting of incidents involving PSCs. The central Contractor Operations Cell is located at MNC-I headquarters at Camp Victory, while the others are located at the tactical operations centers of each of the five divisions that control the corresponding battle space in Iraq. According to MNF-I and MNC-I officials, the Contractor Operations Cells provide a better mechanism for coordination than did the Reconstruction Operations Center, for several reasons. First, as we noted above, the Contractor Operations Cells are co-located with the tactical units responsible for the battle space, making coordination easier. Second, commanders have improved situational awareness because information related to PSCs is now viewed in context with other battle space activities. For example, the State Department provides the Contractor Operations Cells with U.S. Embassy PSC movement information that can be tracked by battlefield commanders using the same system as is used to track military vehicles. This movement information was never provided to the Reconstruction Operations Center when it was responsible for tracking DOD's PSC movements. Third, battle space commanders now control the movement of DOD PSCs in Iraq. According to the MNF-I order establishing the Contractor Operations Cells, the tactical unit responsible for the battle space must approve or deny the movement request submitted by DOD PSCs. Previously, the battlespace commanders may have been made aware of the PSCs' planned movements, but they were not required to approve the movement. Additionally, MNF-I developed common standards for communications between PSCs and government personnel. MNF-I secured funding from U.S. Army Central Command for radios and satellite phones for all DOD PSCs in Iraq in order to standardize communication standards between PSCs and government personnel. Additionally, the Defense Contract Management Agency is currently modifying all PSC contracts in Iraq to incorporate these common standards, and the PSCs will be acquiring standardized radios and satellite phones as contractor furnished equipment in order to meet these new requirements. Figure 4 depicts how the Contractor Operations Cells coordinates U.S. government PSC movements in Iraq.

The Department of Defense and Department of State Have Developed a Memorandum of Agreement to Improve Coordination of PSCs in Iraq

After the Nisour Square incident, DOD and the Department of State recognized the need for a more unified approach toward the oversight and coordination of U.S. government PSCs in Iraq and began to develop, implement,

Figure 4: Overview of the Contractor Operations Cells (CONOC)

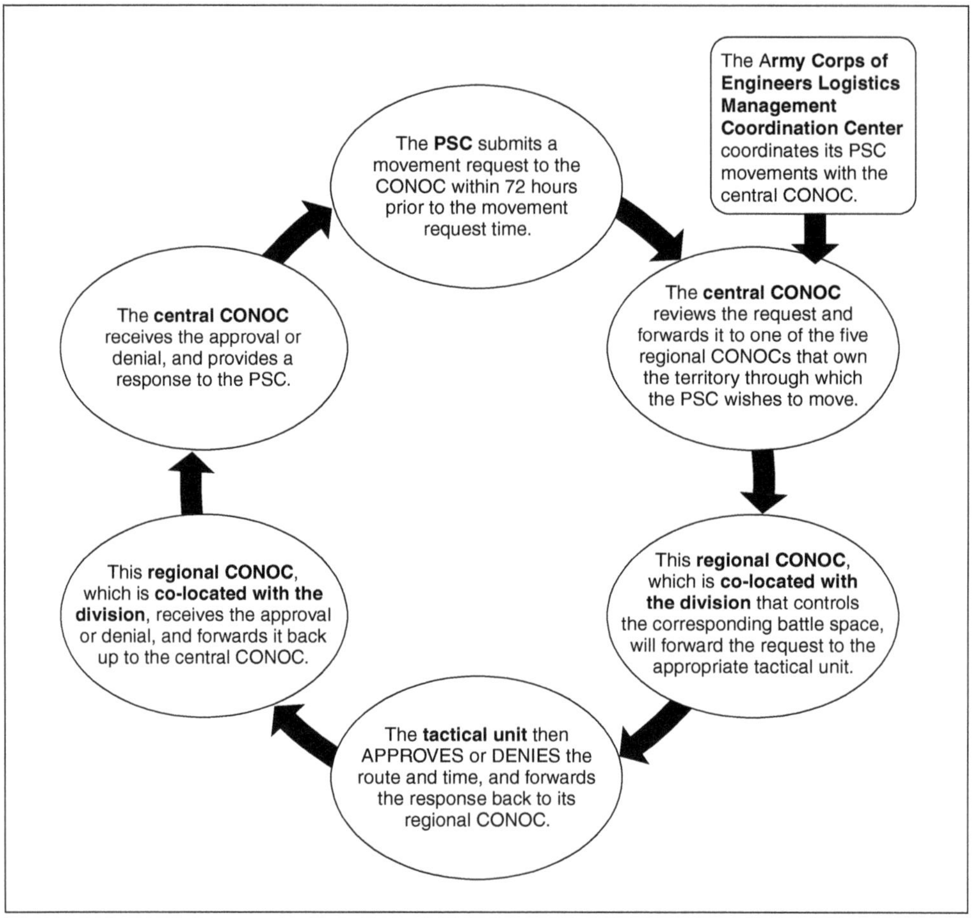

Source: DOD data; GAO presentation.

and follow standards, policies, and procedures for the coordination of PSCs in Iraq. On December 5, 2007, DOD and the State Department signed a memorandum of agreement with the purpose to clearly define the authority and responsibility for the accountability and operations of U.S. government PSCs in Iraq. The memorandum of agreement lays an important groundwork and, as we have discussed, many of its provisions are being implemented. For example, the memorandum of agreement directs the two agencies to

- improve the effectiveness of incident management, response, and follow-up for investigations;

- assure transparent, timely reporting and investigation of incidents between U.S. Embassy in Baghdad and MNF-I, with timely reporting of same to the government of Iraq; and
- synchronize PSC operations between the battle space commander and Regional Security Officer in order to establish real-time oversight, visibility, and coordination of PSC convoy movements outside secure bases.[20]

The memorandum of agreement also directs DOD and the State Department to ensure that their respective PSC contracts and subcontracts contain common language, through contract modifications if necessary, implementing relevant provisions of the memorandum of agreement.

On July 10, 2008, pursuant to Section 861 of the 2008 National Defense Authorization Act, DOD, the State Department and U.S. Agency for International Development (USAID) signed a memorandum of understanding which covers, among other things, contracting and contracting personnel in Iraq, including PSCs. The matters addressed include: identifying each agency's roles and responsibilities pertaining to procedures and coordination for the movement of contractor personnel in Iraq; identifying and maintaining a common database to serve as a repository of information on contracts in Iraq; and collecting data on, and appropriately referring, cases of contractor criminal misconduct.

An Overview of the Legal Framework for Holding Private Security Contractor Employees Accountable for Their Actions in Iraq

Various laws exist to hold PSC employees accountable for criminal acts committed in a wartime environment beyond the borders of the United States. These laws include U.S. criminal laws that may be applied extraterritorially, the Military Extraterritorial Jurisdiction Act[21] (MEJA), the Uniform Code of Military Justice[22] (UCMJ), international law, as well as Iraqi laws. Whether a particular law provides extra-territorial jurisdiction over a criminal act by a PSC employee depends on the specific facts of the incident, such as the time, nature and location of the alleged crime, the nature of the contractor's employment and the nationality of the accused. For example, an employee of a DOD contractor, whether a U.S. citizen or Third Country National, who commits a felony while accompanying the Armed Forces in Iraq during a contingency operation may be charged under the UCMJ

[20] However, according to the memorandum of agreement, when the battle space commander determines there is a need for a PSC to alter routes or abort missions, PSCs are directed to comply with the recommendations of the battlespace commander. While final authority for U.S. Embassy moves rests with the Chief of Mission, he or she will generally honor the MNF-I recommendation.

[21] 18 U.S.C. §§ 3261–3267 (2008).

[22] 10 U.S.C. §§ 801–941 (2008).

or MEJA. With regard to other than DOD contractor employees, a panel of State Department representatives reporting on protective services in Iraq concluded in October 2007 that the legal framework for holding non-Department of Defense contractor employees accountable under U.S. law is inadequate. Congress is presently considering legislation that would clarify and extend U.S. criminal jurisdiction over individuals employed under a contract awarded by any U.S. department or agency where contract performance is located in the area of a contingency operation. In addition to U.S. law, the legal framework for holding PSCs accountable includes applicable international law, including the law of war, and Iraqi law. Also, contract provisions serve to regulate contractor behavior.

U.S. Laws May Be Applied Extraterritorially in Certain Instances

Congress has the authority to enact laws that have effect beyond the territorial boundaries of the United States.[23] However, it is a long standing principle that a law of the United States is meant to apply only within the territorial jurisdiction of the United States, unless there is a clear expression of congressional intent to the contrary.[24] Certain federal statutes prescribe criminal sanctions for offenses committed by or against U.S. nationals overseas, such as the War Crimes Act of 1996, which makes murder, rape, torture, and other grave breaches punishable during an armed conflict.[25] The United States also has jurisdiction over U.S. nationals for crimes committed outside U.S. territory through special maritime and territorial provisions for certain offenses clearly identified in the U.S. Code, such as maiming, assault, kidnapping, murder, and manslaughter. In the U.S. Code, the definition of "special maritime and territorial jurisdiction" includes any lands reserved or acquired for use of the United States or any place acquired by the United States for the erection of a building.[26] In addition, effective October 26, 2001, the definition of the "special maritime and territorial jurisdiction" was expanded to include U.S. diplomatic, consular, military or other U.S. missions or entities in foreign states including leased buildings or residences with respect to offenses committed by or against a U.S. national, except where the offense is committed by a person employed by or accompanying the Armed Forces or a member of the Armed Forces,

[23] *Equal Employment Opportunity Com'n v. Arabian American Oil Co., et al.*, 499 U.S. 244, 248 (1991).

[24] The U.S. Supreme Court has taken this position to avoid encroachment on foreign sovereignty and to protect against unintended clashes between U.S. laws and those of other nations, which could result in international discord. *American Banana Co. v. United Fruit Co., 213 U.S. 347, 356* (1909) and *Equal Employment Opportunity Com'n v. Arabian American Oil Co., et al.*, 499 U.S. 244, 248 (1991).

[25] 18 U.S.C. § 2441 (2008). On November 21, 2001, the President issued a military order, which stated, among other findings, that international terrorists had created a state of armed conflict. President Issues Military Order: Detention, Treatment, and Trial of Certain Non-Citizens in the War Against Terrorism, http://www.whitehouse.gov/news/releases/2001/11/20011113-27.html, last visited 6/24/08.

[26] 18 U.S.C. § 7(3) (2008).

as defined in MEJA.[27] Therefore, the statute essentially exempts people who are already subject to MEJA (in other words, giving preference to MEJA as the source of jurisdiction).

MEJA Applies to Contractors Supporting DOD's Mission Overseas

In 2000, Congress enacted MEJA in part due to a disagreement among federal courts interpreting the breadth of special maritime and territorial jurisdiction.[28] MEJA extended U.S. criminal jurisdiction over civilians employed by or accompanying the Armed Forces outside the United States who commit offenses outside the United States that would have been punishable by imprisonment for more than 1 year had the offense occurred within the special maritime and territorial jurisdiction of the United States. The statute is applicable to DOD contractors, including subcontractors at any tier, and, beginning in 2004,[29] to contractors of any other U.S. agency to the extent that the contractor employee's employment relates to supporting the mission of the DOD overseas. The law is not applicable to individuals who are nationals of or ordinarily resident in the host nation. DOD has issued regulations and an instruction implementing policies and procedures under MEJA.[30] Among other things, the regulation states that the DOD General Counsel shall provide initial coordination and liaison with the departments of Justice and State, on behalf of the military departments, regarding a case for which investigation and/or federal criminal prosecution under MEJA is contemplated.[31] The regulation further states that the DOD Inspector General shall report to the Attorney General whenever the Inspector General has reasonable grounds to believe that a violation of federal criminal law has occurred and to ensure that DOD criminal investigative organizations fulfill their responsibilities outlined in the memorandum of understanding between the Department of Justice and DOD. The regulation also notes that a question remains as to whether MEJA jurisdiction should be applied to persons who are Third Country Nationals but have a tenuous nexus to the United States.

---

27 USA PATRIOT Act, Pub. L. No. 107-56, § 804.

28 In 2000, a federal circuit court refused to interpret 'special maritime and territorial jurisdiction' to include a housing complex leased by the U.S. military on a military base in Germany where a sexual assault was committed by one military dependent upon another. *U.S. v. Gatlin*, 216 F. 3d 207, 209 (2nd Cir. 2000). Later that year, a federal judge in a different circuit interpreted the jurisdiction to include an American citizen tried for a crime that occurred in a private apartment building rented by the U.S. embassy for the use of its employees. *U.S. v. Corey*, 232 F.3d 1166, 1169 (9th Cir. 2000).

29 Effective October 28, 2004, the definition of "employed by the Armed Forces outside the United States," was revised from DOD employees, contractors, and contractor employees, to those of DOD and any other federal agency or any provisional authority to the extent their employment relates to the DOD mission overseas. Ronald Reagan National Defense Authorization Act for Fiscal Year 2005, Pub. L. No. 108-375, § 1088.

30 32 C.F.R. Part 153 and DOD Instruction 5525.11, "Criminal Jurisdiction Over Civilians Employed By or Accompanying the Armed Forces Outside the United States, Certain Service Members, and Former Service Members," March 3, 2005.

31 32 C.F.R. §153.4 (a) & (b).

The Report of the Secretary of State's Panel on Personal Protective Services in Iraq stated among its principal findings that the panel was unaware of a clear legal basis for holding non-Department of Defense contractors accountable under U.S. law and recommended the State Department urgently engage with other administration agencies to establish a clear legal basis for holding contractors accountable under U.S. law. A number of bills have been introduced during the 110th Congress, including one that was passed in the U.S. House of Representatives in October 2007, to broaden the applicability of MEJA beyond members of the Armed Forces and individuals employed by or accompanying the Armed Forces outside the United States, to include individuals employed under a contract or subcontract awarded by any U.S. department or agency where the employment is carried out in or near an area where the Armed Forces are conducting a contingency operation.[32] DOD officials we interviewed expressed concern that the pending legislation is imprecise and contains nebulous language that needs refinement. State, Defense and Justice Department officials we interviewed all confirmed that alternative language is being jointly prepared in an effort to clarify the jurisdictional boundaries under MEJA.

Certain Contractors May Be Subject to Prosecution under the UCMJ

Contractor personnel may be subject to prosecution by court-martial under the Uniform Code of Military Justice (UCMJ) for conduct that takes place during a contingency operation in certain circumstances. The John Warner National Defense Authorization Act for Fiscal Year 2007 broadened the applicability of the UCMJ regarding persons serving with or accompanying an armed force in the field,[33] from "in time of war"[34] to "in time of declared war or a contingency operation." According to DOD officials we interviewed, the trial of civilian contractors by courts-martial will likely be challenged on constitutional grounds, particularly in light of variations between the rules of courts-martial and civilian trials on key issues such as

[32] The House Judiciary Committee has stated this legislation is needed to make contractors not affiliated with DOD accountable for their criminal conduct. House Report 110-352 to accompany H.R. 2740, MEJA Expansion and Enforcement Act of 2007, at 5, Sept. 27, 2007.

[33] "In the field" has been judicially interpreted to refer to the nature of the military's engagement, as opposed to a matter of location. *Hines v. Mikell*, 259 Fed. 28, 34 (4th Cir., 1919). As such, even after the 2007 amendment, the applicability of the UCMJ to civilians accompanying the armed forces would be limited to those contingency operations where the armed forces are engaged in an existing conflict. See *Reid v. Covert*, 354 U.S. 1, 34 (1957) (where the Court, in rejecting the government's assertion that the conditions of world tension present in 1957 permitted military trial of civilians accompanying the armed forces overseas in an area where no actual hostilities were under way, stated "The exigencies which have required military rule on the battlefront are not present in areas where no conflict exists.").

[34] Beginning with a 1957 U.S. Supreme Court case, courts have interpreted the phrase "in time of war" to mean wars declared by Congress. *Reid v. Covert*, 354 U.S. 1 (1957), *Robb v. U.S.* 456 F. 2d 768 (Ct. Cl. 1972).

jury composition and due process. On March 10, 2008, the Secretary of Defense issued guidance regarding expanded UCMJ jurisdiction over DOD contractor personnel and other persons serving with or accompanying the Armed Forces overseas. The memorandum clarifies the broad scope of command authority to act whenever criminal activity may relate to or affect the commander's responsibilities. It requires that when alleged offenses committed by civilians violate U.S. federal criminal laws, DOD notify responsible Department of Justice authorities to afford them the opportunity to pursue prosecution of the case in federal district court. The memorandum also specifically notes that the unique nature of extended UCMJ jurisdiction requires sound management over when, where, and by whom such jurisdiction is exercised. According to MNF-I officials, on June 22, 2008, the Army for the first time tried a civilian defense contractor employee by court-martial under the expanded UCMJ authority. MNF-I officials informed us that an interpreter with U.S. armed forces in Iraq was originally charged with aggravated assault for allegedly stabbing another contractor at a combat outpost, but pleaded guilty to wrongfully taking a soldier's knife, obstructing justice, and lying to investigators. After the military judge accepted the guilty plea, the government dismissed the assault charge and the contractor employee was found guilty of all remaining charges and sentenced to 5 months confinement.

International Law

The part of international law that addresses the conduct of armed hostilities is referred to as the law of war. The law of war encompasses all international law for the conduct of hostilities binding on the United States or its individual citizens, such as treaties and international agreements to which the United States is a party. According to DOD policy, the law of war obligations of the United States are observed and enforced by the DOD components and DOD contractors assigned to or accompanying deployed Armed Forces.[35] This DOD policy also requires the service secretaries to develop internal policies and procedures to forward all reports of suspected or alleged violations of the law of war involving contractors or subcontractors assigned to or accompanying the Armed Forces to the DOD General Counsel for review for prosecutorial action under the criminal jurisdiction of the United States.

PSCs in Iraq Operate under the Law of the Government of Iraq

PSCs who perform services for U.S. agencies, for any member of the multinational force, or for diplomatic entities in Iraq operate under the law of the government of Iraq, which includes orders issued by the Coalition

[35] Department of Defense Directive 2311.01E, "DOD Law of War Program," May 9, 2006.

Provisional Authority (CPA) that have not been rescinded. PSCs, however, currently enjoy legal protections by virtue of CPA Order 17, which was revised on June 27, 2004. CPA Order 17 provides that PSCs are not subject to Iraqi laws or regulations on matters relating to the terms and conditions of their contracts, as long as they comply with CPA Orders and instructions governing the activities of PSCs in Iraq. Those orders and instructions include the registration and licensing of weapons and firearms. One such instruction, CPA Memorandum17, provides binding rules for the use of force and a code of conduct that must be followed by all PSCs. CPA Order 17 further recognizes that the United States shall have the right to exercise within Iraq any criminal and disciplinary jurisdiction conferred by U.S. law over persons subject to U.S. military law.

Contract Provisions Also Regulate Contractor Behavior

Contracts specify the terms of conduct and employment by which contractors must abide. For example, PSC contracts typically provide that a contractor is responsible for ensuring that its personnel who are authorized to carry weapons are adequately trained to carry and use them safely, adhere to the rules on the use of force, comply with law and agreements, and are not barred from possession of a firearm. Inappropriate use of force could subject a contractor, its subcontractors, or its employees to prosecution or civil liability under the laws of the United States and the host nation. A Defense Federal Acquisition Regulation Supplement clause, which is required to be included in contracts that authorize contractor personnel to accompany U.S. Armed Forces outside the United States in contingency operations, reminds such contractor personnel that they must comply with, and ensure that deployed personnel are familiar with and comply with, all applicable laws, rules, and regulations, including those of the host country, all treaties and international agreements, all U.S. regulations, and all orders, directives, and instructions issued by the combatant commander.[36] A Federal Acquisition Regulation clause, which is required to be included in contracts that require contractor personnel to perform outside the United States in a designated operational area during contingency operations, creates similar requirements for contractor personnel supporting a diplomatic or consular mission outside the United States.[37] The requirements of these clauses apply to subcontractors as well. As discussed earlier in this report, Fragmentary Order 07-428 also identifies language that must be incorporated into all DOD contracts where arming of employees is contemplated in Iraq, including a statement that the contractors and their subcontractors

[36] DFARS 252.225-7040(d).

[37] FAR 52.225-19(d).

agree to obey all existing and future laws, regulations, orders, and directives applicable to the use of private security personnel in Iraq.

Conclusions

Given the security situation in Iraq and the shortage of available military personnel and Department of State diplomatic security personnel to provide security, private security contractors play an integral role in providing the security. The September 16, 2007, incident in Nisour Square demonstrated the importance of having in place a coordinated system of oversight and coordination over U.S. government-hired private security contractors. Since that incident, DOD and the State Department have taken steps to increase oversight and coordination over PSCs, including establishing the Armed Contractor Oversight Division and Contractor Operations Cell systems and increasing the number of personnel devoted to PSC oversight functions in Iraq. The improvements DOD and the State Department have made may reduce the number of PSC incidents in Iraq. However, these enhancements may not eliminate incidents. Moreover, while the increase in the number of DOD personnel devoted to PSC oversight in Iraq should improve oversight, more efforts are required to ensure that that these personnel are well-trained and qualified, and that positions are filled and sustained over time. Furthermore, unless DOD ensures that military units deploying to Iraq understand both their expanded oversight and coordination responsibilities problems in managing and overseeing PSCs may continue. By ensuring that these efforts are sustained, the U.S. government can strengthen its framework of PSC oversight and coordination in Iraq and can better prepare to respond effectively to incidents and to apply this framework to future contingency operations, should they occur, and overseas diplomatic missions in high threat areas.

Recommendations for Executive Action

To ensure that DOD sustains its current efforts to strengthen oversight for private security contractors in Iraq, we recommend that the Secretary of Defense develop and implement a strategy to fill authorized positions for the Joint Contracting Command—Iraq/Afghanistan and DCMA.

To ensure that units and military commanders deploying to Iraq are aware of their new oversight and coordination responsibilities, we recommend that the Secretary of Defense direct the service Secretaries to update the information being provided on PSCs at unit mission-rehearsal exercises and predeployment training to include information regarding the operations of the Armed Contractor Oversight Division and the Contractor Operations Cells along with the role of military units in providing contract oversight, incident investigation, and PSC coordination procedures. Further, we recommend that DOD fully implement our 2005 recommendation by including information on PSC typical operating procedures and the military's responsibilities to PSCs.

Agency Comments and Our Evaluations

We provided a draft of this report to DOD and the State Department for their review and comment. DOD's response is provided in appendix III, and the State Department's response and our comments are provided in appendix IV. Both departments also provided us with technical comments, which we incorporated into the report as appropriate.

In commenting on the draft of this report, DOD concurred with our recommendations. First, DOD concurred with our recommendation to develop and implement a strategy to fill authorized positions for the JCCI/A and DCMA. DOD concurred and stated that it has initiated a strategy to deploy 220 personnel by December 15, 2008. DOD also concurred with our second recommendation that the Secretary of Defense direct the Service Secretaries to update the information being provided on PSCs at unit mission rehearsal exercises and pre-deployment training to include information regarding the operation of the Armed Contractor Oversight Division and the Contractor Operations Cells along with the role of military units in providing contract oversight, incident investigation, and PSC coordination procedures. DOD stated that it is actively incorporating contractors and contract support into the exercise schedules. We believe this is a positive step. However, DOD's efforts should also ensure that the training provided is given to a wide audience including senior military leadership, officers, and enlisted personnel. Lastly, DOD concurred with the third recommendation to fully implement our 2005 recommendation by including information on typical PSC operating procedures and the military's responsibilities to PSCs. DOD stated that it continues to swiftly improve its procedures through the rapid dissemination of changes to the MNF-I Fragmentary Order 07-428.

In commenting on our report the State Department noted that in addition to the oversight improvements discussed in this report, the State Department and the Bureau of Diplomatic Security have increased and realigned staff to enhance oversight. According to the State Department, the duties of the increased and realigned staff include assisting in administrating contracts, approving invoices, and increasing oversight of contractor training. In addition, the State Department provided us with some additional information regarding actions it has taken to improve contract oversight for private security contractors in Iraq which we have included in the report. The State Department expressed concern over our depiction of the status of implementation of the Secretary of State's Panel on Personal Protective Services in Iraq in appendix II. In its comments the State Department stated that it has implemented 16 of the 18 recommendations made by the panel. In our draft report we originally assessed 9 recommendations as complete. Based on additional information provided by the State Department we changed our assessment of the status of two recommendations (recommendation numbers 3 and 11 in appendix II) and now we are reporting that the State Department has completed 11 of the 18 recommendations. For example, in comments the State Department noted that it considered the implementation of the panel's recommendation that video recording equipment be installed into each security vehicle, even though to date the equipment has been installed in 140 of 233 vehicles. Therefore, we disagreed with the State Department's assessment and stand by our assertion that the State Department has implemented 11 of the panel's recommendations and have detailed our rationale in appendix II. In addition, the State Department's comments and our detailed responses appear in appendix IV.

We are sending copies of this report to other interested congressional committees, the Secretary of Defense and the Secretary of State. Copies of this report will also be made available to others upon request. In addition, this report will be available at no charge on GAO's Web site at http://www.gao.gov.

If you or your staff has any questions on the matters discussed in this report, please contact me at (202) 512-8365. Contact points for our Offices of Congressional Relations and Public Affairs may be found on the last page of this report. Key contributors to this report are John Needham, Director, Acquisition and Sourcing Management; Carole Coffey, Assistant Director; Vincent Balloon; Laura Czohara; Barbara Hills; Moshe Schwartz; Karen Thornton; Cheryl Weissman; and Natasha Wilder.

William M. Solis
Director, Defense Capabilities and Management

List of Congressional Committees

The Honorable Carl Levin
Chairman
The Honorable John McCain
Ranking Member
Committee on Armed Services
United States Senate

The Honorable Ike Skelton
Chairman
The Honorable Duncan L. Hunter
Ranking Member
Committee on Armed Services
House of Representatives

The Honorable David Price
House of Representatives

Appendix I: Scope and Methodology

To assess the U.S. government's use of PSCs in Iraq as well as to examine the efforts by DOD and the State Department to provide oversight, coordination, and accountability over the actions of the PSCs they employ in Iraq, we took a number of actions.

To determine if the oversight and coordination of PSCs operating in Iraq strengthened between U.S. government agencies, we reviewed several DOD, CENTCOM, Multinational Force-Iraq (MNF-I) and State Department policies and guidance addressing the requirements, procedures and responsibilities for the control, coordination, management and oversight of PSCs, as well as policies and guidance on arming requirements and certification, rules for the use of force, and incident reporting and investigation requirements. Specifically, we reviewed DOD regulations and instructions that relate to the management and oversight of PSCs during contingency operations as well as guidance and fragmentary orders issued by CENTCOM and headquarters MNF-I, including fragmentary order 07-428 entitled 'Armed Contractors/ DOD Civilians and PSCs', and its appendices, which consolidates several prior MNF-I fragmentary orders. We analyzed these documents to gain an understanding of the evolution of oversight roles and responsibilities and the delegation of authority to increase coordination between the agencies. In addition, we reviewed the memorandum of agreement, signed in December 2007, between DOD and the State Department on U.S. Government PSCs in Iraq. We reviewed these policies and documents to determine the authority and responsibility for the oversight, coordination, and accountability over PSC operations in Iraq. We reviewed the National Defense Authorization Act, including Sec. 861 directing the agencies to enter into a Memorandum of Understanding as well as Sec. 862 which outlines regulations on contractors performing private security functions in areas of combat operations.

To understand what actions the agencies have or can take to hold PSCs accountable, we analyzed the legal framework that PSCs hired by the U.S. government must comply with, including applicable international law, Iraqi law, and U.S. law. We reviewed the Military Extraterritorial Jurisdiction Act and the Uniform Code of Military Justice to gain an understanding of the process of how PSCs are held accountable for criminal misconduct. We interviewed officials from DOD's Office of the General Counsel, the State Department's Office of the Legal Adviser and from the Department of Justice to gain an understanding of the process used and the actions taken against PSC employees accused of misconduct in Iraq. Moreover, we also reviewed applicable U.S. government PSC contract provisions that outline and regulate contractor behavior.

Additionally, we met with military officials from the Office of the Under Secretary of Defense, Acquisition, Technology, and Logistics; Office of the

Secretary of Defense, Office of the General Counsel, U.S. Central Command; and the U.S. Army Corps of Engineers; officials from the State Department, including the Bureau of Diplomatic Security, Office of Acquisitions Management, and the Office of the Legal Advisor, and the U.S. Agency for International Development to discuss oversight, coordination, and accountability of PSCs in Iraq. We also met with the Executive Secretary who led the State Department panel to review the State Department's security practices in Iraq to discuss the findings and recommendations of their study.

We also interviewed officials from ten private security firms, located in the United States, the United Kingdom, and/or Baghdad, Iraq, who currently provide or have recently provided private security functions in Iraq. We met with the three firms contracted by the State Department under the Worldwide Personal Protective Service Contract as well as the firm hired by DOD to run the Reconstruction Operations Center, the predecessor to the Contractor Operations Cells. In addition, we interviewed several others to reflect a range of firms that provide private security. The private security firms we met with provided the U.S. government with a variety of private security services, including static security, personal protective detail, high threat protection, and convoy security. Our discussions included qualification and training standards, employee conduct and accountability, coordination with U.S. government agencies and their tactical operations centers, interaction amongst the other PSC firms operating in Iraq, vehicle and weapon tracking, and incident reporting procedures. Additionally, we met with representatives from an Iraq-based private security association to gain an industry perspective on the use, role, oversight, accountability, and legal framework of PSCs operating in Iraq.

We traveled to Iraq to meet with officials from DOD, including Multi-National Force-Iraq, Multi-National Corps-Iraq, and Multi-National Division-Baghdad, and Joint Contracting Command-Iraq/Afghanistan to discuss issues related to oversight, coordination, and accountability of PSCs in Iraq. We met with senior officials responsible for the establishment and operation of the Armed Contractor Oversight Division and the Contractor Operations Cells, as well as the military liaisons who are located in the State Department's Tactical Operations Center. Likewise, we met with officials from the State Department, including senior officials from the U.S. Embassy Baghdad and its Regional Security Office. We met with them to gain an understanding of the delegated responsibility and oversight structure of PSCs in Iraq, procedures for the coordination and communication between MNF-I and US Embassy Baghdad for the movement of PSCs within the MNF-I battle space, procedures for reporting and investigation in the event that a serious incident occurs as well as applicable laws to hold PSCs operating in Iraq accountable for their actions. While in Iraq, we toured DOD's Contracting Operations Cell and the State Department's Tactical Operations

Center, witnessing the planning, oversight and coordination, and tracking of PSC movements throughout Iraq. Additionally, in Iraq, we met with officials from private security firms to gain an industry perspective.

We scoped our work to include only on PSCs that have a direct contractual relationship with the U.S. government. As such, our work excluded PSCs with an indirect relationship with the U.S. government, such as those contracted by reconstruction firms. We reviewed processes but did not evaluate how effectively they were being implemented because the processes reviewed are new. We also did not evaluate how laws were being used to hold contractors accountable. We conducted this performance audit from February 2008 to April 2008, in accordance with generally accepted government auditing standards. Those standards require that we plan and perform the audit to obtain sufficient, appropriate evidence to provide a reasonable basis for our findings and conclusions based on audit objectives. We believe that the evidence obtained provides a reasonable basis for our findings and conclusions based on our audit objectives.

We visited or contacted the following organizations during our review:

The Department of Defense:

- Office of the Under Secretary of Defense, Acquisition, Technology, and Logistics, Washington, D.C.
- Office of General Counsel, Arlington, Va.
- Office of the J4, Washington, D.C.
- U.S. Central Command, Tampa, Fla.
- Defense Contract Management Agency, Baghdad, Iraq
- Multi-National Forces-Iraq, Baghdad, Iraq
- Multi-National Corps-Iraq, Baghdad, Iraq
- Multi-National Division-Baghdad, Baghdad, Iraq
- Joint Contracting Command Iraq/Afghanistan, Baghdad, Iraq

Department of the Army:

- Army Corps of Engineers Gulf Regional Division, Baghdad, Iraq
- Army Corps of Engineers, Logistics Movement Coordination Center, Baghdad, Iraq

Other Government Agencies

- State Department
    - Bureau of Diplomatic Security, Arlington, Va.

    - Office of Acquisitions Management, Arlington, Va.
    - Office of the Legal Adviser, Arlington, VA; Baghdad, Iraq
    - Secretary of State's Panel on Personal Protective Services in Iraq, Washington, D.C.
    - US Embassy Iraq, Baghdad, Iraq
- Department of Justice
    - Criminal Division, Washington, D.C.
    - Federal Bureau of Investigation, Washington, D.C.

Industry Associations:

- Private Security Association of Iraq, Baghdad, Iraq

Private Security Contractors:

- Aegis, London, United Kingdom
- Armor Group, London, United Kingdom
- Blackwater, Baghdad, Iraq; Moyock, N.C.
- Blue Hackle, Baghdad, Iraq
- Control Risks Group, London, United Kingdom
- Dyncorps International, West Falls Church, Va.
- Erinys International, London, United Kingdom
- Olive Group, Baghdad, Iraq
- Raymond Associates, Clifton Park, N.Y.
- Triple Canopy Inc., Herndon, Va.

Appendix II: Implementation Status of Recommendations from the Secretary of State's Panel on Personal Protective Services in Iraq

According to State Department officials, the department has also begun to implement other recommendations made by the panel including the installation of audio and video recording equipment in security vehicles and the creation of an eight person unit to investigate any reported and alleged incidents involving State Department PSCs including those involving injuries or death. In July 2008, officials provided information on the status of the implementation of the recommendations noting that 16 were completed and that others were dependent on other agencies or governments. This appendix provides additional information on all of the panel's recommendations, their implementation status, and our assessment of the implementation status. In certain instances our assessment differed from the State Department's. For example, the panel recommended that the Regional Security Office should be provided video and audio recording equipment for each security vehicle operating in Iraq. According to the State Department, they have fully implemented this recommendation by installing video recording systems into 140 vehicles and installing a radio recording system in the Regional Security Officer's Tactical Operations Center to record all Embassy radio transmissions. However, according to State Department officials the goal is to install the equipment into 233 vehicles by December 2008. Therefore, it is our assessment that implementation of the recommendation is still in progress. Similarly, the panel also recommended that a working group should be established to determine ways to move the Iraqi licensing process forward more transparently. The State Department stated that in its view this recommendation has been completed because it established the working group and that it was not necessary to have improved the licensing process to consider the recommendation implemented.

Table 1: Implementation Status of Recommendations from the Secretary of State's Panel on Personal Protective Services in Iraq

Recommendation	Status of Implementation as Reported by the State Department	GAO Comments
1. The State Department should urgently engage with the Department of Justice and the Office of Management and Budget, and then with the Congress, to establish a clear legal basis for holding contractors accountable under U.S. law	• The Department of State's Office of the Legal Adviser has actively engaged with an inter-agency working group, led by the Department of Justice, to work with Congress on legislation clarifying the Military Extraterritorial Jurisdiction Act (MEJA) in order to hold USG private security contractors overseas accountable for offenses. • The Department of Justice is taking the lead on further discussions of this issue with Senate staff. • The Department of State's Office of the Legal Adviser will stay engaged in this process until legislation is passed. • The Department's actions have met the intent of the recommendation. This recommendation is complete.	We disagree with the State Department's assessment that the recommendation is complete. According to the State Department at least three officials from the Legal Advisor's office have been working continuously on this issue. However, when asked to provide a copy of the legislation, officials stated that no such single draft exists and that the language had evolved over time through discussions within the agency and with Congress. In addition, the interagency working group is still pursuing an effort to establish a clear legal basis for holding contractors accountable under U.S. law. Therefore, we believe that implementation of the recommendation is still in progress.
2. The Department of State should work with the Department of Defense to determine how to commence discussions with the Government of Iraq on a new regulatory framework for PPS contractors.	• U.S. Embassy Baghdad, Multi-National Forces—Iraq (MNF-I), and the Iraqi Ministry of Interior continue to negotiate a Status of Forces Agreement and a Strategic Framework Agreement. • The Department's actions have met the intent of the recommendation. This recommendation is complete.	We disagree with the State Department's assessment that the recommendation is complete. The Status of Forces Agreement and a Strategic Framework Agreement are still being negotiated. Therefore, we believe that implementation of the recommendation is still in progress.

3. The requirement to expand security oversight requires an overall increase in the Diplomatic Security Service's authorized staffing level. The Department of State should approach the Office of Management and Budget and request in the final appropriations action for FY-08 an increase of 100 positions and the requisite salary and operating costs in order to provide the needed staffing in Iraq without stripping other missions of their security resources.	• The FY2008 Supplemental Appropriations Act provides funding for the 4th quarter of FY2008 and all of FY2009. The positions have been regularized in the Department's FY2010 budget request. • This recommendation is complete.	GAO agrees with the State Department's assessment.
4. When the FBI investigation into the September 16, 2007, incident is completed, the Embassy should submit its recommendation as to whether the continued services of the contractor involved is consistent with the accomplishment of the overall United States mission in Iraq	• The Embassy and the Department are awaiting the results of the FBI's investigation.	GAO agrees with the State Department's assessment.
5. The Regional Security Office should be provided with additional Department of State Special Agents so that an Assistant Regional Security Officer can accompany PPS movements. The State Department should ensure that each Assistant Regional Security Officer should complete an Iraq-specific orientation program.	• 45 new full time employee DS Special Agents positions were created for Iraq. Currently, 11 of these new positions are staffed at post and 34 agents are completing High Threat Training. All positions will be filled by Sept. 08. • Additionally, the RSO staff is currently augmented by 16 temporary duty (TDY) DS personnel. • All Diplomatic Security (DS) Special Agents complete Iraq-specific training at the DS Training Center and Foreign Service Institute prior to deployment. • This recommendation is complete.	We disagree with the State Department's assessment that the recommendation is complete as the Department's efforts to fulfill this requirement are ongoing. Therefore, we believe that implementation of the recommendation is still in progress.

Recommendation	Status of Implementation as Reported by the State Department	GAO Comments
6. The Worldwide Personal Protective Service (WPPS) contract should be amended to require the contractor to provide a limited number of Arabic language staff for use as needed.	• The WPPS contract was modified to require eight (8) Protective Security Specialist/ Translators, as requested by the RSO, to serve throughout Iraq. • This recommendation is complete.	GAO agrees with the State Department's assessment.
7. Additional training modules should be added under the Worldwide Protective Services contract to enhance the cultural awareness of assigned personnel, acquaint them with diplomatic structures and procedures, and familiarize them with Multi-National Force-I tactics, techniques, and procedures	• The WPPS contract was modified to require that all WPPS personnel complete the Iraq Cultural Awareness training program developed by the DS Training Center and the online "Working in an Embassy" course offered by the Foreign Service Institute. • This recommendation is complete.	GAO agrees with the State Department's assessment.
8. To tighten the ground rules for the use of deadly force and to ensure greater parallelism with USCENTCOM rules on the use of force by contracted security in Iraq, the U.S. Mission Firearms Policy should be revised to specify, without limiting the inherent right to take action necessary for self-defense, if an authorized employee must fire his/her weapon, he/she must fire only aimed shots; fire with due regard for the safety of innocent bystanders; and make every effort to avoid civilian causalities.	• The Departments of State and Defense agreed upon common principles for the Rules for the Use of Force. • The updated Mission Firearms Policy incorporating these revised Rules for the Use of Force was signed into effect by the Deputy Chief of Mission on February 2, 2008. • This recommendation is complete.	GAO agrees with the State Department's assessment.

9. The Regional Security Office (RSO) should be provided video and audio recording equipment for each security vehicle, audio recording equipment in the Tactical Operations Center to record all radio transmissions and computer enhancements to record all Blue Force Tracking Data	• To date, video recording systems have been installed into 140 mission vehicles throughout Iraq. The remaining installations have been funded and are planned for completion by December 2008. • Each protective mission now includes a vehicle with video recording capability. • Protective vehicle video camera installations have been institutionalized. All new vehicles are now being hard-wired for video recording capability in the assembly line process. • The radio recording system in the RSOs Tactical Operations Center is operational, and all Embassy radio transmissions are recorded. • Post implemented long-term recording of all Blue Force Tracker data. Blue Force Tracker data is stored on external hard drives, expanding retention capabilities. • This recommendation is complete.	We disagree with the State Department's assessment that the recommendation is complete. According to State Department documents, video and audio recording equipment has been installed into 133 vehicles. While officials have stated that the systems have been installed in 140 vehicles, according to State Department officials, the equipment is to be installed into 233 vehicles. Therefore, we believe that implementation of the recommendation is still in progress.

Recommendation	Status of Implementation as Reported by the State Department	GAO Comments
10. The Regional Security Office should place a readable number (like a license plate) on the right rear door of each vehicle utilized, to enable anyone wishing to question its mode of operation to identify the unit of the Regional Security Office, which can then review the matter and take appropriate action.	• The intent of Recommendation 10 is to ensure that Private Security Contractors (PSC) can be easily identified, located, and held accountable for their actions should it be required. The technical systems and procedural measures implemented by the Regional Security Officer (RSO) place Chief of Mission motorcades in full compliance with the scope of the recommendation. • Currently, Chief of Mission (COM) motorcade movements are tracked and monitored real-time by State Department personnel utilizing BFT and Tapestry. COM motorcade radio communications are recorded and monitored by RSO personnel in the RSO TOC. Motorcade vehicles are equipped with video cameras that record and document motorcade movements and events. These technical measures combined with reporting requirements and established operational procedures allow for COM motorcades to be monitored and held accountable. • This recommendation is complete.	We disagree with the State Department's assessment that the recommendation is complete. According to State Department officials, this recommendation was reviewed because of concern that unless all PSCs operating in Iraq, including non-State Department PSCs, were required to use the readable number, placing such a number on the State Department vehicles would make the agency's motorcades more vulnerable to attack. However, during our trip to Iraq, we observed that many non-State Department PSCs, including many with contracts with DOD, affixed readable numbers on their vehicles. While the technical systems and procedural measures being implemented may assist the monitoring of these motorcades by U.S. government officials, these systems and measures will not enable anyone to identify the vehicle via a readable number such as a license plate as stated in the recommendation. Additionally, as stated above, the recording equipment has not been installed into every vehicle. Therefore, we believe that implementation of the recommendation is still in progress.

11. The Regional Security Office should establish a "Go Team" that would proceed as soon as possible to the scene of any weapons discharge to gather information and material and provide an analysis of what happened and why, and prepare a report. The team would work with representatives of the appropriate Government of Iraq offices and the U.S. military unit responsible for the location.	• The RSO established a dedicated Go Team, referred to as the Force Investigation Unit, and reached an agreement with MNF-I for military security support for investigators as needed. • The Go Team is currently staffed with 2 full-time DS Special Agents who are augmented by 4 DS Special Agents assigned to the Investigations and Intelligence section. When the need arises this group is augmented by Special Agents from other sections of the RSO office. • Since January 2008, the Go Team has investigated 49 motor vehicle accidents and 52 escalations of force incidents involving Tier 1 and Tier 2 contractors -- of those 35 were pen flares and 13 were discharge of firearms incidents. • To expand and augment the Go Team, DS awarded a contract on May 22, 2008, to provide additional investigators and translators. • Six investigators and 2 translators have been hired and are now in training. They depart for Iraq on July 27, 2008. • This recommendation is complete.	GAO agrees with the State Department's assessment.

Recommendation	Status of Implementation as Reported by the State Department	GAO Comments
12. An Embassy Joint Incident Review Board should be established to review all incidents involving the use of deadly force that are known or asserted to have caused injury or death or other serious consequences. The Board should be chaired by the Deputy Chief of Mission and other members should be the Regional Security Officer, another civilian embassy officer with a law enforcement background from an agency other than State or Justice, and a military officer designated by MNF-I. The Board would hear from the Assistant Regional Security Officer (A/RSO) who was in the motorcade, review the statements provided by the security personnel involved, as well as any protectee(s), plus the Go Team report, and then make a recommendation to the Ambassador on whether or not the use of force appears justified. If it does not feel that it was justified, the Department should be informed to notify the Department of Justice.	• The Deputy Chief of Mission approved an Action Memo establishing the framework and process for convening an Embassy Joint Incident Review Board. The board has not yet had cause to meet. • This recommendation is complete.	GAO agrees with the State Department's assessment.
13. The Regional Security Office and MNF-I should establish a permanent working group to develop commonly agreed operational procedures; establish a robust liaison element; exchange information; ensure optimal situational awareness; and ensure that any issues are discussed and quickly resolved.	• A permanent working group was established in November 2007. • In December 2007, the Deputy Secretaries of State and Defense signed a memorandum of agreement to define the authority and responsibility for the accountability and operations of private security contractors in Iraq. • This recommendation is complete.	GAO agrees with the State Department's assessment.

In addition to the above, three specific items should be on the agenda for the first meeting: Ensuring that the planning, coordinating and routing information which currently flows from the Regional Security Office's Tactical Operations Center (TOC) to Multi-National Force-Iraq (MNF-1) liaison elements located in the TOC and posted to the U.S. Military's Command Post of the Future system, is available electronically to all operating elements under MNF-I; Providing TOC Spot Reporting electronically to any subordinate military element that wishes to receive it directly; Coordinating the provision of frequencies for the military radios and the RSO has ordered to enhance coordination.	• Electronic tracking issues were addressed to everyone's satisfaction by Command Post of the Future, Blue Force Tracker, and TAPESTRY. (11/16/07) • The RSO and MNC-I exchanged liaison officers in their respective Tactical Operations Centers. • This recommendation is complete. • RSO Spot Report language entered into MNF-I Combined Information Data Network Exchange database by the MNF-I liaison officer. This recommendation is complete. (11/16/07) • The RSO received 142 PRC-152 radios, which have been loaded and configured with DOD-compatible channels. This recommendation is complete.	
14. Coordination with MNF-I elements could be further enhanced if the pending order for Harris Corporation Model PRC-110 radios were received. The Department of State should intervene, including with DOD as necessary, to obtain these units.	• Post received 142 PRC-152 radios. • All radios have been loaded and configured with DOD-compatible channels and were distributed to RSO protective security teams. • This recommendation is complete.	GAO agrees with the State Department's assessment.

Recommendation	Status of Implementation as Reported by the State Department	GAO Comments
15. When the "Go Team" is not involved in investigating incidents, it should be employed in pattern analysis. The Diplomatic Security service in Washington should provide the RSO with a relational database to be used to review incidents and determine potential patterns. Such a database would include: Date and time of incident Destination and GPS coordinates GPS coordinates of incident Mission identifier Vehicle identification numbers Incident type Names of all security personnel involved and their assignments in the motorcade Such other details as would be useful. Data on each event would be input promptly after it occurs. Weekly reports should be generated to look for potential patterns that would call for systemic or individual changes	• Pattern analysis software was identified, tested, modified, and beta tested. • Software was tested locally through May 2008 and milestones were met. The software was deployed to Baghdad on June 19, 2008, and is undergoing various forms of testing with hardwire and encrypted radio networks. • Based on feedback from the field, deployment of the finalized version of pattern analysis software from headquarters with full operational capability is expected by December 2008.	According to State Department officials the software is currently being tested in Baghdad. However, officials could not provide documentation of any evaluations of the software, noting that the software testing and assessment continues.

16. The Embassy should use the venue afforded by the Iraqi-U.S. Joint Commission to establish a working group to determine ways to move the licensing process forward in an open and transparent way	• The Deputy Chief of Mission, Embassy Legal Advisor, RSO, and MNF-I have been involved in discussions with Iraqi officials concerning private security company licensing and registration processes. • Currently the Iraqi licensing process involves the Ministries of Interior and Trade. Security company licenses must be renewed every six months. Worldwide Personal Protective Services (WPPS) contractors Triple Canopy and DynCorp are currently licensed by the central government in Baghdad. Blackwater has submitted an application for a license, which is currently pending. • The Department's actions have met the intent of the recommendation. This recommendation is complete.	We disagree with the State Department's assessment. While State Department officials stated that they have had numerous conversations with Iraqi officials regarding the licensing and registration of PSCs in Iraq, the process is still ongoing and officials were unable to provide formal documentation of the discussions. According to the State Department in its view this recommendation has been completed because it established the working group and it was not necessary to have improved the licensing process to consider the recommendation implemented. We believe that implementation of the recommendation is still in progress.
17. The Regional Security Officer should establish direct channels to senior Iraqi police and security officials in Baghdad and in any other city where Provincial Reconstruction Teams are located. This should be a major step towards providing information on incidents in a timely way so that they can be appropriately investigated.	• The RSO had multiple meetings with senior Iraqi officials at the National Police, Ministry of Interior, and Ministry of Defense and developed working agreements on coordination, liaison, and mutually supportive engagement. • RSO personnel serving at Regional Embassy Offices and Provincial Reconstruction Teams have also established relations with local Iraqi police and security officials. • This recommendation is complete.	GAO agrees with the State Department's assessment.

Recommendation	Status of Implementation as Reported by the State Department	GAO Comments
18. In order to be more responsive to Iraqi customs, the Embassy must actively seek out the families of those innocent Iraqi civilians killed or seriously injured, or those whose property has been damaged by personal protective services personnel. The Regional Security Office "Go Team", assisted by the U.S. military unit responsible for the area in which an incident has occurred, should work with counterparts designated by the Government of Iraq to promptly offer appropriate condolences and compensation.	• As part of the investigative process, the RSO coordinates with MNF-I and the Government of Iraq to facilitate victim access to the Embassy Claims Program. • This recommendation is complete.	GAO agrees with the State Department's assessment. However, our interviews with PSCs with contracts with the State Department found that they were unaware that the Embassy Claims Program existed.

Source: State Department; GAO Analysis.

Appendix III: Comments from the Department of Defense

DEPUTY UNDER SECRETARY OF DEFENSE FOR
LOGISTICS AND MATERIEL READINESS
3500 DEFENSE PENTAGON
WASHINGTON, DC 20301-3500

JUL 28 2008

Mr. William M. Solis
Director, Defense Capabilities and Management
U.S. Government Accountability Office
441 G Street, N.W.
Washington, DC 20548

Dear Mr. Solis:

This is the Department of Defense (DoD) response to the GAO draft report GAO - 08-996, "REBUILDING IRAQ: DoD and State Department Have Improved Oversight and Coordination of Private Security Contractors in Iraq, but Further Actions are Needed to Sustain Improvements," dated July 8, 2008 (GAO Code 351234). We welcome your assistance in improving how the DoD and its contractors can plan for and effectively execute contracts in a complex and changeable security environment. Enclosed are DoD's detailed comments regarding the recommendations on page 31 of your draft report.

We appreciate the opportunity to review and comment on your findings.

Sincerely,

Jack Bell

Jack Bell

Enclosure:
As stated

GAO DRAFT REPORT - DATED JULY 8, 2008
GAO CODE 351234/GAO-08-996

"REBUILDING IRAQ: DoD and State Department Have Improved Oversight and Coordination of Private Security Contractors in Iraq, but Further Actions are Needed to Sustain Improvements"

DEPARTMENT OF DEFENSE COMMENTS TO THE RECOMMENDATIONS

RECOMMENDATION 1: The GAO recommends that the Secretary of Defense develop and implement a strategy to fill authorized positions for the Joint Contracting Command-Iraq/Afghanistan and Defense Contract Management Agency (DCMA).

DOD RESPONSE: Concur. We have initiated a strategy, based on current and projected delegated workload, to deploy 220 personnel by 15 December 2008. Underpinning this strategy is the recent hiring of Emergency Essential employees, current volunteer efforts, and the continued support by the Services to source the Joint Manning Document.

RECOMMENDATION 2: The GAO recommends that the Secretary of Defense direct the Service Secretaries to update the information being provided on PSCs at unit mission-rehearsal exercises and pre-deployment training to include information regarding the operations of the Armed Contractor Oversight Division and the Contractor Operations Cells along with the role of military units in providing contract oversight, incident investigation, and Private Security Contractor (PSC) coordination procedures.

DOD RESPONSE: Concur. DoD is actively incorporating contractors and contract support into the exercise schedules.

RECOMMENDATION 3: The GAO recommends that DoD fully implement their 2005 recommendation by including information on Private Security Contractors (PSC) typical operating procedures and the military's responsibilities to PSCs.

DOD RESPONSE: Concur. DoD continues to swiftly improve its procedures through the rapid dissemination of changes to CENTCOM FRAGO 07-428, *'Overarching FRAGO For Requirements, Procedures, Responsibilities For Control Coordination And Management And Oversight of Armed Contractors DoD Civilian and PSCs'*, which was last updated on July 17, 2008.

Appendix IV: Comments from the Department of State

Note: GAO comments supplementing those in the report text appear at the end of this appendix.

United States Department of State

Assistant Secretary for Resource Management and Chief Financial Officer

Washington, D.C. 20520

JUL 24 2008

Ms. Jacquelyn Williams-Bridgers
Managing Director
International Affairs and Trade
Government Accountability Office
441 G Street, N.W.
Washington, D.C. 20548-0001

Dear Ms. Williams-Bridgers:

We appreciate the opportunity to review your draft report, "REBUILDING IRAQ: DOD and State Department Have Improved Oversight and Coordination of Private Security Contractors in Iraq, but Further Actions are Needed to Sustain Improvements," GAO Job Code 351234.

The enclosed Department of State comments are provided for incorporation with this letter as an appendix to the final report.

If you have any questions concerning this response, please contact Paul Ginsburg, Program Analyst, Bureau of Diplomatic Security at (571) 345-2742.

Sincerely,

B. Higgins

Bradford R. Higgins

cc: GAO – William Solis
DS – Eric Boswell
State/OIG – Mark Duda

Department of State Comments on GAO Draft Report

REBUILDING IRAQ: DOD and State Department Have Improved Oversight and Coordination of Private Security Contractors in Iraq, but Further Actions are needed to Sustain Improvements
(GAO-08-966, GAO Code 351234)

The Department of State (DOS) thanks the Government Accountability Office (GAO) for the opportunity to respond to their draft report resulting from the August 9, 2007, notification letter to review private security contractors in Iraq. In addition to oversight enhancements discussed in this document, the State Department and Bureau of Diplomatic Security (DS) have increased and realigned staff to enhance Post's oversight responsibilities as follows.

- Two in-country Contracting Officer Representatives (CORs) for the Baghdad Embassy Security Force (BESF).
- A third COR at Headquarters assists with the administrative aspects of the contract to include a weekly meeting with the contractor, monthly invoice reviews, and liaison between the Contracting Officer and in-country CORs, and when requested, personnel deployment to assist the in-country CORs with their responsibilities.
- Two in-country CORs in support of the Worldwide Personal Protective Services (WPPS) Iraq task orders who are supported by two CORs at Headquarters that assist with the administrative aspects of the contracts to include weekly meetings with the contractors, monthly invoice reviews, and liaison between the Contracting Officer and in-country CORs.
- The Department increased its staffing by eight personnel to assist with compliance issues, invoice approval, and the Synchronized Pre-Deployment and Operational Tracking System for the WPPS contracts. In support of contract oversight, DS is hiring six additional training instructors to enhance oversight of contractor training.

Comments

Highlights

"The State Department has **completed more than half** of 18 actions recommended in October 2007 by **the Secretary's** panel tasked with

2

reviewing that agency's use of private security contractors in Iraq. **Three (3) recommendations are dependent on other agencies or governments and those remaining will be completed by December 2008."**

See Comment 1.

- **The phrase "begun implementing" is misleading to the extent it sounds like DOS has not actually completed any of the actions. The Department requests this phrase be corrected and information added in the *Highlights* section and on pages 4, 9, and 17.**

Page 2

"On September 16, 2007, an incident **in Nisour Square** involving a PSC firm working for the Department of State resulted in the deaths of Iraqi civilians in Baghdad."

See Comment 2.

- **This is an ongoing DOJ investigation and the number of casualties is not definitive. If GAO wishes to use a specific number, it should provide the source of that information or include a footnote noting the range of reported numbers.**

Pages 5 and 24

"Whether a particular law provides extra-territorial jurisdiction over a criminal act by a PSC contractor depends on the specific facts of the incident, such as the time, nature, and location of the alleged crime, **nature of the contractors' employment,** and the nationality of the accused."

See Comment 3.

- **The Department requests that factors listed regarding whether a particular law applies should include "the nature of the contractors' employment" as this is a very relevant factor to UCMJ and MEJA jurisdiction.**

Page 19

See Comment 4.

"**Since** the Nisour Square incident, DOD and the **DOS have significantly enhanced** communication **and** coordination on the departments' efforts related to PSCs in Iraq, and **both** DOD **and DOS are** coordinating with the Government of Iraq on issues related to PSCs on a regular basis."

3

Pages 24 – 26

See Comment 5.

- **The Department is concerned that the 18 USC 7(9) -- added to the Special Maritime and Territorial Jurisdiction (SMTJ) statute as part of the PATRIOT ACT -- is only mentioned in Footnote 28, but not in the section discussing SMTJ itself. 18 USC 7(9) is a significant source of extra-territorial jurisdiction that may potentially apply in the context of a crime by a PSC in Iraq or elsewhere. By contrast, the discussion of the case law interpreting SMTJ prior to 2001 seems to be of less importance than the current state of the jurisdiction and might be best discussed in a footnote.**

See Comment 6.

- **The description of 18 USC 7(9) in footnote 28 is misleading and suggests there is a major loophole in the law, but the statute essentially exempts people who are *already* subject to MEJA (in other words, giving preference to MEJA as the source of jurisdiction).**

Page 30

"The improvements DOD and DOS have made may reduce the number of **PSC incidents** in Iraq, however, it may not eliminate incidents."

- **The Department believes the more relevant question is whether the PSC incidents are minimized to the extent possible and, if they do occur, are they handled appropriately.**

See Comment 7.

- **The term "PSC incidents" is used without defining what that term means and in a way that sets up a false standard. If the term refers to any instance involving use-of-force, then the DOS goal would be to minimize them rather than eliminate them, as PSCs are authorized to use force under specific conditions. If "PSC incidents" refers to negative incidents involving use-of-force, then again, it seems unfair to suggest that they could ever be eliminated in this context.**

Page 39

Appendix II

4

- **The Department requests revisions to this entire narrative based on comments and technical corrections provided below.**

Recommendation 1 - Status of Implementation

- **The Department requests this section be replaced with the following.**

    - **The Department of State's Office of the Legal Adviser has actively engaged with an interagency working group, led by the Department of Justice, to work with Congress on legislation clarifying the Military Extraterritorial Jurisdiction Act (MEJA) in order to hold USG private security contractors overseas accountable for offenses.**
    - **The Department of Justice is taking the lead on further discussions of this issue with Senate staff.**
    - **The Department of State's Office of the Legal Adviser will stay engaged in this process until legislation is passed.**
    - **The Department's actions have met the intent of the recommendation. This recommendation is complete.**

See Comment 8.

Page 40

Recommendation 2: "The Department of State should work with the Department of Defense to determine how to commence discussions with the Government of Iraq on a new regulatory framework for PPS contractors."

Recommendation 2 - GAO Comment: "The negotiations of the Status of Forces Agreement and a Strategic Framework Agreement are still being negotiated. Therefore, we believe that implementation of the recommendation is still in progress."

See Comment 9.

- **The Department must register disagreement with GAO's interpretation of Recommendation 2. This recommendation is specifically worded not to require DOS to create or negotiate a new regulatory framework, but merely to "commence discussions" with the Government of Iraq on the subject, which has been done. It would not be proper to hold this**

5

- **recommendation open, given that it depends on the actions of another sovereign nation.**
- **The Department's actions have met the intent of the recommendation. This recommendation is complete.**

Recommendation 3 - GAO Comment: "Although State Department officials told us that funding for the positions was in the FY2008 supplemental request and that they would ask for funding in the Department's FY2010 base budget, the Department indicated it was not included in the FY2009 supplemental request currently being considered by Congress."

See Comment 10.

- **The FY2008 Supplemental Appropriations Act provides funding for the 4th quarter of FY2008 and all of FY2009. The positions have been regularized in the Department's FY2010 budget request.**
- **This recommendation is complete.**

Recommendation 5 - Status of Implementation

See Comment 11.

- **The Department requests the addition of a 4th bullet indicating this recommendation is complete.**

Page 41

Recommendation 9 - Status of Implementation

See Comment 12.

- **The Department requests this section be replaced with the following.**
    - **To date, video recording systems have been installed into 140 mission vehicles throughout Iraq. The remaining installations have been funded and are planned for completion by December 2008.**
    - **Each protective mission now includes a vehicle with video recording capability.**
    - **Protective vehicle video camera installations have been institutionalized. All new vehicles are now being hard-**

6

wired for video recording capability in the assembly line process.

- The radio recording system in the RSOs Tactical Operations Center is operational, and all Embassy radio transmissions are recorded.
- Post implemented long-term recording of all Blue Force Tracker (BFT) data. BFT data is stored on external hard drives, expanding retention capabilities.
- This recommendation is complete.

Page 42

Recommendation 10 - Status of Implementation

See Comment 13.

- **The Department requests this section be replaced with the following.**
  - **The intent of Recommendation 10 is to ensure that Private Security Contractors (PSC) can be easily identified, located, and held accountable for their actions should it be required. The technical systems and procedural measures implemented by the Regional Security Officer (RSO) place Chief of Mission motorcades in full compliance with the scope of the recommendation.**
  - **Currently, COM motorcade movements are tracked and monitored real-time by State Department personnel utilizing BFT and Tapestry. COM motorcade radio communications are recorded and monitored by RSO personnel in the RSO TOC. Motorcade vehicles are equipped with video cameras that record and document motorcade movements and events. These technical measures combined with reporting requirements and established operational procedures allow for COM motorcades to be monitored and held accountable.**
  - **This recommendation is complete.**

Recommendation 11 - Status of Implementation

7

- **The Department requests this section be replaced with the following.**

    - **The RSO established a dedicated Go Team, referred to as the Force Investigation Unit (FIU), and reached an agreement with MNF-I for military security support for investigators as needed.**
    - **The Go Team is currently staffed with 2 full-time DS Special Agents who are augmented by 4 DS Special Agents assigned to the Investigations and Intelligence section. When the need arises this group is augmented by Special Agents from other sections of the RSO office.**
    - **Since January 2008, the Go Team has investigated 49 motor vehicle accidents and 52 escalations of force incidents involving Tier 1 and Tier 2 contractors -- of those 35 were pen flares and 13 were discharge of firearms incidents.**
    - **To expand and augment the Go Team, DS awarded a contract on May 22, 2008, to provide additional investigators and translators.**
    - **Six investigators and 2 translators have been hired and are now in training. They depart for Iraq on July 27, 2008.**
    - **This recommendation is complete.**

See Comment 14.

Page 44

Recommendation 15 - Status of Implementation

- **The Department requests this section be replaced with the following.**

    - **Pattern analysis software was identified, tested, modified, and Beta tested.**
    - **Software was tested locally through May 2008 and milestones were met. The software was deployed to Baghdad on June 19, 2008, and is undergoing various forms of testing with hardwire and encrypted radio networks.**
    - **Based on feedback from the field, deployment of the finalized version of pattern analysis software from**

See Comment 15.

8

headquarters with full operational capability is expected by December 2008.

Page 45

Recommendation 16 - Status of Implementation

- **The Department requests this section be replaced with the following.**
  - **The DCM, Embassy Legal Advisor, RSO, and MNF-I have been involved in discussions with Iraqi officials concerning private security company licensing and registration processes.**
  - **Currently the Iraqi licensing process involves the Ministries of Interior and Trade. Security company licenses must be renewed every six months. WPPS contractors Triple Canopy and DynCorp are currently licensed by the central government in Baghdad. Blackwater has submitted an application for a license, which is currently pending.**
  - **The Department's actions have met the intent of the recommendation. This recommendation is complete.**

See Comment 16.

The following are GAO's comments on the State Department's letter dated July 24, 2008.

GAO Comments

1. The State Department commented that it had completed more than half of the 18 recommendations made by the Secretary of State's panel. The department noted that three of the recommendations were dependent on other agencies or governments and the remaining recommendations would be completed by December 2008. In appendix II of the report, we note the State Department's assessment on the status of implementation for each of the panel's 18 recommendations. This information is presented verbatim from information provided by the State Department. We also added an acknowledgement in the report that the State Department has implemented 11 of the 18 recommendations made by the panel.

2. We revised the report to attribute the number of Iraqi civilian deaths caused by the September 16, 2007, incident to the report of the Secretary of State's Panel on Personal Protective Services in Iraq.

3. We revised the report to include "nature of the contractor's employment" among the factors that could affect whether a particular law provides extraterritorial jurisdiction in a specific case.

4. While DOD and the State Department have improved communication and coordination related to PSCs in Iraq, we have no basis to state that these improvements are significant.

5. The report was revised to accept the suggested change.

6. We are unclear how the language in footnote 28 is misleading or suggests a loophole in 18 U.S.C. 7(9). We did change the language as suggested by the State Department to clearly state that "the statute essentially exempts people who are already subject to MEJA (in other words, giving preference to MEJA as the source of jurisdiction)."

7. The State Department misinterpreted our conclusions. Our statement that the improvements made by DOD and the State Department may reduce, but not necessarily eliminate, incidents is intended to demonstrate that regardless of the level of oversight provided, in places with tenuous security situations such as Iraq, incidents involving PSCs may still occur. As we noted in our conclusions, a strengthened framework of PSC oversight and coordination in Iraq will enable the U.S. government to be better prepared to respond effectively when incidents do occur.

8. While we incorporated the requested updated information into the status of implementation column of recommendation 1, we disagree that the State Department has completed implementation of the recommendation.

The State Department noted that the department's Office of the Legal Advisor was actively engaged in this manner through an interagency working group led by the Department of Justice. However, the effort to establish a clear legal basis for holding contractors accountable under U.S. law is still ongoing. Therefore, we assert that this recommendation has not been implemented.

9. The State Department commented that it disagreed with our assertion that the status of implementation of recommendation 2 should be cited as in progress. In its comments the department noted that the recommendation was worded not to require that the State Department create or negotiate a new regulatory framework, but to merely "commence discussions" with the Government of Iraq on this subject. While negotiations with the Government of Iraq are ongoing on a Status of Force Agreement and a Strategic Framework Agreement, it is our assertion that implementation will be complete when an agreement is reached.

10. Based on additional information provided to by the State Department we have changed our assessment of the status of this implementation to "GAO agrees with the State Department's assessment."

11. While we have incorporated the requested updated information into the status of implementation column of recommendation 5, we disagree that the State Department has completed the implementation of this recommendation. We assert that fully implementing the recommendation means that the additional personnel should be recruited, trained, and deployed to Iraq, a process that has not happened yet. Therefore, we believe that implementation of the recommendation is still in progress.

12. The State Department requested that we incorporate updated information into the status of implementation column of recommendation 9. While we updated the column, we disagree that the State Department has completed the implementation of this recommendation because not all of the department's vehicles have been outfitted with the video recording systems as recommended by the panel. According to the State Department, to date the equipment has been installed in 140 of the 233 vehicles it intends to place this equipment in. The State Department noted that it expects this process to be completed by December 2008. As such our assessment of the status of implementation is that implementation is ongoing.

13. While we have incorporated the requested updated information into the status of implementation column of recommendation 10, we disagree that the State Department has completed the implementation of this recommendation. As noted in appendix II, the panel recommended that the State Department place a readable number on the right rear door of each vehicle utilized, to enable anyone wishing to question its mode of operation to identify the unit to the Regional Security Office. The systems and

measures being implemented by the State Department may assist the monitoring of these vehicles by U.S. government officials. However, these systems do not enable any person, such as an Iraqi citizen standing on a street corner, to identify the unit to the Regional Security Office.

14. We incorporated the requested updated information into the status of implementation column for recommendation 11. Based on this additional information we now agree with the State Department that the recommendation has been implemented.

15. We incorporated the requested updated information into the status of implementation column for recommendation 15.

16. While we incorporated the requested updated information into the status of implementation column of recommendation 16, we stand by our initial assertion that the recommendation is ongoing and therefore not complete. According to information provided by the State Department, officials from the department have had numerous conversations with officials from the government of Iraq regarding the licensing and registration of PSCs in Iraq and had established a working group. However, officials were unable to provide a written account for these discussions when asked and stated that it considered the recommendation completed because the intent of the recommendation was to start holding talks and not to have necessarily improved the licensing process.

GAO's Mission

The Government Accountability Office, the audit, evaluation, and investigative arm of Congress, exists to support Congress in meeting its constitutional responsibilities and to help improve the performance and accountability of the federal government for the American people. GAO examines the use of public funds; evaluates federal programs and policies; and provides analyses, recommendations, and other assistance to help Congress make informed oversight, policy, and funding decisions. GAO's commitment to good government is reflected in its core values of accountability, integrity, and reliability.

Obtaining Copies of GAO Reports and Testimony

The fastest and easiest way to obtain copies of GAO documents at no cost is through GAO's Web site (www.gao.gov). Each weekday, GAO posts newly released reports, testimony, and correspondence on its Web site. To have GAO e-mail you a list of newly posted products every afternoon, go to www.gao.gov and select "E-mail Updates."

Order by Mail or Phone

The first copy of each printed report is free. Additional copies are $2 each. A check or money order should be made out to the Superintendent of Documents. GAO also accepts VISA and Mastercard. Orders for 100 or more copies mailed to a single address are discounted 25 percent. Orders should be sent to:

U.S. Government Accountability Office
441 G Street NW, Room LM
Washington, DC 20548

To order by Phone:	Voice:	(202) 512-6000
	TDD:	(202) 512-2537
	Fax:	(202) 512-6061

To Report Fraud, Waste, and Abuse in Federal Programs

Contact:

Web site: www.gao.gov/fraudnet/fraudnet.htm
E-mail: fraudnet@gao.gov
Automated answering system: (800) 424-5454 or (202) 512-7470

Congressional Relations

Ralph Dawn, Managing Director, dawnr@gao.gov, (202) 512-4400
U.S. Government Accountability Office, 441 G Street NW, Room 7125
Washington, DC 20548

Public Affairs

Chuck Young, Managing Director, youngc1@gao.gov, (202) 512-4800
U.S. Government Accountability Office, 441 G Street NW, Room 7149
Washington, DC 20548

DOCUMENT NO. 6

CONTRACTORS' SUPPORT OF U.S. OPERATIONS IN IRAQ

CBO Report

August 2008

Notes:

All dollar amounts are in 2008 dollars.

Unless otherwise indicated, all years referred to in this report are federal fiscal years.

Numbers in the text and tables may not add up to totals because of rounding.

Obligations are a legally binding commitment by the federal government that will result in outlays, immediately or in the future.

Preface

Contractors play a substantial role in supporting the United States' current military, reconstruction, and diplomatic operations in Iraq. That support has raised questions regarding the costs, quantities, functions, and legal status of contractor personnel working in the Iraq theater.

This Congressional Budget Office (CBO) paper, which was prepared at the request of the Senate Committee on the Budget, examines the use of contractors in the Iraq theater from 2003 through 2007. It provides an overview of the federal government's costs of employing contractors in Iraq and in nearby countries, the type of products and services they provide, the number of personnel working on those contracts, comparisons of past and present use of contractors during U.S. military operations, and the use of contractors to provide security. CBO also investigated the command-and-control structure between the U.S. government and contract employees and the legal issues surrounding contractor personnel working in Iraq.

This paper was prepared by Daniel Frisk and R. Derek Trunkey of CBO's National Security Division under the supervision of J. Michael Gilmore and Matthew Goldberg. Adam Talaber contributed to the analysis, and Adebayo Adedeji and Victoria Liu provided additional assistance. Robert Dennis, Theresa Gullo, and Frank Sammartino provided helpful comments. Robert Murphy reviewed the section on legal issues, as did Jennifer Elsea of the Congressional Research Service. Victoria A. Greenfield, a professor at the United States Naval Academy, reviewed the entire study. (The assistance of external reviewers implies no responsibility for the final product, which rests solely with CBO.)

Sherry Snyder edited the study, and Loretta Lettner proofread it. Cindy Cleveland produced drafts of the manuscript. Maureen Costantino prepared the report for publication and designed the cover. Lenny Skutnik printed the initial copies, Linda Schimmel handled the print distribution, and Simone Thomas prepared the electronic version for CBO's Web site (www.cbo.gov).

Peter R. Orszag
Director

August 2008

Contractors' Support of U.S. Operations in Iraq

Introduction and Summary

Contractors play a substantial role in supporting the United States' current military, reconstruction, and diplomatic operations in Iraq, accounting for a significant portion of the manpower and spending for those activities. The Congressional Budget Office (CBO), at the request of the Senate Committee on the Budget, has studied the use of contractors in the Iraq theater to support U.S. activities in Iraq.[1]

This paper, which covers the period from 2003 through 2007, provides an overview of the federal costs of employing contractors in Iraq and in nearby countries, the type of products and services they provide, the number of personnel working on those contracts, comparisons of past and present use of contractors during U.S. military operations, and the use of contractors to provide security. CBO also examined the command-and-control structure between the U.S. government and contract employees and the legal issues surrounding contractor personnel working in Iraq.

[1] For this study, the Congressional Budget Office considers the following countries to be part of the Iraq theater: Iraq, Bahrain, Jordan, Kuwait, Oman, Qatar, Saudi Arabia, Turkey, and the United Arab Emirates. CBO found that in-theater contracts to support operations in Iraq were almost entirely performed in those countries, all of which are located within the U.S. Central Command's area of operations.

The findings of CBO's study include the following:

- From 2003 through 2007, U.S. agencies awarded $85 billion in contracts for work to be principally per formed in the Iraq theater, accounting for almost 20 percent of funding for operations in Iraq. (Dollar amounts in this paper are in 2008 dollars.) More than 70 percent of those awards were for contracts per formed in Iraq itself.
- The Department of Defense (DoD) awarded contracts totaling $76 billion, of which the Army (including the Joint Contracting Command—Iraq/Afghanistan) obligated 75 percent. The U.S. Agency for International Development and the Department of State obligated roughly $5 billion and $4 billion, respectively, over the same period.
- Contractors provide a wide range of products and services in-theater. Most contract obligations over the 2003–2007 period were for logistics support, construction, petroleum products, or food. The contract for the Army's Logistics Civil Augmentation Program (LOGCAP) is the largest one in the Iraq theater, with obligations totaling $22 billion.
- Although personnel counts are rough approximations, CBO estimates that as of early 2008 at least 190,000 contractor personnel, including subcontractors, were working on U.S.-funded contracts in the Iraq theater. Just under 40 percent of them are citizens of the country where the work is being performed (primarily Iraq); about 20 percent are U.S. citizens.
- The United States has used contractors during previous military operations, although not to the current extent. According to rough historical data, the ratio of about one contractor employee for every member of the U.S. armed forces in the Iraq theater is at least 2.5 times higher than that ratio during any other major U.S. conflict, although it is roughly comparable with the ratio during operations in the Balkans in the 1990s.

Private security contractors have been a particular focus of attention. CBO finds that:

- Total spending by the U.S. government and other contractors for security provided by contractors in Iraq from 2003 through 2007 was between $6 billion and $10 billion, CBO estimates. As of early 2008, approximately 25,000 to 30,000 employees of private security contractors were operating in Iraq. Those contractors worked for the U.S. government, the Iraqi government, other contractors, and other customers.
- The costs of a private security contract are comparable with those of a U.S. military unit performing similar functions. During peacetime, however, the private security contract would not have to be renewed, whereas the military unit would remain in the force structure.

Regarding the legal issues associated with contractor personnel, CBO finds that:

- Military commanders have less direct authority over the actions of contractor personnel than over their military or civilian government subordinates. Contractors' duties are set out in their contract, which is managed by a government contracting officer, not the military commander.
- The legal status of contractor personnel in Iraq is uncertain, particularly for those who are armed. Contractor personnel are potentially subject to a number of laws and jurisdictions, including the Uniform Code of Military Justice, the Military Extraterritorial Jurisdiction Act of 2000, the Special Maritime and Territorial Jurisdiction Act of the United States, and the USA Patriot Act. However, there have been few tests in courts of how those laws apply to contractors.

Costs, Functions, and Numbers of Contractor Personnel in the Iraq Theater

Using available data, CBO assessed the costs of in-theater contractor support for operations in Iraq and summarized the primary types of products and services they provide. CBO estimated the number of contractor personnel working for the United States in the Iraq theater and compared the current ratio of contractor to military personnel with that of previous conflicts. CBO also estimated the costs and numbers of contractor personnel providing security, including those working as subcontractors. Such personnel are referred to in this paper as private security contractors (PSCs).

The U.S. Government's Obligations for Contracts Principally Performed in the Iraq Theater

From 2003 through 2007, U.S. government agencies obligated a total of $85 billion for contracts principally performed in the Iraq theater, CBO estimates.[2] In-theater support for operations in Iraq occurred in multiple countries, including $63 billion of obligations for contracts principally performed in Iraq, $14 billion for contracts principally performed in Kuwait, and $8 billion for contracts principally performed in other nearby countries (see the top panel of Figure 1). New obligations for contracts performed in the Iraq theater have totaled about $17 billion to $21 billion annually since 2004.[3]

---

[2] Principal place of performance is defined as "the location of the principal plant or place of business where the items will be produced, supplied from stock, or where the service will be performed." If more than one location is involved, the principal place of performance is the location where the most dollars are spent. See *FPDS-NG User's Manual*, Version 1.0 (May 2006), p. 23, www.fpds.gov.

[3] Because this paper focuses on Iraq, CBO's estimate excludes about $10 billion in obligations for contracts performed in Afghanistan over the 2003–2007 period.

Figure 1: The U.S. Government's Obligations for Contracts Performed in the Iraq Theater, 2003 to 2007

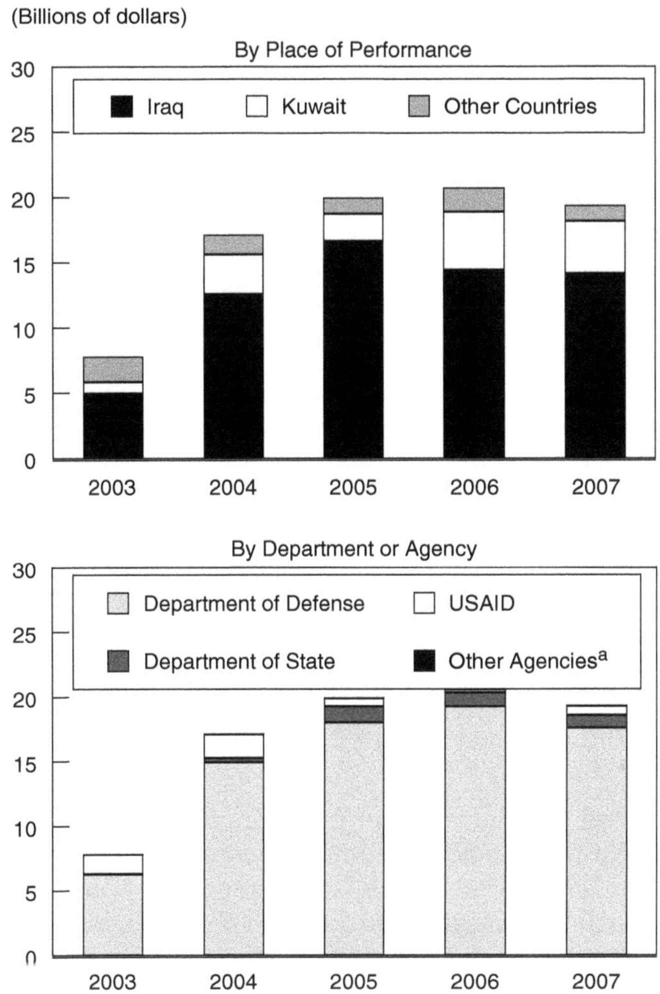

Source: Congressional Budget Office based on data from the Federal Procurement Data System—Next Generation and the Joint Contracting Command—Iraq/Afghanistan.

Notes: For this study, the Congressional Budget Office considers the following countries to be part of the Iraq theater: Iraq, Bahrain, Jordan, Kuwait, Oman, Qatar, Saudi Arabia, Turkey, and the United Arab Emirates.

USAID = U.S. Agency for International Development.

[a] Includes the Departments of Agriculture, Commerce, Health and Human Services, the Interior, Justice, Transportation, and the Treasury, as well as the Broadcasting Board of Governors and the General Services Administration. Obligations of other agencies totaled $113 million or less in each year.

The $85 billion in obligations for contracts performed in the Iraq theater accounts for almost 20 percent of the $446 billion of U.S. appropriations for activities in Iraq from 2003 through 2007 (CBO 2008, p. 7, converted to 2008 dollars). However, the $85 billion estimate does not capture the total share of U.S. spending on Iraq that goes to contractors. CBO's estimate excludes the costs of contracts supporting operations in Iraq that are performed in countries outside the Iraq theater, including the United States (such as the manufacture of mine-resistant ambush-protected vehicles, or MRAPs, and any of the other military equipment used in the Iraq theater).

CBO's estimates come with additional qualifications and assumptions. First, the accuracy and completeness of the available data on procurement directly influence the accuracy of CBO's estimates of contract obligations (see Box 1). Second, the Department of Defense is the only U.S. government agency employing significant numbers of contractor personnel who support operations in Iraq but are located elsewhere in the Iraq theater; CBO's estimates therefore exclude all non-DoD contracts performed outside Iraq. Third, CBO assumed that some of DoD's contract obligations supported programs and facilities located in the Iraq theater that existed before the war, such as the Incirlik Air Base in Turkey. The estimates of obligations to support operations in Iraq exclude that prewar level of contracting effort, about $1.5 billion annually.[4] Last, CBO assumed that all of DoD's obligations above prewar amounts for contracts performed in Bahrain, Jordan, Kuwait, Oman, Qatar, Saudi Arabia, Turkey, and the United Arab Emirates were to support operations in Iraq but not those in Afghanistan or elsewhere.

DoD's obligations for contracts performed in the Iraq theater are substantially larger than those made by other agencies (see the bottom panel of Figure 1). DoD's $76 billion in obligations represents almost 90 percent of all dollars awarded from 2003 through 2007 for such contracts. Of that amount, $54 billion was for contracts performed in Iraq, $14 billion was for contracts performed in Kuwait, and $8 billion was for contracts performed in other nearby countries. The U.S. Agency for International Development (USAID) and the Department of State (DoS) obligated $5 billion and $4 billion, respectively, for contracts in Iraq over the same period.[5] Other U.S. departments and agencies obligated a total of less than $300 million. That category includes the Departments of Agriculture, Commerce, Health and Human Services, the Interior, Justice, Transportation,

[4] In Saudi Arabia, average annual contract obligations made before the war were larger than those made after operations in Iraq began. Consequently, CBO's estimates exclude all obligations for contracts performed in Saudi Arabia.

[5] USAID is an independent federal agency but reports to the Secretary of State. Part of USAID's budget is managed jointly with the Department of State.

and the Treasury, as well as the Broadcasting Board of Governors and the General Services Administration.

Within DoD, the Department of the Army is by far the largest obligator of funds for contracts in the Iraq theater (see Figure 2). The Army awarded $57 billion for such contracts from 2003 through 2007. The Departments of the Air Force and the Navy (which includes the Marine Corps) awarded $6 billion and $1 billion, respectively. Defensewide agencies obligated an

Box 1. The Federal Procurement Data System—Next Generation

The Congressional Budget Office's (CBO's) estimates of federal contract obligations are largely based on data collected from the Web-based Federal Procurement Data System—Next Generation (FPDS-NG).[1] It is the only government wide system that tracks federal spending on procurement. Federal Acquisition Regulations require executive departments and agencies to report all unclassified procurement data to FPDS-NG shortly after a contract has been awarded. The FPDS-NG database allows queries based on dozens of contract parameters, including the name of the department or agency awarding the contract, the dates on which the contract was signed and completed, a description of the products or services in the contract, the vendor's name, and the principal place where the contract will be performed. FPDS-NG is continually updated; CBO obtained most of the data used in this paper by querying the database in April 2008.

FPDS-NG has some limitations. A number of organizations—including the Government Accountability Office, the RAND Corporation, and the Acquisition Advisory Panel—have issued reports that criticize the accuracy of procurement data contained in FPDS-NG.[2] Among their concerns were the timeliness of the availability of data, inaccuracies in the data due to human or technological errors, and a lack of detail in how products and services in the contract were classified. Those reports also highlighted difficulties that the Department of Defense (DoD)—the largest contracting entity in the government—was experiencing in attempting to electronically interface with FPDS-NG.

1. The Federal Procurement Data System—Next Generation and its associated documentation are available at www.fpds.gov.

2. Government Accountability Office, *Improvements Needed to the Federal Procurement Data System-Next Generation*, GAO-05-960R (September 27, 2005); Lloyd Dixon and others, *An Assessment of Air Force Data on Contract Expenditures* (Santa Monica, Calif.: RAND Corporation, 2005); Acquisition Advisory Panel, *Report of the Acquisition Advisory Panel to the Office of Federal Procurement Policy and the United States Congress* (January 2007). The panel's report also provides a history of the Federal Procurement Data System.

Continued

Box 1. The Federal Procurement Data System—Next Generation

The General Services Administration (the executive agency responsible for FPDS-NG) and the Office of Management and Budget have recently taken steps to improve the quality of the data in FPDS-NG. Nearly all government offices, including most of those within DoD, now send data to FPDS-NG via a machine-to-machine interface with their systems for writing contracts, reducing the possibility of human error. (That interface does not address any deficiencies with agency-unique databases that feed into FPDS-NG, however.) All agencies are required to certify the data they report in FPDS-NG and to submit plans for improving the quality of their data.[3] DoD, the last agency to certify, provided an interim confirmation of its 2007 data in April 2008.

In light of those apparent improvements, and because no other government wide procurement databases exist, CBO determined that FPDS-NG was the most comprehensive and accessible source of data on federal contract obligations in Iraq. Although FPDS-NG may contain some inaccuracies in the details of individual contracts, CBO's analysis is based on aggregated data, so errors should be relatively small in the context of billions of dollars of reported obligations. CBO did not audit the FPDS-NG data used in this report.

One important exception to FPDS-NG's reporting requirements is the Joint Contracting Command—Iraq/Afghanistan (JCC-I/A). In part because of limitations on Internet bandwidth, JCC-I/A currently provides information to FPDS-NG in a bulk fashion, rather than reporting individual contract actions as they occur.[4] As of June 2008, JCC-I/A had not yet reported all of its 2007 procurement actions to FPDS-NG; CBO collected those data directly from JCC-I/A.

3. Office of Management and Budget, "Improving Acquisition Data Quality—FY 2008 FPDS Data" (memorandum from Paul A. Denett, Administrator, Office of Federal Procurement Policy, to chief acquisition officers, senior procurement executives, and small agency council members, May 9, 2008).

4. JCC-I/A uses its own system, the Joint Contingency Contracting System, to maintain a current record of its contracts. See Joint ContractingCommand—Iraq/Afghanistan, *Acquisition Instruction* (December 15, 2007), p. 18.

additional $12 billion over that period, primarily for contracts awarded by the Defense Logistics Agency.

The Army's obligations have been much larger than those of the other DoD services for two reasons. Most U.S. military personnel (roughly 125,000 of the 200,000 total military personnel in Iraq as of December 2007) are Army service members. In addition, contracts awarded by the Joint Contracting Command—Iraq/Afghanistan (JCC-I/A) are attributed to the Army because that command operates under the Army's acquisition authority.

Figure 2: The Department of Defense's Obligations for Contracts Performed in the Iraq Theater, by Department or Agency Awarding the Contract, 2003 to 2007

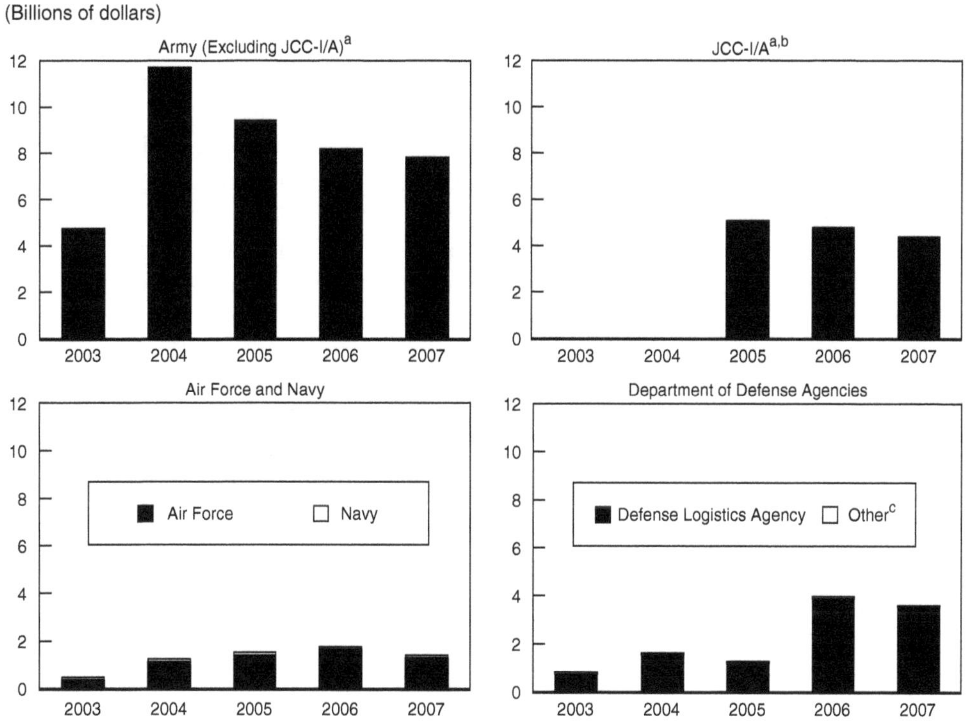

Source: Congressional Budget Office based on data from the Federal Procurement Data System—Next Generation and the Joint Contracting Command—Iraq/Afghanistan.

Note: For this study, the Congressional Budget Office considers the following countries to be part of the Iraq theater: Iraq, Bahrain, Jordan, Kuwait, Oman, Qatar, Saudi Arabia, Turkey, and the United Arab Emirates.

a. The Joint Contracting Command—Iraq/Afghanistan (JCC-I/A) operates under the Army's acquisition authority.

b. The Department of Defense formed JCC-I/A in 2005.

c. Obligations of other agencies within the Department of Defense totaled $93 million or less in each year.

JCC-I/A, a major subordinate command of Multi-National Force—Iraq, awards in-theater contracts to support coalition military forces as well as reconstruction and economic development in Iraq and Afghanistan. Those contracts typically address immediate needs and rely on the local vendor base.[6] Created in early fiscal year 2005, JCC-I/A obligated about $15 billion through 2007 for contracts performed in Iraq. The Department of the Navy's

[6] JCC-I/A also reviews all contracts for work in Iraq and Afghanistan to ensure that the correct terms and conditions are included in the contract language and that the contracted work is consistent with the plans of the in-country commander.

contract obligations have been low relative to its manpower presence in the Iraq theater, in part because the Marine Corps is receiving some logistics support through the Army's Logistics Civil Augmentation Program. (The Marine Corps reimburses the Army for support received from LOGCAP; FPDS-NG does not capture interagency contract agreements.)

LOGCAP is the Army's primary means of providing support services for military personnel.[7] Contractor personnel provide a wide range of services under LOGCAP, such as operating food service and dining facilities, storing and supplying ammunition, distributing fuel, maintaining equipment, and managing procurement and property. From 2003 through 2007, the Army obligated more than $22 billion to the LOGCAP contract for services rendered in the Iraq theater. CBO previously conducted a detailed analysis of LOGCAP, including a description of its functions and a comparison of the costs of contractor and military personnel to provide those services (CBO 2005). In that study, CBO determined that Army support units could perform LOGCAP tasks during wartime for virtually the same costs as contractors. During peacetime, however, the costs of contractors would be substantially lower than those of Army units.

Products and Services Provided by Contractors in the Iraq Theater

Contractors provide a wide variety of services and products in support of U.S. government agencies operating in the Iraq theater. Examples of services performed by contractors include logistics, construction, engineering and technical support, linguist services, economic development, humanitarian assistance, and security. Examples of products provided by contractors include food, fuel, vehicles, and communications equipment. Contractor personnel are involved in many aspects of U.S. operations in Iraq, with the notable exception of roles defined as "inherently governmental" or "military essential." Those roles, and the restrictions on services provided by contractors, are described later in this paper.

The Federal Procurement Data System—Next Generation (FPDS-NG) classifies contract functions using the North American Industrial Classification System (NAICS) and a system of product and service codes. Product and service codes, though still general, are more specific than NAICS in the context of government procurement.[8] Nonetheless, both systems of classification have weaknesses. Some experts claim that the functional categories

---

[7] The Army awarded LOGCAP III, contract number DAA09-02D-0007, to Kellogg Brown and Root, Inc., on December 14, 2001.

[8] The FPDS-NG Web site explains the benefit of having two classification systems: "The NAICS classifies commercial activity into broad service categories, e.g., farming, manufacturer, wholesaler, retail, services. Contracts, on the other hand, generally purchase specific goods (such as cameras or telephones) and services. Therefore, FPDS has a second set of codes called Products and Services Codes." See Question 16, www.fpdsng.com/questions.html .

lack sufficient specificity and are too broad to allow detailed analyses of procurement spending. In addition, FPDS-NG, which allows only a single product and service code and a single NAICS code for each contract, does not capture the diversity of functions that some contracts provide. Large umbrella contracts providing a range of services, such as the Army LOGCAP contract, are particularly affected by that shortcoming. Under a more precise classification system, agencies could select multiple codes to classify a contract. To be most useful, however, such a system would also require assigning a portion of that contract's obligations to each of its assigned product and service codes.

CBO's analysis of contractors' functions in the Iraq theater is also hindered by the fact that data on about $19 billion in contract obligations have not been categorized by function, have not been entered in the FPDSNG database, or both. Almost all obligations made by JCC-I/A and entered in FPDS-NG were coded under the nonspecific product and service code "miscellaneous" and the NAICS code "other general government support," even though those obligations were probably used to procure a wide but identifiable variety of products and services. In addition, contract data provided directly to CBO by JCC-I/A and USAID were neither recorded in FPDS-NG nor classified by function. Consequently, without investigating each of those uncategorized contract actions, CBO cannot classify the functions provided by about one-fifth of obligations for contracts performed in the Iraq theater over the 2003–2007 period.

Notwithstanding those limitations, grouping contracts by FPDS-NG product and service codes provides some insight into the breadth of work that contractors perform in the Iraq theater, as well as a rough indication of the functions that contractors most often provide (see Figure 3). From 2003 through 2007, U.S. government agencies obligated funds to perform 99 of 102 possible principal product and service codes.[9] Total obligations for each of those categories ranged from only a few thousand dollars to billions of dollars. CBO estimates that, on the basis of contract classifications in FPDS-NG, nearly 80 percent of categorized U.S. obligations for contractors' activities in the Iraq theater over that period were for services.

Eleven product and service codes (excluding the "uncategorized or miscellaneous" category) each received over $1 billion in contract obligations in the Iraq theater from 2003 through 2007. The category "professional, administrative, and management support" accounted for the largest share—nearly $26 billion, or about 30 percent of all obligations. Most obligations in that category have been in the subcategory "logistics support services," which primarily consists of the Army LOGCAP contract. To date, that

[9] For a complete list of product and service codes and their subcategories, refer to General Services Administration (1998).

Figure 3: U.S. Government Contracts Performed in the Iraq Theater, by Product and Service Code, 2003 to 2007

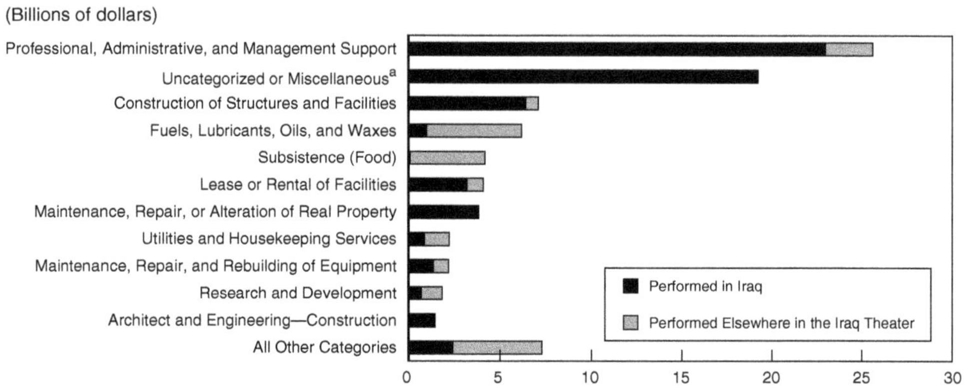

Source: Congressional Budget Office based on data from the Federal Procurement Data System—Next Generation and the Joint Contracting Command—Iraq/Afghanistan (JCC-I/A).

Note: For this study, the Congressional Budget Office considers the following countries to be part of the Iraq theater: Iraq, Bahrain, Jordan, Kuwait, Oman, Qatar, Saudi Arabia, Turkey, and the United Arab Emirates.

[a] Consists mostly of contracts awarded by JCC-I/A.

contract is the largest one performed in Iraq. Although logistics support is a reasonable, albeit broad, description of the LOGCAP contract, portions of that contract could also be classified under other categories, such as construction, equipment and property maintenance, subsistence (food), and housekeeping services.

Other categorized product and service codes accounted for much smaller shares of obligations. Over $7 billion was obligated for "construction of structures and facilities," primarily buildings in Iraq. "Fuels, lubricants, oils, and waxes" received over $6 billion, about three-quarters of which was used to purchase petroleum-based liquid propellants outside Iraq. Contracts for food; leasing or renting of facilities; and property maintenance, repair, or alteration each totaled nearly $4 billion. (Private security services, the costs of which have been considerably lower than those of the most heavily contracted functions, are distributed across several product and service codes.)

Counting and Tracking Contractor Personnel in the Iraq Theater

On the basis of data collected from DoD, DoS, and USAID, CBO estimates that at least 190,000 contractor personnel work in the Iraq theater on contracts funded by the United States.[10] The ratio of U.S.-funded contractor employees to members of the U.S. military in the Iraq theater is therefore

[10] CBO did not collect data on contractor personnel from other agencies because they represent a very small percentage of total contract obligations for work in the Iraq theater.

approximately 1 to 1. The 190,000 estimate includes personnel who work directly for the U.S. government as prime contractors and, to the extent possible, the personnel of subcontractors who work for other contractors. (Only DoD included subcontractor personnel in its data.)

About 20 percent (38,700) of all contractor personnel working in the Iraq theater are U.S. citizens (see Table 1). Local nationals, defined as citizens of the country in which they are working, and third-country nationals, who are neither U.S. citizens nor local nationals, each account for roughly 40 percent of the theater's contractor population (70,500 and 81,000, respectively). The majority of contractor personnel—at least 160,000—work in Iraq. DoD is the only U.S. agency employing significant numbers of contractor personnel who support operations in Iraq but are located in countries elsewhere in the Iraq theater, such as Kuwait.

DoD employs the bulk of contractor personnel in the Iraq theater, and its U.S. Central Command (CENTCOM) estimates the number of those personnel by means of a quarterly manual census of contractors. That census is a synthesis of headcounts at project and military sites across the theater. CENTCOM's census data categorize contractor personnel working in Iraq (but not in other countries within the Iraq theater) according to the service they provide and their nationality (see Figure 4). More than one-half of the estimated 149,000 DoD-funded contractor personnel in Iraq perform base support functions, and 20 percent provide construction services.

The Department of State also provided CBO with a categorization of its contractor personnel in Iraq based on job function (see Figure 5). As of late 2007, about 40 percent of the approximately 6,700 contractor personnel working for DoS in Iraq were providing security.

Counts of contractor personnel in Iraq and nearby countries are only rough approximations. Government agencies indicate that counting contractor personnel in-theater is a difficult task. The contracting effort to support operations in Iraq is extensive, involving hundreds of U.S., Iraqi, and international firms employing tens of thousands of people of various nationalities. Contract work is continuously awarded and completed as requirements dictate; numbers, nationalities, and functions of contractor personnel fluctuate over time. In addition, prime contractors may subcontract portions of their contract to other firms. Subcontracting may run several tiers deep, further decentralizing administration of the workforce and reducing the likelihood of an accurate tally of all contractor personnel. (CBO does not have an estimate of the percentage of federal obligations for contracts in Iraq that have been subcontracted.)

Although U.S. agencies attempt to closely account for contract obligations, their mechanisms for determining the number of nongovernment personnel have not been well established. Headcounts of contractor personnel have

Table 1. Number of Contractor Personnel Working in the Iraq Theater, by Department or Agency Awarding the Contract

		Nationality			
	Location	U.S. Citizens	Local Nationals	Third-Country Nationals	Total
Department of Defense[a]	Iraq	29,400	62,800	57,300	149,400
	Elsewhere in the Iraq Theater[b]	6,700	3,500	20,100	30,300
Department of State[c]	Iraq	2,300	1,300	3,100	6,700
U.S. Agency for Interna tional Development[d]	Iraq	200	2,900	300	3,500
Other Agencies[e]	Iraq	200	100	200	500
Total	**Iraq Theater**	**38,700**	**70,500**	**81,000**	**190,200**

Source: Congressional Budget Office based on data from U.S. Central Command, *2nd Quarter Contractor Census Report* (April 30, 2008); Department of State; U.S. Agency for International Development.

Notes: Estimates of numbers of personnel in Iraq and nearby countries are rough approximations; numbers, nationalities, and functions of contractor personnel continually fluctuate. Including subcontractors who work on contracts for the Department of State and the U.S. Agency for International Development would increase the totals.

For this study, the Congressional Budget Office considers the following countries to be part of the Iraq theater: Iraq, Bahrain, Jordan, Kuwait, Oman, Qatar, Saudi Arabia, Turkey, and the United Arab Emirates.

Local nationals are citizens of the country in which they are working. Third-country nationals are neither U.S. citizens nor local nationals.

a. Data include both prime contractors and subcontractors; they also include contractors working for the Army Corps of Engineers.

b. The Department of Defense is the only government agency with a significant number of contractor personnel who are supporting operations in Iraq but are located in countries elsewhere in the Iraq theater. Although CBO's estimates exclude contractor personnel working in Afghanistan, some personnel located in the Iraq theater may be supporting operations in Afghanistan.

c. The Department of State counts only prime contractors and was therefore unable to provide estimates of the number of subcontractors working on its contracts. The department's data do not include contractors working under its Personal Service Agreements (such individuals are treated as employees of the U.S. government).

d. The U.S. Agency for International Development (USAID) counts only prime contractors and was therefore unable to provide estimates of the number of subcontractors working on its contracts. Those data, collected in the summer of 2007, also exclude USAID grantees and an estimated 75,000 Iraqis (as of fall 2007) who were working on programs sponsored by USAID in Iraq.

e. Includes the Departments of Agriculture, Commerce, Health and Human Services, the Interior, Justice, Transportation, and the Treasury, as well as the Broadcasting Board of Governors and the General Services Administration. Data are CBO estimates using contract obligations from the Federal Procurement Data System—Next Generation.

Figure 4: Number of Contractor Personnel Working on Contracts in Iraq Funded by the Department of Defense, by Function and Nationality

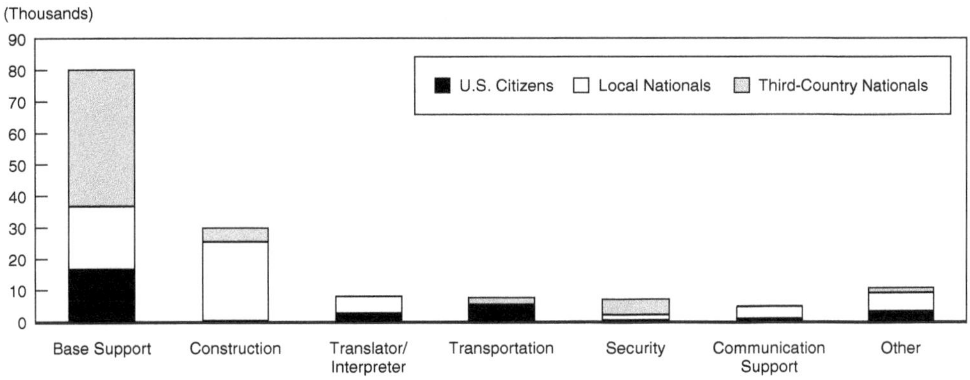

Source: Congressional Budget Office based on data from U.S. Central Command, 2nd Quarter Contractor Census Report (April 30, 2008).

Note: Data include people working for subcontractors.

typically been the responsibility of their employers. Increased use of performance-based contracting—a procurement model that emphasizes outcomes rather than specification of work processes—has further reduced the government's ability to know how many people are working on a given contract. (Performance-based contracts are described in Federal Acquisition Regulation (FAR), subpart 37.6.)

As operations in Iraq and elsewhere continue, however, government agencies have strengthened their efforts to account for contractor personnel.[11] DoD, for example, believes that the accuracy of the data in CENTCOM's quarterly census of contractors has improved since the census's inception in August 2006.[12] (According to DoD, the counts of contractor personnel are the most accurate for U.S. citizens and the least accurate for Iraqis.) DoD is also working to fully implement a Web-based system for tracking contractor personnel (known as the Synchronized Predeployment and Operational Tracker, or SPOT) before the end of calendar year 2008.

[11] Legislation has spurred improved tallying and tracking of contractor personnel in Iraq. For example, sections 815 and 854 of the National Defense Authorization Act for Fiscal Year 2007 (Public Law 109-364); section 3305 of the U.S. Troop Readiness, Veterans' Care, Katrina Recovery, and Iraq Accountability Appropriations Act, 2007 (Public Law 110-28); and section 861 of the National Defense Authorization Act for Fiscal Year 2008 (Public Law 110-181) have each required DoD to issue reports detailing the use of contractors operating in-theater and the policies that govern them.

For a detailed description of DoD's initiatives to improve its management of contractors accompanying the force, refer to Department of Defense (2007b); DoD (2008b).

[12] Although CENTCOM had collected six quarters of census data as of April 2008, trends in the number of contractor personnel are not meaningful because of low confidence in the accuracy of the early quarterly counts and inconsistencies in how the data have been collected. An increase in the number of contractors, for example, could be due to actual growth in the number of contract personnel in Iraq, more complete reporting, or a combination of both factors.

Figure 5: Number of Contractor Personnel Working on Contracts in Iraq Funded by the Department of State, by Function

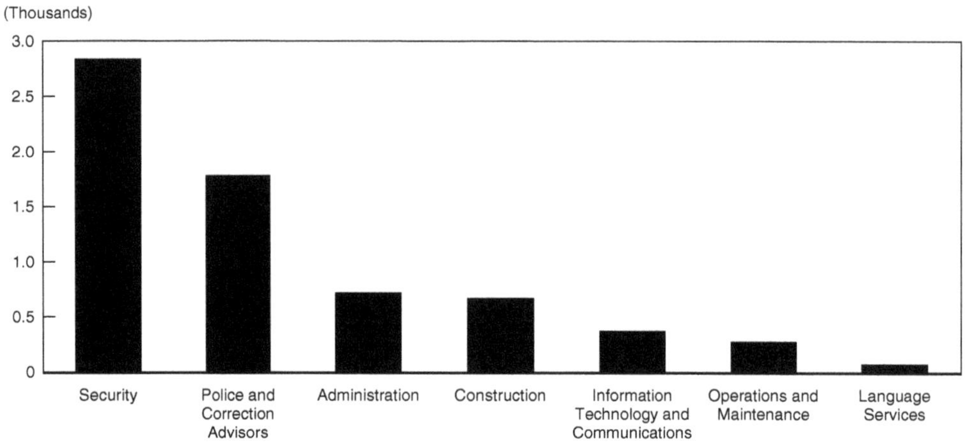

Source: Congressional Budget Office based on data from the Department of State.

Note: Data include U.S. citizens, local nationals, and third-country nationals; they exclude people working for subcontractors and people working under the Department of State's Personal Service Agreements (people in the latter group are treated as employees of the U.S. government).

A March 2007 update to the Defense Federal Acquisition Regulation Supplement (DFARS) requires contractors to report counts of their personnel into that system.[13] SPOT currently contains roughly half of the contractor personnel counted in CENTCOM's manual census, including all personnel of prime contractors employed on DoD's contracts to provide security, translator, and linguist services in Iraq (DoD 2008c). CENTCOM's manual counting will continue until SPOT is robust. When fully implemented, SPOT will track all contractor personnel working on both new and existing contracts that are funded by DoD, DoS, and USAID.[14]

Some Members of Congress have expressed concern that contractors' recruitment of government personnel is depleting the supply of specific in-demand skills and experience within the federal workforce (see, for example, House Committee on Armed Services, 2004). In particular, during the first few years of operations in Iraq, private security firms increased their size by drawing on former special operations forces for additional personnel. The Government Accountability Office (GAO) found in 2005, however,

[13] Refer to DFARS clause 252.225-7040. DFARS is a DoD supplement to the U.S. government's Federal Acquisition Regulation, which sets the policies and procedures for acquisition by all agencies in the executive branch.

[14] Section 861 of the National Defense Authorization Act for Fiscal Year 2008, Public Law 110-181, required DoD, DoS, and USAID to identify a common database for information on contracts and contractor personnel in Iraq and Afghanistan. SPOT has been selected as that database.

that the expanded use of private security contractors did "not appear to be increasing attrition among military personnel" (GAO 2005, p. 35). More recently, DoD officials have said that the hiring of experienced military and government personnel by contractors is not causing significant shortages of certain categories of military personnel at this time.[15] Because of a lack of data, CBO was unable to determine the number of contractor personnel who are former U.S. military or U.S. government civilians.

Comparing Past and Present Use of Contractors During Military Operations

Throughout the history of U.S. military conflicts, contractor personnel have worked alongside military and government civilian personnel in the theater of operations. The United States has hired contractors to perform noncombat functions beginning with the Revolutionary War and continuing to the present day.[16] Contractors typically provide services judged too menial or too specialized for government personnel to accomplish themselves. Those services generally fall under the following broad categories (Epley 1990):

- Transportation (moving people, supplies, and equipment);
- Engineering and construction (building and repairing bases, bridges, roads, railways, and communications systems);
- Maintenance (providing technical support for increasingly complex equipment);
- Base operations (providing food and housekeeping services on bases); and
- Medical (using civilian surgeons, nurses, and attendants).

Contractors continue to provide most of those services in-theater today, with the exception of medical support, almost all of which is now provided by military personnel. Contractors also perform some functions, such as security, that traditionally have been reserved for the military.

Although the use of contractors during military operations is well established, most experts agree that the scale of the deployment of contractor personnel in the Iraq theater (relative to the number of military personnel in the country) is unprecedented in U.S. history. Historical data on numbers of contractor personnel in-theater, though sparse and inexact, support that conclusion.[17] The current ratio of contractor to military personnel in

[15] Interview with officials from the Office of the Assistant Deputy Secretary of Defense (Program Support) and DoD's Office of the General Counsel, February 21, 2008, and follow-up communications.

[16] For a more detailed discussion of the support that contractors have provided during past contingency operations, see CBO (2005), Chapter 1. For the historical use of armed contractors, see Parks (2005) and Tabarrok (2007).

[17] CBO does not have historical data on numbers of contractor personnel used by DoS during earlier contingency operations. Other U.S. agencies, such as USAID, do not have a history of working in-theater until after military operations have ended.

the Iraq theater is 1 to 1—higher than it has been during any other major U.S. military operation (see Table 2). In the 1990s, however, U.S. operations in the Balkans illustrated the potential extent of the use of contractors during future conflicts. The ratio of contract to military personnel in the Balkans was also about 1 to 1, but those operations involved no more than 20,000 U.S. military personnel at any time, about one-tenth of the total in the Iraq

Table 2. Presence of Contractor Personnel During U.S. Military Operations

Conflict	Estimated Personnel (Thousands)		Estimated Ratio of Contractor to Military Personnel[a]
	Contractor[a]	Military	
Revolutionary War	2	9	1 to 6
War of 1812	n.a.	38	n.a.
Mexican-American War	6	33	1 to 6
Civil War	200	1,000	1 to 5
Spanish-American War	n.a.	35	n.a.
World War I	85	2,000	1 to 24
World War II	734	5,400	1 to 7
Korea	156	393	1 to 2.5
Vietnam	70	359	1 to 5
Gulf War	9[b]	500	1 to 55[b]
Balkans	20	20	1 to 1
Iraq Theater as of Early 2008[c]	190	200	1 to 1

Source: Congressional Budget Office based on data from William W. Epley, "Civilian Support of Field Armies," *Army Logistician*, vol. 22 (November/December 1990), pp. 30–35; Steven J. Zamparelli, "Contractors on the Battlefield: What Have We Signed Up For?" *Air Force Journal of Logistics*, vol. 23, no. 3 (Fall 1999), pp. 10–19; Department of Defense, *Report on DoD Program for Planning, Managing, and Accounting for Contractor Services and Contractor Personnel During Contingency Operations* (October 2007), p. 12.

Note: n.a. = not available.

a. For some conflicts, the estimated number of contractor personnel includes civilians employed by the U.S. government. However, because most civilians present during military operations are contractor personnel, the inclusion of government civilians should not significantly affect the calculated ratio of contractor personnel to military personnel.

b. The government of Saudi Arabia provided significant amounts of products and services during Operations Desert Shield and Desert Storm. Personnel associated with those provisions are not included in the data or the ratio.

c. For this study, the Congressional Budget Office considers the following countries to be part of the Iraq theater: Iraq, Bahrain, Jordan, Kuwait, Oman, Qatar, Saudi Arabia, Turkey, and the United Arab Emirates.

theater as of December 2007. The Army used the LOGCAP contract in the Balkans, and logistics support was also provided through the Balkans Support Contract.

The historically high ratio of contractor personnel to military personnel in the Iraq theater is the result of several factors. In response to reductions in the size of the post–Cold War military, DoD has augmented its force structure by relying more heavily on contractors for support functions, for example, through LOGCAP (CBO 2005, pp. 16–21). Those contractors perform functions in-theater that would otherwise require the deployment of additional military personnel. The extent of DoD's contracting is particularly evident during prolonged, large-scale operations—like those in Iraq—where there may not be enough military personnel available to provide logistics support.

More generally, the U.S. government has placed greater emphasis in recent decades on outsourcing activities to the private sector that are not inherently governmental. The government's policy is to subject services identified as commercial to the forces of competition.[18] In addition, the ratio of contractor personnel to military personnel reflects the United States' attempt to reconstruct Iraq while military activities are under way, rather than delaying rebuilding until hostilities have ended. As a result, that ratio includes thousands of contractor personnel associated with Iraq's reconstruction, not with military operations.

Private Security Contractors

Providing security for all personnel, including contractors, is an inescapable aspect of U.S. operations in Iraq because of the instability and violence in that country. Under current DoD policy in Iraq, the military provides security to contractors and government civilians only if they deploy with the combat force or directly support the military's mission (GAO 2005, p. 10).[19] Unless special arrangements are made, U.S. government agencies and contractors, such as reconstruction contractors, that do not meet that requirement must provide their own security. As a result, the use of contractors to provide security has increased—a well-publicized and controversial aspect of contractor support in Iraq.

Private security contractors, or PSCs (also referred to as private security companies), protect people and property in Iraq for U.S. agencies, the Iraqi government, and private businesses, namely, other contractors working in Iraq. Virtually all PSCs in the Iraq theater work in Iraq. They provide

[18] See Office of Management and Budget (2003) for federal policy on determining whether services should be provided by government or commercial sources.

[19] DFARS Procedures, Guidance, and Information, PGI 225.7402. The Army provides security for LOGCAP contractor personnel under that policy. The LOGCAP contract does not permit the hiring of subcontractors to provide security.

personal security details for high-ranking officials, security escorts for government and contractor personnel, security for convoys and at fixed sites, and advice and planning related to security (GAO 2005, p. 9).

Costs for Private Security Contractors and Subcontractors

CBO estimates that total spending by U.S. agencies and U.S.-funded contractors for private security services ranged between $6 billion and $10 billion over the 2003–2007 period. Between $3 billion and $4 billion of that spending was for obligations made directly by the U.S. government for private security services in Iraq.[20] The government's obligations for those services have amounted to roughly between $500 million and $1.2 billion annually since 2005. DoD, DoS, and USAID have awarded all of the U.S. government contracts for security services in Iraq. Since Iraq's transition to sovereignty, DoS's security contracts have also protected USAID employees, so USAID is not obligating new funds for PSCs in Iraq.

Contractors hired by the U.S. government that are not protected by the U.S. military generally hire PSCs as subcontractors to provide security. Neither FPDS-NG nor U.S. agencies explicitly track the costs of those subcontracts because those costs are not direct government obligations. Consequently, estimating the costs associated with subcontracts for security services in Iraq generates a wide range of values.

CBO estimates that U.S.-funded contractors spent $3 billion to $6 billion for subcontractors to provide security services over the 2003–2007 period. That spending makes up the balance of CBO's $6 billion to $10 billion estimate of total spending for those services. CBO calculated that range by first estimating the value of the government's service contracts performed in Iraq that required nonmilitary security. That estimate—$32 billion—is based on the assumptions that the military provides security for the LOGCAP contract, that contracts for products do not have significant security costs, and that JCC-I/A contracted for products or services at a ratio similar to that for all other in-theater contracts supporting operations in Iraq. CBO then determined that contractors spend between 10 percent and 20 percent of that $32 billion on security subcontracts.[21]

Costs for PSC Personnel Compared with a Military Alternative

A widely reported aspect of private security contractors is the perception that PSC personnel cost significantly more than equivalent military personnel.

[20] CBO's estimate, based on data from FPDS-NG and JCC-I/A, is a range because some obligations that may be for security contracts are not clearly categorized or described. Security services are distributed across several categories of product and service codes.

[21] For example, a $100 million contract would allocate between $10 million and $20 million for security. That range is based on information from Department of State (2006); GAO (2006); and discussions with officials of the Army Corps of Engineers.

For example, in Joseph Stiglitz and Linda Bilmes's estimates of the overall cost of the war in Iraq, they state that "In 2007, private security guards working for companies such as Blackwater and DynCorp were earning up to $1,222 a day; this amounts to $445,000 a year. By contrast, an Army ser geant was earning $140 to $190 a day in pay and benefits, a total of $51,100 to $69,350 a year."[22]

Those figures, however, are not appropriate for comparing the cost-effectiveness of contracting the security function or performing it using military personnel. The figure of $1,222 a day represents the contractor's billing rate, not the amount paid to the contractor's employees. The billing rate is greater than an employee's pay because it includes the contractor's indirect costs, overhead, and profit. A better comparison would involve estimating a soldier's "billing rate"—the total cost to the government of having a soldier fill a deployed security position for one year. Further, contractors generally bid various numbers of personnel in different labor categories, so focusing on a single labor category—such as the security guards—gives an incomplete picture of the total cost of providing security. A better comparison would also reflect all types of personnel as well as non-labor costs (such as vehicles and other equipment) that a security contractor includes in its bid.

CBO performed such an analysis, comparing the costs of a private security contractor with those of a military alternative. That analysis indicates that the costs of the private contractor did not differ greatly from the costs of having a comparable military unit performing similar functions. During peacetime, however, the military unit would remain in the force structure and continue to accrue costs at a peacetime rate, whereas the private security contract would not have to be renewed (see Box 2).

Number of PSC Personnel in Iraq

Reported tallies of the total number of PSC personnel in Iraq vary. In 2005, DoD estimated that at least 60 private security providers were operating in Iraq, with as many as 25,000 employees working for the U.S., Iraqi, and coalition governments, businesses, and other customers (GAO 2005, p. 8). The Private Security Company Association of Iraq (PSCAI), an industry association with 40 member companies, puts that number at about 30,000 in 2008. That estimate, which excludes some Kurdish areas where PSCAI

[22] See Stiglitz and Bilmes (2008), p. 12. Their figures appear to come from a memorandum to members of the House Committee on Oversight and Government Reform, *Additional Information About Blackwater USA* (October 1, 2007), http://oversight.house.gov/documents/20071001121609.pdf. The committee's report sources the contractors' figures to invoices from a particular contract that Blackwater had with the Department of State; the committee posted that information on its Web site (http://oversight.house.gov/story.asp?ID=1509 , accessed June 20, 2008). The report sources the military's figures to an online compensation calculator of the Department of Defense (subsequently moved to www.defenselink.mil/militarypay/pay/calc , accessed June 20, 2008).

Box 2. Costs of a Private Security Contract and a U.S. Military Alternativeb

The Congressional Budget Office (CBO) analyzed available information on a security contract between Blackwater and the Department of State for the one-year period beginning June 11, 2004. Because the terms of security contracts vary in the work to be performed and the qualifications of contractor personnel, the Blackwater contract is not necessarily representative of other security contracts.

Private Security Contractor Personnel

Nearly 80 percent of personnel on the Blackwater contract were bid as "protective security specialists" (PSS) and billed at $1,222 per day, or $1,325 in 2008 dollars. The contract included other types of personnel—those who supervise the PSS (such as project managers and detail leaders) and those who support their activities (such as administrative personnel and emergency medical technicians). Blackwater bid 314 operational positions and 7 positions in project management and administration but did not propose to fill every position every day; the contract would deliver 189 full-time equivalent (FTE) operational personnel. The contract also included about $1.7 million to lease nine personnel carriers (vehicles) and provide spare parts. Other equipment costs were not shown explicitly but were presumably rolled into the labor rates.[1] Finally, the contract included about $2.1 million for insurance, yielding a total cost of $99 million for the 189 FTEs for one year (in 2008 dollars, and excluding aviation support, which CBO did not analyze).

Military Personnel

To compare the costs of private security contractor personnel (PSCs) and military personnel, CBO assumed that an equivalent U.S. military force would be composed of units of light infantry (units not equipped with heavy armored vehicles). Using infantry as a substitute for PSCs is supported by the fact that U.S. Marines have traditionally provided infantry personnel to guard U.S. missions overseas; since 1986, however, private companies have also been allowed to compete for security contracts.[2] The differences between Marine and Army infantry units would not be relevant for performing a security mission; CBO assumed that the Army, because of its greater size, would be more likely to provide units to replace PSCs.

[1] Testimony of Erik D. Prince, chairman and CEO of Blackwater USA, before the House Committee on Oversight and Government Reform (October 2, 2007). Prince said, "They [the contractor personnel] need uniforms, equipment, body armor, boots, everything you wear from head to toe, their training, their travel, their insurance, [and] sometimes their food." See the preliminary transcript, p. 128, http://oversight.house.gov/story.asp?ID=1509.

[2] Omnibus Diplomatic Security and Antiterrorism Act of 1986, Public Law 99-399.

Box 2. Costs of a Private Security Contract and a U.S. Military Alternative

Typically, an Army unit would not be organized in the same way as a contractor's workforce. To calibrate the two, CBO identified a hypothetical Army unit that could deliver roughly the same 189 FTEs as Blackwater. The precise mix of personnel in the two workforces would differ because Army doctrine implies support elements in different proportions than those observed in Blackwater's contract. Delivering 189 FTEs would require about one-third of an Army light infantry battalion—a rifle company plus one-third of the battalion's headquarters company.[3] The headquarters company would include not only command elements but also medics, scouts, snipers, and others who functionally correspond to some of Blackwater's specialized personnel.[4]

Costs Included in the Analysis

CBO included three types of costs in its analysis: military personnel costs, operating costs, and equipment costs. The military pay rates ($140 to $190 a day) correspond to cash pay (basic pay, subsistence and housing allowances, plus a federal tax advantage because those allowances are not taxed) but exclude non-cash benefits, such as free health care for military families back home, and deferred benefits, such as pay and health care for those who receive military retirement benefits. Cash pay accounts for about half of total peacetime compensation for typical enlisted personnel.[5] CBO therefore roughly doubled cash pay when estimating annual personnel costs for the Army to perform functions in Iraq and then added the costs of providing special pays to deployed soldiers.[6]

---

[3] Such a battalion also has a weapons company, but security personnel would probably not need the additional heavy machine guns, grenade launchers, and antitank missiles that a weapons company provides.

[4] The typical soldier would be a corporal (pay grade E-4); virtually all soldiers of that rank have served for at least three years. All PSS contractor personnel have at least one year's experience in protective security work, which may have been gained in the Army or Marine Corps infantry or, alternatively, in other federal agencies such as the Federal Bureau of Investigation, Secret Service, or the Department of State (see statement of Richard J. Griffin, Assistant Secretary of State, Bureau of Diplomatic Security, before the House Committee on Oversight and Government Reform, October 2, 2007). Army infantry personnel would have much of the training required to perform the PSS function, except possibly in skills such as motorcade operations and evasive driving.

[5] Congressional Budget Office, *Evaluating Military Compensation* (June 2007), Table 2.

[6] Those special pays are Hostile Fire and Imminent Danger Pay, $225 a month; Hardship Duty Pay, $100 a month; and, for soldiers who have dependents and are away from their family for at least 30 consecutive days, Family Separation Pay, $250 a month.

Box 2. Costs of a Private Security Contract and a U.S. Military Alternative

	Cost of Army Infantry Units (Millions of 2008 dollars)					Blackwater's Costs (Millions of 2008 dollars)
		Case 1—1.2 Units in Rotation Base		Case 2—2.0 Units in Rotation Base		
Type of Cost	Deployed Units	Rotational Units	Total Cost	Rotational Units	Total Cost	
Military Personnel	21.8	24.9	46.6	41.5	63.2	
Operations	33.2	7.4	40.6	12.4	45.6	
Equipment	0.4	0.5	0.9	0.8	1.2	
Total Costs	**55.4**	**32.8**	**88.2**	**54.6**	**110.1**	**98.5**

Source: Congressional Budget Office based on Blackwater's invoice for contract S-AQMPD-04-D-0061.

The Army's goal is to have two units at home station (that is, in the rotation base) for each unit deployed overseas.[7] The time at home lets units recuperate from their deployment, reconstitute personnel and equipment, and train for their next deployment.[8] The Army, however, has not been achieving its rotation goal. CBO previously estimated that the ratio of units at home station to units deployed was 1.2 as of April 2007 (just before the "surge" in U.S. forces in Iraq), and the ratio has averaged about that value as far back as 2004.[9] To capture the costs of maintaining a rotation base for infantry units assigned to provide security in Iraq, CBO analyzed two cases: Case 1 adds the cost of 1.2 soldiers at home for each soldier deployed; Case 2 adds the cost of 2.0 soldiers at home. CBO included only peacetime costs for soldiers at home station, not wartime special pays.

Operating costs would be paid out of the Army's operations and maintenance (O&M) appropriation. CBO estimated O&M costs separately for the deployed unit and for the 1.2 or 2.0 units at home station.

[7] Statement of Richard Cody, Vice-Chief of Staff, U.S. Army, before the Subcommittee on Military Personnel of the House Committee on Armed Services (February 2, 2005). www.army.mil/leaders/leaders/vcsa/testimony/20050202.html.

[8] Blackwater deploys its security personnel to Iraq for at most 90 days, then flies them back to the United States; they must wait another 90 days before Blackwater will redeploy them. Blackwater does not pay its personnel during their 90-day layovers and therefore, unlike the Army, does not have an explicit rotation base. However, Blackwater implicitly maintains its workforce by paying its employees enough during their 90-day deployment that they can afford the layover. Those costs are captured by the in-theater billing rates in Blackwater's contract.

[9] Congressional Budget Office, *Some Implications of Increasing U.S. Forces in Iraq* (April 2007), Figure 1 and Table 1.

Box 2. Costs of a Private Security Contract and a U.S. Military Alternative

Finally, CBO assumed that equipment for the deployed unit, and its counterparts at home station, would have a useful life of 20 years. Thus, CBO amortized one-twentieth of the total equipment cost for a single year's operations.[10]

Comparison of the Estimated Costs

CBO estimated the Army's total costs at $88 million to maintain 1.2 units at home station and $110 million to have 2.0 units at home station for each deployed unit (see the table above). Those costs bracket Blackwater's total cost of $99 million to perform the same security function.

The costs of the two organizations would be different in peacetime. The Blackwater contract would not have to be renewed once the Iraq conflict ends, except possibly for a small retainer to allow Blackwater to maintain a capability to meet the demands for security in a future conflict. The Army units would stay in the force structure, although they would accrue costs at a peacetime rate without the wartime special pays or the elevated rate of O&M spending. CBO estimates the Army's annual peacetime cost at $60 million to maintain 2.2 units (where "unit" again represents about one-third of an Army light infantry battalion) and $82 million to maintain 3.0 units. During peacetime, however, the Army units need not devote themselves to security missions that parallel Blackwater's contract. Army infantry units can serve many other functions in peacetime or in other conflicts.

[10] If the Army added infantry units to its force structure, and particularly if this analysis was scaled to replace more than a single private security contract with infantry units, a large up-front outlay would have to be made to initially equip those units. CBO reports instead the recurring annual amortization to equip the units.

has no presence, includes approximately 5,000 U.S. citizens, 15,000 Iraqis, and 10,000 third-country nationals.[23]

Approximately 30 percent to 40 percent of PSC personnel work directly for the U.S. government as prime contractors. That share assumes that estimates of the total number of PSC personnel (25,000 to 30,000) are accurate. According to CENTCOM's April 2008 census of contractors, almost 7,300

[23] CBO phone interview with PSCAI in February 2008. Although PSCAI does not maintain a formal database of contractors, the association has frequent contact with its members and the Iraqi and coalition governments. One of PSCAI's functions is to help PSCs register with the Iraqi Minister of Interior and to verify that registry with U.S. contracting authorities. See PSCAI, www.pscai.org/moikrgreg.html , accessed February 26, 2008.

PSC personnel (including all nationalities) work on DoD-funded contracts or subcontracts. Nearly 3,000 additional PSC personnel (including all nationalities) work directly for DoS as prime contractors.[24] The remaining 15,000 to 20,000 work for the Iraqi government, other coalition governments such as Great Britain, or private companies. (CBO does not have estimates of how many PSC personnel work for each of those customers.) Among some of the larger non-U.S. employers are Baghdad International Airport, which employs approximately 1,000 PSC personnel, and the 43 diplomatic missions in Iraq (most of which hire private security contractors).

PSC Personnel Who Are Armed

Given the nature of their work, many PSC personnel are armed. CENTCOM's census reports that about three-quarters of the 7,300 PSC personnel working for DoD in Iraq carry weapons. A similar proportion of armed personnel probably holds for all other PSCs in Iraq.

The presence of armed contractor personnel—hired by various governments, agencies, and businesses—has created significant challenges for the United States in overseeing contractors and managing the combat zone in Iraq (GAO 2006). As events in that country have shown, the presence of armed contractors introduces the possibility of shooting incidents between contractor personnel and military or local civilian personnel. In response to those issues and to requirements instituted by the National Defense Authorization Act for Fiscal Year 2008, DoD and DoS signed a memorandum of agreement in December 2007 to jointly develop policies and procedures for vetting, training, and using PSC personnel.[25] Under that agreement, PSCs working for the U.S. government will follow common principles regarding the use of force, and details of all of their movements will be provided in advance to the appropriate military commander. The role of private security contractors in Iraq, including their possession and use of weaponry, has also generated questions about their legal status, as described in the next section.

---

[24] Meeting with DoS officials, November 2007. About 1,700 contractor personnel provide local guard services for DoS in Iraq. An additional 1,150 contractor personnel in Iraq work as bodyguards and provide security for fixed sites under DoS's Worldwide Personal Protective Services umbrella contract.

[25] Memorandum of Agreement (MOA) between the Department of Defense and the Department of State on USG [U.S. Government] Private Security Contractors (December 5, 2007), as required by section 862 of the 2008 defense authorization act. Section 861 of that act further requires DoD, DoS, and USAID to enter into a memorandum of understanding (MOU) by July 2008 that establishes policy, guidance, and regulations covering all contracts and contractor personnel in Iraq and Afghanistan.

Legal Issues Associated with Contractor Personnel Supporting U.S. Operations

The restrictions on how contractor personnel are used and the mechanisms by which they are controlled are different from the corresponding restrictions and mechanisms for uniformed military personnel or civilian government employees. Contractor personnel have a different legal status than government employees and are subject to different regulations and laws (both U.S. and international). Those differences have led some Members of Congress to express concern about using contractors as part of military operations—concerns that date back to the use of contractors in the Revolutionary War (Cahlink 2002; Continental Congress 1781, p. 591; GAO 2008b; Pincus 2008; Senate Committee on Armed Services 2007; Shrader 1999; Zamparelli 1999).

The legal issues regarding the government's use of contractors to support military operations are encapsulated in the following four questions:

- What restrictions are placed on the use of contractors?
- What authority does the U.S. military have over the actions of contractor personnel?
- What is the legal status of contractor personnel supporting military operations such as those in Iraq?
- What laws govern the actions of contractor personnel?

The Congress and the President have enacted legislation and DoD has changed its policies in response to problems and concerns that have arisen in recent military operations overseas, and that process is ongoing. This section discusses in greater detail several of the legal issues that have come to light under the framework of those four questions. The new laws and policies, and assertions of jurisdiction related to them, may be challenged in U.S. and international courts. Because of those potential challenges, CBO's assessment provides only tentative answers to some of the questions posed above.

Restrictions on the Use and Arming of Contractor Personnel

The federal government uses several approaches to identify which functions should be performed only by government personnel and which others may be contracted to the private sector.[26] The Federal Activities Inventory Reform Act of 1998 (FAIR) and guidance provided by the Office

[26] This section focuses on the types of functions that must be performed by government employees rather than on the broader question of which functions should be paid for by government funds. For example, building and repairing roads is a function often paid for by public funds but performed by private companies.

of Management and Budget require functions classified as "inherently governmental" to be performed by government personnel. Inherently governmental functions are those that are "so intimately related to the public interest" as to mandate performance by government personnel; such activities generally require either exercising sovereign government authority or establishing procedures and processes related to the oversight of monetary transactions (Office of Management and Budget 2003, p. A-2).[27] Applying those constraints, the Department of Defense characterizes some functions—those directly linked to the military's warfighting mission or requiring personnel who have recent hands-on experience in a military position—as "core" or "military essential" and may also reserve them for government personnel.[28]

DoD's core or military essential functions can be defined narrowly as those associated directly with the use of physical force (and thereby also meet the definition of inherently governmental as an exercise of sovereign government authority). However, the term "core" is sometimes used more broadly and subjectively to include functions less directly related to warfighting, such as those defined as "core business missions" of the Defense Business Transformation Agency (DoD 2008a) and "core depot maintenance" for weapon systems (DoD 2007a).[29] Those designations are sometimes applied to commercial-type functions that are required by law or policy to be performed by government employees. For example, federal law requires that DoD perform at least half its annual volume of depot maintenance activities at in-house facilities.[30] The difference between the two interpretations of core functions leaves ambiguous the classification of particular support functions, such as maintenance, and whether or to what extent having contractors perform such support functions is appropriate (CBO 1995, p. xi; GAO 2003, pp. 3, 11).

In instances in which the classification is ambiguous, additional factors must be considered to determine whether a particular function can or should be performed by contractors. Those factors include cost, risk, flexibility, the government's ability to draft an enforceable contract, and the availability of government employees (for example, in cases like Iraq, in which there may not be enough military personnel to perform logistics support) (Camm and Greenfield 2005, p. 56; CBO 2005, p. 32). In practice, most classifications based on the above criteria exclude certain functions that involve making financial or policy decisions, overseeing contractors, conducting offensive military operations, and performing police functions.

---

[27] Federal Activities Inventory Reform Act of 1998 § 5, 31 U.S.C. § 501 note.

[28] For one definition of "core," see DoD (2001), p. 53; for other definitions, see GAO (2003), p. 1. "Military essential" is defined in Camm and Greenfield (2005), p. 179.

[29] 10 U.S.C. § 2464.

[30] 10 U.S.C. § 2466.

Contractors, however, sometimes provide support to government personnel who perform those functions (GAO 2008a, p. 8).

The U.S. government often reserves certain functions, such as those involving a high risk of physical harm or the likely application of physical force, for uniformed law enforcement agencies (for example, federal marshals or customs agents) or for the military. There are many exceptions, however, including contractor personnel who accompany military forces, private bounty hunters, and security guards (Drimmer 2006, p. 734; Industrial College of the Armed Forces 2006, p. 2; Sklansky 1999, p. 1175). In a military operation like the current one in Iraq, contractor personnel performing logistics functions, such as driving trucks, may encounter enemy forces and be at risk of physical harm above and beyond what they would face in most domestic occupations (Debusmann 2007, p. 13).[31]

When DoD contractor personnel are at risk of physical harm, the Combatant Commander may authorize contractor personnel to be armed for self-defense (DoD 2005, sections 6.3.4 and 6.3.5).[32] The Combatant Commander must determine on an individual basis whether military forces can adequately protect contractor personnel, whether military protection is inadequate and contractor personnel need to be armed to provide for their safety, or whether the function is so dangerous that it should instead be performed only by military personnel. A condition for arming contractor personnel is that they must be eligible to possess weapons under U.S. laws or under the laws of their home nation. Eligibility mainly requires the lack of any felony convictions. Armed contractor personnel must also be trained in the proper use of weapons and must voluntarily accept weapons for self-defense. With the exception of contractor personnel performing certain security functions discussed in the next paragraph, DoD policy limits contractor employees to carrying a sidearm (a pistol). As of February 28, 2008, 638 contractor employees in Iraq and Afghanistan were armed in that manner for self-defense. About 200 DoD civilians have also been armed for self-defense.[33]

Additional issues arise for some types of contractor personnel, such as private security contractors, who perform functions that are similar to those of military combat forces (Northam 2007). When contractor personnel perform security functions, they may use small arms (with a caliber of 7.62 mm or smaller) similar to those used by infantry soldiers, but the contractors

[31] For a comparison of fatality rates for people in dangerous domestic occupations with rates for military personnel and logistics contractors in Iraq, see CBO (2005), p. 13.

[32] That policy applies to defense contractors, their employees, and subcontractors at all tiers who are authorized to accompany the U.S. armed forces.

[33] Interview with officials from the Office of the Assistant Deputy Under Secretary of Defense (Program Support) and DoD's Office of the General Counsel, February 21, 2008, and follow-up communications.

are subject to "rules of the use of force" that are more restrictive than the "rules of engagement" governing military forces.[34] Specifically, PSCs are not allowed to engage in any offensive military operations.[35] As of April 2008, 5,613 of DoD's 7,259 security contractor personnel in Iraq were authorized to be armed (U.S. Central Command 2008).

Under DoD policy, contractors may provide security for fixed-perimeter defenses and private convoys as well as perform some police functions.[36] Thus, PSCs are sometimes positioned in a defensive posture adjacent to military forces, and those contractors—as well as contractor personnel performing other support functions—may drive armored vehicles into areas subject to attack. DoD recognizes the potential for problems to arise when placing contractor personnel in a position in which they are likely to be physically harmed or need to employ force, but DoD relies on the discretion of commanders rather than a clear policy rule to guide the use of contractors in such cases. "Contracts [for security services] shall be issued cautiously in contingency operations where major combat operations are ongoing or imminent," and the security contractor personnel are not to guard military personnel or property unless authorized specifically by the Combatant Commander, an authority that cannot be delegated (DoD 2005, section 6.3.5). A local commander may also restrict the movement of security contractor personnel according to the threat level.

Military Authority Over Contractor Personnel

Although military commanders can directly control the actions of military personnel and government civilians, their control over individual contractor personnel is less direct. Military personnel are subject to criminal punishment if they fail to obey a lawful order from their military commanders (Turner and Norton 2001, p. 35).[37] Government civilians may fall under the control of military commanders either permanently or temporarily during a conflict, but only under extraordinary circumstances would they be subject to administrative actions, such as suspension or termination, if they failed to obey an order (Turner and Norton 2001, p. 35). Military commanders may

[34] *Ibid.* For other statutory restrictions on using contractors to perform security functions, see 10 U.S.C. § 2465. Additional policy guidance in implementing those restrictions is found in Army Materiel Command (2000), p. 40–1; DoD (2006b); Office of Management and Budget (2003), p. A-3.

[35] DoD policy also prohibits using contractors as mercenaries. See Army Materiel Command (2000), p. 40–2; 73 Fed. Reg. 16764-16765 (2008). Security contractor personnel are not generally considered mercenaries because their mission is to protect property and personnel, not to overthrow governments or undermine the order of the state. See De Wolf (2006), p. 323.

[36] Interview with officials from the Office of the Assistant Deputy Under Secretary of Defense (Program Support) and DoD's Office of the General Counsel, February 21, 2008, and follow-up communications; DoD (2006b); Elsea and Serafino (2007), p. 12.

[37] Applying the Uniform Code of Military Justice to contractor personnel could mean criminal prosecution for disobeying an order, but that would be an unusual case. (Interview with officials from the Office of the Assistant Deputy Under Secretary of Defense (Program Support) and DoD's Office of the General Counsel, February 21, 2008, and follow-up communications.)

change the daily tasks and duties of military and civilian DoD employees within the usual military chain of command, subject broadly to the laws and regulations of the United States.[38] In practice, that authority enables the military commander to allocate the personnel under his or her command among any number of tasks those personnel are able and trained to do. The military commander may also request that additional personnel be reassigned from other parts of the government if necessary.

By contrast, the duties of contractor personnel are set out in a fixed written contract (DoD 2005, section 6.1.4; Vernon 2004, p. 369).[39] The military commander generally lacks the authority either to increase the scope (dollar value) of the contract or to change the contractor's duties except in ways anticipated in the contract language. However, using a task-order arrangement may enhance the flexibility of a contract by enabling the military com - mander to add new tasks, sometimes quickly, to an existing contract within overall resource bounds (Army Regulation 700-137, "Logistics Civil Augmentation Program (LOGCAP)," December 16, 1985; CBO 2005, p. 25; Wilkinson 2007, p. 259). Task orders are particularly useful if the types of functions can be anticipated but not their timing or precise quantity. The LOGCAP contract is a task-order contract.

The contracting officer is the official designee of the head of the agency for binding the government on matters related to a particular contract (DoD 2005, section 6.3.3).[40] Typically a civilian, the contracting officer is not always colocated with the military commander or the contractor personnel and may not even be within the theater of operations (Douglas 2004, p. 139). The contracting officer may not have access to the place of performance if that place is remote or dangerous or if it covers a large geographic area (GAO 2007). Instead, he or she may rely on a technical representative, usually a military officer on the staff of the military unit being supported and colocated with the contractor. The technical representative interacts frequently, sometimes daily, with the contractor about details of performance but not about the scope or size of the contract.[41] In one example that a security contractor provided to CBO, the technical representative often directed the location to which contractor personnel were assigned but did not determine the number of such personnel.

---

[38] The commander can only give orders that are consistent with the laws and regulations of the United States (*Manual for Courts, United States*, 2008 ed., www.usapa.army.mil/pdffiles/mcm.pdf, p. iv–24). The commander and employees may also be subject to local laws, depending on the content of treaties and status-offorces agreements.

[39] Contracts are also governed by the Federal Acquisition Regulation and the Defense FAR Supplement. The regulations governing contractor personnel authorized to accompany U.S. armed forces under contracts performed outside the United States were recently revised along with the standard contract provisions. See 73 Fed. Reg. 10943-10959 (2008) and 73 Fed. Reg. 16764-16777 (2008).

[40] FAR, 48 C.F.R. 1.602 (1995).

[41] DFARS, 48 D.F.R. 201.602 (1991).

The military commander has less direct authority over the actions of contractor employees than over military or government civilian subordinates. The contractor, not the commander, is responsible for ensuring that employees comply with laws, regulations, and military orders issued in the theater of operations. Short of criminal behavior by contractor personnel, the military commander has limited authority for taking disciplinary action (DoD 2005, section 6.3.3).

Legal Status of Contractor Personnel

The Laws of Armed Conflict (LOAC), primarily as embodied in the Third and Fourth Geneva Conventions, govern the status and treatment of people who come under the control of enemy forces engaged in a declared war or other armed conflict.[42] U.S. policy is to follow those laws even in cases in which they may not apply, but enemy forces, such as the insurgency forces in Iraq, might not follow them (DoD 2006a).[43] Thus, even if DoD contractor personnel in Iraq qualified for protection under the LOAC, they might not receive it. The nature of the hostilities in Iraq may change, however, and enemies in future conflicts may recognize the LOAC. Therefore, the distinctions in legal status under the LOAC are still an important consideration in using contractor and government civilian personnel in positions in which they are subject to risk of capture. This section looks at distinctions in legal status and how that status changes when contractor and government civilian personnel are armed.

General Distinctions in Legal Status. The legal status of contractor personnel is not only different from that of military or government civilian personnel but is also subject to less agreement among legal scholars (CBO 2005, p. 12). It also depends on many factors such as their nationality, the phase of military operations, where they work, and what type of work they do (Davidson 2000; Elsea 2007, p. 7; Parks 2005; Rivkin and Casey 2008; Turner and Norton 2001, p. 24; Vernon 2004).

Under the LOAC, legal status determines whether personnel in a particular group can be targeted legitimately by enemy forces; how they should be treated if captured by enemy forces; and who would have the legal jurisdiction to punish their behavior if they committed offenses against the laws, regulations, or policies of the United States, the country where the work was performed, or international agreements (Vernon 2004). DoD has issued policies regarding the legal rights and responsibilities of contractor

[42] Third Geneva Convention Relative to the Treatment of Prisoners of War, August 12, 1949, 6 U.S.T. 3316; Fourth Geneva Convention Relative to the Protection of Civilian Persons in Time of War, August 12, 1949, 6 U.S.T. 3516.

[43] For U.S. citizens who are captured and taken hostage, U.S. government policy is to "use every appropriate resource to gain" their safe return but will "make no concessions to individuals or groups" holding the hostages (Department of State 2002).

personnel, but some experts believe those policies are likely to face court challenges when DoD implements them (Elsea and Serafino 2007, p. 21).

Prisoner-of-War Status. Under the Laws of Armed Conflict, primarily as embodied in the Third Geneva Convention, the highest level of protection given to people who come under the control of enemy forces while engaged in a declared war or other armed conflict is called prisoner-of-war (POW) status. Uniformed military personnel, government civilians, and contractor personnel can all qualify for POW status under some conditions.[44] Most military personnel qualify if they meet the criteria for being a lawful combatant, but contractor and government civilian personnel generally have to remain noncombatants and carry appropriate identification cards (Army Materiel Command 2000, p. 11–2; Elsea 2007, p. 5; Turner and Norton 2001, pp. 25, 35). Under the LOAC, POW status affords protections such as humane treatment, the right to communications, and a safe return at the end of hostilities (Turner and Norton 2001, p. 66; Vernon 2004). Even when POW status does not apply, other provisions of the Geneva Conventions still call for some protections, such as humane treatment (Elsea and Serafino 2007).

Lawful Combatants. Lawful combatants are identified primarily by four criteria: clearly wearing particular types of uniforms or other distinguishing markings, carrying their weapons openly, operating under a clear command structure, and obeying the Geneva Conventions or other Laws of Armed Conflict. Military personnel, except for medical personnel and chaplains, usually qualify as lawful combatants under the Geneva Conventions, meaning that they are legitimate military targets of enemy forces.[45] They also obtain some immunity from prosecution for hostile actions taken during combat and receive POW status (Elsea 2007, p. 6). Contractor personnel are not classified as lawful combatants because they do not wear military uniforms and are not in the military chain of command.

Noncombatants. If contractor personnel take "no active part in hostilities," they probably qualify as noncombatants (Guillory 2001, p. 115). As such, they would not be legitimate military targets of enemy forces, although they might be injured or killed during a military action against a legitimate target.

[44] The details of those conditions are complex and often in dispute, and they do not have equal authority and effect. One important determination is the current state of hostilities and the nature of the parties (such as international war, civil war, or occupation). This discussion does not attempt to comprehensively address the subject, but it does point out some differences in the treatment of military, government civilian, and contractor personnel. For more information, see Adedeji and Rosen (2000); Army Sustainment Command, www.aschq.army.mil/gc/battle2.asp ; Davidson (2000); Elsea (2007); Parks (2005); Rivkin and Casey (2008); Rosky (2004); Turner and Norton (2001).

[45] Medical personnel and chaplains have separate protections. See the Geneva Convention Relative to the Treatment of Prisoners of War, August 12, 1949, 6 U.S.T. 3317, art. 33.

Illegal Combatants and Uncertain Status. The legal status of government civilians and contractor personnel performing functions closely linked to military operations— such as analyzing intelligence data, maintaining weapon systems, and resupplying forward-based forces—is less certain than that of contractor personnel performing purely commercial functions such as laundry or food services (Guillory 2001, pp. 134–136). Many contractor personnel deploy as systems technicians, helping to maintain, repair, and operate weapon systems. Others operate unmanned aerial vehicles that can provide reconnaissance or even fire weapons. Still others analyze intelligence data, which they may transmit in the form of targeting coordinates to unmanned aerial vehicles or other manned or unmanned platforms that fire weapons. Government civilians and contractor personnel performing such functions could be deemed to have taken an active part in hostilities, in which case they would no longer qualify as noncombatants. But they also do not meet the definition of a lawful combatant, and some experts argue that those personnel could be classified as illegal combatants and could be criminally prosecuted for actions taken during a conflict (Adedeji and Rosen 2000; Guillory 2001, pp. 134–136; Zamparelli 1999).[46] Illegal combatants are entitled to humane treatment, but they may be subject to more intensive interrogation than a POW and may not be entitled to be released after hostilities have ceased (Elsea 2007, pp. 19–43).

DoD's position is that most of its contractor personnel in Iraq are neither combatants nor noncombatants and that they fall into a special category called "civilians authorized to accompany the force" (DoD 2000, p. V-6; DoD 2005, section 6.1.1).[47] DoD's interpretation of the LOAC is that the combatant and noncombatant classifications apply only to military forces, but some experts disagree (Turner and Norton 2001, p. 30). According to DoD, civilians accompanying the force are entitled to some, but not all, protections afforded to noncombatants in addition to some protections afforded to combatants (McCullough and Edmonds 2004). For example, they qualify for humane treatment (and possibly POW status) yet may be subject to criminal prosecution under local laws for actions taken during the conflict (Davidson 2000, p. 245). Those contractor personnel are not legitimate targets of enemy forces, but the functions they perform are (Fortner 2000). For example, the equipment the personnel are using may be targeted, but not the personnel themselves.

The distinctions among combatant, noncombatant, civilian, and illegal combatant classifications for personnel working for the U.S. military may not have practical significance for a conflict like the current operation in Iraq.

[46] *Ex parte Quirin*, 317 U.S. 1, 31 (1942).

[47] Interview with officials from the Office of the Assistant Deputy Under Secretary of Defense (Program Support) and DoD's Office of the General Counsel, February 21, 2008, and follow-up communications.

Insurgency forces have not been following the Laws of Armed Conflict; for example, they have detonated explosives in public areas that are as likely to result in the death of noncombatants (including Iraqi civilians) as well as combatants. The issues raised in this section involving the status of contractors who are captured will matter only when the United States faces an enemy that recognizes the LOAC. Even if that occurs, many related issues are subject to different interpretations that will take time to resolve.

Distinctions in Legal Status When Armed. The legal status of government civilians and contractor personnel becomes even less certain when they are armed. The in-theater military commander may authorize them to be armed for their own protection or to use arms in security guard functions (DoD 2005, sections 6.3.4 and 6.3.5).[48] Even if those personnel shot at enemy forces in self-defense, their noncombatant status could be open to challenge (Guillory 2001; Turner and Norton 2001, p. 27). The distinction between performing security functions and taking "no active part in hostilities" may be ambiguous in an atmosphere of frequent attacks (Elsea and Serafino 2007, p. 13).

Laws Governing the Conduct of Contractor Personnel Supporting Military Operations

Contractor personnel are potentially subject to a number of sources of law and jurisdiction.[49] Determining which laws govern contractor personnel depends on a variety of factors, including citizenship, location, and the particular laws they may have broken. Recent changes to U.S. law may make it easier to apply U.S. jurisdiction to contractor personnel in Iraq, but attempts to apply that jurisdiction could lead to challenges in court (Elsea and Serafino 2007, p. 21; GAO 2008b, p. 28).[50]

Also, criminal jurisdiction is not exclusive to one country. In general, the concept of "dual sovereigns" means that in cases in which one sovereign (a foreign government, the U.S. government, or state government) has asserted jurisdiction, other sovereigns are not precluded from also attempting to assert jurisdiction.[51] However, because assertions of jurisdiction have thus far been rare, dual sovereignty has been only a theoretical consideration to date.

[48] DFARS, 48 C.F.R. 252.225-7040 (2005).

[49] This section does not address civil cases, such as contract cases against U.S. companies that may apply to contractors in Iraq.

[50] Even in the recent changes, jurisdictional holes remain for some types of crimes and some types of contractors—notably, DoD contractors who are working outside U.S. territory and not during a war or contingency operation. Contractors working for agencies other than DoD who do not provide support to DoD's mission would also not fall under U.S. jurisdiction.

[51] *United States v. Wheeler*, 435 U.S. 313, 317 (1978).

Iraqi and International Law. Contractor personnel who commit crimes in Iraq could be tried in local Iraqi courts or International Criminal Courts except for the immunity agreement that the United States obtained from the Coalition Provisional Authority (CPA) and the U.N. Security Council (Garcia 2008, p. 5).[52] The United States can waive that immunity but has chosen not to do so in any case thus far. The immunity, which also applies to contractors of other coalition partners, is set to expire in December 2008; the United States is negotiating to extend it (Byrne and McNett 2008).

Uniform Code of Military Justice. One type of jurisdiction that could be applied to contractor personnel is the Uniform Code of Military Justice (UCMJ), which outlines procedures for prosecuting members of the military who commit crimes in the United States or abroad.[53] Traditionally, DoD civilian and contractor personnel have been subject to the UCMJ only when they participate in a declared war or are "retired members of a regular component of the armed forces who are entitled to pay." Thus, retired service members serving as contractors or as government civilians may be subject to the UCMJ and could be court-martialed for criminal violations (Ives and Davidson 2003).

In 2006, Congress expanded the jurisdiction of the UCMJ over "persons serving with or accompanying an armed force in the field" to include times of a contingency operation.[54] Thus, the UCMJ may cover DoD contractor personnel in Iraq (Elsea and Serafino 2007, p. 20).[55] On March 27, 2008, DoD used that expanded jurisdiction to bring charges against a contractor employee accused of assault with a dangerous weapon against another contractor employee. The employee pleaded guilty to lesser charges at a court-martial on June 22, 2008. A military judge sentenced him to five months of confinement. That was the first conviction of a civilian under the UCMJ during the current operation in Iraq (Multi-National Corps—Iraq 2008). Using the UCMJ to prosecute civilians, even during a war, may generate constitutional challenges based on the standards of due process applicable to military courts.[56]

In addition to the offenses specified in the punitive articles of the UCMJ (articles 77 through 134) that apply to "any person" (not just military members), the UCMJ also incorporates the LOAC by reference.[57] Thus, civilians

---

[52] All CPA orders remain in effect until amended or rescinded by the Iraqi government. See De Wolf (2006), p. 349, note 118.

[53] 10 U.S.C. ch. 47.

[54] Section 552 of the John Warner National Defense Authorization Act for Fiscal Year 2007, Public Law 109-364.

[55] However, not all portions of the UCMJ apply to civilians. Some portions apply only to military personnel, such as the provisions covering desertion and absence without leave.

[56] On initial guidance, see DoD (2008c). On potential challenges, see Baker (2008); Elsea and Serafino (2007), p. 21; Gensheimer (2008).

[57] 10 U.S.C. § 818.

(including contractor personnel) subject to the UCMJ are also subject to the LOAC. Before the 2006 expansion of the UCMJ jurisdiction, however, the military lacked a general mechanism for trying DoD civilians or contractor personnel who were not retired service members for crimes committed during contingency operations.

Military Extraterritorial Jurisdiction Act of 2000. The Military Extraterritorial Jurisdiction Act of 2000 (MEJA) extended jurisdiction of the U.S. courts to DoD civilians or contractor personnel supporting DoD missions who commit a felony (an offense punishable by more than one year in prison) outside sovereign U.S. territory while accompanying U.S. forces (Elsea and Serafino 2007; GAO 2008b).[58] The defendants may be tried in federal court after being brought to the United States. MEJA jurisdiction applies only if civilians (including contractor personnel) have not been prosecuted by the host nation's legal system or under the UCMJ. It does not apply to civilians working for foreign governments or for federal departments or agencies other than DoD; it also does not apply to nationals of the host country (in this case, Iraq). For example, employees of security contractors working for the Department of State would not be subject to MEJA.

The statute has been used infrequently. Since enactment of MEJA in 2000 and through March 2008, DoD has referred 58 cases to the Department of Justice, 12 of which have been charged in federal court and one in state court (Department of Justice 2008; Singer 2004, p. 537).[59] Of those, 8 resulted in a conviction and 5 await trial.

Special Maritime and Territorial Jurisdiction of the United States. Certain federal criminal statutes govern actions in U.S. facilities overseas, including the premises of the U.S. military in foreign states that qualify as part of the special maritime and territorial jurisdiction (SMTJ) of the United States (Elsea and Serafino 2007, pp. 17–18). Examples of such statutes include those addressing murder, torture, and assault committed by or against U.S. nationals. The United States has also asserted jurisdiction over crimes committed against U.S. government property or personnel, regardless of where the crimes occur (Doyle 2007). The Department of Justice is responsible for prosecuting such crimes in U.S. courts. That jurisdiction has been used sparingly, but it was used recently to convict a Central Intelligence Agency contractor who assaulted a detainee in Afghanistan (Elsea and Serafino 2007, p. 18).

---

[58] 18 U.S.C. §§ 3261–3267.

[59] Interview with officials from the Office of the Assistant Deputy Under Secretary of Defense (Program Support) and DoD's Office of the General Counsel, February 21, 2008, and follow-up communications.

Other Statutes. Two recent statutes prescribing sanctions for offenses committed outside U.S. territory may also apply to civilians accompanying U.S. forces. The USA Patriot Act expanded extraterritorial jurisdiction in two ways.[60] First, it augmented the list of federal statutes that apply federal extraterritorial criminal jurisdiction, adding some computer-related crimes and the transportation of illegal drugs and explosives related to terrorism. Second, the act expanded the coverage of SMTJ to include the "premises of the United States diplomatic, consular, military, or other United States government missions or entities in foreign States" with respect to offenses committed by or against a citizen of the United States.

Another statute covering actions overseas is the War Crimes Act of 1996, as amended by the Military Commissions Act of 2006. That act provides that "whoever, whether inside or outside the United States, commits a war crime . . . shall be fined under this title or imprisoned for life or any term of years, or both, and if death results to the victim, shall also be subject to the penalty of death."[61] The law applies to members of the U.S. armed forces as well as to any U.S. citizen, regardless of his or her employment. It would not apply to contractor personnel who are not U.S. citizens.

[60] Pub. L. 107-56, 115 Stat. 272 (2001), codified in various sections of 18 U.S.C.
[61] 18 U.S.C. § 2441.

References

Adedeji, Adebayo M., and Mark E. Rosen. 2000. *Outsourcing on Aircraft Carriers: An Idea Whose Time Has Come*. CMR D000119 A2. Alexandria, Va.: CNA Corporation, March.

Army Materiel Command. 2000. *Contracts and Contractors Supporting Military Operations*. AMC-P 715-18. June.

Baker, Melinda. 2008. "Military Law on Trial: The First Civilian Contractor to Be Prosecuted Under UCMJ Since Vietnam." *Journal of International Peace Operations*, vol. 3, no. 6 (May–June), p. 21.

Byrne, John, and Gavin McNett. 2008. "U.S. Quietly Demands Iraq Give Defense Contractors, U.S. Military Immunity from Prosecution." *The Raw Story*. January 25. http://rawstory.com.

Cahlink, George. 2002. "Army of Contractors." *Government Executive Magazine*. February 1. www.govexec.com/features/0202/0202s5.htm.

Camm, Frank, and Victoria A. Greenfield. 2005. *How Should the Army Use Contractors on the Battlefield: Assessing Comparative Risk in Sourcing Decisions* (Santa Monica, Calif.: RAND Corporation).

(CBO) Congressional Budget Office. 1995. *Public and Private Roles in Maintaining Military Equipment at the Depot Level*. July.

——. 2005. *Logistics Support for Deployed Military Forces*. October.

——. 2008. *The Budget and Economic Outlook: Fiscal Years 2008 to 2018*. January.

Continental Congress. 1871. *Journals of the Continental Congress, 1774–1789*. Ed. Worthington C. Ford and others (vol. 11, June 1778, p. 591). Washington, D.C., 1904–1937. http://memory.loc.gov/ammem/amlaw/lwjclink.html .

Davidson, Michael J. 2000. "An Introduction to the Legal Issues Associated with Civilian Contractors on the Battlefield." *Public Contract Law Journal*, vol. 29 (Winter), pp. 233–263.

Debusmann, Bernd. 2007. "In Outsourced U.S. Wars, Contractor Deaths Top 1,000." Reuters. July 3. www.reuters.com/article/politicsNews/idUSN0318650320070703?sp=true.

De Wolf, Antenor Hallo. 2006. "Modern Condottieri in Iraq: Privatizing War from the Perspective of International and Human Rights Law." *Indiana Journal of Global Legal Studies*, vol. 13, no. 2, pp. 315–356.

DoD (Department of Defense). 2000. *Doctrine for Logistic Support of Joint Operations*. Joint Publication 4-0. April 6.

——. 2001. *Quadrennial Defense Review Report*. September 30. www.defenselink.mil/pubs/pdfs/ qdr2001.pdf.

——. 2005. "Contractor Personnel Authorized to Accompany the U.S. Armed Forces." DoD Instruction 3020.41. October 3. www.dtic.mil/whs/directives/corres/pdf/302041p.pdf.

——. 2006a. "DoD Law of War Program." DoD Directive 2311.01E. May 9. www.dtic.mil/whs/directives/corres/pdf/231101p.pdf.

——. 2006b. "Request to Contract for Private Security Companies in Iraq." Memorandum from the Office of the General Counsel to Staff Judge Advocates. January 10.

——. 2007a. "Depot Maintenance Core Capabilities Determination Process." DoD Instruction 4151.20. January 5. www.acq.osd.mil/log/mrmp/4151.20.pdf.

——. 2007b. *Report on DoD Program for Planning, Managing, and Accounting for Contractor Services and Contractor Personnel During Contingency Operations.* October.

——. 2008a. "Core Business Missions." Business Transformation Agency, May. www.pentagon.gov/dbt/mission_core-missions.html.

——. 2008b. *Department of Defense Program for Planning, Managing, and Accounting for Contractor Services and Contractor Personnel During Contingency Operations.* Report to Congress. April. www.acq.osd.mil/log/PS/p_vault/final_section854_report_Congress_Apr08.pdf.

——. 2008c. "Implementation Guidance for the Synchronized Predeployment and Operational Tracker (SPOT) to Account for Contractor Personnel Performing in the United States Central Command Area of Responsibility (AOR)." Memorandum from the Office of the Under Secretary of Defense, Acquisition Technology and Logistics, to Directors of Defense Agencies. January 28.

——. 2008d. "UCMJ Jurisdiction Over DoD Civilian Employees, DoD Contractors, and Other Persons Serving With or Accompanying the Armed Forces Overseas During Declared War and in Contingency Operations." Memorandum on initial guidance issued by the Secretary of Defense to the military departments and Chairman of the Joint Chiefs of Staff. March 10. www.dtic.mil/whs/directives/corres/pdf/sec080310ucmj.pdf.

Department of Justice. 2008. *Closing Loopholes: Prosecuting Sexual Assaults and Other Violent Crimes Committed by American Civilians in a Combat Environment.* Statement of Sigal P. Mandelker, Deputy Assistant Attorney General, Criminal Division, before the Senate Committee on Foreign Relations. April 9.

Department of State. 2002. "International Terrorism: American Hostages." Press release, February 20. www.state.gov/r/pa/prs/ps/2002/8190.htm .

——. 2006. *Report to Congress, Section 2207 Report on Iraq Relief and Reconstruction.* January. www.state.gov/p/nea/rls/rpt/2207/jan2006/pdf.

Douglas, Karen L. 2004. "Contractors Accompanying the Force: Empowering Commanders with Emergency Change Authority." *Air Force Law Review*, vol. 55, pp. 127–155.

Doyle, Charles. 2007. *Extraterritorial Application of American Criminal Law.* CRS Report for Congress 94-166 A. Congressional Research Service. September 10.

Drimmer, Jonathan. 2006. "When Man Hunts Man: The Rights and Duties of Bounty Hunters in the American Criminal Justice System." *Houston Law Review*, vol. 33, no. 651, pp. 731–793.

Elsea, Jennifer K. 2007. *Treatment of "Battlefield Detainees" in the War on Terrorism.* CRS Report for Congress RL31367. Congressional Research Service. January 23.

Elsea, Jennifer K., and Nina M. Serafino. 2007. *Private Security Contractors in Iraq: Background, Legal Status, and Other Issues.* CRS Report for Congress RL32419. Congressional Research Service. July 11.

Epley, William W. 1990. "Civilian Support of Field Armies," *Army Logistician*, vol. 22 (November/ December), pp. 30–35.

Fortner, Joe A. 2000. "Managing, Deploying, Sustaining, and Protecting Contractors on the Battlefield." *Army Logistician*, vol. 32, no. 5 (September/October). www.almc.army.mil/alog/issues/SepOct00/ms571.htm .

Garcia, Michael, R. Chuck Mason, and Jennifer K. Elsea. 2008. *Congressional Oversight and Related Issues Concerning the Prospective Security Agreement Between the United States and Iraq.* CRS Report for Congress RL34362. Congressional Research Service, May 28.

GAO (General Accounting Office). 2003. *Defense Management: DoD Faces Challenges Implementing Its Core Competency Approach and A-76 Competitions.* GAO-03-818. July.

GAO (Government Accountability Office). 2005. Rebuilding Iraq: *Actions Needed to Improve Use of Private Security Providers.* GAO-05-737. July.

——. 2006. *Rebuilding Iraq: Actions Still Needed to Improve the Use of Private Security Contractors.* Statement of William Solis, Director, Defense Capabilities and Management, before the Subcommittee on National Security, Emerging Threats, and International Relations of the House Committee on Government Reform. GAO-06-865T. June 13.

——. 2007. *Stabilizing and Rebuilding Iraq: Conditions in Iraq Are Conducive to Fraud, Waste, and Abuse.* Statement of David M. Walker, Comptroller General, before the Subcommittee on Defense of the House Committee on Appropriations. GAO-07-525T. April 23.

——. 2008a. *Defense Contracting: Army Case Study Delineates Concerns with Use of Contractors as Contract Specialists.* GAO-08-360. March.

——. 2008b. *Rebuilding Iraq: DoD and State Department Have Improved Oversight and Coordination of Private Security Contractors in Iraq, but Further Actions Are Needed to Sustain Improvements.* GAO-08-966. July.

General Services Administration. 1998. *Federal Procurement Data System: Product and Service Codes Manual.* August. www.fpdsng.com/downloads/service_product_codes.pdf.

Gensheimer, Lydia. 2008. "War Zone Crimes: Accountability MIA." *CQ Weekly* (May 12), pp. 1230–1232.

Guillory, Michael E. 2001. "Civilianizing the Force: Is the United States Crossing the Rubicon?" *Air Force Law Review*, vol. 51, pp. 111–142.

House Committee on Armed Services. 2004. *Special Operations Command Personnel Issues*. Opening statement of Jim Saxton, Chairman, Subcommittee on Terrorism, Unconventional Threats and Capabilities. July 20.

Industrial College of the Armed Forces. 2006. *Privatized Military Operations*. Washington, D.C.: National Defense University. Spring.

Ives, J. Mackey, and Michael J. Davidson. 2003. "Court-Martial Jurisdiction Over Retirees Under Articles 2(4) and 2(6): Time to Lighten Up and Tighten Up?" *Military Law Review*, vol. 175 (March), pp. 1–85.

McCullough, James J., and Courtney J. Edmonds. 2004. *Contractors on the Battlefield Revisited: The War in Iraq and Its Aftermath*. Briefing Paper 04–6, Second Series. Washington, D.C.: West, a Thomson Business.

Multi-National Corps—Iraq. 2008. "Civilian Contractor Convicted at Court-Martial." Press release, Baghdad. June 23. www.mnf-iraq.com/index.php?option=com_content&task=view&id=20671&Itemid=128.

Northam, Jackie. 2007. "Private Contracting Industry Set for Regulation." *NPR Morning Edition*. October 26. www.npr.org/templates/story/story.php?storyId=15655334.

Office of Management and Budget. 2003. *Performance of Commercial Activities*. Circular A-76. Revised, May 29.

Parks, W. Hays. 2005. "Evolution of Policy and Law Concerning the Role of Civilians and Civilian Contractors Accompanying the Armed Forces." Summary of a presentation at the Third Meeting of Experts on direct participation in hostilities, Geneva, October 25.

Pincus, Walter. 2008. "U.S. Cannot Manage Contractors in Wars, Officials Testify on Hill," *Washington Post*, January 25, p. A5.

Rivkin, David B., and Lee A. Casey. 2008. "Combatant States Under the Laws of War." *National Security Law Report* (American Bar Association), vol. 30, no. 1 (March), pp. 1–7.

Rosky, Clifford J. 2004. "Force, Inc.: The Privatization of Punishment, Policing, and Military Force in Liberal States." *Connecticut Law Review*, vol. 36, no. 3 (Spring), pp. 879–1032.

Senate Committee on Armed Services. 2007. "Senate Armed Services Committee Completes Conference of National Defense Authorization Bill for Fiscal Year 2008." Press release, December 6.

Shrader, Charles R. 1999. *Contractors on the Battlefield*, Landpower Essay Series, No. 99–6. Arlington, Va.: Association of the United States Army, Institute of Land Warfare May.

Singer, Peter W. 2004. "War, Profits, and the Vacuum of Law: Privatized Military Firms and International Law," *Columbia Journal of Transnational Law*, vol. 42, no. 2 (Spring), pp. 521–550.

Sklansky, David A. 1999. "The Private Police." *UCLA Law Review*, vol. 46, pp. 1165–1287.

Stiglitz, Joseph E., and Linda J. Bilmes. 2008. *The Three Trillion Dollar War: The True Cost of the Iraq Conflict*. New York: W.W. Norton.

Tabarrok, Alexander. 2007. "The Rise, Fall, and Rise Again of Privateers." *Independent Review*, vol. 11, no. 4 (Spring), pp. 565–577.

Turner, Lisa L., and Lynn G. Norton. 2001. "Civilians at the Tip of the Spear." *Air Force Law Review*, vol. 51, pp. 1–110.

U.S. Central Command. 2008. *2nd Quarter Contractor Census Report*. April 30.

Vernon, Rebecca. 2004. "Battlefield Contractors: Facing the Tough Issues." *Public Contract Law Journal*, vol. 33, no. 2 (Winter), pp. 369–421.

Wilkinson, Kevin J. 2007. "More Effective Federal Procurement Response to Disasters: Maximizing the Extraordinary Flexibilities of IDIQ Contracting." *Air Force Law Review*, vol. 59, pp. 231–286.

Zamparelli, Steven J. 1999. "Contractors on the Battlefield: What Have We Signed Up For?" *Air Force Journal of Logistics*, vol. 23, no. 3 (Fall), pp. 10–19.

CONTRACTOR ACCOUNTABILITY IN THE WAR AGAINST TERRORISTS

Commentary

By
Douglas C. Lovelace, Jr.

The need to hold civilian contractors supporting military operations accountable for their actions is not a recent development. The Uniform Code of military Justice (UCMJ), the document containing the U.S. armed forces body of criminal law, has long provided that civilian contractors accompanying military forces during time of war were subject to the UCMJ's provisions and could be prosecuted and punished, under the Code, for offenses they committed; in fact, many have been. On the surface, that provision of the UCMJ appears to provide military commanders the authority they need to discipline contractors who support military operations.

However, the United States has not declared war in over a half- century, and some analysts argue it never will again—that war declaration is an anachronism. For brevity, this volume does not delve into that argument in depth, but acknowledges its validity nonetheless. Obviously, the total absence of U.S. war declarations in recent history has not precluded frequent and often substantial applications of military force around the globe in places like the Korean Peninsula, Vietnam, Lebanon, Grenada, Panama, the Balkans, Afghanistan, and Iraq. Contractors participated in almost all of those operations. Until recently, the UCMJ did not cover civilian contractors who accompanied military forces on operations other than declared war.

However, the UCMJ was amended at the end of 2006 by language sponsored by Senator Lindsey Graham (R-SC), who also is a reserve member of the U.S. Air Force's Judge Advocate General Corps. The Graham amendment made contractors accompanying military forces in declared war *and contingency operations* (emphasis added) subject to the UCMJ. "Contingency operations" is a military term that covers virtually all military deployments. So, the Graham amendment would appear to have closed the loophole that existed in the prior iteration of the UCMJ. Unfortunately, the closing of the loophole has been slow in coming, because the Defense Department did not draft and promulgate implementing guidance until March 10, 2008 and then did so in an arguably inadequate memorandum, rather than via a sufficiently comprehensive implementing regulation developed through notice and comment rule making. Therefore, the gap in accountability existed for much longer than it needed to, and incidents of contractor misconduct went unpunished since, absent the implementing regulations, field commanders had insufficient guidance for implementing the Graham amendment. Making the situation even more opaque is an Iraqi law, allegedly passes pursuant to an order issued by U.S. officials in 2004 that grants prosecutorial immunity to foreign contractors. Reports are that the Status of Forces Agreement currently under negotiation between Iraqi and U.S. officials would significantly reduce or even eliminate such immunity.

The slowness in taking steps to remove the loopholes preventing contractors from being held accountable for alleged wrongdoings occurred against the backdrop of perceptions of grievous contractor misconduct, especially that of private security contractors. For example, a September 2007 shooting incident that involved guards from Blackwater USA (now Blackwater International), a company that provides security for U.S. Embassy officials, left at least 17 Iraqis dead and outraged the Iraqi population and government leaders. The investigation continues. In November 2007, a private security contractor based in Dubai, United Arab Emirates, that has contracts with the U.S. Department of Defense to provide bases with essentials such as food, water and tents, was involved in the non-fatal shooting of an Iraqi woman. The shooting apparently occurred when the contractor was providing security for a convoy under a contract with an Iraqi company. That incident also evoked very negative public and political reactions.

While the Graham amendment to the UCMJ remained generally inoperable, the U.S. Congress moved on a parallel track to pass the Military Extraterritorial Jurisdiction Act of 2000. This section of the volume presents a constellation of brief documents that address extraterritorial jurisdiction over contractor crimes and DoD's guidance for breathing life into the Graham amendment. They include the Military Extraterritorial Jurisdiction Act of 2000, the 2007 version of Chapter 212 of Title 18 of the United States Code, a 2002 CRS Report for Congress on *Terrorism and Extraterritorial Jurisdiction in Criminal Cases: Recent Developments in Brief,* the MEJA Expansion and Enforcement Act of 2007, and the March 10, 2008 Secretary of Defense Memorandum for the Secretaries of the Military Departments, Chairman of the Joint Chiefs of Staff, Undersecretary of Defense, and Commanders of the Combatant Commands on UCMJ Jurisdiction over DoD Civilian Employees, DoD Contractor Personnel and other Persons Serving with or Accompanying the Armed Forces Overseas during Declared War and in Contingency Operations. Together, the documents provide the reader an excellent summary of the measure taken to improve contractor accountability in the war against terrorists.

DOCUMENT NO. 7

MILITARY EXTRATERRITORIAL JURISDICTION

18 USC CHAPTER 212

January 3, 2007

TITLE 18—CRIMES AND CRIMINAL PROCEDURE
PART II—CRIMINAL PROCEDURE
CHAPTER 212—MILITARY EXTRATERRITORIAL JURISDICTION

Sec.

CITE: 18 USC Sec. 3261

01/03/2007

AMENDMENTS: 2004—Par. (1)(A). Pub. L. 108-375 amended subpar. (A) generally. Prior to amendment, subpar. (A) read as follows: "employed as a civilian employee of the Department of Defense (including a nonappropriated fund instrumentality of the Department), as a Department of Defense contractor (including a subcontractor at any tier), or as an employee of a Department of Defense contractor (including a subcontractor at any tier)."

Sec. 3261. Criminal offenses committed by certain members of the Armed forces and by persons employed by or accompanying the Armed Forces outside the United States

(a) Whoever engages in conduct outside the United States that would constitute an offense punishable by imprisonment for more than 1 year if the conduct had been engaged in within the special maritime and territorial jurisdiction of the United States—

(1) while employed by or accompanying the Armed Forces outside the United States; or

(2) while a member of the Armed Forces subject to chapter 47 of title 10 (the Uniform Code of Military Justice),

shall be punished as provided for that offense.

(b) No prosecution may be commenced against a person under this section if a foreign government, in accordance with jurisdiction recognized by the United States, has prosecuted or is prosecuting such person for the conduct constituting such offense, except upon the approval of the Attorney General or the Deputy Attorney General (or a person acting in either such capacity), which function of approval may not be delegated.

(c) Nothing in this chapter may be construed to deprive a court-martial, military commission, provost court, or other military tribunal of concurrent jurisdiction with respect to offenders or offenses that by statute or by the law of war may be tried by a court-martial, military commission, provost court, or other military tribunal.

(d) No prosecution may be commenced against a member of the Armed Forces subject to chapter 47 of title 10 (the Uniform Code of Military Justice) under this section unless—

(1) such member ceases to be subject to such chapter; or

(2) an indictment or information charges that the member committed the offense with one or more other defendants, at least one of whom is not subject to such chapter.

(Added Pub. L. 106-523, Sec. 2(a), Nov. 22, 2000, 114 Stat. 2488.)

SHORT TITLE OF 2000 AMENDMENT, Pub. L. 106-523, Sec. 1, Nov. 22, 2000, 114 Stat. 2488, provided that: "This Act [enacting this chapter] may be cited as the 'Military Extraterritorial Jurisdiction Act of 2000.'"

Sec. 3262. Arrest and commitment

(a) The Secretary of Defense may designate and authorize any person serving in a law enforcement position in the Department of Defense to arrest, in accordance with applicable international agreements, outside the

United States any person described in section 3261(a) if there is probable cause to believe that such person violated section 3261(a).

(b) Except as provided in sections 3263 and 3264, a person arrested under subsection (a) shall be delivered as soon as practicable to the custody of civilian law enforcement authorities of the United States for removal to the United States for judicial proceedings in relation to conduct referred to in such subsection unless such person has had charges brought against him or her under chapter 47 of title 10 for such conduct.

(Added Pub. L. 106-523, Sec. 2(a), Nov. 22, 2000, 114 Stat. 2489.)

Sec. 3263. Delivery to authorities of foreign countries

(a) Any person designated and authorized under section 3262(a) may deliver a person described in section 3261(a) to the appropriate authorities of a foreign country in which such person is alleged to have violated section 3261(a) if—

(1) appropriate authorities of that country request the delivery of the person to such country for trial for such conduct as an offense under the laws of that country; and

(2) the delivery of such person to that country is authorized by a treaty or other international agreement to which the United States is a party.

(b) The Secretary of Defense, in consultation with the Secretary of State, shall determine which officials of a foreign country constitute appropriate authorities for purposes of this section.

(Added Pub. L. 106-523, Sec. 2(a), Nov. 22, 2000, 114 Stat. 2489.)

Sec. 3264. Limitation on removal

(a) Except as provided in subsection (b), and except for a person delivered to authorities of a foreign country under section 3263, a person arrested for or charged with a violation of section 3261(a) shall not be removed—

(1) to the United States; or

(2) to any foreign country other than a country in which such person is believed to have violated section 3261(a).

(b) The limitation in subsection (a) does not apply if—

(1) a Federal magistrate judge orders the person to be removed to the United States to be present at a detention hearing held pursuant to section 3142(f);

(2) a Federal magistrate judge orders the detention of the person before trial pursuant to section 3142(e), in which case the person shall be promptly removed to the United States for purposes of such detention;

(3) the person is entitled to, and does not waive, a preliminary examination under the Federal Rules of Criminal Procedure, in which case the person shall be removed to the United States in time for such examination;

(4) a Federal magistrate judge otherwise orders the person to be removed to the United States; or

(5) the Secretary of Defense determines that military necessity requires that the limitations in subsection (a) be waived, in which case the person shall be removed to the nearest United States military installation outside the United States adequate to detain the person and to facilitate the initial appearance described in section 3265(a).

(Added Pub. L. 106-523, Sec. 2(a), Nov. 22, 2000, 114 Stat. 2489.)

REFERENCES IN TEXT: The Federal Rules of Criminal Procedure, referred to in subsec. (b)(3), are set out in the Appendix to this title.

Sec. 3265. Initial proceedings

(a)(1) In the case of any person arrested for or charged with a violation of section 3261(a) who is not delivered to authorities of a foreign country under section 3263, the initial appearance of that person under the Federal Rules of Criminal Procedure—

(A) shall be conducted by a Federal magistrate judge; and

(B) may be carried out by telephony or such other means that enables voice communication among the participants, including any counsel representing the person.

(2) In conducting the initial appearance, the Federal magistrate judge shall also determine whether there is probable cause to believe that an offense under section 3261(a) was committed and that the person committed it.

(3) If the Federal magistrate judge determines that probable cause exists that the person committed an offense under section 3261(a), and if no motion is made seeking the person's detention before trial, the Federal magistrate judge shall also determine at the initial appearance the conditions of the person's release before trial under chapter 207 of this title.

(b) In the case of any person described in subsection (a), any detention hearing of that person under section 3142(f)—

(1) shall be conducted by a Federal magistrate judge; and

(2) at the request of the person, may be carried out by telephony or such other means that enables voice communication among the participants, including any counsel representing the person.

(c)(1) If any initial proceeding under this section with respect to any such person is conducted while the person is outside the United States, and the person is entitled to have counsel appointed for purposes of such proceeding, the Federal magistrate judge may appoint as such counsel for purposes of such hearing a qualified military counsel.

(2) For purposes of this subsection, the term "qualified military counsel" means a judge advocate made available by the Secretary of Defense for purposes of such proceedings, who—

(A) is a graduate of an accredited law school or is a member of the bar of a Federal court or of the highest court of a State;

and

(B) is certified as competent to perform such duties by the Judge Advocate General of the armed force of which he is a member.

(Added Pub. L. 106-523, Sec. 2(a), Nov. 22, 2000, 114 Stat. 2490.)

REFERENCES IN TEXT: The Federal Rules of Criminal Procedure, referred to in subsec. (a)(1), are set out in the Appendix to this title.

Sec. 3266. Regulations

(a) The Secretary of Defense, after consultation with the Secretary of State and the Attorney General, shall prescribe regulations governing the apprehension, detention, delivery, and removal of persons under this chapter and the facilitation of proceedings under section 3265. Such regulations shall be uniform throughout the Department of Defense.

(b)(1) The Secretary of Defense, after consultation with the Secretary of State and the Attorney General, shall prescribe regulations requiring that, to the maximum extent practicable, notice shall be provided to any person employed by or accompanying the Armed Forces outside the United States who is not a national of the United States that such person is potentially subject to the criminal jurisdiction of the United States under this chapter.

(2) A failure to provide notice in accordance with the regulations prescribed under paragraph (1) shall not defeat the jurisdiction of a court of the United States or provide a defense in any judicial proceeding arising under this chapter.

(c) The regulations prescribed under this section, and any amendments to those regulations, shall not take effect before the date that is 90 days after the date on which the Secretary of Defense submits a report containing those regulations or amendments (as the case may be) to the Committee on the Judiciary of the House of Representatives and the Committee on the Judiciary of the Senate.

(Added Pub. L. 106-523, Sec. 2(a), Nov. 22, 2000, 114 Stat. 2491.)

Sec. 3267. Definitions

As used in this chapter:

(1) The term "employed by the Armed Forces outside the United States" means—

(A) employed as—

(i) a civilian employee of—

(I) the Department of Defense (including a nonappropriated fund instrumentality of the Department); or

(II) any other Federal agency, or any provisional authority, to the extent such employment relates to supporting the mission of the Department of Defense overseas;

(ii) a contractor (including a subcontractor at any tier) of—

(I) the Department of Defense (including a nonappropriated fund instrumentality of the Department); or

(II) any other Federal agency, or any provisional authority, to the extent such employment relates to supporting the mission of the Department of Defense overseas; or

(iii) an employee of a contractor (or subcontractor at any tier) of—

(I) the Department of Defense (including a nonappropriated fund instrumentality of the Department); or

(II) any other Federal agency, or any provisional authority, to the extent such employment relates to supporting the mission of the Department of Defense overseas;

(B) present or residing outside the United States in connection with such employment; and

(C) not a national of or ordinarily resident in the host nation.

(2) The term "accompanying the Armed Forces outside the United States" means—

(A) a dependent of—

(i) a member of the Armed Forces;

(ii) a civilian employee of the Department of Defense (including a nonappropriated fund instrumentality of the Department); or

(iii) a Department of Defense contractor (including a subcontractor at any tier) or an employee of a Department of Defense contractor (including a subcontractor at any tier);

(B) residing with such member, civilian employee, contractor, or contractor employee outside the United States; and

(C) not a national of or ordinarily resident in the host nation.

(3) The term "Armed Forces" has the meaning given the term "armed forces" in section 101(a)(4) of title 10.

(4) The terms "Judge Advocate General" and "judge advocate" have the meanings given such terms in section 801 of title 10.

(Added Pub. L. 106-523, Sec. 2(a), Nov. 22, 2000, 114 Stat. 2491; amended Pub. L. 108-375, div. A, title X, Sec. 1088, Oct. 28, 2004, 118 Stat. 2066.)

DOCUMENT NO. 8

TERRORISM AND EXTRATERRITORIAL JURISDICTION IN CRIMINAL CASES: RECENT DEVELOPMENTS IN BRIEF

CRS Report
RS21306

September 6, 2002

Charles Doyle
Senior Specialist
American Law Division

Summary

Most crime is territorial. It is proscribed, investigated, tried, and punished under the law of the place where it occurs. As a general rule, no nation's laws apply within the territory of another. Yet in a surprising number of instances, federal criminal law does apply overseas to U.S. citizens and foreign nationals. As long as there is some nexus to the United States, federal law authorizes prosecution—practical, diplomatic, and procedural impediments notwithstanding.

In the 107th Congress, the USA PATRIOT Act and the legislation implementing the international conventions on terrorist bombings and on financing terrorism have extended the substantive authority for federal prosecution of crimes occurring elsewhere. This is an abridged version of CRS Report RL31557, *Terrorism and Extraterritorial Jurisdiction in Criminal Cases: Recent Developments*, stripped of its footnotes and most citations.

Extraterritorial Jurisdiction: The Constitution provides the power to enact criminal laws with extraterritorial application. It vests Congress with, among other things, the power "to regulate commerce with foreign nations . . . to define and punish piracies and felonies committed on the high seas, and offenses against the law of nations . . ." and gives Congress legislative jurisdiction over places acquired "for the erection of forts, magazines, arsenals, dock-years, and other needful buildings."

The Constitution also limits the manner in which this authority may be exercised. The due process clause of the Fifth Amendment, for instance, bars the extraterritorial application of federal criminal laws in the absence of a connection between the crime, the defendant, and the United States. Prosecution requires personal jurisdiction over the defendant and subject matter jurisdiction over the crime. Nevertheless, neither due process nor any other Constitutional limitation have posed any serious obstacle to the enactment and enforcement of federal law for crimes committed abroad. In fact, the extraterritorial application of federal law is frequently said to be a matter of intent rather than power, of statutory construction rather than constitutional limitation.

When a statute contains a statement of its extraterritorial application, Congress's intent is clear. When the statute is silent, the courts begin with a presumption against extraterritorial application. The nature of the statute, however, may be sufficient to overcome the presumption, so long as the application beyond the borders of the United States does not offend the principles of international law. The courts will find no offense to international law as long as the application features reasonable contacts between the crime and the nation asserting jurisdiction. That standard is often judged by whether the case comes within one of five circumstances or "principles" under which international law recognizes a nation's prerogative to assert the application of its laws: (1) the objective territorial principle where external conduct has a substantial effect within the country; (2) the protective principal where the outside conduct is directed against the country's national security; (3) the nationality principle where the offender is one on the country's nationals; (4) the passive personality principle where the victim is one of the country's nationals; and (5) the universality principle where the conduct, such as piracy, is universally condemned and may be prosecuted by any country that can capture the offender.

The inventory of federal crimes with extraterritorial application already includes prohibitions on crimes of violence committed against federal officials and employees, the theft or destruction of federal property, efforts to smuggle drugs or foreign nationals into this country, and aircraft hijacking, to name a few. Legislation during the 107th Congress augments the store with authority to prosecute: (a) crimes committed by or against Americans on military and diplomatic installations and residences overseas; (b) fraud involving American credit cards or other "access devices" committed abroad; (c) laundering the proceeds of various federal crimes in a foreign bank; (d) laundering in this country of the proceeds of foreign political corruption and of an expanded list of other foreign crimes; (e) terrorist bombings abroad; and (f) the overseas financing of terrorism.

Common Law Crimes on American Facilities Overseas: Section 804 of the USA PATRIOT Act addresses a difference of opinion among the lower federal appellate courts over whether the federal laws that outlaw such crimes as murder, rape, and robbery when committed within federal enclaves in this country also apply on American governmental installations abroad. With the enactment of section 804, they do; at least when either the victim or the offender is a U.S. national. The dispute centers on the construction of 18 U.S.C. 7(3) which defines the special territorial jurisdiction of the United States. The Fourth and Ninth Circuits contend that the definition in subsection 7(3) includes areas in other countries over which the host nation has afforded the United States privileges akin to sovereignty. The Second Circuit argues that the subsection is intended to encompass only those areas over which Congress may exercise legislative jurisdiction of the kind ordinarily vested in the Several States.

The Fourth Circuit has held that at least some areas located in other countries might be considered within the special territorial jurisdiction of the United States as described in subsection 7(3), *United States v. Erdos*, 474 F.2d 157 (4th Cir. 1973). *Erdos* upheld the conviction of an American diplomat for the crime of manslaughter committed in the American embassy in Equatorial Guinea. *Erdos* saw two grounds for territorial jurisdiction within subsection 7(3): [1] "Any lands reserved or acquired for the use of the United States, and under the exclusive or concurrent jurisdiction thereof, or" [2] "any place purchased or otherwise acquired by the United States by consent of the legislature of the State in which the same shall be, for the erection of a fort, magazine, arsenal, dockyard, or other needful building." It concluded that by virtue of "the practical usage and dominion exercised over the embassy or other federal establishment by the United States government 18 U.S.C. 7(3) is a proper grant of special territorial jurisdiction embracing an embassy in a foreign country acquired for the use of the United States and under its concurrent jurisdiction," 474 F.2d at 159-60.

Courts in the Second Circuit read subsection 7(3) differently. *United States v. Bin Laden*, 92 F.Supp.2d 189 (S.D.N.Y. 2000) involved the terrorist bombing of American embassies in Kenya and Tanzania. Unlike *Erdos*, it held that the American embassies abroad were not within the special territorial jurisdiction of the United States and that statutes outlawing murder and maiming within the territorial jurisdiction of the United States (18 U.S.C. 1111, 114) had no extraterritorial application, 92 F.Supp.2d at 204-16. The Court of Appeals for the Second Circuit came to much the same conclusion. It reversed a conviction under 18 U.S.C. 2243 (sexual abuse of a minor within the territorial jurisdiction of the United States) for a statutory rape which occurred in a housing complex on a U.S. military base in Germany, *United States v. Gatlin*, 216 F.3d 207 (2d Cir. 2000). *Gatlin* based its conclusion that subsection 7(3) has no extraterritorial application on three factors. First, a statute is presumed to have no extraterritorial application absent a clear indication to the contrary. Second, *Gatlin* read the subsection's legislative history as an indication that Congress intended the subsection to apply solely within the United States. Third, it pointed out that after *Reid* and *Kinsella*, Congress, the Executive Branch, and commentators had all described as beyond federal jurisdiction those crimes committed by dependents and contractors on overseas military bases—all assuming that subsection 7(3) had no extraterritorial application, 216 F.3d at 214–22.

The Ninth Circuit could not agree, *United States v. Corey*, 232 F.3d 1166 (9th 2000). *Corey* involved the conviction of a civilian postal employee for sexual abuse committed in military housing in Japan and in a residence rented by the U.S. embassy in the Philippines. *Corey* found the presumption against extraterritoriality unpersuasive and not particularly relevant. In its mind, jurisdiction was territorial (not extraterritorial) no matter where the property was located as long as it was acquired for "needful" purposes and as long as U.S. legislative jurisdiction over the property was exclusive or concurrent, 232 F.3d at 1170-171. It found support in the history of subsection 7(3) which had been applied over time to territory beyond the confines of any admitted state or beyond the continental boundaries of the United States, 232 F.3d at 1173–176.

Congress resolved the dispute, or at least greatly mitigated its consequences, when it enacted section 804 of the USA PATRIOT Act and the Military Extraterritorial Jurisdiction Act of 2000. The Military Extraterritorial Jurisdiction Act treats felonies, committed anywhere overseas by members of the armed forces or those accompanying or employed by them, as if they were committed within the territorial jurisdiction of the United States, 18 U.S.C. 3261. Section 804 of the USA PATRIOT Act creates a new territorial subsection in 18 U.S.C.7: the special territorial jurisdiction of the United States includes the overseas business premises of federal governmental entities and the residences of the members of their staffs, but only for crimes committed by or against Americans (other than those who come within the military extension of 18 U.S.C. 3261). The split in the circuits remains of consequence for crimes committed in federal overseas facilities by foreign nationals who are not associated with the U.S. armed forces. In the Fourth and Ninth Circuits, such crimes may come within the territorial jurisdiction of the United States. In the Second Circuit, they do not.

Credit Card Fraud Overseas (Fraud and Related Activity in Connection with Access Devices Abroad): Section 1029 of title 18 proscribes counterfeiting or trafficking in counterfeit or unauthorized "access devices" or attempting or conspiring to do so "if the offense affects interstate or foreign commerce." Thus, prior to the addition of subsection (h), the section would have been thought to have extraterritorial application when the offense affected the interstate or foreign commerce of the United States. Subsection (h) might be construed to limit the overseas application of section 1029 to circumstances involving an American issuer of the depicted "access device" *and* some contact between the United States and the material used in the offense or the profits from it. Alternatively, it might be construed as an explicit confirmation that the section applies under these circumstances, but without intending to foreclose other circumstances justifying application abroad.

Money Laundering: The money laundering provisions of 18 U.S.C. 1956 proscribe money laundering or more exactly, "financial transactions" related in various ways to a "specified unlawful activity." It creates six distinct crimes: (1) laundering with intent to promote an illicit activity; (2) laundering to evade taxes; (3) laundering to conceal or disguise; (4) smurfing (structuring transactions to avoid reporting requirements); (5) international laundering; and (6) laundering part of a law enforcement sting.

The extraterritorial aspects of section 1956 come in two forms. First, the statute prohibits transactions in this country related to certain crimes in other countries. Second, the section specifically asserts extraterritorial jurisdiction over transactions in other countries which involve more than $10,000 and either the participation of an American or conduct occurring within the United States, 18 U.S.C. 1956(f).

Section 318 of the USA PATRIOT Act expressly eliminates any requirement that the triggering financial transactions occur in an American bank or other American financial institution by changing the applicable definition of financial institution to include foreign banks. Whether this is intended as an implicit repeal of the requirements subsection 1956(f) is unclear. The amendment allows for extraterritorial application in instances where subsection 1956(f) would not. Subsection 1956(f), for example, does not reach transactions of less than $10,000 or foreign transactions by a foreign national relating to specified illegal activity committed in the United States. The report of the House committee in which this proposal originated makes it clear that the provision was crafted to fill in gaps in existing law. On the other hand, the courts do not favor repeal by implication, *J.E.M. AG Supply, Inc. v. Pioneer Hi-Bred International, Inc.*, 122 S.Ct. 593, 606 (2001)("the only permissible justification for a repeal by implication is when the earlier and later statutes are irreconcilable"). Yet it is possible to read the amendment and subsection 1956(f) consistently, i.e., each independently describes circumstances under which extraterritorial jurisdiction may be asserted without reference to the other.

Section 315 of the Act supplements the 18 U.S.C. 1956 definition of "specified unlawful activity" to include (when the financial transaction occurs at least in part in the U.S.) a wider range of foreign crimes such as crimes of violence, foreign official corruption, various smuggling offenses, and crimes for which we have extradition obligations under a multinational treaty. It also adds sundry smuggling offenses, gun running, computer fraud and abuse, and felony violations of the Foreign Agents Registration Act of 1938 to the definition of the specified unlawful activity.

Treaty Implementation: Contemporaneous with Senate approval of the International Conventions for the Suppression of Terrorist Bombings and of the Financing of Terrorism, Congress enacted implementing criminal provisions that feature extraterritorial components. Subsection 2332f(a) bans the use of nuclear materials, chemical weapons, explosives, or biological weapons against public places or governmental facilities and utilities or attempting or conspiring to do so. Violations are punishable in the same manner as violations of 18 U.S.C. 2332a(a)(use of weapons of mass destruction against federal property or an American abroad), i.e., imprisonment for any term of years or life and if death results from commission of the offense the offender may also be subject to the death penalty.

The extraterritorial reach of the new statute runs parallel to several existing statues which prohibit international terrorism; the unlawful use of chemical or biological weapons, nuclear materials, explosives, or weapons of mass destruction; or attacks on aircraft, airports, mass transit, diplomatic officials, or federal employees. It is somewhat distinctive in that it may be enforced when the offense is committed overseas and subsequently the offender is found here or has been brought here. No other connection to the United States is needed. The section does not become effective, however, until the treaty provisions it implements come into effect for the United States—a limitation without which any claim to legislative jurisdiction in some instances might be suspect.

Newly enacted section 2339C condemns (1) providing or collecting funds to be used for terrorist purposes or (2) concealing information concerning funds used to support terrorism. Subsection 2339C(a), the financing provision which also outlaws attempts and conspiracies, applies where the funds are to be used in support of the commission of either an offense covered in any of the various specified anti-terrorism treaties or an act of terrorism intended to cause death or serious injury. The underlying treaty offenses include the following federal crimes and their foreign equivalents: 18 U.S.C. 32 (destruction of aircraft or aircraft facilities); 18 U.S.C. 37 (violence at international airports); 18 U.S.C. 112, 878, 1116, 1117, 1201 (assault, threats, murder, manslaughter, attempted murder, kidnaping of internationally protected persons); 18 U.S.C. 831 (nuclear materials offenses); 18 U.S.C. 1203 (hostage taking); 18 U.S.C. 2280 (violence against maritime navigation); 18 U.S.C. 2281 (violence against fixed maritime platforms); and 49 U.S.C. 46502 (aircraft piracy). Violations are punishable by imprisonment for not more than 20 years, a fine of not more than $250,000 for individuals or not more than $500,000 for organizations, and/or a civil penalty of at least $10,000, 18 U.S.C. 2339C(d)(1),(f).

The financing subsection applies overseas if the offender is an American, if the target of the underlying terrorism is the United States government, an American, or an American entity, or (when the Financing Convention becomes effective for the U.S.) if the offender is subsequently found in the United States, 18 U.S.C. 2339C(c). The subsection has several counterparts elsewhere in federal law, most notably 18 U.S.C. 2339B (providing material support to terrorists organizations), 18 U.S.C. 2339A (providing material support to terrorists), and 18 U.S.C. 2 (aiding and abetting). The extraterritorial reach of subsection 2339C(a) when it may be based on the presence of the offender of the United States is more sweeping than the most expansive of these. Section 2339B proscribes aid to groups designated foreign terrorist organizations by the Secretary of State as threats to U.S. national security or the national security of U.S. nationals and has a general extraterritorial jurisdiction provision, 18 U.S.C. 2339B(d) ("There is extraterritorial federal jurisdiction over an offense under this section"). Subsection 2339C(a) is limited neither to designated terrorist organizations nor to terrorism directed against American national security interests—the subsequent presence of the financier in the U.S. is enough.

Section 2339A prohibits aid to a terrorist in the commission of any of a list designated for federal predicate offenses. It has no explicit extraterritorial provisions but almost certainly has extraterritorial application by virtue of the extraterritorial features of its predicate offenses. Subsection 2339C(a)'s predicate offense list is more extensive than that of section 2339A and consequently its extraterritorial reach is greater.

Section 2 imposes the same criminal liability upon those who aid and abet the commission of a crime as those who actually commit it. It carries the extraterritorial reach of the underlying offenses. Although more extensive than the predicate offense list of section 2339A, section 2 cannot stand on the full range of foreign law offenses available to subsection 2339C(a). Moreover, this section requires a completed predicate federal crime. There is ordinarily no crime to attempt to aid and abet nor to aid and abet an unsuccessful criminal effort. Subsection 2339C(a) suffers from neither limitation.

Prior to the Convention for the Suppression of the Financing of Terrorism entering into force for the United States, however, subsection 2339C(a) will not reach those overseas acts of financial support for terrorism offenses whose only connection to the United States is the subsequent presence of the offender in this country.

Concealment: Section 2339C also contains a concealment offense with extraterritorial application. Subsection 2339C(c)(concealment) only extends to those violations abroad that are committed by U.S. nationals or American entities. Section 2 appears to offer broader extraterritorial coverage, since its parallel prohibition on aiding and abetting violations of subsection 2339C(a)(financing terrorism) and 2339B enjoys the benefit of their extraterritorial application without any offender citizenship requirement. On the other hand, where their proscriptions overlap subsection 2339C(c) provides an additional penalty option since section 2 carries the same criminal penalties as the underlying offense (i.e., imprisonment for not more than 20 years plus fine) but not a civil penalty.

DOCUMENT NO. 9

MEJA EXPANSION AND ENFORCEMENT ACT OF 2007 (H.R. 2740)

110th Congress, First Session

October 4, 2007

SYNOPSIS:

A bill to require accountability for contractors and contract personnel under Federal contracts, and for other purposes

DATE OF INTRODUCTION: June 15, 2007

SPONSOR(S):

Sponsor and Cosponsors as of 06/20/2007
Price, David E. (D-NC) - Sponsor
Woolsey, Lynn (D-CA) - Cosponsor
Filner, Bob (D-CA) - Cosponsor
DeFazio, Peter A. (D-OR) - Cosponsor
HALL, JOHN (D-NY) - Cosponsor
Grijalva, Raul (D-AZ) - Cosponsor
McGovern, Jim (D-MA) - Cosponsor
Stark, Fortney H. (Pete) (D-CA) - Cosponsor
Brady, Robert (D-PA) - Cosponsor
Spratt, Jr., John (D-SC) - Cosponsor
Davis, Danny (D-IL) - Cosponsor
Schakowsky, Jan (D-IL) - Cosponsor
HIRONO, MAZIE (D-HI) - Cosponsor
ELLISON, KEITH (D-MN) - Cosponsor
Bishop, Tim (D-NY) - Cosponsor
Blumenauer, Earl (D-OR) - Cosponsor

TEXT:

HR 2740 EH
110th Congress, First Session
H.R. 2740

AN ACT

To require accountability for contractors and contract personnel under Federal contracts, and for other purposes.

Be it enacted by the Senate and House of Representatives of the United States of America in Congress assembled,

SECTION 1. SHORT TITLE.

This Act may be cited as the 'MEJA Expansion and Enforcement Act of 2007.'

SEC. 2. LEGAL STATUS OF CONTRACT PERSONNEL.

(a) Clarification of the Military Extraterritorial Jurisdiction Act—

(1) INCLUSION OF CONTRACTORS—Subsection (a) of section 3261 of title 18, United States Code, is amended—

(A) by striking 'or' at the end of paragraph (1);

(B) by striking the comma at the end of paragraph (2) and inserting'; or'; and

(C) by inserting after paragraph (2) the following:

'(3) while employed under a contract (or subcontract at any tier) awarded by any department or agency of the United States, where the work under such contract is carried out in an area, or in close proximity to an area (as designated by the Department of Defense), where the Armed Forces is conducting a contingency operation.'

(2) DEFINITION—Section 3267 of title 18, United States Code, is amended by adding at the end the following:

'(5) The term 'contingency operation' has the meaning given such term in section 101(a)(13) of title 10..'

(b) Department of Justice Inspector General Report—

(1) REPORT REQUIRED—Not later than 180 days after the date of the enactment of this Act, the Inspector General of the Department of Justice shall submit to Congress a report in accordance with this subsection.

(2) CONTENT OF REPORT—The report under paragraph (1) shall include—

(A) a description of the status of Department of Justice investigations of alleged violations of section 3261 of title 18, United States Code, to have been committed by contract personnel, which shall include—

(i) the number of complaints received by the Department of Justice;

(ii) the number of investigations into complaints opened by the Department of Justice;

(iii) the number of criminal cases opened by the Department of Justice; and

(iv) the number and result of criminal cases closed by the Department of Justice;

(B) findings and recommendations about the number of criminal cases prosecuted by the Department of Justice involving violations of section 3261 of title 18, United States Code; and

(C) with respect to covered contracts where the work under such contracts is carried out in Iraq or Afghanistan—

(i) a list of each charge brought against contractors or contract personnel performing work under such a covered contract, including—

(I) a description of the offense with which a contractor or contract personnel were charged; and

(II) the disposition of such charge; and

(ii) a description of any legal actions taken by the United States Government against contractors or contract personnel as a result of—

(I) a criminal charge brought against such contractors or contract personnel; or

(II) a complaint received regarding the activities of such contractors or contract personnel.

(3) FORMAT OF REPORT—The report under paragraph (1) shall be submitted in unclassified format, but may contain a classified annex as appropriate.

SEC. 3. FEDERAL BUREAU OF INVESTIGATION INVESTIGATIVE UNIT FOR CONTINGENCY OPERATIONS.

(a) Establishment of Theater Investigative Unit—The Director of the Federal Bureau of Investigation shall ensure that there are adequate personnel through the creation of Theater Investigative Units to investigate allegations of criminal violations of section 3261 of title 18, United States Code, by contract personnel.

(b) Responsibilities of Theater Investigative Unit—The Theater Investigative Unit established for a theater of operations shall—

(1) investigate reports that raise reasonable suspicion of criminal misconduct by contract personnel;

(2) investigate reports of fatalities resulting from the potentially unlawful use of force by contract personnel; and

(3) upon conclusion of an investigation of alleged criminal misconduct, refer the case to the Attorney General of the United States for further action, as appropriate in the discretion of the Attorney General.

(c) Responsibilities of Federal Bureau of Investigation—

(1) RESOURCES—The Director of the Federal Bureau of Investigation shall ensure that each Theater Investigative Unit has adequate resources and personnel to carry out its responsibilities.

(2) NOTIFICATION—The Director of the Federal Bureau of Investigation shall notify Congress whenever a Theater Investigative Unit is established or terminated in accordance with this section.

(3) SECURITY—The Director of the Federal Bureau of Investigation shall request security assistance from the Secretary of Defense in any case in which a Theater Investigative Unit does not have the resources or is otherwise unable to provide adequate security to ensure the safety of such Unit. The Director may not request or provide for security for a Theater Investigate Unit from any individual or entity other than the Federal Bureau of Investigation or the Secretary of Defense.

(d) Assistance on Request of Attorney General—In consultation with the Director of the Federal Bureau of Investigation, the Attorney General may request assistance from the Secretary of State, the Secretary of Defense, the Secretary of Homeland Security, or the head of any other Executive agency, notwithstanding any statute, rule, or regulation to the contrary, including the assignment of additional personnel and resources to a Theater Investigative Unit.

(e) Annual Report—Not later than one year after the date on which the Director of the Federal Bureau of Investigation ensures compliance with the provisions of this Act pursuant to section 5(c), and annually thereafter, the Director of the Federal Bureau of Investigation shall submit to Congress a report containing—

(1) the number of reports received by Theater Investigative Units relating to suspected criminal misconduct by contractors or contract personnel;

(2) the number of reports received by Theater Investigative Units relating to fatalities resulting from the use of force by contractors or contract personnel;

(3) the number of cases referred by Theater Investigative Units to the Attorney General for further investigation or other action; and

(4) any recommended changes to Federal law that the Director considers necessary to perform the duties of the Director under this Act.

SEC. 4. DEFINITIONS.

In this Act:

(1) COVERED CONTRACT—The term 'covered contract' means an agreement—

(A) that is—

(i) a prime contract awarded by an agency;

(ii) a subcontract at any tier under any prime contract awarded by an agency; or

(iii) a task order issued under a task or delivery order contract entered into by an agency; and

(B) according to which the work under such contract, subcontract, or task order is carried out in a region outside the United States in which the Armed Forces are conducting a contingency operation.

(2) AGENCY—The term 'agency' has the meaning given the term 'Executive agency' in section 105 of title 5, United States Code.

(3) CONTINGENCY OPERATION—The term 'contingency operation' has the meaning given the term section 101(13) of title 10, United States Code.

(4) CONTRACTOR—The term 'contractor' means an entity performing a covered contract.

(5) CONTRACT PERSONNEL—The term 'contract personnel' means persons assigned by a contractor (including subcontractors at any tier) to perform work under a covered contract.

SEC. 5. EFFECTIVE DATE.

(a) Applicability—The provisions of this Act shall apply to all covered contracts and all covered contract personnel in which the work under the contract is carried out in an area, or in close proximity to an area (as designated by the Department of Defense), where the Armed Forces is conducting a contingency operation on or after the date of the enactment of this Act.

(b) Immediate Effectiveness—The provisions of this Act shall enter into effect immediately upon the enactment of this Act.

(c) Implementation—With respect to covered contracts and covered contract personnel discussed in subsection (a)(1), the Director of the Federal Bureau of Investigation, and the head of any other agency to which this Act applies, shall have 90 days after the date of the enactment of this Act to ensure compliance with the provisions of this Act.

SEC. 6. RULE OF CONSTRUCTION.

Nothing in this Act shall be construed to affect intelligence activities that are otherwise permissible prior to the enactment of this Act.

Passed the House of Representatives October 4, 2007.

Attest:

Clerk.

110th Congress, 1st Session

H.R. 2740

AN ACT

To require accountability for contractors and contract personnel under Federal contracts, and for other purposes.

DOCUMENT NO. 10

DOD MEMO: UCMJ JURISDICTION OVER DOD CIVILIAN EMPLOYEES

Secretary of Defense

March 10, 2008

MEMORANDUM FOR SECRETARIES OF THE MILITARY DEPARTMENTS CHAIRMAN OF THE JOINT CHIEFS OF STAFF UNDER SECRETARIES OF DEFENSE COMMANDERS OF THE COMBATANT COMMANDS

SUBJECT: UCMJ Jurisdiction Over DoD Civilian Employees, DoD Contractor Personnel, and Other Persons Serving With or Accompanying the Armed Forces Overseas During Declared War and in Contingency Operations

References: (a) Section 552 of the John Warner National Defense Authorization Act for Fiscal Year 2007 (Public Law 109-364, October 17, 2006)

(b) Uniform Code of Military Justice (Chapter 47 of title 10, United States Code)

(c) Manual for Courts-Martial, United States (Executive Order 12473, July 13, 1984, as amended)

(d) Military Extraterritorial Jurisdiction Act (MEJA), Chapter 212 of title 18, United States Code

(e) Department of Defense Instruction 5525.11, "Criminal Jurisdiction Over Civilians Employed By or Accompanying the Armed Forces Outside the United States, Certain Service Members, and Former Service Members," March 3, 2005

Military operations in support of the Global War on Terrorism (GWOT) increasingly require U.S. military forces to operate alongside DoD civilian employees and DoD contractor personnel who serve with or accompany our armed forces as integral parts of that unified effort. This memorandum provides additional guidance to commanders on the exercise of their UCMJ authority during contingency operations, including those supporting the GWOT.

Commanders retain authority to respond to an incident, restore safety and order, investigate, apprehend suspected offenders, and otherwise address the immediate needs of the situation. Commanders possess significant authority to act whenever criminal activity may relate to or affect the commander's responsibilities, including situations in which the alleged offender's precise identity or actual affiliation is to that point undetermined. Attachment 1, "Command Law Enforcement Authority," summarizes the broad scope of this command authority. I expect commanders and their law enforcement authorities to act accordingly.

On October 17, 2006, the Uniform Code of Military Justice (UCMJ) was amended to extend UCMJ jurisdiction over persons serving with or accompanying U.S. armed forces in the field in times of declared war or a contingency operation (references (a) and (b)). Since then, commanders have had available this additional UCMJ disciplinary authority.

The unique nature of this extended UCMJ jurisdiction over civilians requires sound management over when, where, and by whom such jurisdiction is exercised. There is a particular need for clarity regarding the legal framework that should govern a command response to any illegal activities by Department of Defense civilian employees and DoD contractor personnel overseas with our Armed Forces. Accordingly, pursuant to my authority under Article 22, UCMJ (reference (b)), and Rules for Courts-Martial 401 and 601 of the Manual for Courts-Martial (reference (c)), the requirements of Attachment 2, "Article 2(a)(10), UCMJ, Authority Over Persons Serving With or Accompanying the Armed Forces," apply to all disciplinary actions under this UCMJ amendment.

When offenses alleged to have been committed by civilians violate U.S. federal criminal laws, the Department shall notify responsible Department of Justice (DoJ) authorities, and afford DoJ the opportunity to pursue its prosecution of the case in federal district court (references (d) and (e)). To expedite that process, the notification requirements and procedures of attachment 3 shall apply in all cases.

While the DoJ notification and decision process is pending, commanders and military criminal investigators should continue to address the alleged crime. Commanders should ensure that any preliminary military justice procedures that would be required in support of the exercise of UCMJ jurisdiction over civilians continue to be accomplished during the concurrent DoJ notification process. Commanders should be prepared to act, as appropriate, should possible U.S. federal criminal jurisdiction prove to be unavailable to address the alleged criminal behavior.

DoD regulations and other guidance, the regulations and other guidance of the Secretaries of the Military Departments (including the U.S. Coast Guard when it is operating as a Service in the Navy), publications and other guidance of the Joint Chiefs of Staff, and, by agreement, regulations and other guidance of the Department of Homeland Security for the U.S. Coast Guard, when it is not operating as a Service in the Navy, shall incorporate the guidance provided by this memorandum and its attachments. The General Counsel of the Department of Defense is authorized to issue additional guidance implementing this memorandum.

Command Law Enforcement Authority

The following summarizes some of the commander's authority and the military law enforcement authority available when a crime is committed within that commander's geographic area of responsibility outside the United States.

1. Commanders have authority to cause an inquiry or investigation to be conducted of any crime allegedly committed by persons subject to Uniform Code of Military Justice (UCMJ) jurisdiction, as well as a person subject to Military Extraterritorial Jurisdiction Act (MEJA) jurisdiction until such time as civilian law enforcement officials have assumed sole investigative responsibility. (References: Rule for Courts-Martial 303, Manual for Courts-Martial; DoD Instruction 5525.11; DoD Instruction 5525.07).

2. Military law enforcement officers and military criminal investigators are authorized to apprehend persons subject to UCMJ jurisdiction, and arrest and temporarily detain persons subject to MEJA jurisdiction, when there is probable cause that an offense has been committed and that the person committed it. (References: Rules for Courts-Martial 301-305, Manual for Courts-Martial; 10 U.S.C. §§ 807–814, 1585a, 4027, 7480, 9027; 18 U.S.C. § 3262; Paragraph 6.2, DoD Instruction 5525.11; DoD Instruction 5525.07).

3. All commissioned, warrant, petty, and noncommissioned officers on active duty may apprehend offenders subject to UCMJ jurisdiction. (References: 10 U.S.C. § 807; Rule for Courts-Martial 302, Manual for Courts-Martial).

4. Any person authorized to make an apprehension may use such force and means as are reasonable under the circumstances to accomplish the apprehension. (References: 10 U.S.C. § 807; Rule for Courts-Martial 302, Manual for Courts-Martial).

5. Federal law enforcement officials have independent authority to apprehend persons, whether or not subject to trial by court-martial, to the extent their authority is permitted by applicable statutes and other law. (References: 10 U.S.C. § 807; Rule for Courts-Martial 302, Manual for Courts-Martial; DOD Instruction 5525.07).

Article 2(a)(10), UCMJ, Authority

Over Persons Serving With or Accompanying the Armed Forces

1. Within the Department of Defense, only the Secretary of Defense shall possess authority to exercise court-martial convening authority and impose nonjudicial punishment over persons subject to Article 2(a)(10), Uniform Code of Military Justice (UCMJ), jurisdiction with respect to:

a. Offenses committed within the "United States", meaning the several States of the United States, the District of Columbia, and the commonwealths, territories, and possessions of the United States;

b. Persons who were not at all times during the alleged misconduct located outside the "United States", as defined above; and

c. Persons who are, at the time court-martial charges are initiated (preferred) or notice of Article 15, UCMJ proceedings is given, located within the "United States", as defined above.

2. Subject to the above, the commanders of geographic combatant commands, and only those commanders assigned or attached to the combatant command who possess general court-martial convening authority, may exercise court-martial convening authority and impose nonjudicial punishment over persons subject to Article 2(a)(10), UCMJ, jurisdiction with respect to offenses committed outside the "United States," as defined above. The commander of the combatant command may further withhold such authority within the combatant command.

3. Authority to initiate (prefer) court-martial charges and nonjudicial punishment is withheld until the required notification requirements established in attachment 3 are accomplished for Article 2(a)(10), UCMJ, cases. Law enforcement, criminal investigations, and other military justice procedures that precede the initiation (preferral) of court-martial charges should continue, as applicable, during this notification process.

4. Authority to initiate (prefer) court-martial charges and nonjudicial punishment over an offense pursuant to this UCMJ authority is withheld whenever the Department of Justice (DoJ) provides notice to the Department of Defense that it intends to pursue U.S. federal criminal prosecution for what is substantially the same offense or a related offense, and such withholding shall remain in effect while DoJ is pursuing its

federal prosecution of the case, and until such prosecution is completed or terminated prior to its completion.

Article 2(a)(10), UCMJ, Notification Requirements and Procedures

Because of the unique nature of this Uniform Code of Military Justice (UCMJ) jurisdiction over civilians, it is important that the exercise of this jurisdiction be based on military necessity to support an effective fighting force and be called for by circumstances that meet the interests of justice, such as:

- When U.S. federal criminal jurisdiction otherwise does not apply or federal prosecution is not pursued, and/or
- When the person's conduct is adverse to a significant military interest of the United States (e.g., alleged misconduct that may jeopardize good order and discipline or discredit the armed forces and thereby have a potential adverse effect on military operations).

Nevertheless, before initiating a disciplinary action pursuant to this UCMJ authority, commanders shall comply with the following notification procedures to determine whether U.S. federal criminal jurisdiction under the Military Extraterritorial Jurisdiction Act (MEJA) or other federal laws applies and will be pursued:

1. The notification procedures and information requirements of DoD Instruction 5525.11 shall be followed in all cases intended to be pursued under Article 2(a)(10), UCMJ, jurisdiction, to include providing all reasonably available information regarding the investigation and the location of the alleged offender's last known residence in the United States.

2. Commanders who are not general court-martial convening authorities (GCMCA) have had their UCMJ authority withheld by attachment 2. As such, those commanders shall, before initiating any disposition action under Rules for Courts-Martial 306-308 or 401-406 of the Manual for Courts-Martial (MCM), forward expeditiously all available information regarding the alleged misconduct that is potentially subject to this jurisdiction to the first GCMCA in the chain of command for that GCMCA's disposition consideration under Rule for Courts-Martial 407, MCM. The notification shall include the reasoning in support of a UCMJ disposition.

3. *Combatant Command GCMCA Notification Requirements.* All GCMCAs assigned or attached to the geographic combatant commands shall notify in writing (including by email or facsimile) their respective geographic combatant command commander of their intended disposition by court-martial or nonjudicial punishment over persons subject to Article 2(a)(10), UCMJ, jurisdiction. This notification affords the commander of

the geographic combatant command concerned the opportunity to accomplish the following notification requirements, as well as the opportunity to exercise authority under Rule for Courts-Martial 601(f), MCM.

4. *Combatant Command Notification Requirements*. Before initiating (preferring) court-martial charges and nonjudicial punishment based on Article 2(a)(10), UCMJ, jurisdiction, and regardless of whether the suspected offense may also be an offense under federal criminal laws, reference (e), the geographic combatant commander shall first provide notice of the case in writing (including by email or facsimile), in accordance with the procedures established in DoD Instruction 5525.11. This notification enables the Department of Defense to formally notify the Department of Justice (DoJ) of the case and any potential U.S. federal criminal jurisdiction, and affords DoJ an opportunity to determine if it intends to pursue U.S. federal criminal prosecution and to advise DoD accordingly.

a. Commanders should continue law enforcement, criminal investigations, and other military justice procedures that precede the initiation (preferral) of court-martial charges and nonjudicial punishment during this notification process, as applicable.

b. After DoD's formal notification to DoJ, DoJ shall expeditiously (but in no case longer than 14 calendar days) determine whether it intends to exercise jurisdiction over the case.

(1) If, within that 14-day review period, DoJ determines that extraordinary circumstances warrant additional time to complete its review, the Deputy Attorney General shall communicate that assessment to the Deputy Secretary of Defense and an extension shall be granted as mutually agreed upon.

(2) If, after this review period (to include any extension to which the Deputy Attorney General and Deputy Secretary of Defense agreed upon), DoJ does not advise DoD that it intends to pursue prosecution of the case, DoD may notify DoJ that it intends to authorize the initiation of UCMJ proceedings and may then inform the geographic combatant commander that, as a matter of command discretion, disciplinary action pursuant to Article 2(a)(10), UCMJ, may be initiated.

(3) When notifying the respective GCMCA who intends to take disciplinary action, the combatant commander shall also advise the respective GCMCA whether the combatant commander will, instead, exercise UCMJ authority pursuant to Rule for Courts-Martial 601(f), MCM. Similar procedures shall apply when DoJ advises DoD that the

(4) exercise of U.S. federal criminal jurisdiction is not applicable, or when DoJ indicates it does not intend to pursue prosecution.

c. Even where DoJ intends to pursue prosecution, continued DOD investigative assistance may be necessary. Thus, criminal investigative activity by DOD should continue in coordination with DoJ unless and until civilian law enforcement officials assume sole investigative responsibility for the matter.

d. When DoJ elects to exercise jurisdiction over the case, further action by the combatant command concerned, and all GCMCAs assigned or attached to that combatant command, to convene a court-martial or administer nonjudicial punishment is withheld, as stated in attachment 2.

e. The required notification process does not rescind or negate general court-martial convening authority over cases subject to Article 2(a)(10), UCMJ, jurisdiction and, in the event that U.S. federal criminal jurisdiction of the case is later declined or terminated, GCMCAs may then exercise this authority, as appropriate.

ADDITIONAL CONCERNS OVER THE USE OF CONTRACTORS ON THE BATTLEFIELD

Commentary

By
Douglas C. Lovelace, Jr.

We conclude this volume with two additional documents that shed light on issues associated with the use of contractors in the war against terrorists. The first is a March 2008 Government Accountability Office (GAO) report on testimony before the U.S. House of Representatives' Armed Services Committee's Subcommittee on Readiness. The second document is a GAO Report to Congressional Committees that addresses a particular concern with the management of contracts and the relationship between contractors and contracting officers. Each report addresses contemporary concerns and helps provide better understanding of the state concern regarding increased reliance on contractors.

The GAO report, *DEFENSE MANAGEMENT: DoD Needs to Reexamine Its Extensive Reliance on Contractors and Continue to Improve Management and Oversight*, summarizes a GAO study conducted to review longstanding issues associated with determining the appropriate roles for contractors and their management, particularly within and by the Department of defense (DoD.) It also identifies and discusses the increased number and severity of challenges confronting U.S. agencies who rely more and more on contractors. Understandably, the report focuses on DoD's problems in managing its increased reliance on contractors supporting deployed forces. The reader will find informative the report's review of some of the GAO's past recommendations to improve DoD's management, and measures taken by DoD to address them.

In this study, GAO correctly concludes that problems associated with increased reliance on contractors to perform core agency missions are greater in contingency operations such as in Iraq, in disaster relief operations such as those following hurricane Katrina, and in other *in extremis* cases requiring efforts beyond the government's organic capabilities or capacity. As suggested in earlier sections of this volume, the business case for relying extensively on contractors has come under increasing challenge. That analysis has several dimensions, some of which this report highlights. First, DoD must determine which are its core functions and ensure the capabilities to address them are resident in the Department. One could reasonably argue that increased capacity to perform core functions may me acquired through the use of contractors. But, as the report implies, DoD should never entirely relinquish a capability to perform a core function. Additionally, the capabilities required to perform certain core functions, such as the use of violence to achieve tactical, operational, and strategic objectives should remain the sole province of DoD. Nevertheless, we have seen the emergence and significant growth of the use of private security contractors over the past five years.

The key then, as the report correctly concludes, is to develop a workforce strategy that provides a blend of contractor and government personnel that addresses accountability, risk, ethical and professional concerns, oversight requirements and the apportionment of roles and missions. The report correctly notes that the most significant challenges confronting DoD have been in the areas of oversight, adherence to planning guidance, failure to lean institutionally, and inadequate training for military commanders and contract oversight personnel. The report provides evidence that these problems have had negative impacts on operations and have increased cost unnecessarily. As for cost, the report reinforces the observation often made elsewhere that the extent to which, if any, reliance on contractors had resulted in overall cost savings has yet to be shown.

The final document in this volume, *Defense Contracting: Army Case Study Delineates Concerns with Use of Contractors as Contract Specialists*, Is a March 2008 GAO report on a study conducted in collaboration with the Army Contracting Agency's (ACA) Contracting Center of Excellence (CCE). The report focuses on a particular role performed by contractors: the use of contractors as contract specialists; that is, to assist in awarding and managing contracts performed by other contractors. The study examined CCE reliance on contractor contract specialists, what the risk of doing so is and how is it managed. The report also addresses the relative cost of the practice and whether the contracts were appropriate. The report presents several significant findings.

GAO found that since the practice began in 2003, the use of contractors as contract specialists has grown considerably. When measured in August 2007, 42% of the contract specialist population was provided by contractors. The dramatically increased use of contractors in this role has given rise to many issues, and the GAO report addresses many of them. CCE officials stated an understandable preference for using government employees as contract specialists. CCE also reported difficulty in hiring and retaining government contractor specialists due to competition from the private sector and also from other government agencies. This is not surprising. The duties of a contracting specialist are highly sensitive and quite technical. Therefore, contracting specialists must be extensively trained. Often the government will hire and train a contracting specialist only to lose the person to private industry.

That suggests a second issue associated with the use of contractor contracting specialists; they cost more in the long run. This also should come as no surprise. When contracting specialist jobs are filled by contractors as opposed to direct government hiring, overall cost must increase, assuming market forces determine what a contracting specialist costs the government, as well as private contractors. When a private contractor supplies comparable personnel to fill contracting specialist positions, it must add a surcharge to assure a profit for the company providing the contracting specialists. Since it must compensate the contracting specialists it provides the same that the government would compensate them, the resulting cost to the government must be higher, unless the company provides less qualified personnel. Such contractors sometimes "buy-in low" by initially submitting bids too low to provide adequate profit, with the intent of escalating the costs in the future. This practice makes the use of contractors as contracting specialists initially seem attractive, but the final steady-state cost can be much higher. In fact, GAO found that CCE is paying almost 27 percent more for its contractor-provided contract specialists than for similarly graded government employees.

The GAO found other significant issues with the use of contractor contracting specialists. The GAO correctly reported that although federal regulations require that contractors be clearly distinguished from government employees, frequently they are not. Additionally, the Federal Acquisition Regulations' (FAR) general prohibition of personal services contracts appears to be violated frequently. GAO also found that Joint Ethics Regulation (JER) conflict of interest proscriptions have been violated. Furthermore, notwithstanding warnings from its legal counsel, GAO found that CCE has used an inappropriate Government Services Contract (GSA) to order contract specialists and unauthorized contractor advertising on the GSA website. The brief recommendations the report offers addresses the problems GAO discusses in the report and indications are that the U.S. Army and GSA are committed to implementing them.

DOCUMENT NO. 11

DEFENSE MANAGEMENT: DOD NEEDS TO REEXAMINE ITS EXTENSIVE RELIANCE ON CONTRACTORS AND CONTINUE TO IMPROVE MANAGEMENT AND OVERSIGHT

GAO Report
GAO-08-572T

March 11, 2008

Statement of David M. Walker
Comptroller General of the United States

Testimony Before the Subcommittee on Readiness, Committee on Armed Services, House of Representatives

What GAO Found

While there are benefits to using contractors to perform services for the government—such as increased flexibility in fulfilling immediate needs—GAO and others have raised concerns about the increasing reliance on contractors to perform agency missions. GAO's body of work shows that agencies face challenges with increased reliance on contractors to perform core agency missions, and these challenges are accentuated in contingency operations such as Iraq, in emergency situations such as Hurricane Katrina, or in cases where sufficient government personnel are not available. In making the decision to use contractors, agencies have experienced challenges such as: determining which functions and activities should be contracted out and which should not to ensure institutional capacity; developing a total workforce strategy to address the extent of contractor use and the appropriate mix of contractor and government personnel; identifying and distinguishing the roles and responsibilities of contractors and civilian and military personnel; and ensuring appropriate oversight, including addressing risks, ethics concerns, and surveillance needs.

DOD's increased reliance on contractors to support forces deployed for military operations and to perform maintenance and other logistic support for weapon systems has highlighted challenges that DOD faces in managing this component of its total force. With regard to contractor support for deployed forces, DOD's primary challenges have been to provide effective management and oversight, including failure to follow planning guidance, an inadequate number of contract oversight personnel, failure to systematically capture and distribute lessons learned, and a lack of comprehensive training for military commanders and contract oversight personnel. These challenges have led to negative operational and monetary impacts at deployed locations. For example, several military commanders GAO met with in 2006 said their pre-deployment training did not provide them with sufficient information on the extent of contractor support that they would be relying on in Iraq and were therefore surprised by the substantial number of personnel they had to allocate to provide on-base escorts, convoy security, and other force protection support to contractors. Although DOD has taken some steps to address these issues, many of these issues remain a concern and additional actions are needed. With respect to weapon system support, the challenges have been to resolve questions about how much depot maintenance and other logistics work needs to be performed in-house and to what extent outsourcing for DOD logistics has been cost-effective. While DOD has a process for defining core maintenance capability, GAO has identified shortcomings with this process and found that core maintenance capability has not always been developed. Finally, although increased contractor reliance for maintenance and other logistics activities was justified by DOD based on the assumption that there would be significant cost savings, it is uncertain to what extent cost savings have occurred or will occur.

Mr. Chairman and Members of the Subcommittee:

I am pleased to be here today to discuss the increased reliance on contractors to conduct more and more of the business of the federal government. In fiscal year 2007, the federal government spent about $254 billion on contractor services, an amount that has more than doubled over the past decade. The Department of Defense's (DOD) obligations on service contracts, expressed in constant fiscal year 2006 dollars, rose from $85.1 billion in fiscal year 1996 to more than $151 billion in fiscal year 2006, a 78 percent increase. With this growth in spending, DOD has become increasingly reliant on contractors both overseas and in the United States. For example, the department has relied extensively on contractors for services that include communication services, interpreters who accompany military patrols, base operations support (e.g., food and housing), weapon systems maintenance, and intelligence analysis to support military operations in Southwest Asia. The U.S. military has long used contractors to provide supplies and services to deployed forces, but the scale of contractor support DOD relies on in deployed locations today has increased considerably. DOD has recently estimated the number of contractors in Iraq and Afghanistan to be about 196,000. Further, DOD currently has the equivalent of three brigades of contractors providing security services in Iraq, as well as another brigade equivalent supporting these contractors—a total of about 12,000 personnel. Put another way, there are more private security contractors in Iraq today than the total number of contractors (about 9,200) that were deployed to support military operations in the 1991 Gulf War. In addition to the support contractors provide for military forces deployed overseas, DOD has also increasingly relied on contractors for other services. For example, we have reported in recent years on DOD's increasing reliance on the private sector for various aspects of weapon system logistics support, including depot-level maintenance.

While contractors, along with military personnel and civilians, are part of DOD's total force and fulfill many vital functions that enable DOD to accomplish its missions, the increased reliance on contractors has raised a number of issues and concerns that warrant continued attention. Our previous work has highlighted long-standing problems regarding the appropriate role and management and oversight of contractors in the federal workforce—particularly at DOD—and I have identified 15 systemic acquisition challenges facing DOD (see app. I). These challenges range from separating agency wants from needs to creating a capable workforce and holding it accountable. Since 1992, we have designated DOD contract management as a high-risk area, in part due to concerns over the adequacy of the department's acquisition workforce, including contract oversight personnel. Congress has expressed increasing concerns about DOD's management and oversight of contractors as well. For example, the National Defense Authorization Act for Fiscal Year 2008 called for the creation of a Commission on Wartime Contracting to make assessments of the government's reliance on contractors in Iraq and Afghanistan and certain contract performance and management issues related to those contracts. The act also created a contingency contractor training requirement for military personnel outside the acquisition workforce. Congress also has taken steps to improve oversight by increasing the budgets for the Defense Contract Audit Agency, Defense Contract Management Agency, and the Defense Department's Inspector General in the fiscal year 2008 DOD appropriations. As I have noted previously, given DOD's heavy and increasing reliance on contractors in Iraq and elsewhere, and the risks this reliance entails, it may be appropriate to ask if DOD has become too reliant on contractors to provide essential services.[1] To help frame this issue today, I will highlight

[1] GAO, *Stabilizing and Rebuilding Iraq: Conditions in Iraq Are Conducive to Fraud, Waste, and Abuse,* GAO-07-525T (Washington, D.C.: Apr. 23, 2007).

governmentwide challenges we have identified related to the increased reliance on contractors. Next, I will focus more specifically on challenges DOD has had in managing the increased reliance on contractors who support deployed troops and who provide logistics support for weapons systems. I will conclude with some broad observations that Congress and DOD may wish to consider in addressing these important issues.

My statement today is based primarily on our prior work and the work of others at agencies across the federal government. Our work includes reviews at the Departments of Defense, Homeland Security, and Energy, the Environmental Protection Agency, and the National Aeronautics and Space Administration. The work of others includes the congressionally mandated Acquisition Advisory Panel and the Defense Acquisition University. A list of related GAO products is provided at the end of this statement. As part of ongoing work, we obtained updated information on DOD's actions to address issues we have previously raised. We developed this statement from February to March 2008 in accordance with generally accepted government auditing standards. Those standards require that we plan and perform the audit to obtain sufficient, appropriate evidence to provide a reasonable basis for our findings and conclusions based on our audit objectives. We believe that the evidence obtained provides a reasonable basis for our findings and conclusions based on our audit objectives.

Summary

While there are benefits to using contractors to perform services for the government—such as increased flexibility in fulfilling immediate needs—GAO and others have raised concerns about the increasing reliance on contractors to perform agency missions. Our body of work shows that agencies face challenges with increased reliance on contractors to perform core agency missions, and these challenges are accentuated in contingency operations such as Iraq, in emergency situations such Hurricane Katrina, or in cases where sufficient government personnel are not available. In making the decision to use contractors, agencies have experienced challenges such as: determining which functions and activities should be contracted out and which should not to ensure institutional capacity; developing a total workforce strategy to address the extent of contractor use and the appropriate mix of contractor and government personnel; identifying and distinguishing the roles and responsibilities of contractors and civilian and military personnel; and ensuring appropriate oversight, including addressing risks, ethics concerns, and surveillance needs.

DOD's increased reliance on contractors to support forces deployed for military operations and to perform maintenance and other logistic support for weapon systems has highlighted challenges that DOD faces in managing this component of its total force. With regard to contractor support for deployed forces, DOD's primary challenges have been to provide effective management and oversight. These challenges include failure to follow planning guidance, an inadequate number of contract oversight personnel, failure to systematically capture and distribute lessons learned, and a lack of comprehensive training for military commanders and contract oversight personnel. These challenges have led to negative operational and monetary impacts at deployed locations. For example, several military commanders we met with in 2006 said their pre-deployment training did not provide them with sufficient information on the extent of contractor support that they would be relying on in Iraq and were therefore surprised by the substantial number of personnel they had to allocate to provide on-base escorts, convoy security, and other force protection support to contractors. Although DOD has taken some steps to address these issues, many of these issues remain a concern and additional actions are needed. For example, in response to our 2003 recommendation that DOD develop comprehensive guidance to help the services manage contractors supporting deployed forces, the department issued the first comprehensive guidance dealing with contractors who support deployed forces in October 2005. However, as we recently testified, DOD's leadership needs to ensure implementation of and compliance with this guidance and other guidance.[2] With respect to weapon system support, the challenges have been to resolve questions about how much depot maintenance and other logistics work needs to be performed in-house and to what extent outsourcing for DOD logistics has been cost-effective. While DOD has a process for defining core maintenance capability, we have identified shortcomings with this process and found that core maintenance capability has not always been developed. Further, DOD does not have a process for defining core capability requirements for other logistics functions and activities, such as supply chain management and engineering. Finally, although increased contractor reliance for maintenance and other logistics activities was justified by DOD based on the assumption that there would be significant cost savings, it is uncertain to what extent cost savings have occurred or will occur.

Background

Acquisition of products and services from contractors consumes about a quarter of discretionary spending governmentwide, with services making up roughly 60 percent. These services range from basic functions, such as landscaping and janitorial, to those that are more complex, like intelligence analysis, acquisition support, security services, and program office support. The acquisition of services differs from that of products in several key

[2] GAO, *Military Operations: Implementation of Existing Guidance and Other Actions Needed to Improve DOD's Oversight and Management of Contractors in Future Operations*, GAO-08-436T (Washington, D.C.: Jan. 24, 2008).

respects and can be particularly challenging in terms of defining requirements and assessing contractor performance. DOD is by far the largest federal purchaser of service contracts—ranging from housing to intelligence to security.

Contractors can play an important part in helping agencies accomplish their missions. For example, agencies use service contracts to acquire special knowledge and skills not available in the government, obtain cost-effective services, or obtain temporary or intermittent services. The congressionally mandated Acquisition Advisory Panel[3] has cited a number of developments that have led federal agencies to increase the use of contractors as service providers: limitations on the number of authorized full-time equivalent positions; unavailability of certain capabilities and expertise among federal employees; desire for operational flexibility; and the need for "surge" capacity. According to DOD and service officials, several factors have contributed to the department's increased use of contractors for support services: (1) the increased requirements associated with the Global War on Terrorism and other contingencies; (2) policy to rely on the private sector for needed commercial services that are not inherently governmental in nature; and (3) DOD initiatives, such as competitive sourcing and utility privatization programs.

The Office of Management and Budget (OMB), procurement law, and the Federal Acquisition Regulation (FAR) provide guidance on contracting for services. OMB Circular A-76 details a process for federal agencies to obtain commercially available services currently performed by government employees from the private sector when it is cost-effective to do so.[4] The Circular reinforces that government personnel shall perform inherently governmental activities. This process does not apply to private sector performance of a new requirement, expanded activity, or continued performance of a commercial activity. As such, this process effectively applies to a small percentage of the government's contracting activity. Most of the growth in service contracting has occurred outside of the A-76 process. The Federal Activities Inventory Reform (FAIR) Act of 1998 further requires agencies annually to determine and list which government-provided agency activities are not inherently governmental functions.[5] Federal procurement regulation states that functions that are so intimately related to the public interest are considered inherently governmental and should only be performed by government personnel. These functions include

[3] The Panel was established by section 1423 of the Services Acquisition Reform Act of 2003, Pub. L. No. 108-136, Title XIV. The Report of the Acquisition Advisory Panel to the Office of Federal Procurement Policy and the United States Congress was dated January 2007.

[4] Office of Management and Budget Circular A-76 (Revised) (May 29, 2003).

[5] Pub. L. No. 105-270, §2(a) (1998). In 1999, OMB incorporated the FAIR Act requirements into the A-76 process.

those activities which require either the exercise of discretion in applying government authority or the use of value judgment in making decisions for the government, and should not be performed by contractors.[6] The FAR and OMB also require agencies to provide greater scrutiny and management oversight when contracting for services that closely support the performance of inherently governmental functions.[7] The closer contractor services come to supporting inherently governmental functions, the greater the risk of their influencing the government's control over and accountability for decisions that may be based, in part, on contractor work. This may result in decisions that are not in the best interest of the government, and may increase vulnerability to waste, fraud, and abuse.

Before I go into more detail on the issues surrounding the federal government's and DOD's reliance on contractors, I would like to touch on another subject of interest to the Subcommittee—DOD's application of enhanced use leases. DOD's longstanding leasing authority is codified at 10 U.S.C. 2667. The law provides general authority for the Secretary of a military department to enter into a lease upon such terms he considers will promote the national defense or be in the public interest. The Secretary of a military department is authorized to lease real property up to five years unless the Secretary determines that a lease for a longer period will promote the nation defense or be in the public interest. Over time, Congress has expanded DOD's leasing authority several times to provide a lessee the first right to buy the property and provide for payment in cash or in kind by the lessee of consideration in an amount not less than the fair market value. Most recently, the National Defense Authorization Act for Fiscal Year 2008 amended 10 U.S.C. 2667 in several ways; for example, the authority to accept facilities operation support as in-kind consideration was eliminated, and a requirement that leases meeting certain criteria be competitively awarded was added.[8] The services have leased real property on their bases for years as a means to reduce infrastructure and base operating costs. For example, the military services have leased space for banks, credit unions, ATMs, storage, schools, and agricultural grazing. As you know, Mr. Chairman, we are conducting a review of DOD's land use planning activities, and will have more to say on this issue later.

Federal Agencies Have Faced Challenges with Increased Reliance on Contractors to Perform Agency Missions

While there are benefits to using contractors to perform services for the government—such as increased flexibility in fulfilling immediate

[6] FAR § 2.101.

[7] FAR § 37.114; OFPP Policy Letter 93-1: Management Oversight of Services Contracting, Office of Federal Procurement Policy, May 18, 1994.

[8] National Defense Authorization Act for Fiscal Year 2008, Pub. L. No. 110-181, § 2823 (2008).

needs—GAO and others have raised concerns about the increasing reliance on contractors to perform agency missions. Our work shows that agencies face challenges with increased reliance on contractors to perform core agency missions, especially in contingency or emergency situations or in cases where sufficient government personnel are not available. As I have previously stated, prior to making the decisions to use contractors, agency officials should focus greater attention on which functions and activities should be contracted out and which should not. To guide this approach, agencies need to consider developing a total workforce strategy to meet current and future human capital needs, and address the extent of contractor use and the appropriate mix of contractor and civilian and military personnel. I have also noted that identifying and distinguishing the responsibilities of contractors and civilian and military personnel are critical to ensure contractor roles are appropriate. Finally, once contractors are in place, agencies must ensure appropriate oversight of contractors, including addressing risks, ethics concerns, and surveillance needs.

Institutional Capacity: Agencies Face Challenges in Determining What Functions and Activities Can be Contracted Out and What Should be Provided by Government Personnel

In order to determine what functions and activities can be contracted out, the FAIR Act requires agencies annually to identify government-performed agency activities that are not inherently governmental functions. At GAO's 2006 forum on federal acquisition challenges and opportunities, some participants noted that it might be more appropriate for agencies to develop guiding principles or values to determine which positions could be contracted out and which should be performed in-house. Forum participants further noted that many corporate organizations carefully deliberate upfront and at the highest management levels about what core functions they need to retain and what non-core functions they should buy, and the skill sets needed to procure non-core functions.[9]

DOD's Panel on Contracting Integrity, in its 2007 report to Congress, noted that the practice of using contractors to support the government acquisition function merits further study because it gives rise to questions regarding the appropriate designation of government versus nongovernment functions.[10] A November 2005 report by the Defense Acquisition University warned that the government must be careful when contracting for the acquisition support function to ensure that the government retains thorough

[9] GAO, *Highlights of a GAO Forum: Federal Acquisition Challenges and Opportunities in the 21st Century*, GAO-07-45SP (Washington, D.C.: Oct. 6, 2006).

[10] The Panel was established by section 813 of the John Warner National Defense Authorization Act for Fiscal Year 2007, Pub. L. No. 109-364 (2006). Its 2007 Report to Congress was the first of three annual reports mandated by the act.

control of policy and management decisions and that contracting for the acquisition support function does not inappropriately restrict agency management in its ability to develop and consider options.[11] Additionally, our prior work has found that when federal agencies, including DOD, believe they do not have the in-house capability to design, develop, and manage complex acquisitions, they sometimes turn to a systems integrator to carry out these functions, creating an inherent risk of relying too much on contractors to make program decisions. For example, the Army's Future Combat System program is managed by a lead systems integrator that assumes the responsibilities of developing requirements; selecting major system and subsystem contractors; and making trade-off decisions among costs, schedules, and capabilities. While this management approach has some advantages for DOD, we found that the extent of contractor responsibility makes DOD vulnerable to decisions being made by the contractor that are not in the government's best interests.[12]

In September 2007, we reported that an increasing reliance on contractors to perform services for core government activities challenges the capacity of federal officials to supervise and evaluate the performance of these activities. I recently noted that this may be a concern in the intelligence community.[13] Specifically, while direction and control of intelligence and counter-intelligence operations are listed as inherently governmental functions, the Director of National Intelligence reported in 2006 that the intelligence community finds itself in competition with its contractors for employees and is left with no choice but to use contractors for work that may be "borderline inherently governmental."[14] We have also found problems with contractors having too much control at other federal agencies.[15] Unless the federal government pays the needed attention to the types of functions and activities performed by contractors, agencies run the risk of losing accountability and control over mission-related decisions.

---

[11] Defense Acquisition University, *Contracting Out Procurement Functions: An Analysis*, DAU Research Report 06-001 (Fort Belvoir, VA.: November 2005).

[12] GAO, *Defense Acquisitions: Role of Lead Systems Integrator on Future Combat Systems Program Poses Oversight Challenges*, GAO-07-380 (Washington, D.C.: June 6, 2007).

[13] GAO, *Intelligence Reform: GAO Can Assist the Congress and the Intelligence Community on Management Reform Initiatives*, GAO-08-413T (Washington, D.C.: Feb. 29, 2008).

[14] The U.S. Intelligence Community's Five Year Strategic Human Capital Plan.

[15] See for example, GAO, *Civil Servants and Contractor Employees: Who Should Do What for the Federal Government?* FPCD-81-43 (Washington, D.C.: June 19, 1981); GAO, *Energy Management: Using DOE Employees Can Reduce Costs for Some Support Services*, GAO/RCED 91-186 (Washington, D.C.: Aug. 16, 1991); GAO, Government Contractors: Are Service Contractors Performing Inherently Governmental Functions? GAO/GGD-92-11 (Washington, D.C.: Nov. 18, 1991).

Workforce Planning: Agencies Face Challenges in Developing an Appropriate Mix of Contractor and Government Personnel to Meet Current and Future Needs

Along with determining the functions and activities to be contracted out, agencies face challenges in developing a total workforce strategy to address the extent of contractor use and the appropriate mix of contractor and civilian and military personnel. We have found that agencies need appropriate workforce planning strategies that include contractor as well as federal personnel and are linked to current and future human capital needs. These strategies should be linked to the knowledge, skills, and abilities needed by agencies and how the workforce will be deployed across the organization. Deployment includes the flexible use of the workforce, such as putting the right employees in the right roles according to their skills, and relying on staff drawn from various organizational components and functions using "just-in-time" or "virtual" teams to focus the right talent on specific tasks.[16]

As agencies develop their workforce strategies, they also need to consider the extent to which contractors should be used and the appropriate mix of contractor and federal personnel. Over the past several years, there has been increasing concern about the ability of agencies to ensure sufficient numbers of staff to perform some inherently governmental functions. The Department of Homeland Security's human capital strategic plan notes the department has identified core mission-critical occupations and plans to reduce skill gaps in core and key competencies. However, it is unclear how this will be achieved and whether it will inform the department's use of contractors for services that closely support inherently governmental functions. The Department of Homeland Security has agreed with the need to establish strategic-level guidance for determining the appropriate mix of government and contractor employees to meet mission needs.[17]

Roles and Responsibilities: Agencies Face Challenges in Defining the Relationship between Contractors and Government Employees

Agencies are challenged to define the roles and responsibilities of contractors vis-à-vis government employees. Defining the relationship between contractors and government employees is particularly important when contracting for professional and management support services since contractors often work closely with government employees to provide these services. This definition begins during the acquisition planning process

[16] GAO, *Human Capital: A Self-Assessment Checklist for Agency Leaders*, GAO/GGD-99-179 (Washington, D.C.: Sept. 1, 1999).

[17] GAO, *Department of Homeland Security: Improved Assessment and Oversight Needed to Manage Risk of Contracting for Selected Services*, GAO-07-990 (Washington, D.C.: Sept. 17, 2007).

when contract requirements are determined. We have recommended that agencies define contract requirements to clearly describe roles, responsibilities, and limitations of selected contractor services. Well-defined contract requirements can also help minimize the risk of contractors performing inherently governmental functions. Yet contracts, especially service contracts, often do not have definitive or realistic requirements at the outset. Because the nature of contracted services can vary widely, from building maintenance to intelligence, a tailored approach should be used in defining requirements to help ensure that risks associated with a requirement are fully considered before entering into a contract arrangement.[18] In our recent review of the Department of Homeland Security's service contracts, we found that some contracts included requirements that were broadly defined and lacked detail about activities that closely support inherently governmental functions. We found instances in which contractors provided services that were integral to the department's mission or comparable to work performed by government employees, such as a contractor directly supporting the department's efforts to hire federal employees, including signing offer letters.[19]

Our work on contractors in acquisition support functions has found that it is now commonplace for agencies to use contractors to perform activities historically performed by federal government contract specialists. Although these contractors are not authorized to obligate government funds, they provide acquisition support to contracting officers, the federal decision makers who have the authority to bind the government contractually. Contract specialists perform tasks that closely support inherently governmental functions, such as assisting in preparing statements of work; developing and managing acquisition plans; and preparing the documents the contracting officer signs, such as contracts, solicitations, and contract modifications. Therefore, it is important to clearly define the roles contractors play in supporting government personnel to ensure they do not perform inherently governmental functions.

Management and Oversight: Agencies Face Challenges in Assessing Risks, Minimizing Potential Ethics Concerns, and Ensuring Quality Surveillance

Our work has also identified a number of practices that are important to effectively managing and overseeing contractors once contractors are in place. These include assessing risks, minimizing potential ethics concerns,

[18] GAO, *Defense Acquisitions: Tailored Approach Needed to Improve Service Acquisition Outcomes*, GAO-07-20 (Washington, D.C.: Nov. 9, 2006).
[19] GAO-07-990.

and ensuring quality through adequate surveillance. However, agencies face challenges in all these areas.

Risk is innate when contractors closely support inherently governmental functions. Federal procurement policy requires enhanced oversight of services that closely support the performance of inherently governmental functions to ensure that government decisions reflect the independent judgment of agency officials and that agency officials retain control over and remain accountable for policy decisions that may be based on contractor work products. However, our work has shown that agency officials do not always assess these risks to government decision making. For example, in 2007 we reported that while Department of Homeland Security program officials generally acknowledged that their professional and management support services contracts closely supported the performance of inherently governmental functions, they did not assess the risk that government decisions may be influenced by rather than independent from contractor judgments. Further, most of the program officials and contracting officers we spoke with were not aware of the requirement to provide enhanced oversight, and did not believe that their professional and management support services needed enhanced oversight.

Contractors are generally not subject to the same ethics rules as government employees even when they are co-located and work side-by-side with federal employees and perform similar functions. Federal ethics rules and standards have been put in place to help safeguard the integrity of the procurement process by mitigating the risk that employees entrusted to act in the best interest of the government will use their positions to influence the outcomes of contract awards for future gain. In addition, as we reported in 2005, contractors we met with indicated that DOD did not monitor their recruiting, hiring, and placement practices for current and former government employees. Consequently, DOD could not be assured that potential conflicts of interest would be identified. A lack of awareness among government employees of procurement integrity rules and conflict-of interest considerations creates additional risk. For example, in 2005 we reported that DOD did not know the content or frequency of ethics training and counseling or which employees received information on conflict-of-interest and procurement integrity. DOD also lacked knowledge on reported allegations of potential misconduct.[20] In 2007, the Acquisition Advisory Panel recommended training for contractors and government employees, and the development of standard conflicts of interest clauses to include in solicitations and contracts.

[20] GAO, *Defense Ethics Program: Opportunities Exist to Strengthen Safeguards for Procurement Integrity*, GAO-05-341 (Washington, D.C.: Apr. 29, 2005).

Quality assurance, especially regular surveillance and documentation of its results, is essential to determine whether goods or services provided by the contractor satisfy the contract requirements and to minimize risks that the government will pay the contractor more than the value of the goods and services. However, DOD officials have expressed concerns about the current state of the acquisition workforce to support surveillance and mentioned that surveillance remains an "other duty as assigned" and, consequently, is a low-priority task. We have also reported wide discrepancies in the rigor with which officials responsible for surveillance perform their duties, particularly in unstable environments. For example, in the aftermath of Hurricanes Katrina and Rita, the number of government personnel monitoring contracts was not always sufficient or adequately deployed to provide effective oversight.[21] Unfortunately, attention to oversight has not always been evident in a number of instances, including during the Iraq reconstruction effort. We have reported that, particularly in the early phases of the Iraq reconstruction effort, several agencies including the Army lacked an adequate acquisition workforce in Iraq to oversee billions of dollars for which they were responsible. Further, Army personnel who were responsible for overseeing contractor performance of interrogation and other services were not adequately trained to properly exercise their responsibilities. Contractor employees were stationed in various locations around Iraq, with no assigned representative on site to monitor their work. An Army investigative report concluded that the number and training of officials assigned to monitor contractor performance at Abu Ghraib prison was not sufficient and put the Army at risk of being unaware of possible misconduct by contractor personnel.[22]

DOD Faces Challenges in Managing the Increased Role of Contractors Performing Support Functions for Military Operations and Weapons Systems

DOD's increasing use of contractors to perform mission-support functions, including contractors who support forces deployed for military operations and contractors who perform maintenance and other logistic support for weapon systems, has highlighted several challenges that DOD faces in managing the increased role of this component of its total force. With regard to contractor support to deployed forces, DOD's primary challenges have been to provide effective management and oversight. With respect to weapon system support, the challenges have been to resolve questions about how much depot maintenance and other logistic work needs to be

[21] GAO, *Agency Management of Contractors Responding to Hurricane Katrina and Rita*, GAO-06-461R (Washington, D.C.: Mar. 16, 2006).

[22] GAO, *Interagency Contracting: Problems with DOD's and Interior's Orders to Support Military Operations*, GAO-05-201 (Washington, D.C.: Apr. 25, 2005).

performed in-house and about to what extent outsourcing for DOD logistics has been cost-effective.

DOD has Experienced Long-Standing Problems with its Management and Oversight of Contractors Supporting Deployed Forces, But Has Taken Some Actions to Address these Problems

Since 1997, we have reported on DOD's management and oversight challenges related to its use of contractor support to deployed forces. In December 2006, we issued a comprehensive review of DOD's management and oversight of contractor support to deployed forces.[23] We reported that despite making progress in some areas, DOD continued to face long-standing problems that hindered its management and oversight of contractors at deployed locations. Those problems included issues regarding visibility of contractors, numbers of contract oversight personnel, lessons learned, and training of military commanders and contract oversight personnel. More recently, we testified that DOD's leadership needs to ensure implementation of and compliance with guidance on the use of contractors to support deployed forces.

While DOD has long relied on contractors to support forces deployed for military operations, the large influx of contractors in support of operations in Iraq has exacerbated problems that DOD has had in managing and overseeing their activities. Significantly, the individual services and a wide array of DOD and non-DOD agencies can award contracts to support deployed forces. For example, although DOD estimated that as of the first quarter of fiscal year 2008, 163,590 contractors were supporting deployed forces in Iraq, no one person or organization made a decision to send 163,590 contractors to Iraq. Rather, decisions to send contractors to support forces in Iraq were made by numerous DOD activities both within and outside of Iraq. This decentralized process, combined with the scope and scale of contract support to deployed forces, contributes to the complexity of the problems we have identified in our past work on this topic.

DOD has taken a number of actions to implement recommendations that we have made to improve its management of contractors. For example, in response to our 2003 recommendation that DOD develop comprehensive guidance to help the services manage contractors supporting deployed forces, the department issued the first comprehensive guidance dealing with contractors who support deployed forces in October 2005. Additionally, in October 2006, DOD established the office of the Assistant Deputy Under Secretary of Defense for Program Support to serve as the office with

[23] GAO, *Military Operations: High-Level DOD Action Needed to Address Long-standing Problems with Management and Oversight of Contractors Supporting Deployed Forces*, GAO-07-145 (Washington, D.C.: Dec. 18, 2006).

primary responsibility for contractor support issues. This office has led the effort to develop and implement a database which, when fully implemented, will allow by-name accountability of contractors who deploy with the force. This database implements recommendations we made in 2003 and 2006 to enhance the department's visibility over contractors in locations such as Iraq and Afghanistan. Although DOD has taken these and other steps to address these issues, we recently testified that many of these issues remain a concern and additional actions are needed.[24]

DOD Has Not Followed Long-Standing Planning Guidance Regarding the Use of Contractors to Support Deployed Forces

As we have noted in previous reports and testimonies, DOD has not followed long-standing planning guidance, particularly by not adequately factoring the use and role of contractors into its planning. For example, we noted in 2003 that the operations plan for the war in Iraq contained only limited information on contractor support.[25] However, Joint Publication 4-0,[26] which provides doctrine and guidance for combatant commanders and their components regarding the planning and execution of logistic support of joint operations, stresses the importance of fully integrating into logistics plans and orders the logistics functions performed by contractors along with those performed by military personnel and government civilians.

Additionally, we reported in 2004 that the Army did not follow its planning guidance when deciding to use the Army's Logistics Civil Augmentation Program (LOGCAP) in Iraq.[27] This guidance stresses the need to clearly identify requirements and develop a comprehensive statement of work early in the contingency planning process. Because this Army guidance was not followed, the plan to support the troops in Iraq was not comprehensive and was revised seven times in less than 1 year.

Our 2003 report also concluded that essential contractor services had not been identified and backup planning was not being done.[28] DOD policy requires DOD and its components to determine which contractor-provided services will be essential during crisis situations, develop and implement plans and procedures to provide a reasonable assurance of the continuation of essential services during crisis situations, and prepare a contingency plan for obtaining the essential service from an alternate source should the contractor be unable to provide it. Without such plans, there is no

[24] GAO-08-436T.

[25] GAO, *Military Operations: Contractors Provide Vital Services to Deployed Forces but Are Not Adequately Addressed in DOD Plans*, GAO-03-695 (Washington, D.C.: June 24, 2003).

[26] The Joint Chiefs of Staff, *Doctrine for Logistic Support of Joint Operations*, Joint Publication 4-0 (Washington, D.C.: April 2000).

[27] GAO, *Military Operations: DOD's Extensive Use of Logistics Support Contracts Requires Strengthened Oversight*, GAO-04-854 (Washington, D.C.: July 19, 2004).

[28] GAO-03-695.

assurance that the personnel needed to provide the essential services would be available when needed.

Moreover, as we reported in 2003 and 2006,[29] senior leaders and military commanders need information about the contractor services they are relying on in order to incorporate contractor support into their planning. For example, senior military commanders in Iraq told us that when they began to develop a base consolidation plan for Iraq, they had no source to draw upon to determine how many contractors were on each installation. Limited visibility can also hinder the ability of commanders to make informed decisions about base operations support (e.g., food and housing) and force protection for all personnel on an installation.

DOD has taken some action to address this problem. DOD is developing a database of contractors who deploy with U.S. forces. According to senior DOD officials familiar with this database, as of February 2008, the database had about 80,000 records. DOD is working with the State Department to include additional contractors, including private security contractors, in the database. In addition, Joint Contracting Command Iraq/Afghanistan has created the Theater Business Clearance process that reviews and approves all contracts for work in Iraq or Afghanistan. Joint Contracting Command Iraq/Afghanistan officials stated that this has helped military commanders know ahead of time when contractors are coming to work on their bases and ensure sufficient facilities are available for them. According to senior DOD officials, the department is also developing a cadre of contracting planners to ensure that contractor support is included in combatant commanders' operational and contingency planning.

DOD Lacks an Adequate Number of Trained Contract Oversight Personnel

As we noted in several of our previous reports, having the right people with the right skills to oversee contractor performance is crucial to ensuring that DOD receives the best value for the billions of dollars spent each year on contractor-provided services supporting forces deployed to Iraq and elsewhere. However, since 1992, we have designated DOD contract management as a high-risk area, in part due to concerns over the adequacy of the department's acquisition workforce, including contract oversight personnel. While this is a DOD-wide problem, having too few contract oversight personnel presents unique difficulties at deployed locations given the more demanding contracting environment as compared to the United States.

[29] GAO-03-695 and GAO-07-145.

Having an inadequate number of contract oversight personnel has hindered DOD's ability to effectively manage and oversee contractors supporting deployed forces and has had monetary impacts as well. For example, in 2004 we reported that DOD did not always have enough contract oversight personnel in place to manage and oversee its logistics support contracts such as LOGCAP and the Air Force Contract Augmentation Program (AFCAP).[30] As a result, the Defense Contract Management Agency was unable to account for $2 million worth of tools that had been purchased using the AFCAP contract. During our 2006 review, several contract oversight personnel we met with told us DOD does not have adequate personnel at deployed locations.[31] For example, a contracting officer's representative for a linguistic support contract told us that although he had a battalion's worth of people with a battalion's worth of problems, he lacked the equivalent of a battalion's staff to deal with those problems. Similarly, an official with the LOGCAP Program Office told us that, had adequate staffing been in place early, the Army could have realized substantial savings through more effective reviews of the increasing volume of LOGCAP requirements.

More recently, we reported that the Army did not have adequate staff to oversee an equipment maintenance contract in Kuwait.[32] According to Army officials, vacant and reduced inspector and analyst positions meant that surveillance was not being performed sufficiently in some areas and the Army was less able to perform data analyses, identify trends in contractor performance, and improve quality processes. In addition, the 2007 report of the Commission on Army Acquisition and Program Management in Expeditionary Operations stated that the Army lacks the leadership and military and civilian personnel to provide sufficient contracting support to either expeditionary or peacetime missions.[33] As a result, the commission found that the vital task of post-award contract management is rarely being done. As we noted in our 2006 report,[34] without adequate contract oversight personnel in place to monitor its many contracts in deployed locations such as Iraq, DOD may not be able to obtain reasonable assurance that contractors are meeting their contract requirements efficiently and effectively.

DOD has taken some actions to address this problem. In February 2007, the Deputy Assistant Secretary of the Army (Policy and Procurement) issued guidance that required, among other things, contracting officers to appoint certified contracting officer's representatives in writing before contract performance begins, identify properly trained contracting officer's

[30] GAO-04-854.
[31] GAO-07-145.
[32] GAO, *Defense Logistics: The Army Needs to Implement an Effective Management and Oversight Plan for the Equipment Maintenance Contract in Kuwait*, GAO-08-316R (Washington, D.C.: Jan. 22, 2008).
[33] Commission on Army Acquisition and Program Management in Expeditionary Operations, *Urgent Reform Required: Army Expeditionary Contracting* (Oct. 31, 2007).
[34] GAO-07-145.

representatives for active service contracts, and ensure that a government quality assurance surveillance plan is prepared and implemented for service contracts exceeding $2,500. Joint Contracting Command Iraq/Afghanistan officials stated they are in the process of adding 39 personnel to provide additional contractor oversight. Similarly, the Defense Contract Management Agency has deployed an additional 100 people and plans to deploy approximately 150 more people to provide contract oversight and management to both ongoing and future contracts in Iraq. The agency is providing oversight for DOD's private security contracts as well as other theaterwide contracts. Additionally, senior DOD officials stated that the department has created a task force to address the recommendations of the October 2007 report by the Commission on Army Acquisition and Program Management in Expeditionary Operations.

DOD Is Not Systematically Collecting and Distributing Lessons Learned

Although DOD and its components have used contractors to support deployed forces in several prior military operations, DOD does not systematically ensure that institutional knowledge on the use of contractors to support deployed forces, including lessons learned and best practices, is shared with military personnel at deployed locations. We previously reported that DOD could benefit from systematically collecting and sharing its institutional knowledge to help ensure that it is factored into planning, work processes, and other activities.[35] Although DOD has policy requiring the collection and distribution of lessons learned to the maximum extent possible, we found in our previous work that no procedures were in place to ensure that lessons learned are collected and shared.

Moreover, although the Army regulation which establishes policies, responsibilities, and procedures for the implementation of the LOGCAP program makes customers that receive services under the LOGCAP contract responsible for collecting lessons learned, we have repeatedly found that DOD is not systematically collecting and sharing lessons learned on the use of contractors to support to deployed forces. Despite years of experience using contractors to support forces deployed to the Balkans, Southwest Asia, Iraq, and Afghanistan, DOD has made few efforts to leverage this institutional knowledge. As a result, many of the problems we identified in earlier operations have recurred in current operations.

During the course of our 2006 work, we found no organization within DOD or its components responsible for developing procedures to capture lessons

[35] GAO, *Information Technology: DOD Needs to Leverage Lessons Learned from Its Outsourcing Projects*, GAO-03-371 (Washington, D.C.: Apr. 25, 2003); and *Military Training: Potential to Use Lessons Learned to Avoid Past Mistakes Is Largely Untapped*, GAO/NSIAD-95-152 (Washington, D.C.: Aug. 9, 1995).

learned on the use of contractor support at deployed locations.[36] We noted that when lessons learned are not collected and shared, DOD and its components run the risk of repeating past mistakes and being unable to build on the efficiencies and effectiveness others have developed during past operations that involved contractor support. We also found a failure to share best practices and lessons learned between units as one redeploys and the other deploys to replace it. As a result, new units essentially start at ground zero, having to resolve a number of difficulties until they understand contractor roles and responsibilities.

DOD Does Not Comprehensively Train Military Commanders and Contract Oversight Personnel

DOD does not routinely incorporate information about contractor support for deployed forces in its pre-deployment training of military personnel, despite the long-standing recognition of the need to provide such information. We have discussed the need for better pre-deployment training of military commanders and contract oversight personnel since the mid-1990s and have made several recommendations aimed at improving such training. Moreover, according to DOD policy, personnel should receive timely and effective training to ensure they have the knowledge and other tools necessary to accomplish their missions. Nevertheless, we continue to find little evidence that improvements have been made in terms of how DOD and its components train military commanders and contract oversight personnel on the use of contractors to support deployed forces prior to their deployment. Without properly trained personnel, DOD will continue to face risks of fraud, waste, and abuse.

Limited or no pre-deployment training on the use of contractor support can cause a variety of problems for military commanders in a deployed location. As we reported in 2006, with limited or no pre-deployment training on the extent of contractor support to deployed forces, military commanders may not be able to adequately plan for the use of those contractors.[37] Similarly, in its 2007 report, the Commission on Army Acquisition and Program Management in Expeditionary Operations concluded that the Army needs to educate and train commanders on the important operational role of contracting. Several military commanders we met with in 2006 said their pre-deployment training did not provide them with sufficient information on the extent of contractor support that they would be relying on in Iraq and were therefore surprised by the substantial number of personnel they had to allocate to provide on-base escorts, convoy security, and other force protection support to contractors. In addition, limited

[36] GAO-07-145.
[37] GAO-07-145.

or no pre-deployment training for military commanders can result in confusion over their roles and responsibilities in managing and overseeing contractors. For example, we found some instances where a lack of training raised concerns over the potential for military commanders to direct contractors to perform work outside the scope of the contract, something commanders lack the authority to do. This can cause the government to incur additional charges because modifications would need to be made to the contract.

We also found that contract oversight personnel such as contracting officer's representatives received little or no pre-deployment training on their roles and responsibilities in monitoring contractor performance. Many of the contracting officer's representatives we spoke with in 2003 and 2006 said that training before they assumed these positions would have better prepared them to effectively oversee contractor performance. In most cases, deploying individuals were not informed that they would be performing contracting officer's representative duties until after they had deployed, which hindered the ability of those individuals to effectively manage and oversee contractors. For example, officials from a corps support group in Iraq told us that until they were able to get a properly trained contracting officer's representative in place, they experienced numerous problems regarding the quality of food service provided by LOGCAP. In addition, the 2007 report of the Commission on Army Acquisition and Program Management in Expeditionary Operations discussed the need to train contracting officer's representatives and warned that the lack of training could lead to fraud, waste, and abuse.

DOD has taken some steps to address this problem. In DOD's response to our 2006 report, the Director of Defense Procurement and Acquisition Policy stated that the Army is making changes to its logistics training programs that would incorporate contracting officer's representatives training into its basic and advanced training for its ordnance, transportation, and quartermaster corps.[38] In addition, the Defense Acquisition University has updated its contingency contracting course to include a lesson on contractors accompanying the force. Further, the Defense Contract Management Agency is adding personnel to assist in the training and managing of contracting officer's representatives.

Increased Reliance on Contractors for Weapon System Support Raises Questions about Core Functions and Cost Effectiveness

DOD has moved over the years toward greater use of the private sector to perform maintenance and other logistics support for weapon systems. Factors influencing this increased reliance on contractors include changes

[38] GAO-07-145.

in DOD's guidance and plans that emphasized the privatization of logistics functions, a lack of technical data and modernized facilities needed to perform maintenance on new systems, and reductions in maintenance workers at government-owned depots. The move toward greater reliance on contractors has raised questions regarding how much depot maintenance and other logistics work needs to be performed in-house and about the cost-effectiveness of outsourcing DOD logistics.

DOD Has Increasingly Relied on Contractors for Maintenance and Other Logistic Support of Weapon Systems

DOD has increasingly relied on contractors for maintenance and other logistic support of weapon systems. For example, funding for private sector contractors to perform depot maintenance[39] increased in then-year dollars from about $4.0 billion in fiscal year 1987 to about $13.8 billion in fiscal year 2007, or 246 percent. In contrast, during this same time period, the amount of funding for depot maintenance performed at government (public) depots increased from about $8.7 billion to about $16.1 billion, or 85 percent. This trend toward greater reliance on the private sector for depot maintenance was most evident during the period from fiscal years 1987 to 2000, when the amount of funding for public depot maintenance largely stayed flat and private sector funding increased by 89 percent. Since 2001, military operations in support of the Global War on Terrorism have resulted in large funding increases for maintenance performed by both public and private sector activities.

One potential future limitation to continued contracting out of depot maintenance activities is the statutory limit on the amount of funding for depot maintenance work that can be performed by private sector contractors. Under 10 U.S.C. 2466(a), not more than 50 percent of funds made available in a fiscal year to a military department or defense agency for depot-level maintenance and repair may be used to contract for the performance by non-government personnel of such workload for the military departments and defense agencies. As the contractors' share has increased over time, managing within this limitation has become more challenging—particularly for the Air Force and, to a lesser extent, the Army. Another potential limitation to contracting out is a requirement that DOD maintain a core logistics capability within government facilities.[40] However, as I will

[39] Depot maintenance is the highest level of maintenance within DOD and generally refers to major maintenance and repairs, such as overhauling, upgrading, or rebuilding parts, assemblies, or subassemblies. Depot maintenance has long been provided by a mix of government-owned depots and private contractors.

[40] Section 2464 of Title 10 of the U.S. Code provides that it is essential for the national defense that DOD maintain a core logistics capability that is government-owned and government-operated to ensure the existence of a ready and controlled source of technical competence and resources necessary to ensure a timely and effective military response to mobilizations, national defense emergencies, and contingencies.

discuss, our work has revealed problems in DOD's implementation of this requirement.

DOD also has experienced significant growth in the overall use of contractors for long-term logistics support of weapon systems.[41] While the department does not collect and aggregate cost data specifically on these support arrangements, available data illustrate this growth. For example, Air Force data show an increase in funding for these support arrangements from $910 million in fiscal year 1996 to a projected $4.1 billion in fiscal year 2013. Many DOD acquisition program offices have been adopting long-term support strategies for sustaining new and modified systems that rely on contractors. Our ongoing review of core logistics capability indicates that performance-based logistics or some other type of partnership is a frequently used weapon system sustainment approach.

Multiple Factors Have Influenced DOD's Increased Reliance on Contracting

The move toward increased use of contractors to perform maintenance and other logistics support for weapon systems has been influenced by multiple factors. A significant factor has been the shift in DOD's guidance and plans that placed greater emphasis on privatizing logistics functions. In 1996, for example, DOD issued a report, *Plan for Increasing Depot Maintenance Privatization and Outsourcing*, which provided a framework for substantially increasing reliance on the private sector for depot maintenance. In addition, both the 1995 report by the Commission on Roles and Missions[42] and a 1996 report by a Defense Science Board[43] task force recommended that DOD outsource almost all depot maintenance and other logistics activities. Both study teams assumed large cost savings would result from increased privatization. Today, DOD guidance provides that performance-based logistics is now DOD's preferred approach for providing long-term total system support for weapon systems. DOD describes performance-based logistics as the process of (1) identifying a level of performance required by the warfighter and (2) negotiating a performance-based arrangement to provide long-term total system support for a weapon system at a fixed level of annual funding.

---

[41] Contractor logistics support arrangements may involve the contractor performing maintenance, assuming responsibility for life-cycle management of the system, and performing sustainment activities, including parts management. These arrangements may take various forms, including performance-based logistics.

[42] Commission on Roles and Missions, *Directions for Defense* (May 24, 1995).

[43] Defense Science Board, *Report of the Defense Science Board Task Force on Outsourcing and Privatization* (August 1996). Also see Defense Science Board, *Report on the Defense Science Board 1996 Summer Study on Achieving an Innovative Support Structure for 21st Century Military Superiority: Higher Performance at Lower Costs* (November 1996).

Another factor in the move toward greater reliance on contractors has been the lack of technical data and other elements of support, such as modernized facilities, required to establish a maintenance capability for new systems. Technical data for weapon systems include drawings, specifications, standards, and other details necessary to ensure the adequacy of item performance, as well as manuals that contain instructions for installation, operation, maintenance, and other actions needed to support weapon systems. As a result of not having acquired technical data rights from the equipment manufacturers, the military services in some instances have had difficulty establishing a maintenance capability at government depots. For example, the Air Force identified a need to develop a core capability to perform maintenance on the C-17 aircraft at government depots, but lacked the requisite technical data rights. Consequently, the Air Force has sought to form partnerships with C-17 subvendors to develop a depot maintenance capability, but these efforts have had mixed results. Based on our ongoing review of DOD core capability, we found that the Air Force continues to have challenges establishing core capability for C-17 commodities because of technical data issues.

A third factor influencing DOD's increasing reliance on contractor support has been reductions in government depot maintenance personnel available to perform the work. Personnel downsizing has greatly reduced the number of depot maintenance workers and has limited the amount of work that could be performed in the depots. Since 1987 the number of depot-level maintenance personnel was reduced by 56 percent from a high of 163,000 in 1987 to about 72,000 in 2002, after which the depots began to see some personnel increases to support the Global War on Terrorism. In comparison, in the 13 years between 1989 and 2002, DOD's total civilian workforce had a 38 percent reduction. While some downsizing was essential, given reductions in depot maintenance workloads over the same period, mandated reductions in the number of personnel were taken even though the depots may have had funded workload to support an increased number of personnel. For example, in a review of Army depot personnel reductions in 1998, we found that efforts to implement the reductions at the Corpus Christi Army Depot were poorly managed and more direct labor employees were reduced than intended—adversely affecting the depot's productivity. We found that while Army regulations on manpower management provide that staffing levels are to be based on the workloads performed, the Army's reduced staffing plan was developed in response to affordability concerns and a desire to lower the depot's rates and did not support the depot's funded workload requirement.[44]

[44] GAO, *Army Industrial Facilities: Workforce Requirements and Related Issues Affecting Depots and Arsenals*, GAO/NSIAD-99-31 (Washington, D.C.: Nov. 30, 1998).

Uncertainties Exist About Maintaining Core Capability for Depot Maintenance and Other Logistics Work

Because DOD has not clearly and comprehensively identified what depot maintenance and other logistics activities the department should be performing itself, it is unclear how much of the work that has been contracted out may be work that should be done in-house by government personnel. Additionally, DOD has not identified core logistics capability requirements for other logistics functions, such as supply chain management and engineering.

With regard to depot maintenance, we previously reported that DOD lacks assurance that core logistics capabilities were being maintained as needed to ensure timely and effective response to national defense emergencies and contingencies, as required by 10 U.S.C. 2464, noting that several factors precluded this assurance.[45] First, DOD's existing policy, which establishes a process for identifying core maintenance capability, was not comprehensive in that it did not provide for a forward look at new weapon systems and associated future maintenance capability requirements. Second, the various procedures and practices being used by the services to implement the existing policy were also affecting the establishment of core capability. For example, the Air Force reduced its core requirement as a result of its consideration of maintenance work performed in the private sector, even though core work is supposed to be performed in military facilities and by government personnel. In addition, we have noted that DOD has had other limitations, including a lack of technical data rights and a lack of sufficient investment in facilities, equipment, and human capital to ensure the long-term viability of the military depots.

To improve its process for identifying core maintenance capability requirements, in January 2007 DOD issued an instruction on how to identify required core capabilities for depot maintenance, which generally mirrored previous guidance.[46] Also, in March 2007 DOD issued its depot maintenance strategy, which delineated the actions DOD is undertaking to identify and sustain core maintenance capability. We have an ongoing engagement to assess the effectiveness of the current policy and procedures as well as the services' implementation.

To address issues inhibiting the establishment of core capability, Congress has taken recent actions to address problems with technical data and depot facilities. We previously recommended that DOD improve its acquisition

[45] GAO, *Defense Logistics: Actions Needed to Overcome Capability Gaps in the Public Depot System*, GAO-02-105 (Washington. D.C.: Oct. 12, 2001).

[46] DOD Instruction 4151.20 (Jan. 5, 2007) states that pursuant to DOD policy, DOD components must apply the core capability requirements determination process to identify required core capabilities and the workloads necessary to sustain effectively the core capabilities.

policies for assessing technical data needs to support weapon systems.[47] The John Warner National Defense Authorization Act for Fiscal Year 2007 (2007 Defense Authorization Act) mandated that DOD require program managers for major weapon systems to assess long-term technical data needs for weapon systems and to establish corresponding acquisition strategies that provide for technical data rights needed to sustain such systems over their life cycle.[48] DOD subsequently issued a new policy in July 2007 to implement this requirement.[49] Potential benefits from this action are long term because of the time frames required for developing and acquiring weapon systems, and it is uncertain what actions may have been taken by program offices as a result of this policy change or the extent in which any actions taken could improve the availability of required data in the future. To address inadequacies in the military's investments in its maintenance depots, the 2007 Defense Authorization Act required military departments to invest each fiscal year in the capital budgets of certain depots a total amount equal to at least 6 percent of the average total combined workload funded at all of the depots over the preceding 3 fiscal years.[50] As a part of an ongoing engagement, we are reviewing the military departments' implementation of this mandate.

We have also reported that DOD has not established policies or processes for determining core requirements for non-maintenance logistics capabilities for activities such as supply support, engineering, and transportation.[51] Without identifying those core logistics activities that need to be retained in-house, the services may not be retaining critical capabilities as they proceed with contracting initiatives. For example, if DOD implements performance-based logistics—its preferred weapon system support arrangement—at the platform level, this can result in contracting out the program integration function, a core process which the private sector firms we interviewed during a 2004 review considered integral to their successful business operations. Another potential adverse effect of awarding a performance-based contract at the platform level is the loss of management control and expertise over the system that private sector companies told us were essential to retain in-house. In an earlier engagement, Army, Navy, and Air Force operational command officials told us that among their concerns with various types of long-term contractor logistics support arrangements were

[47] GAO, *Weapons Acquisition: DOD Should Strengthen Policies for Assessing Technical Data Needs to Support Weapon Systems*, GAO-06-839 (Washington, D.C.: July 14, 2006).
[48] Pub. L. No. 109-364, § 802 (2006).
[49] A July 19, 2007 memorandum from the Under Secretary of Defense (Acquisition, Technology, and Logistics) for the service acquisition executives required that program managers assess the long-term technical data needs of their systems and reflect that assessment in a data management strategy which must be integrated with other life-cycle sustainment planning, assess certain data requirements, and address the merits of a priced contract option for the future delivery of technical data.
[50] Pub. L. No. 109-364, § 332 (2006).
[51] GAO-02-105.

(1) retaining the ability to maintain and develop critical technical skills and knowledge, (2) limiting operational authority, and (3) reducing the program office's ability to perform essential management functions. Thus, without well-defined policy and procedures for identifying core requirements for critical logistics areas, the department may not be in a position to ensure that it will have the needed capabilities for the logistics system to support essential military weapons and equipment in an emergency.

Uncertainties Exist About Projected Cost Effectiveness of Outsourcing Initiatives for DOD Logistics

Although DOD justified its logistics outsourcing initiatives based on the assumption that there would be significant cost savings, it is uncertain to what extent cost savings have occurred or will occur. Overall funding for depot maintenance costs and other logistics support costs are increasing significantly, both for work that is performed in military depots and by contractors. However, sufficient data are not available to determine whether increased contracting has caused DOD's costs to be higher than they would have been had the contracted activities been performed by DOD civilians. As noted earlier, assumptions about savings were a key part of DOD's shift in policy toward the performance of defense logistics by the private sector.

While the 1995 Commission on Roles and Missions projected savings of 20 percent from outsourcing, we questioned this group's savings assumptions, noting that its data did not support its depot privatization savings assumptions.[52] These assumptions were based on reported savings from public-private competitions for commercial activities under Office of Management and Budget Circular A-76. The commercial activities were generally dissimilar to depot maintenance activities because they involved relatively simple, routine, and repetitive tasks that did not generally require large capital investments or highly skilled and trained personnel. Public activities were allowed to compete for these workloads and won about half the competitions. Additionally, many private sector firms generally made offers for this work due to the highly competitive nature of the private sector market, and estimated savings were generally greater in situations where there were larger numbers of private sector offerors. In contrast, most depot maintenance work is awarded without competition to the original equipment manufacturer. We noted that in the absence of a highly competitive market, privatizing unique, highly diverse, and complex depot maintenance workloads that require large capital investments, extensive technical data, and highly skilled and trained personnel would not likely achieve expected savings and could increase the costs of depot

[52] GAO, *Defense Depot Maintenance: Commission on Roles and Mission's Privatization Assumptions Are Questionable*, NSIAD-96-161 (Washington, D.C.: July 15, 1996).

maintenance operations. We also questioned the Defense Science Board's projections of $30 billion in annual savings from privatizing almost all logistics support activities.

We have also reported that whereas DOD expected to achieve large savings from its contracting out of more of its depot-level maintenance work, depot maintenance contracting represented a challenge to relying on commercial market forces. Whereas DOD was attempting to rely on competitive market forces, about 91 percent of the depot maintenance contracts we reviewed were awarded noncompetitively. We also noted that difficulties in precisely defining requirements also affected DOD's efforts to rely on competitive market forces. Further, we cautioned that DOD would need to increase the use of competitively awarded depot maintenance contracts and to address how best to assure product quality and reasonable prices when competitive market forces were not present.

We have also raised questions about cost savings from DOD's increased use of performance-based logistics. Although DOD guidance recommends that program offices perform a business case analysis before adopting a performance based logistics approach to support weapon system, our reviews of the implementation of this approach show these analyses are not often done and DOD program offices could not demonstrate that they had achieved cost savings.[53] Of the 15 programs we reviewed, 11 program offices had developed a business case analysis—prior to entering into a performance-based logistics arrangement—which projected achieving significant cost savings. Only one of these programs offices had updated its business case analysis with actual cost data as recommended by DOD guidance. The one program office that did update its business case analysis determined that the contract did not result in the expected cost savings and subsequently restructured the program. Program office officials acknowledged limitations in their own information systems in providing reliable data to closely monitor contractor costs. While existing systems are capable of collecting some cost information, they are not capturing sufficiently detailed cost information for monitoring the performance-based logistics contracts.

Our 2005 report on DOD's implementation of performance-based logistics included a recommendation on the validation of business case decisions to demonstrate whether they are resulting in reduced costs and increased performance. Also, given the stated limitations in cost information, we recommended that program offices be required to improve their monitoring of performance-based logistics arrangements by verifying the reliability of contractor cost and performance data. Although DOD concurred with our

[53] GAO, *Defense Management: DOD Needs to Demonstrate That Performance-Based Logistics Contracts Are Achieving Expected Benefits*, GAO-05-966 (Washington, D.C.: Sept. 9, 2005).

recommendations, we are currently evaluating the corrective actions taken. In addition, DOD currently does not require detailed reporting of contractor logistics support costs, including for performance based arrangements.

Concluding Observations

In closing, I believe that we must engage in a fundamental reexamination of when and under what circumstances we should use contractors versus civil servants or military personnel. This is a major and growing concern that needs immediate attention. In general, I believe there is a need to focus greater attention on what type of functions and activities should be contracted out and which ones should not. Inherently governmental functions are required to be performed by government personnel, not private contractors. Government officials, in making decisions about whether to use contractors for services closely supporting inherently governmental functions, should assess risk and consider the need for enhanced management and oversight controls. Once the decision to contract has been made, we must address challenges we have observed in ensuring proper oversight of these arrangements—especially considering the evolving and enlarging role of contractors in federal acquisitions. These concerns, identified in our work at several federal agencies including DOD, are more complex to address and may take on greater significance in contingency or military operations. As we have witnessed with contractors in Iraq, a specific decision made by a contractor can impact U.S. strategic and operational objectives in ways that were not considered in making the initial contracting decision.

To address these concerns with regard to contractor support to deployed forces, we believe that in the immediate future, DOD's leadership needs to ensure implementation of and compliance with relevant existing guidance. In the longer term, we believe a broader examination of the use and role of contractors to support deployed forces is in order. As I stated in April 2007, it may be appropriate to ask if DOD has become too reliant on contractors to provide essential services.[54] What is needed is a comprehensive, forward-looking, and integrated review of contractor support to deployed forces that provides the proper balance between contractor support and the core capabilities of military forces over the next several years. In a November 2007 briefing on DOD transformation, I called on DOD to employ a total force management approach to planning and execution (e.g. military, civilian, and contractors).[55] Many of the problems we have identified regarding the management and oversight of contractor support to deployed forces stem from DOD's reluctance to plan for contractors as an integral part of the

[54] GAO-07-525T.

[55] GAO, *Defense Transformation: Challenges and Opportunities*, GAO-08-323CG (Washington, D.C.: Nov. 29, 2007).

total force. One way DOD could begin to address this issue is by incorporating the use and role of contractors into its readiness reporting. DOD regularly reports on the readiness status, capabilities assessments, and other reviews of the status and capabilities of its forces. Given the reality that DOD is dependent on contractors for much of its support in deployed locations, the department should include information on the specific missions contractors will be asked to perform, the operational impacts associated with the use of contractors, and the personnel necessary to effectively oversee and manage those contractors.

Mr. Chairman, this concludes my prepared statement. I would be happy to respond to any questions you or other Members of the Subcommittee may have at this time.

Contacts and Acknowledgments

For further information regarding this testimony, please contact William M. Solis at (202) 512-8365 or (solisw@gao.gov) or John Hutton at (202) 512-4841 or (huttonj@gao.gov). Contact points for our Offices of Congressional Relations and Public Affairs may be found on the last page of this product. Staff making key contributions to this statement were Julia Denman, Tom Gosling, Amelia Shachoy, Assistant Directors; Carleen Bennett, Laura Holliday, Randy Neice, Janine Prybyla, James Reynolds, Bill Russell, Karen Sloan, and Karen Thornton.

Appendix I: Systemic Acquisition Challenges at the Department of Defense

1. Service budgets are allocated largely according to top line historical percentages rather than Defense-wide strategic assessments and current and likely resource limitations.

2. Capabilities and requirements are based primarily on individual service wants versus collective Defense needs (i.e., based on current and expected future threats) that are both affordable and sustainable over time.

3. Defense consistently overpromises and underdelivers in connection with major weapons, information, and other systems (i.e., capabilities, costs, quantities, and schedule).

4. Defense often employs a "plug and pray approach" when costs escalate (i.e., divide total funding dollars by cost per copy, plug in the number that can be purchased, then pray that Congress will provide more funding to buy more quantities).

5. Congress sometimes forces the department to buy items (e.g., weapon systems) and provide services (e.g., additional health care for non-active beneficiaries, such as active duty members' dependents and military retirees and their dependents) that the department does not want and we cannot afford.

6. DOD tries to develop high-risk technologies after programs start instead of setting up funding, organizations, and processes to conduct high-risk technology development activities in low-cost environments, (i.e., technology development is not separated from product development). Program decisions to move into design and production are made without adequate standards or knowledge.

7. Program requirements are often set at unrealistic levels, then changed frequently as recognition sets in that they cannot be achieved. As a result, too much time passes, threats may change, or members of the user and acquisition communities may simply change their mind. The resulting program instability causes cost escalation, schedule delays, smaller quantities and reduced contractor accountability.

8. Contracts, especially service contracts, often do not have definitive or realistic requirements at the outset in order to control costs and facilitate accountability.

9. Contracts typically do not accurately reflect the complexity of projects or appropriately allocate risk between the contractors and the taxpayers (e.g., cost plus, cancellation charges).

10. Key program staff rotate too frequently, thus promoting myopia and reducing accountability (i.e., tours based on time versus key milestones). Additionally, the revolving door between industry and the department presents potential conflicts of interest.

11. The acquisition workforce faces serious challenges (e.g., size, skills, knowledge, and succession planning).

12. Incentive and award fees are often paid based on contractor attitudes and efforts versus positive results (i.e., cost, quality, and schedule).

13. Inadequate oversight is being conducted by both the department and Congress, which results in little to no accountability for recurring and systemic problems.

14. Some individual program and funding decisions made within the department and by Congress serve to undercut sound policies.

15. Lack of a professional, term-based Chief Management Officer at the department serves to slow progress on defense transformation and reduce the chance of success in the acquisitions/contracting and other key business areas.

Related GAO Products

Acquisition Management

Defense Contracting: Additional Personal Conflict of Interest Safeguards Needed for Certain DOD Contractor Employees. GAO-08-169. Washington, D.C.: March. 7, 2008.

Intelligence Reform: GAO Can Assist the Congress and the Intelligence Community on Management Reform Initiatives. GAO-08-413T. Washington, D.C.: February 29, 2008.

Federal Acquisition: Oversight Plan Needed to Help Implement Acquisition Advisory Panel Recommendations. GAO-08-160. December 20, 2007.

Department of Homeland Security: Improved Assessment and Oversight Needed to Manage Risk of Contracting for Selected Services. GAO-07-990. Washington, D.C.: September 17, 2007.

Federal Acquisitions and Contracting: Systemic Challenges Need Attention. GAO-07-1098T. Washington, D.C.: July 17, 2007.

Defense Acquisitions: Role of Lead Systems Integrator on Future Combat Systems Program Poses Oversight Challenges. GAO-07-380. Washington, D.C.: June 6, 2007.

Highlights of a GAO Forum: Federal Acquisition Challenges and Opportunities in the 21st Century. GAO-07-45SP. Washington, D.C.: Oct. 6, 2006.

Contract Management: DOD Vulnerabilities to Contracting Fraud, Waste, and Abuse. GAO-06-838R. Washington, D.C.: July 7, 2006.

Agency Management of Contractors Responding to Hurricane Katrina and Rita, GAO-06-461R. Washington, D.C.: March 16, 2006.

Defense Ethics Program: Opportunities Exist to Strengthen Safeguards for Procurement Integrity. GAO-05-341. Washington, D.C.: April 29, 2005.

Interagency Contracting: Problems with DOD's and Interior's Orders to Support Military Operations. GAO-05-201. Washington, D.C.: April 25, 2005.

Rebuilding Iraq: Fiscal Year 2003 Contract Award Procedures and Management Challenges. GAO-04-605. Washington, D.C.: June 1, 2004.

Human Capital: Key Principles for Effective Strategic Workforce Planning. GAO-04-39. Washington, D.C.: December 11, 2003.

Human Capital: A Self-Assessment Checklist for Agency Leaders. GAO/GGD-99-179. Washington, D.C.: September 1, 1999.

Government Contractors: Are Service Contractors Performing Inherently Governmental Functions? GAO/GGD -92-11. Washington, D.C.: November 18, 1991.

Energy Management: Using DOE Employees Can Reduce Costs for Some Support Services. GAO/RCED 91-186. Washington, D.C.: August 16, 1991.

Civil Servants and Contractor Employees: Who Should Do What for the Federal Government? FPCD-81-43. Washington, D.C.: June 19, 1981.

Reliance on Contractors to Support Deployed Forces

Military Operations: Implementation of Existing Guidance and Other Actions Needed to Improve DOD's Oversight and Management of Contractors in Future Operations. GAO-08-436T. Washington, D.C.: January 24, 2008.

Defense Logistics: The Army Needs to Implement an Effective Management and Oversight Plan for the Equipment Maintenance Contract in Kuwait. GAO-08-316R. Washington, D.C.: January 23, 2008.

Defense Acquisitions: Improved Management and Oversight Needed to Better Control DOD's Acquisition of Services. GAO-07-832T. Washington, D.C.: May 10, 2007.

Military Operations: High-Level DOD Action Needed to Address Long-standing Problems with Management and Oversight of Contractors Supporting Deployed Forces. GAO-07-145. Washington, D.C.: December 18, 2006.

Rebuilding Iraq: Continued Progress Requires Overcoming Contract Management Challenges. GAO-06-1130T. Washington, D.C.: September 28, 2006.

Military Operations: Background Screenings of Contractor Employees Supporting Deployed Forces May Lack Critical Information, but U.S. Forces Take Steps to Mitigate the Risks Contractors May Pose. GAO-06-999R. Washington, D.C.: September 22, 2006.

Rebuilding Iraq: Actions Still Needed to Improve the Use of Private Security Providers. GAO-06-865T. Washington, D.C.: June 13, 2006.

Rebuilding Iraq: Actions Needed to Improve Use of Private Security Providers. GAO-05-737. Washington, D.C.: July 28, 2005.

Interagency Contracting: Problems with DOD's and Interior's Orders to Support Military Operations. GAO-05-201. Washington, D.C.: April 29, 2005.

Defense Logistics: High-Level DOD Coordination Is Needed to Further Improve the Management of the Army's LOGCAP Contract. GAO-05-328. Washington, D.C.: March 21, 2005.

Contract Management: Opportunities to Improve Surveillance on Department of Defense Service Contracts. GAO-05-274. Washington, D.C.: March 17, 2005.

Military Operations: DOD's Extensive Use of Logistics Support Contracts Requires Strengthened Oversight. GAO-04-854. Washington, D.C.: July 19, 2004.

Military Operations: Contractors Provide Vital Services to Deployed Forces but Are not Adequately Addressed in DOD Plans. GAO-03-695. Washington, D.C.: June 24, 2003.

Contingency Operations: Army Should Do More to Control Contract Cost in the Balkans. GAO/NSIAD-00-225. Washington, D.C.: September 29, 2000.

Contingency Operations: Opportunities to Improve the Logistics Civil Augmentation Program. GAO/NSIAD-97-63. Washington, D.C.: February 11, 1997.

Reliance on Contractors for Weapon System Logistic Support

Defense Management: DOD Needs to Demonstrate That Performance-Based Logistics Contracts Are Achieving Expected Benefits. GAO-05-966. Washington, D.C.: September 9, 2005.

Defense Management: Opportunities to Enhance the Implementation of Performance-Based Logistics. GAO-04-715. Washington, D.C.: August 16, 2004.

Depot Maintenance: Key Unresolved Issues Affect the Army Depot System's Viability. GAO-03-682. Washington, D.C.: July 7, 2003.

Depot Maintenance: Public-Private Partnerships Have Increased, but Long-Term Growth and Results Are Uncertain. GAO-03-423. Washington, D.C: April 10, 2003.

Defense Logistics: Opportunities to Improve the Army's and the Navy's Decision-making Process for Weapons Systems Support. GAO-02-306. Washington, D.C.: February 28, 2002.

Defense Logistics: Actions Needed to Overcome Capability Gaps in the Public Depot System. GAO-02-105. Washington D.C.: October 12, 2001.

Defense Logistics: Air Force Lacks Data to Assess Contractor Logistics Support Approaches. GAO-01-618. Washington, D.C.: September 7, 2001.

Army Industrial Facilities: Workforce Requirements and Related Issues Affecting Depots and Arsenals. GAO/NSIAD-99-31. Washington. D.C.: November 30, 1998.

Defense Depot Maintenance: DOD Shifting More Workload for New Weapon Systems to the Private Sector. GAO/NSIAD-98-8. Washington, D.C.: March 31, 1998.

Defense Depot Maintenance: Commission on Roles and Missions' Privatization Assumptions Are Questionable. GAO/NSIAD-06-161. Washington, D.C.: July 15, 1996.

Defense Depot Maintenance: DOD's Policy Report Leaves Future Role of Depot System Uncertain. GAO/NSIAD-96-165. Washington, D.C.: May 21, 1996.

Defense Depot Maintenance: Privatization and the Debate Over the Public-Private Mix. GAO/T-NSIAD-96-146. Washington, D.C.: April 16, 1996.

Depot Maintenance: Issues in Allocating Workload Between the Public and Private Sectors. GAO/T-NSIAD-94-161. Washington, D.C.: April 12, 1994.

Depot Maintenance: Issues in Management and Restructuring to Support a Downsized Military. GAO/T-NSIAD-93-13. Washington, D.C.: May 6, 1993.

GAO's Mission

The Government Accountability Office, the audit, evaluation, and investigative arm of Congress, exists to support Congress in meeting its constitutional responsibilities and to help improve the performance and accountability of the federal government for the American people. GAO examines the use of public funds; evaluates federal programs and policies; and provides analyses, recommendations, and other assistance to help Congress make informed oversight, policy, and funding decisions. GAO's commitment to good government is reflected in its core values of accountability, integrity, and reliability.

Obtaining Copies of GAO Reports and Testimony

The fastest and easiest way to obtain copies of GAO documents at no cost is through GAO's Web site (www.gao.gov). Each weekday, GAO posts newly released reports, testimony, and correspondence on its Web site. To have GAO e-mail you a list of newly posted products every afternoon, go to www.gao.gov and select "E-mail Updates."

Order by Mail or Phone

The first copy of each printed report is free. Additional copies are $2 each. A check or money order should be made out to the Superintendent of Documents. GAO also accepts VISA and Mastercard. Orders for 100 or more copies mailed to a single address are discounted 25 percent. Orders should be sent to:

U.S. Government Accountability Office
441 G Street NW, Room LM
Washington, DC 20548

To order by Phone:	Voice:	(202)512-6000
	TDD:	(202)512-2537
	Fax:	(202)512-6061

To Report Fraud, Waste, and Abuse in Federal Programs

Contact:

Web site: www.gao.gov/fraudnet/fraudnet.htm
E-mail: fraudnet@gao.gov
Automated answering system: (800) 424-5454 or (202) 512-7470

Congressional Relations

Ralph Dawn, Managing Director, dawnr@gao.gov, (202) 512-4400
U.S. Government Accountability Office, 441 G Street NW, Room 7125
Washington, DC 20548

Public Affairs

Chuck Young, Managing Director, youngc1@gao.gov, (202) 512-4800
U.S. Government Accountability Office, 441 G Street NW, Room 7149
Washington, DC 20548

DOCUMENT NO. 12

DEFENSE CONTRACTING: ARMY CASE STUDY DELINEATES CONCERNS WITH USE OF CONTRACTORS AS CONTRACT SPECIALISTS

GAO Report
GAO-08-360

March 2008

What GAO Found

CCE has relied on contractor contract specialists since it began hiring them in 2003. In August 2007, contractors—who work side by side and perform the same functions as their government counterparts—comprised 42 percent of CCE's contract specialists. CCE officials cited difficulties hiring and retaining government personnel in light of the competition from government and the private sector for this competency. While CCE officials said that they prefer to use government employees, they have not considered the appropriate balance of contractor versus government contract specialists. Furthermore, CCE has not addressed the need for more training of its government employees to strengthen their skills in conducting CCE's increasingly more complex procurements.

Methods to mitigate the risks of using contractors have been mixed in effect. First, the line separating contractor from government employee is blurry, and contractors did not always clearly identify themselves as such when dealing with the public. Second, the potential for the work being done under a personal services contract, which the *Federal Acquisition Regulation* generally prohibits because of the government-contractor relationship it creates, was clearly present. While contractor managers retained control over matters such as approving leave requests, CCE took steps to further strengthen the management distinction between government and contractor employees based on GAO's findings. Finally, risks of organizational and personal conflicts of interest were mitigated to some extent, but in practice the government relies on individual contractor employees to identify potential conflicts. These types of risks must be mitigated to ensure that the government does not lose accountability over policy and program decisions.

CCE is paying up to almost 27 percent more for its contractor-provided contract specialists than for similarly graded government employees. This comparison took into account government salary, benefits, and overhead and the loaded hourly labor rates paid to contractors. Our review of available résumés showed that six contractor employees supporting CCE in fiscal year 2007 had on average more contracting experience than CCE's five recent government hires.

Despite CCE's legal counsel's concerns, CCE has been inappropriately ordering contract specialists under a GSA contract because the services were out of scope of those contracts. GAO found additional problems, such as a contractor advertising contract specialist services on GSA's Web site that it was not authorized to provide. Due to what it characterizes as the growing demand by federal agencies for contractor contract specialists, GSA recently posted a revised contract category, under which government agencies can procure contract specialists to provide acquisition management services, such as cost estimating and proposal evaluation support. In response to GAO's findings, GSA contacted each of the contractors involved in our review about their out-of-scope services and plans further follow-ups with them.

Abbreviations

ACA	Army Contracting Agency
BPA	blanket purchase agreement
CCE	Contracting Center of Excellence
DAU	Defense Acquisition University
DAWIA	Defense Acquisition Workforce Improvement Act
DOD	Department of Defense
FAR	*Federal Acquisition Regulation*
GAO	Government Accountability Office
GSA	General Services Administration
JCC-I/A	Joint Contracting Command-Iraq/Afghanistan
MOBIS	Mission Oriented Business Integrated Services
OCI	organizational conflict of interest
RFQ	request for quotations

United States Government Accountability Office
Washington, DC 20548

March 26, 2008

Congressional Committees

Over the past 10 years, Department of Defense (DOD) spending on services has increased 76 percent—to $158.3 billion in fiscal year 2007—and now outpaces its spending on supplies and equipment, including major weapon systems.[1] One effect of the escalation in service spending has been to place greater demands on a shrinking acquisition workforce, which is increasingly faced with the need to manage more complex contracting approaches. Agencies have dealt with these trends by relying more heavily on contractors, particularly those that provide professional, administrative, and management support services, an area where DOD's spending more than tripled from fiscal years 1998 through 2007. One example of a function DOD is acquiring through contracts is contract specialists, who perform a range of acquisition services in support of government contracting officers.

The decision to turn to contractors can, in some cases, create risks that the government needs to consider and manage. Of key concern is the risk of loss of government control over and accountability for mission-related policy and program decisions when contractors provide services that closely support inherently governmental functions. Contract specialist services are an example of such a service, whereas the contracting officer, who obligates the government's money, is performing an inherently governmental function that cannot be obtained through a contract. Other concerns include an increased potential for conflicts of interest, both organizational and personal; the potential for improper use of personal services contracts, which the *Federal Acquisition Regulation* (FAR) generally prohibits because of the employer-employee relationship they create between the government and contractor personnel; and the cost to the government of hiring contractors rather than government personnel.

To learn more about the use and roles of contractors providing contract specialist services, we conducted a case study, under the authority of the Comptroller General to conduct evaluations on his own initiative, of the Army's Contracting Center of Excellence's (CCE) use of contractors in this role. Organizationally, CCE falls under the Army Contracting Agency (ACA), a field operating agency reporting to the Assistant Secretary of the Army for Acquisition, Logistics, and Technology. We determined (1) the

[1] We have reported that to a large extent, DOD has not proactively managed this growth, meaning that it cannot know whether its investments in service contracts are achieving the desired outcomes. GAO, *Defense Acquisitions: Tailored Approach Needed to Improve Service Acquisition Outcomes*, GAO-07-20 (Washington, D.C.: Nov. 9, 2006).

extent to which and the reasons CCE is relying on contractors, (2) what actions have been taken to mitigate the risks associated with using contractors in contract specialist roles, (3) how the costs of CCE's contract specialists compared to that of its government contract specialists, and (4) whether the contract vehicles used to acquire the specialists were appropriate. This report presents our findings at CCE as an example of the challenges faced by agencies in an environment of increased reliance on contractors to help meet the contracting mission.

We identified CCE as a government agency using contractors as contract specialists through a bid protest that involved CCE's predecessor organization awarding a contract for contract specialists.[2] In fiscal year 2007, CCE obligated almost $1.8 billion in contract actions. To conduct our work, we interviewed CCE and ACA officials and contractor representatives. We obtained information on CCE's contract specialist staffing levels in fiscal year 2007, and we reviewed CCE's orders issued under blanket purchase agreements (BPA)[3] established in 2006 for contract specialist services, as well as billing information. To identify the roles and responsibilities of contractor contract specialists, we interviewed government and contractor contract specialists and government contracting officers, and we reviewed 42 randomly selected CCE contract files for work performed by the contractor contract specialists in fiscal years 2006 and 2007 to understand the contractors' day-to-day duties. We also reviewed contractor policies and procedures regarding organizational and personal conflicts of interest. In addition, we reviewed FAR provisions pertaining to conflicts of interest, as well as those relating to personal services contracts. To compare costs, we calculated an average loaded hourly rate (including benefits, overhead, and other costs) for CCE's government contract specialists who perform the same tasks and have similar qualifications as the contractor-provided contract specialists, and compared it to the weighted average labor hour rate that two contractors charged CCE for contract specialists in August 2007. The contractors' labor hour rates include wages, benefits, overhead, general and administrative expenses, and profit. We also reviewed résumés to compare experience levels of contractor and government contract specialists. Résumés were available for six contractor contract specialists who had supported the agency for at least 6 months; we also reviewed the résumés of the five contract specialists CCE had recently hired. We reviewed CCE's contracting strategies to determine whether new contracts were awarded to obtain contract specialists or whether interagency contracts through

[2] *LEADS Corporation*, B-292465, September 26, 2003, 2003 CPD 197 at 1. The protest was denied.

[3] BPAs are a simplified method of filling anticipated repetitive needs for supplies and services. For example, agencies can establish "charge accounts" with qualified vendors. FAR 13.303-1(a). BPAs established under a Federal Supply Schedule apply the BPA procedures under subpart 8.4 of the FAR.

other federal agencies, such as the General Services Administration's (GSA) schedule program, were used. We analyzed contract documents, including CCE's BPAs with four contractors, related task orders, and underlying GSA schedule contracts. We spoke with GSA officials responsible for overseeing the Mission Oriented Business Integrated Services (MOBIS) schedule and with CCE officials. We also examined the FAR section on the use of GSA schedules.

While CCE has established BPAs with four contractors to provide contract specialist services, nearly all of the contractor-provided contract specialists at CCE during our review were employees of CACI International, Inc. (CACI); thus, our primary focus was on the CACI contract, related BPA, and orders.

We conducted this performance audit from May 2007 to March 2008 in accordance with generally accepted government auditing standards. Those standards require that we plan and perform the audit to obtain sufficient, appropriate evidence to provide a reasonable basis for our findings and conclusions based on our audit objectives. We believe that the evidence obtained provides a reasonable basis for our findings and conclusions based on our audit objectives. See appendix I for additional information on our scope and methodology.

Results in Brief

CCE has relied on contractor contract specialists since it began hiring them in 2003 to help meet its increasing workload and plans to continue doing so, although officials told us that they would prefer an all-government workforce. CCE's contractor employees supported from 24 to 30 percent of its contract actions from fiscal years 2005 through 2007 and, in August 2007, represented 42 percent of the agency's contract specialists. The contractors work side by side with government contract specialists and perform the same activities. CCE and ACA officials noted that they face chronic difficulties in recruiting and retaining contract specialists, given the high demand for this skill set in the Washington, D.C., area. They said that it is a struggle to compete with other agencies as well as with the contractors supplying the specialists to the government. Further, while the agency has a 2-year training program for interns, it lacks a formal training program for its other contract specialists, despite officials' acknowledgment that skills need to be improved. Finally, CCE has not considered what would be an appropriate and feasible balance of the number of contractor and government employees. A recent Defense Acquisition University (DAU) study recommended that agencies assess the proper balance of contractor to government contract specialists to avoid overreliance on contractors.

We found mixed results in terms of policies, procedures, and actions in place to mitigate the risks of using contractors in the contract specialist role at CCE:

- The line separating contractor from government employee is blurry, and we found situations in which contractor employees were not clearly identified as such to the general public and cases where they were listed as the government's point of contact on contract documents. In situations such as these, contractor employees may appear to be speaking for the government, a situation that could create the impression in the general public that they are government employees. As a result of our findings, CCE has taken initial steps to more clearly delineate the contractor employees.
- The work being done by CCE's contractor contract specialists reflects each of the descriptive elements listed in the FAR as a guide in assessing the existence of personal services contracts—which are generally prohibited unless authorized—including work performed under the direct, day-to-day supervision of the government. However, determinations as to whether a personal services contract is present must be made based on the facts and circumstances of each situation. In this case, the contractor maintains control over a number of supervisory and management functions, such as the approval of time cards and leave requests. As a result of our review, CCE has taken several actions, such as reorganizing the contractor employees so that their work is now assigned by a supervisor employed by the contractor. We found no DOD guidance that elaborated on the factors to be considered in determining whether a personal services contract exists or how to mitigate that risk when contractors work side by side with their government counterparts.
- To mitigate the risk of organizational and personal conflicts of interest, CCE requires contractors to submit mitigation plans when appropriate, and contractor employees sign agreements not to disclose proprietary or sensitive information belonging to the government or other contractors, such as cost and pricing data, government spend plan data, and contractor technical proposal data, and not to engage in any conduct prohibited by provisions of the Procurement Integrity Act as implemented by the FAR.[4] In practice, the government must rely heavily on individual contractor employees to identify potential organizational conflicts of interest, such as where they are assigned to a procurement on which their company is bidding. The same holds true for personal conflicts of interest, because, although a new FAR subpart states that contractors should have a written code of business ethics

[4] 41 U.S.C. § 423, FAR 3.104.

> and conduct, neither the FAR nor DOD contracting policy requires that contractor employees be free from conflicts of interest or that they deploy other safeguards to help ensure that the advice and assistance the employees provide is not tainted by personal conflicts of interest.

CCE is paying more on average for contractor-provided contract specialists than for its government contract specialists who are doing equivalent work. We found that on average and taking into account benefits and overhead rates, the cost of a GS-12 CCE contract specialist is $59.21 per hour, as compared to the contractors' average loaded hourly labor rate of $74.99, or about 17 percent more. The average cost of CCE's GS-13 specialists is $72.15 per hour, while it is paying the contractor specialists $84.38 per hour, or about 27 percent more. We also reviewed available résumés of six contract employees supporting CCE for at least 6 months and found that they had from 5 to 32 years, or an average of 18 years, of contracting-related experience. In comparison, the five CCE government contract specialists hired in fiscal year 2007 had from 6 to 17 years, or an average of about 12 years, of contracting-related experience. All six contract employees had previously worked for, and were trained by, the federal government before being hired by the contractor.

The contract vehicles CCE has used since 2003 to acquire its contract specialists—orders issued under GSA's MOBIS schedule contracts—were inappropriate because the services were out of scope of those contracts. The labor category descriptions in the vendors' GSA schedule contracts are, in most cases, substantially different from the descriptions in CCE's performance work statements and did not accurately represent the work that the contractors were performing. For example, one contractor's negotiated GSA contract was for "senior business analysts," but it is providing CCE with contract specialist support—a completely different description. Acquiring services outside the scope of the underlying contract circumvents the government's competition requirements and limits the government's ability to know if it is paying a fair and reasonable price. CCE's legal counsel and a senior procurement analyst raised concerns about the scope of services, but the agency issued the BPAs without resolving their concerns. When we brought the issue of the out-of-scope services to GSA's attention, as well as other issues we found, such as a contractor that had advertised services on GSA's Web site that it was not under contract to provide, GSA began contacting the contractors to rectify the situations. Because of the high demand for contract specialists, GSA has revised the MOBIS schedule to add acquisition management support services, including assistance in supporting proposal evaluations and reviews of contractor performance. Finally, CCE failed to follow Army policy for certifying that work ordered under a non-DOD contract—in this case, a GSA contract—is within scope of the contract.

We are recommending that the Secretary of the Army direct ACA to work with CCE to take several actions, including identifying the appropriate mix of contractor and government personnel and developing a plan to achieve the desired balance, implementing a training program for its employees, and putting in place procedures to ensure that contractors identify themselves as such in all interactions external to CCE. We are also recommending that DOD issue guidance to clarify the circumstances under which contracts risk becoming improper personal services contracts and to provide direction on how the risk should be mitigated. Finally, we are recommending that GSA, as the entity responsible for the MOBIS schedules, strengthen controls to guard against situations where contractors improperly advertise services on GSA's Web site that they are not under contract to provide. In written comments on a draft of this report, DOD and GSA concurred with the recommendations and outlined actions they plan to take or have taken to address them. DOD's and GSA's comments are reprinted in their entirety in appendixes II and III, respectively.

Background

CCE, which falls organizationally under ACA, provides contracting support to 125 DOD customers in the National Capitol Region, including the Joint Chiefs of Staff, TRICARE Management Activity, Defense Information Systems Agency, DOD Inspector General, Pentagon Renovation Office, and Office of the Judge Advocate General. During fiscal year 2007, the agency awarded about 5,800 contract actions and obligated almost $1.8 billion. CCE is one of many government agencies that have turned to contractors to support their contracting functions.

While use of contractors provides the government certain benefits, such as increased flexibility in fulfilling immediate needs, we and others have raised concerns about the federal government's services contracting, in particular for professional and management support services.[5] A major concern is the risk of loss of government control over and accountability for mission-related policy and program decisions when contractors provide services that closely support inherently governmental functions. Inherently governmental functions require discretion in applying government authority or value judgments in making decisions for the government, such as approving contractual requirements; as such, they must be performed by government employees, not private contractors. The closer contractor services come to supporting inherently governmental functions, the greater the risk of their influencing the government's control over and accountability for decisions that may be based, in part, on contractor work.

[5] GAO, *Department of Homeland Security: Improved Assessment and Oversight Needed to Manage Risk of Contracting for Selected Services*, GAO-07-990 (Washington, D.C.: Sept. 17, 2007).

Decisions may be made that are not in the best interest of the government and may increase vulnerability to waste, fraud, or abuse.

The FAR[6] sets forth examples of services closely supporting inherently governmental functions. These include acquisition support services, such as

- services in support of acquisition planning,
- services that involve or relate to the evaluation of another contractor's performance,
- contractors providing assistance in contract management (such as where the contractor might influence official evaluations of other contractors), and
- contractors working in any situation that permits or might permit them to gain access to confidential business information, any other sensitive information, or both.

It is now commonplace for agencies to use contractors to perform activities historically performed by federal government contract specialists. Although these contractors are not authorized to obligate government money, they provide acquisition support to contracting officers, the federal decision makers who have the authority to bind the government contractually. Among other things, contract specialists perform market research, assist in preparing statements of work, develop and manage acquisition plans, and prepare the documents the contracting officer signs, such as contracts, solicitations, and contract modifications.

In its 2007 report to Congress, DOD's Panel on Contracting Integrity[7] noted that the practice of using contractors to support the contracting mission merits further study because it gives rise to questions regarding potential conflicts of interest and appropriate designation of governmental versus nongovernmental functions. The panel concluded that potential vulnerabilities may exist that could result in fraud, waste, and abuse.

A November 2005 DAU study[8] cited four top reasons that federal agencies are contracting out for procurement services: (1) to meet workload surge requirements, (2) inability to hire adequate resources to meet workload, (3) relative speed of contracting versus hiring to meet workload, and (4) ability to select specific required expertise. The DAU data showed that contractors performed duties across the spectrum of contracting functions,

[6] The FAR is the primary regulation for use by all federal executive agencies in their acquisition of supplies and services with appropriated funds.

[7] Department of Defense, Office of the Under Secretary of Defense for Acquisition, Technology, and Logistics, *Panel on Contracting Integrity, 2007 Report to Congress.* Also, see the John Warner National Defense Authorization Act for Fiscal Year 2007, § 813.

[8] Defense Acquisition University, Contracting Out Procurement Functions: An Analysis, DAU Research Report 06-001 (Fort Belvoir, Va.: Defense Acquisition University Press, November 2005).

from acquisition planning to contract closeout. The study's authors noted that as DOD's personnel levels have dropped, activity rates for procurement organizations have increased, driving a gap between the requirements and government capability in many DOD contracting offices. The report warned that the government must be careful when contracting for the procurement function to ensure that government leaders retain thorough control of policy and management functions and that contracting does not inappropriately restrict agency management in its ability to develop and consider options.[9]

CCE Is Using Contractors to Supplement Its Workforce without Considering the Right Balance of Contractors versus Government Employees

CCE has relied on contractors to help meet its increasing workload requirements since 2003 and plans to continue doing so, although agency officials would prefer an all-government workforce. The roles and responsibilities of the contractor contract specialists mirror those of the government contract specialists. In fact, contractor and government contract specialists work side by side and perform the same duties. CCE has not taken into consideration what constitutes a reasonable and feasible balance of the number of government versus contractor personnel or developed a training program for its permanent government employees.

CCE Has Relied on Contractors to Meet Its Increasing Workload and Plans to Continue Doing So

According to agency officials, CCE began using contractor contract specialists in 2003 as a stopgap measure to meet an increase in workload, but the agency has continued to rely heavily on their support. Our analysis of CCE's contract actions showed that contractors supported from 24 to 30 percent of all actions from fiscal year 2005 through 2007. In fiscal year 2007, CCE spent over $2.8 million on over 32,600 hours (approximately 15.6 full-time-equivalent employees)[10] of contracting support services from two contractors—CACI and The Ravens Group. In August 2007, 42 percent

[9] In *Urgent Reform Required: Army Expeditionary Contracting* (November 2007), the Commission on Army Acquisition and Program Management in Expeditionary Operations reported similar findings specifically for the Army. It noted that there were significant reductions in the Army's contracting workforce from 1990 to 2006, while workload increased over 654 percent from 1992 to 2006. The commission recommended increasing the stature, quantity, and career development of military and civilian contracting personnel. In response to the commission's report, the Army approved the creation of an Army Contracting Command, which will fall under the Army Materiel Command and be led by a two-star officer. The Army also plans to increase its contracting workforce by approximately 400 military personnel and 1,000 civilian personnel.

[10] Based on 2087 hours for a full-time-equivalent employee.

of CCE's contract specialists were contractors.[11] CCE officials stated that the agency plans to continue relying on contractors, although they would prefer an all-government workforce.

CCE officials told us that prior to 2005, the majority of the agency's contracting activity consisted of issuing orders against GSA schedule contracts—a relatively simple contracting method. After a DOD policy memorandum placed limitations on the use of non-DOD contract vehicles because of widely reported misuse of interagency contracts, CCE began relying less on using contract vehicles awarded by other agencies. Our analysis of Federal Procurement Data System-Next Generation data found that from fiscal years 2005 to 2007, the number of CCE contract actions through other agency contract vehicles decreased by 55 percent and obligations through use of these vehicles decreased by 45 percent. According to agency officials, CCE began awarding more of its own contracts through full and open competition, but the contracting staff generally lacked experience with these more complex types of procurements. Much of the workload had to be assigned to a limited number of more experienced staff, creating a situation where officials believed they had no choice but to turn to contractor support.

Activities and Responsibilities of Contractor Contract Specialists Mirror Those of Government Personnel

Contractor contract specialists at CCE perform the same tasks as government contract specialists. Typical tasks include pre-procurement research and planning, preparing contract documents, monitoring contracts, assisting with negotiations, and closing out contracts. These "cradle-to-grave" procurement activities are performed as support for a government contracting officer, who performs an inherently governmental function with the ability to bind the government by contract. According to CCE contracting officers, the work is generally assigned based on knowledge and experience, not whether the specialist is a government or contractor employee, with the only exception being cases where there could be a potential organizational conflict of interest (such as when the contractor employee's company could bid on the contract in question).

We reviewed contract files for 42 randomly selected contract actions on which contractor contract specialists worked during fiscal years 2006 and 2007 and found that the contractors had prepared a range of contracting documents, such as contract modifications, requests for legal review, small business coordination records, cover sheets to route contract actions for approval, award decision memorandums, and memorandums to the file.

[11] This percentage does not include three contractor employees for whom CCE was billed 16 hours or less in August 2007.

Contractors also had requested or received documents from vendors or other DOD entities, such as proposals, technical evaluations, and past performance questionnaires, and assisted in preparing statements of work.

The contracting officers and government and contractor-provided contract specialists we interviewed at CCE emphasized that while the contractors can recommend a course of action, the contracting officers make the decisions, such as deciding on an acquisition strategy and making contract award determinations. The contracting officers and specialists also told us that although contractors may assist in negotiations, the contracting officer takes the lead role in negotiating the terms of the contract.

CCE Has Faced Difficulties Hiring Government Contract Specialists

CCE officials informed us that the agency has had trouble recruiting and retaining government contract specialists. For example, an official told us that as of October 2007 the agency had 10 contract specialist positions that have been vacant for as long as 5 months, as well as another 12 vacancies, such as procurement analysts and a cost/price analyst. According to the official, from August 2006 through August 2007, 24 contract specialists—more than one-quarter of its government contracting workforce[12] during the period—left the agency. Agency officials stated that some of these personnel retired, but many had gone to work for private contractors that support the federal government. In fact, CCE officials said that they cannot compete with the private sector when it comes to offering some employment incentives. Additionally, both CCE and ACA officials stated that the government's hiring process takes too long and that potential candidates are often hired by a contractor or another agency before CCE can make an offer. For example, it took CCE over 5 months, from solicitation to job offer and placement, for two recent contract specialist hires. In contrast, a CCE official told us that they can order and have a contractor employee in place within as little as a couple of weeks.

CCE officials stated that the agency's recruitment difficulties are in large part caused by the high demand for contract specialists—by both the many federal agencies in Washington, D.C., and contractors from which the government purchases these services—making it difficult to compete for them. Contractor representatives, too, reiterated that the employment market for well-qualified contract specialists is extremely competitive. CACI employees who were supporting CCE as contract specialists confirmed that there is a high demand for their skill set, and several of these individuals stated that a well-qualified person can be selective when searching for a new employer. In addition, these employees said CACI offers some better

[12] CCE's government contracting workforce includes contract specialists, procurement analysts, and cost/price analysts.

benefits than the federal government, including higher salaries, fewer responsibilities, and shorter work weeks (because of contract restrictions on extended hours). Senior managers from The Ravens Group told us that their firm recruits contract specialists who have worked for and been trained by the government and hires them at a higher rate of pay.

CCE Has Not Considered the Appropriate Balance of Contractor to Government Employees and Lacks a Training Plan to Help Build Government Staff's Skills

CCE plans to continue relying on contractors to help meet its mission, but has not considered the appropriate and feasible ratio of government employees to contractors. In a November 2005 study on contracting out the procurement function, DAU concluded that it is reasonable to contract out functions or tasks that are not inherently governmental to meet a sudden or temporary increase in workload or when special expertise is required. However, the study cautioned that contracted procurement support needs to be maintained at a "reasonable" level. The study recommended that each contracting activity be limited in the percentage of its workforce that may be contractors, acknowledging that the appropriate limitation is a matter for debate.[13] It noted that using contractors only in limited situations would

- provide contracting agencies with flexibility to quickly react to surge workload situations,
- enable managers to assign the contractors to lower-priority tasks so that government employees would handle the more sensitive procurement tasks, and
- help address the concern that extensive contracting out of the contracting function could reduce, in the long term, the opportunity to develop adequate numbers of government personnel with a full range of contracting experience.

Defining the right mix of contractor to government contract specialists is not just a matter of numbers, but also of skill sets. The DAU study envisions contractors playing a limited role and performing lower-priority tasks. However, at CCE, complex, high-priority work is often assigned to the contractors, whose role has been ongoing since 2003. In part, according to agency officials, this is because many of the government employees lack experience with complex procurements. However, we found that while CCE has implemented a 2-year training program for its contract specialist

[13] The authors suggested that contractor employees should not exceed 25 percent of an activity's total procurement workforce in other than exceptional situations. The authors did not specifically set forth their rationale for recommending this percentage.

interns, the agency does not have in place a training program for its permanent staff. In fact, according to CCE's former Commander and the current Director of Contracting, contracting staff have had to learn these practices on the job, which has resulted in some performance problems. An agency's overall training strategy—including planning, developing, implementing, and continuous improvement of its programs—is an important factor in ensuring that the staff has the skills, knowledge, and experience to meet agency missions.

Risks Associated with Using Contractors for Acquisition Services Are Being Mitigated to a Mixed Degree

Three broad areas of risk of using contractors as contract specialists are present at CCE, with the risks being mitigated to various degrees. First, we found that the blurred lines demarcating contractor from government personnel could result in creating the impression that contractor employees are government personnel. Contractor employees were not always identified as such to the public and in some cases were named on documents as the government's point of contact. Second, the work being done reflects the descriptive elements listed in the FAR as guidance for assessing the existence of personal services contracts, which are prohibited unless authorized. However, a determination as to whether a personal services contract exists must be made on a case-by-case basis; here, CACI's on-site managers retain control over supervisory and managerial functions, such as approving time cards and making hiring and firing decisions, thus negating the existence of a personal services contract. We found no DOD guidance that elaborated on the factors to be considered in determining whether an unauthorized personal services contract exists or how to mitigate that risk. Finally, although policies and procedures are in place to help mitigate organizational and personal conflicts of interest, in practice, CCE relies on contractor employees to self-identify potential conflicts.

Contractor Contract Specialists Not Always Identified as Such

To avoid confusion by vendors and customers over whether they are speaking to a government employee, it is important to clearly distinguish between contractors and government employees in all interactions. Contractor personnel attending meetings, answering government telephones, and working in other situations where their contractor status is not obvious to third parties should identify themselves as such to avoid creating the impression that they are government officials.[14] In addition, the FAR states that agencies must ensure that all documents or reports contractors produce are suitably marked as contractor products or that contractor participation

[14] FAR 37.114(c).

is appropriately disclosed. Further, in December 2005, the Assistant Secretary of the Army issued a memorandum, "Contractors in the Government Workplace," stating that "while it is preferred that contractor personnel work in company office space, if Government and contractor personnel must be co-located in the same office space, then, to the maximum extent possible, the contractor personnel should have separate, and separated, space."

At CCE, we found the line separating government from contractor personnel to be blurry. There is no physical separation; the two work side by side in identical office space, and contractor employees are not identified as such on their cubicles. The only apparent distinction is their different badge color.

In addition, contractors were not always identified as such on contracting documents they had prepared. We reviewed 23 contract modifications[15] prepared by contractor employees and found that their status as contractors was not indicated on the documents. Further, on 16 of these modifications, the contractor was identified as administering the contract, and on four, the contractor was listed as the point of contact without identification as a contractor—for example, as the "CCE contact" or "government point of contact." Instances such as these, where the contractor is not identified as such or is misidentified, can cause confusion about the contractor's status and create an impression that the contractor is speaking or acting for the government. For example, we found a situation in which a vendor, in submitting a proposal to the government, listed the contractor contract specialist as the contracting officer, who has the contract source selection authority for the government. Another contract file contained e-mails between a contractor employee and third-party entities—correspondence with a CCE customer agency and notification to a vendor that its bid would not be considered—with no contractor identification at all.

CCE officials told us that the agency has no requirement that contractor employees identify themselves as contractors in the e-mail signature line, which could help ensure that outside parties know they are dealing with a contractor. Further, although the FAR and CCE's orders for contract specialists under the BPAs specifically cite telephone contacts as situations in which contractors should identify themselves as such, a CCE management official did not know whether this was occurring in practice.

When we brought these issues to CCE's attention, the agency began to establish policies to mitigate the risk of contractors being mistaken for government employees and appearing to be speaking for the government. It

[15] Contract modifications are documents that amend or modify existing contract conditions and are signed by the government contracting officer. Bilateral contract modifications are also signed by the vendor providing the goods or services.

has since issued a policy that contractor support personnel are not to communicate orally or in writing with other contractors, such as vendors. The contractor contract specialists will still communicate with CCE's federal customers. In addition, the CACI on-site senior manager notified CACI employees at CCE that they are to identify themselves as contractors in all correspondence, including e-mail and voice mail, and documents.

Determination of Whether Personal Services Contract Exists Must Be Made on Case-by-Case Basis

At CCE, the work of the contractor contract specialists, performed in direct support of the government contracting officer and under his or her day-to-day supervision, results in an arrangement that can have characteristics of a personal services contract. Personal services contracts are generally prohibited, unless authorized by statute. The government is normally required to obtain its employees by direct hire under competitive appointment or other procedures required by the civil service laws. Section 37.104 of the FAR lists six descriptive elements to be used as a guide in assessing the existence of a personal services contract.[16] The presence of any or all of these elements does not necessarily establish the existence of a personal services contract. Such a finding can only be established based on a case-by-case analysis of the totality of the circumstances of each case. The FAR elements are shown in table 1 along with the working environment of the contract employees at CCE. We found that the actual working environment for the contractor contract specialists at CCE touched on all six elements.

The FAR provides that each contract arrangement be judged in the light of its own facts and circumstances, with the key question always being whether the government will exercise relatively continuous supervision and control over the contractor personnel performing the contract.[17] For example, GAO bid protest decisions have considered, along with the existence of other factors, the fact that government "managers interviewed and selected contractor personnel for assignment to positions, and routinely requested pay increases and promotions for contractor personnel" to be contributing factors in the existence of a personal services contract.[18] Another bid protest decision considered that "the contractor's right to hire and fire employees, to grant or deny individual leave requests, and to reassign employees negate the existence of a personal services contract as defined in the FAR."[19] CACI's performance, in this case, of supervisory and management functions, such as approving time cards and leave requests, preparing performance evaluations, and making hiring and firing decisions,

[16] FAR Subpart 37.104(d).
[17] FAR 37.104(c)(2).
[18] *Encore Management, Inc.*, B-278903.2, February 12, 1999, 99-1 CPD ¶ 33 at 3.
[19] *W.B. Joley*, B-234146, March 31, 1989, 89-1 CPD ¶ 339 at 2.

Table 1. The Six FAR Personal Services Contract Elements Compared with CCE's Working Environment

FAR Elements Suggesting Personal Services Contracts Exist	CCE Contracting Environment
1. Performance on-site.	Contractors are on-site at CCE and sit among government personnel performing the same tasks.
2. Principal tools and equipment furnished by the government.	Contractors use government equipment and facilities.
3. Services are applied directly to the integral effort of the agency or an organizational subpart in the furtherance of its assigned function or mission.	CCE's core mission is providing contract support directly to DOD entities. Contractors fulfill capability and workforce gaps at CCE.
4. Comparable services, meeting comparable needs, are performed in the same or similar agencies using civil service personnel.	Other than reassigning work when a potential organizational conflict of interest exists, there is no difference between the work of a government employee and a contractor employee.
5. The need for the type of service provided can reasonably be expected to last beyond 1 year.	CCE has contracted for contract specialist support on an ongoing basis since 2003.
6. The inherent nature of the service, or the manner in which it is provided, reasonably requires, directly or indirectly, government direction or supervision of contractor employees in order to (1) adequately protect the government's interest, (2) retain control of the function involved, or (3) retain full personal responsibility for the function supported in a duly authorized federal officer or employee.	CCE uses time-and-materials contracts for these services. Because there is no profit incentive for cost control or labor efficiencies when these contracts are used, they require the government to ensure appropriate surveillance over the contractor's performance. Contractor tasks are issued by the government directly to the contractor employee performing the work. The contractors' work is directly reviewed by the government contracting officer. The contractors are performing tasks that are defined by the FAR as closely supporting inherently governmental functions. CCE contracting officers retain the responsibility for making contract awards.

Sources: FAR subpart 37.104(d), CCE data, and GAO analysis.

means a personal services contract does not exist, even if the six FAR elements are present. Although the distinction between a personal services contract and a non-personal services contract is somewhat murky and requires a case-by-case analysis based on the facts of each circumstance, we found no additional DOD guidance that elaborated on the factors contracting officers or program officials should consider in determining whether a personal services contract exists and how to mitigate against this risk when contractors are working side by side with their government counterparts, perhaps even receiving their daily task assignments from a government supervisor. Because of the type of contract and nature of the contract services provided along with the presence of the FAR's descriptive elements, the CACI contract runs the risk of becoming a personal services contract if the government does not carefully monitor the manner in which services are provided.[20]

When we brought these issues to the attention of CCE, the agency began to take actions to strengthen the management distinction between government and contractor personnel. Before, the contractor personnel were assigned to a team consisting of government and contractor employees, and they generally worked for one contracting officer most of the time. Now, all of the contractor personnel are on a separate team, and the contractors' managers on-site are responsible for assigning work to the contractor employees—unlike the previous situation where the government contracting officer assigned the work. Under this arrangement, contractor contract specialists can work for several different contracting officers, according to a CCE official. In addition, CCE has plans to situate contractors together in an area separate from government personnel and to put nameplates on cubicles to clearly distinguish between contractor and government employees, but these plans have not yet been implemented.

The Acquisition Advisory Panel[21] recently reported that as the extent of service contracting has grown, the current ban on personal services contracts has created two responses—government managers may find themselves crafting cumbersome and inefficient processes to manage the work of contractor personnel to avoid the appearance that they are exercising continuous supervisory control, or they may simply ignore the ban. The panel recommended replacing the ban with guidance on the appropriate and

[20] We note the inherent tension between the government's responsibility to refrain from exercising relatively continuous supervision and control over contractor employees under FAR 37.104, the government's obligation to ensure sufficient surveillance of contractor performance for time-and-materials contracts under FAR 16.601(c)(1), and the government's responsibility to ensure enhanced oversight when contracting for functions that closely support inherently governmental functions. See FAR 7.503(d) and FAR 37.114(b).

[21] Acquisition Advisory Panel, *Report of the Acquisition Advisory Panel to the Office of Federal Procurement Policy and the United States Congress* (January 2007). Also, see National Defense Authorization Act for Fiscal Year 2004, Pub. L. No. 108-136, § 1423 (2003).

effective use of personal services contracts. The panel stated that in implementing the recommendation, the government should be allowed to supervise the work performed by the contractor workforce, but current prohibitions on government involvement in purely supervisory or management activities—such as hiring, leave approval, and performance ratings—should be retained.

Mitigations of Organizational and Personal Conflicts of Interest Must Rely Heavily on Individual Contractor Specialists

Reliance on contractor support to meet agency missions can raise the risk of organizational and personal conflicts of interest.[22] In fact, the Acquisition Advisory Panel noted that the government's increased reliance on contractors, coupled with increased contractor consolidations, has escalated the potential for organizational conflicts of interest (OCI). With respect to protecting contractor confidential or proprietary data, the panel recognized the increased threat of improper disclosure as more contractor employees support the government's acquisition function. The panel also found that while there are numerous statutory and regulatory provisions that apply to federal employees to protect against personal conflicts of interest, most do not apply to contractor personnel.

An OCI may be present when a contractor organization has other interests that either directly or indirectly (because of business or relationships with other contractor organizations) relate to the work to be performed under a contract and (1) may diminish its capacity to give impartial, technically sound, objective assistance or advice or (2) may result in it having an unfair competitive advantage. The FAR and GAO bid protest decisions provide guidance for contracting officers to mitigate three types of OCIs: unequal access to nonpublic information as part of its performance under a government contract that might provide the contractor firm unfair competitive advantage in a future competition; biased ground rules, such as the firm being in a position to write a statement of work that might provide it an unfair advantage in a future competition; and impaired objectivity when the contractor firm's work under a contract entails evaluating its own work or that of a competitor either through an assessment of performance under another contract or through an evaluation of proposals.[23]

As required under its BPA with CCE, CACI submitted an OCI risk mitigation plan, which lays out the elements of its plan to mitigate the risk of an OCI. According to the plan, the contractor has established a separation, or

[22] Whether the contractor providing contract specialist support had an adequate organizational conflict of interest mitigation plan in place has been the subject of GAO bid protests, for example, *The LEADS Corporation v. CACI*, B-292465, September 26, 2003.

[23] FAR Subpart 9.5.

"firewall," between the business unit that provides contract specialists and program support services to CCE and all other divisions and corporations owned by the company. As a part of the firewall, the business unit's employees are physically separated from the company's other operating groups, proposal databases are separated, and the business unit's employee financial incentives do not depend on the performance of the company's other operating organizations. Also, the business unit providing contract specialists is precluded from submitting proposals in response to solicitations issued by CCE, except for those related to the BPA for contract specialists. In addition, the company provides its employees with OCI training and instructions to immediately notify the contracting officer of a potential OCI; requires them to sign conflict of interest and nondisclosure agreements to protect proprietary or sensitive information belonging to the government or other contractors—for example, cost and pricing data, government spend plan data, and contractor technical proposal data—and not use this information to violate procurement integrity rules; and limits where employees can work within CACI for 2 years after leaving CCE. The nondisclosure agreement also addresses personal conflicts of interest, as the contractor employee must agree not to engage in any conduct prohibited by the Procurement Integrity Act as implemented in FAR 3.104. Finally, a group internal to the company conducts annual reviews of the effectiveness of and adherence to the OCI risk mitigation plan.

Although CCE and the contractor have taken steps to mitigate OCI risks, in practice, identifying and mitigating the risks necessarily relies, to a large extent, on individual contractor personnel. Contractor officials indicated that it is the responsibility of the contractor contract specialists to immediately notify the company supervisor and contracting officer of potential OCIs. CACI officials and employees told us of cases where contractor contract specialists had been exposed to potential conflicts of interest, that is, they were assigned to procurements that the company planned to bid on. We were told these employees were subsequently removed from working on the procurements after notifying contractor management and government officials of a potential conflict. Despite these instances, CCE officials told us that they are careful about what procurements they assign to the contractors. For example, the CCE contracting officer's representative[24] told us that she screens requirements packages to determine which ones would present a potential conflict if assigned to a contractor. However, she does not have visibility to the subcontract level, where the contractor could be a subcontractor to a potential bidder.

[24] If contract performance will be ongoing, a contracting officer's representative—generally an official at the requiring agency with relevant technical expertise—is normally designated by the contracting officer to monitor the contractor's performance and serve as the liaison between the contracting officer and the contractor.

For purposes of this report, we define a personal conflict of interest as a situation when an individual, employed by an organization in a position to materially influence research findings, recommendations, or both, may lack objectivity or be perceived to potentially lack objectivity because of his or her personal activities, relationships, or financial interests. For example, a conflict can occur when a government employee contacts an offeror during the conduct of an acquisition since this could be construed as seeking employment. Defense contractor employees are not subject to the same laws and regulations that are designed to prevent federal employee conflicts of interests. Moreover, although a new FAR subpart states that contractors should have a written code of business ethics and conduct, neither the FAR nor DOD contracting policy requires that contractor employees be free from conflicts of interest or that they deploy other safeguards to help ensure that the advice and assistance the employees provide is not tainted by personal conflicts of interest.[25] Therefore, mitigating the risks associated with personal conflicts of interest depends on the integrity of the contractors and their employees. For example, one of the contractors providing contract specialists to CCE has an internal policy for standards of employee ethics and business conduct that addresses personal conflicts of interest. In addition, the company provides mandatory ethics training that covers personal conflicts of interest. According to a company official, rather than having a formal financial disclosure process, its employees are equipped with knowledge of what constitutes a personal conflict of interest, and it is the employees' responsibility to self-report if they have a personal conflict of interest. The company also has a moonlighting policy that requires employees to obtain company approval prior to forming any relationship with a for-profit company.

CCE Is Paying More for Contractor Contract Specialists Than Its Government Employees

CCE is paying more on average for contractor-provided contract specialists than for its government specialists. We reviewed the hours of contractor services CCE purchased under orders pursuant to the four BPAs it established at the end of fiscal year 2006. By the end of fiscal year 2007, CCE had purchased contract support services only from CACI and The Ravens Group, with the vast majority being from CACI. Agency officials informed us that CCE has purchased services of two types of contract specialists: (1) contract specialists II, which are Defense Acquisition Workforce Improvement Act (DAWIA)[26] II-certified/GS-12 equivalents, and

[25] See GAO, *Defense Contracting: Additional Personal Conflict of Interest Safeguards Needed for Certain DOD Contractor Employees*, GAO-08-169 (Washington, D.C.: Mar. 7, 2008).

[26] In 1990, Congress enacted DAWIA to enhance the quality and professionalism of the defense acquisition workforce (Pub. L. No. 101-510). Most of DAWIA was codified in Title 10 of the United States

(2) contract specialists III, which are DAWIA III-certified/GS-13 equivalents. Because the orders issued pursuant to the BPAs are time-and-materials contracts, payments to contractors are based on the number of labor hours billed at a fixed hourly rate—which includes wages, benefits, and the company's overhead; general and administrative expenses; and profit.[27] Because agency officials stated that CCE has government contract specialists with the same certifications and GS levels as the contractor contract specialists, we determined that these specialists were comparable. Therefore, we compared the costs and experience of the government and contractor employees within these two categories. We found that the average hourly cost of a contract employee is higher than a government specialist performing the same duties, as shown in table 2.

Key elements of our analysis were as follows:

- The loaded hourly cost of a government employee includes salary, costs of the government's contributions to the employee's benefits, the costs to train the employee, the employee's travel expenses, and the costs of operations overhead—which are the costs of government employees who provide support services, such as budget analysts or human capital staff.
- Government employee salaries and benefits were based on actual data from one pay period. These data were then compared to hourly cost of contractor employees ordered during that same pay period. The cost of a contractor employee is the fully loaded hourly rate the government pays for these services. We reported the weighted average of those hourly rates because the agency used two contractors at two different rates during that pay period.
- We excluded the costs that the government incurs for both government and contractor-provided specialists. These include the costs of supplies, facilities, utilities, information technology, and communications.

Based on a limited number of résumés we reviewed, the contractors generally had more contracting experience than their government counterparts. Résumés were available for six CACI employees supporting CCE as contract specialists for at least 6 months during fiscal year 2007; they had

Code, and it has been amended a few times since enactment. DAWIA requires the Secretary of Defense to establish the minimum qualification standards of those personnel performing functions integral to the acquisition process, formalizes career paths for personnel who wish to pursue careers in acquisition, and defines critical or senior management acquisition positions. See GAO, *Defense Space Activities: Management Actions Are Needed to Better Identify, Track and Train Air Force Space Personnel*, GAO-06-908 (Washington, D.C.: Sept. 21, 2006). The certification levels are based on an individual's education, experience, and training. National Defense Authorization Act for Fiscal Year 1991, Pub. L. No. 101-510 (1990). *See also* DOD Manual 5000.52M.

[27] We recently reported on DOD's use of time-and-materials and labor-hour contracts. GAO, *Defense Contracting: Improved Insight and Controls Needed over DOD's Time-and-Materials Contracts*, GAO-07-273 (Washington, D.C.: June 29, 2007).

Table 2. Comparison of the Average Cost of CCE's Government and Contractor Contract Specialists

DAWIA Certification/ GS Level or Equivalent	Average Hourly Cost of a Government Employee[a]	Average Hourly Cost of a Contract Employee[b]	Percentage Difference
II/GS-12	$59.21	**$74.99**	26.65
III/GS-13	72.15	**84.38**	16.95

Source: GAO analysis based on government information.

[a]This rate is based on actual salaries and benefits paid during the pay period ending on August 18, 2007, and 68.3 productive hours per pay period. The rate does not include the government's costs of managing the payroll of government employees.

[b]This rate is based on the weighted average rate CCE paid during August 2007 and does not include CCE's cost of managing the contracts for these services.

from 5 to 32 years, or an average of about 18 years, of contracting-related experience. In contrast, the five CCE government contract specialists hired during fiscal year 2007 had from 6 to 17 years, or an average of about 12 years, of contracting-related experience prior to joining the agency. All six contract employees previously worked for, and were trained by, the federal government before being hired by the contractor.

Contract Vehicles Inappropriately Issued and Used to Order Contract Specialists

CCE's issuance of the BPAs with four contractors for contract specialists under GSA's MOBIS schedule was inappropriate as some of the services required in CCE's performance work statements were outside the scope of the underlying contracts. The labor category descriptions in the vendors' GSA schedule contracts were, in most cases, significantly different from the description on CCE's performance work statements and, for the two contractors who have been issued task orders, did not accurately represent the work performed.[28] A GSA official confirmed that contract specialist services were not within the scope of the MOBIS schedule but said it is the responsibility of the ordering agency to ensure that orders are within scope. In addition, we found that one of the other contractors had improperly advertised on GSA's Web site that its contract contained contract specialist services. GSA has initiated corrective actions with the four contractors based on our findings. Because of federal agencies' demand for contract

[28] Contract specialists are available under GSA's Temporary Administrative and Professional Staffing Support Services Schedule, but these services are limited to a maximum of 240 work days.

support services, GSA recently implemented a revised MOBIS category for acquisition management support, which includes contract specialist services. Finally, CCE did not comply with Army policy requiring an assertion that work performed by a contractor under a non-DOD contract is within scope of the contract.

Orders for Contract Specialists Were Out of the Scope of the Underlying Contract

The four contractors' BPAs with CCE (CACI, The Ravens Group, Tai Pedro & Associates, and Government Contracts Consultants), established under the GSA schedule contracts, were inappropriately issued as some of the services required in the performance work statements were outside the scope of these underlying contracts. Specifically, their labor category descriptions differed significantly from those required in CCE's performance work statements, and they did not accurately represent the work that the contractor was to perform. Moreover, CCE has issued task orders for contract specialists against CACI's and The Ravens Group's MOBIS contracts that were outside the scope of those contracts. Where an agency announces its intention to order from an existing GSA contractor, all items ordered are required to be within the scope of the vendors' contracts.[29] Orders issued outside the scope of the underlying GSA contract do not satisfy legal requirements under the Competition in Contracting Act for competing the award of government contracts and limit the government's ability to know if it is paying a fair and reasonable price. In such cases, the out-of-scope work should have been awarded using competitive procedures or supported with a justification and approval for other than full and open competition.[30]

CCE has issued task orders for contract specialists against CACI's and The Ravens Group's MOBIS contracts. Table 3 provides examples of the differences between the GSA schedule contract labor category descriptions and CCE's statements of work for these contractors for a contract specialist—level 3 position. Although the performance work statement does not delineate responsibilities that are specific to the contract specialist, level 3 position, it contains responsibilities for all contract specialist positions as described in the table.

Our review of the contract file shows that during acquisition planning, CCE's policy and legal offices raised concerns about the use of the GSA MOBIS schedule to meet CCE's requirements.[31] Specifically, in a

[29] *Tarheel Specialties, Inc.*, B-298197, 298197.2, July 17, 2006, 2006 CPD ¶ 140.

[30] *See generally*, FAR Subpart 6.3.

[31] Although CCE has been procuring contract specialists from the GSA MOBIS schedule since 2003, it established the BPAs with four contractors in September 2006; the contract files contained no evidence of legal objections prior to 2006.

Table 3. Comparison of Labor Categories in Two Contractors' GSA MOBIS Contracts with Requirement in CCE's Performance Work Statement

MOBIS Labor Category Description	CCE Requirements
CACI: senior program control analyst **Responsibilities:** Maintains current project documentation and record of changes, including status reports. Assists in establishing budgets and monitoring performance. Directs all or most activities related to financial and administrative functions, such as budgeting, manpower and resource planning, and financial reporting. May research, report on, and recommend solutions to contractual issues. Provides expert functional advice and direction to functional/user area management and project teams working on complex systems. **Experience/education:** Experience in the preparation and analysis of financial statements, working with acquisition systems, or complex vertical business, purchasing applications, or both. General experience required includes progressively more responsible experience in general accounting, acquisition, or management activities. **The Ravens Group: senior budget/ business analyst** **Responsibilities:** Reviews expenditures and prepares operating budgets for various departments to ensure conformance to budgetary limits. Performs a variety of tasks. **Experience/education:** Requires a bachelor's degree in business, finance, accounting or economics with 8 years of experience in federal government budgeting; the DOD Planning, Programming and Budgeting System; or equivalent budgeting experience. Knowledge of automated systems used in budget formulations and execution is required. Relies on extensive experience and judgment to plan and accomplish goals.	**Contract specialist – level 3** **Responsibilities:** Provides support and assistance in essentially all areas of FAR-based federal procurement in which advanced or complex knowledge and expertise is required, such as preparing or reviewing pre-procurement packages; actively participating in integrated process teams; developing and managing acquisition plans; preparing/researching support documentation; making recommendations to the contracting officer; handling complex problems through resolution; validating data; and otherwise completing actions needed to successfully advertise, solicit, construct, award, administer, and close out government contract vehicles. **Experience/education:** Master's degree. An advanced degree or acquisition certification is preferred. Eight years of progressive experience supporting and developing large, major, or complex government procurements. In-depth knowledge of the FAR, agency-specific regulations, and current and demonstrated experience with acquisition streamlining initiatives and reforms. Practical knowledge of various acquisition approaches. Ability to formulate appropriate documentation for the various approaches. Experience leading and managing other acquisition professionals.

Source: GAO analysis based on GSA contracts and CCE BPAs.

September 1, 2006, letter to the contracting officer and government contract specialist, CCE's Acting Chief Attorney expressed concern that the schedule "may not provide the right personnel for this requirement," and cited an applicable GAO decision in which the protest was sustained on the basis that vendors' quoted services were outside the scope of their GSA contracts.[32] The CCE attorney determined that the request for quotations (RFQ) was "legally insufficient" because of this and other issues and indicated that the out-of-scope issue, among others, should be considered. According to the legal office, despite this determination, CCE contracting personnel issued the RFQ without returning it to the attorney for further review. According to the Army's internal policies and a March 2006 CCE memorandum regarding legal review procedures, where the contracting officer makes a decision or takes a proposed action that is contrary to legal advice, the contract file must include written evidence to that effect, including a statement of the contracting officer's rationale for proceeding contrary to such legal advice. No such evidence was included in the contract file in this case.

Contractor representatives told us that the linkage between labor categories and the work to be performed is more of an art than a clean-cut science. They told us that they attempted to match the labor categories as best they could by using their GSA labor rates and CCE's requirements. Although acknowledging that the mapping was strained, CACI officials pointed out that it was disclosed in their proposal to CCE and that the company provided CCE with résumés that more closely matched the agency's requirements. CACI officials told us that they have had discussions in the past with GSA about offering contracting support skill sets and what schedule is appropriate. The Ravens Group officials said that the key is the evaluation of the qualifications and level of effort required and relating those factors to the various MOBIS schedule job descriptions and labor rates.

GSA agreed that CCE's orders for contract specialists were issued out of scope of the vendors' underlying MOBIS contracts, but a senior official stated that it is the responsibility of the ordering agency to ensure that orders are within scope of the vendors' contracts. The official told us that while GSA has ownership of the MOBIS schedule, it is only able to perform limited oversight of the orders issued under schedule contracts. The official acknowledged that GSA is aware of instances where agencies have

---

[32] In *American Systems Consulting, Inc.*, B-294644, December 13, 2004, 2004 CPD ¶ 247, GAO determined that an award of a BPA based on a competition of GSA schedule contract vendors, using schedule program procedures, was improper because the awardee's quotation contained services not identified in its contract. We found the services offered to be outside of the contract's scope because the labor categories identified in the awardee's schedule contract as "most nearly equating" to the labor categories in the performance work statement did not match the positions as described in the performance work statement.

improperly used the MOBIS schedule to hire contract specialists, although it does not know the extent to which this has occurred.

We found that other DOD agencies had used the MOBIS schedule to procure contract specialists but stopped doing so because of concerns about out-of-scope work. In 2004, ACA's Capital District Contracting Center in Fort Belvoir, Virginia, used the MOBIS schedule to hire contract specialists in support of what is now the Joint Contracting Command-Iraq/Afghanistan (JCC-I/A). However, in 2005, the contracting center changed its approach, awarding a similar contract for additional support using full and open competition instead of continuing to issue orders under the MOBIS contract. When the period of performance expired, JCC-I/A awarded its own contract in 2006 for contract specialists, again using full and open competition. According to a former JCC-I/A official involved in the award, the driving factor in the decision to issue a competitive solicitation was the determination that contract specialist services were not in the scope of the MOBIS schedule.[33]

Based on our findings, CCE is planning to solicit a new contract for contract specialists using full and open competition, under the FAR's commercial item acquisition procedures, with a target award date of June 30, 2008. In the interim, according to a CCE official, no more orders are being placed under the current BPAs for contract specialists.

Although CCE has not placed orders for contract specialists with two other firms with which it has established BPAs—Tai Pedro & Associates and Government Contracts Consultants—we found troublesome issues related to their schedule contracts as well. Tai Pedro & Associates' MOBIS contract actually includes a labor category for "contract specialist" services under a category for competitive sourcing support, which allows contractors to perform competitive sourcing surveys or to assist agencies in developing A-76 procurement strategies.[34] According to GSA officials, the competitive sourcing support category allows contractor contract specialists to assist with A-76 projects and outsourcing efforts, but not with other efforts.

[33] We and others have raised concerns about the use of interagency contracts, such as GSA schedule contracts, for the acquisition of services. For example, in April 2005, we reported on breakdowns in the issuance and administration of task orders, issued by the Department of the Interior under a GSA schedule information technology contract, for interrogation and other services in Iraq on behalf of DOD. These breakdowns included issuing task orders that were beyond the scope of underlying contracts, in violation of competition rules, and not properly justifying the decision to use interagency contracting. GAO, Interagency Contracting: *Problems with DOD's and Interior's Orders to Support Military Operations, GAO-05-201* (Washington, D.C.: Apr. 29, 2005). Also see GAO, *Interagency Contracting: Improved Guidance, Planning, and Oversight Would Enable the Department of Homeland Security to Address Risks*, GAO-06-996 (Washington, D.C.: Sept. 27, 2006). We placed interagency contracting on our high-risk list in January 2005.

[34] Office of Management and Budget Circular A-76 prescribes policies and procedures for use by agencies as they select service providers through competitions among public and private sector sources.

Government Contracts Consultants' MOBIS contract did not contain acquisition support categories. However, the contractor advertised that its contract contained these categories—including contract specialists—on the GSA Advantage Web site, the agency's portal for Web-based procurement. The contractor took this action despite having affirmed in writing to GSA prior to its contract award its understanding that "contract support services are not authorized" under the contract. Until we informed GSA officials of this situation in September 2007, they were unaware that it had occurred. They told us that they normally check postings on GSA Advantage against awarded contracts to ensure that inappropriate services are not advertised, but in this case the situation was overlooked.

GSA Has Initiated Corrective Actions

Based on our findings, GSA began in the fall of 2007 to notify the four contractors that contract specialist services are out of scope of their schedule contracts. For example, GSA notified Government Contracts Consultants that it had been found to be performing out-of-scope services. GSA sent its internal reviewers to the company's facilities to review its task orders to determine what services the company was offering federal customers under its GSA contract. GSA also directed Government Contracts Consultants to remove the incorrect labor categories from its posting on the GSA Advantage Web site, which the company has since done. GSA also notified both CACI and The Ravens Group that they had been found to be performing services outside the scope of their schedule contracts and informed Tai Pedro & Associates that acquisition support services are out of the scope of its MOBIS schedule contract, which is limited to support for competitive sourcing efforts. GSA told CACI, The Ravens Group, and Tai Pedro & Associates that internal reviewers would visit their facilities in fiscal year 2008 to ensure that they are performing within the scope of their contracts and that GSA may periodically ask for copies of recently awarded task orders to be reviewed for scope appropriateness. GSA advised all four companies—Government Contracts Consultants, The Ravens Group, CACI, and Tai Pedro & Associates—that if any new out-of-scope work is performed, GSA will take appropriate action, up to and including canceling their contracts or initiating termination for cause proceedings.

Because of the demand for contract support services, GSA recently implemented a revised Special Item Number category—Acquisition Management Support—under the MOBIS schedule. Contract specialist services can be ordered under this category to perform functions such as cost estimating; preparing price negotiation memorandums and statements of work; assisting with acquisition planning, including performing market research and recommending procurement strategies; providing expert assistance in supporting proposal evaluations; assisting with reviews of contractor performance; and investigating reports of contract discrepancies. GSA has links on its Web site for special ordering instructions and an ordering guide for the revised category. These documents primarily discuss mitigating conflicts of interest and ensuring that contractors do not perform inherently governmental functions.

CCE Did Not Properly Justify Use of Interagency Contracting Vehicle

In placing the orders for contract specialist services, CCE did not follow ACA policy and guidance pertaining to interagency contracts. After a number of reports by inspectors general and others regarding problems with interagency contracting, DOD established requirements in October 2004[35] for reviewing and approving the use of non-DOD contract vehicles when procuring supplies and services for amounts greater than the simplified acquisition threshold.[36] These requirements included determining that the tasks to be accomplished or supplies to be provided were within the scope of the contract to be used. ACA's implementing guidance, issued before CCE established the BPAs with the four contractors, required that specific certifications be made when using non-DOD contracts, including procedures for direct acquisitions (i.e., orders placed by an Army contracting or ordering officer against a non-DOD contract), such as CCE's orders against the vendors' GSA schedule contracts. Prior to the contracting officer's placement of a direct acquisition order for supplies and services, the head of the requiring activity must execute, among other things, a written certification that the supplies, services, or both, are within the scope of the non-DOD contract. Additionally, for the acquisition of services, (1) the requiring activity must obtain written concurrence from the non-DOD contracting officer at the servicing organization (in this case, GSA) that the services to be provided are within the scope of the non-DOD contract, unless the DOD contracting office has access to the non-DOD contract, and (2) the contracting officer must obtain written coordination from supporting legal counsel prior to placement of the order.

CCE's certification for use of a non-DOD contract was undated but signed by the contracting officer. It stated that the services were within the scope of the non-DOD contract, despite the fact that there was a clear disconnect between the descriptions in the contractors' GSA contract labor categories and the services CCE required. In addition, we could find no evidence that CCE obtained written concurrence from a GSA contracting officer,

[35] Memorandum from the Office of the Secretary of Defense, "Proper Use of Non-DOD Contracts," October 29, 2004.

[36] The simplified acquisition threshold is $100,000, except for acquisitions of supplies or services that as determined by the head of the agency, are to be used to support a contingency operation or to facilitate defense against or recovery from nuclear, biological, chemical, or radiological attack. FAR 2.101.

as required, or written coordination from its legal counsel. In fact, the certification listed the point of contact at the non-DOD agency as "to be determined."

Conclusion

The CCE example delineates two major areas of concern in today's environment: hiring contractors for sensitive positions in reaction to a shortfall in the government workforce rather than as a planned strategy to help achieve an agency mission, and the need to properly manage those contractors once they are hired. When contractors are performing duties closely supporting inherently governmental functions—such as those performed by contract specialists at CCE—risks are present that can result in loss of government control and decision making, absent proper mitigation and government vigilance. CCE and its contractors alike bear responsibility for helping to mitigate risks, such as ensuring that measures are in place to prevent conflicts of interest and that contractor personnel are clearly identified as such. Given the blurred lines separating government from contractor employees in such situations as that at CCE, an additional risk is that the work may be done under an improper personal services contract. DOD guidance on this issue—which could help contracting and program officials look beyond the FAR elements to determine the condition and mitigate the risk—is lacking. Because CCE has not considered the appropriate balance of contractor and government personnel performing specific functions, or adequately trained its government workforce, the agency runs the risk of over reliance on contractors to meet its mission and of paying more in the long run. If CCE relies too heavily on contractors and cannot adequately develop its own workforce, it may not be able to support its DOD customers. The cost of decreased mission capability could be far higher than paying more for contractors. And GSA, as the agency responsible for the schedule program, needs to take steps to ensure that contractors appropriately advertise their available services.

Recommendations for Executive Action

We recommend that the Secretary of Defense issue guidance to clarify the circumstances under which contracts risk becoming improper personal services contracts and to provide direction on how the risk should be mitigated.

To help ensure that CCE has sufficient qualified government personnel to meet its mission, and uses contractors appropriately, we recommend that the Secretary of the Army direct ACA to work with CCE in taking the following three actions:

- identify the appropriate mix of contractor and government contract specialists over the long term and develop a plan to help fill positions to achieve the desired balance;
- implement a training program designed to ensure that CCE's permanent employees develop and maintain needed skills; and
- implement formal oversight procedures to ensure that contractors identify themselves as such in all interactions external to CCE, including telephone communications, e-mail signature lines, and documents, as required by the FAR.

Finally, we recommend that the Administrator of GSA strengthen internal controls to guard against situations where contractors advertise services on the GSA Advantage Web site that are not in their underlying GSA schedule contracts.

Agency Comments and Our Evaluation

DOD and GSA provided written comments on a draft of this report. Their comments are reprinted in appendixes II and III, respectively.

DOD's Director, Defense Procurement, Acquisition Policy, and Strategic Sourcing, concurred with all four of our recommendations and outlined actions DOD plans to take or has taken to address them. The Director stated that contractors performing as contract specialists is viewed as a matter of grave concern. While one of our recommendations called for ACA to work with CCE to identify the appropriate mix of contractor and government contract specialists over the long term, the Director stated that he plans to meet with the Army's Senior Procurement Executive in an effort to eliminate, within 180 days, contractors acting as contract specialists at CCE. If this time frame cannot be met, the Director plans to urge the Army to transfer the workload within CCE to other DOD contracting agencies or sister federal agencies so that contract specialist functions are performed solely by government employees. In response to our recommendation that formal oversight procedures be implemented to ensure that contractors are identified as such in all interactions external to CCE, DOD stated that CCE had recently distributed to its government personnel and support contractors an information paper reinforcing such a policy. DOD's response states that CCE provided GAO with this information paper in February 2008. We did not receive such a paper. After seeing this reference in DOD's comments, we contacted CCE to request a copy of this document, but as of our report issuance date, we had not received it.

GSA agreed with our recommendation that the agency strengthen controls to guard against situations where contractors advertise services on the GSA Advantage Web site that are not in their underlying schedule contracts. GSA noted that while it provides limited oversight of the orders issued under schedule contracts, it takes actions to educate customers about how best to use the contracts. GSA also pointed out that because the revised Special Item Number category "Acquisition Management Support" has been implemented under the MOBIS schedule, contracting for contract specialist work is now within the scope of that schedule.

We are sending copies of this report to interested congressional committees; the Secretary of Defense; the Secretary of the Army; the Commander, ACA; the Commander, CCE; the Administrator of GSA; and the Director, Office of Management and Budget. We will provide copies to others on request. This report will also be available at no charge on GAO's Web site at http://www.gao.gov.

If you or your staff have any questions about this report or need additional information, please contact me at (202) 512-4841 or huttonj@gao.gov. Contact points for our Offices of Congressional Relations and Public Affairs may be found on the last page of this report. Staff acknowledgments are provided in appendix IV.

John Hutton
Director
Acquisition and Sourcing Management

List of Congressional Committees

The Honorable Carl Levin
Chairman
The Honorable John McCain
Ranking Member
Committee on Armed Services
United States Senate

The Honorable Joseph I. Lieberman
Chairman
The Honorable Susan M. Collins
Ranking Member
Committee on Homeland Security and Governmental Affairs
United States Senate

The Honorable Daniel K. Inouye
Chairman
The Honorable Ted Stevens
Ranking Member

Subcommittee on Defense
Committee on Appropriations
United States Senate

The Honorable Ike Skelton
Chairman
The Honorable Duncan L. Hunter
Ranking Member
Committee on Armed Services
House of Representatives

The Honorable Henry A. Waxman
Chairman
The Honorable Tom Davis
Ranking Member
Committee on Oversight and Government Reform
House of Representatives

The Honorable John P. Murtha
Chairman
The Honorable C.W. Bill Young
Ranking Member
Subcommittee on Defense
Committee on Appropriations
House of Representatives

The Honorable Bernard Sanders
United States Senate

Appendix I: Scope and Methodology

To learn more about the use and roles of contractors providing contract specialist services, we conducted a case study under the authority of the Comptroller General to conduct evaluations on his own initiative. We selected the Army's Contracting Center of Excellence (CCE), in the Washington, D.C., area, as one Department of Defense (DOD) agency using contractors in this role based on a bid protest that had been submitted to our office. The protest, which was denied, challenged the Defense Contracting Command-Washington's (now known as CCE) acceptance of CACI, International's (CACI) organizational conflict-of-interest mitigation plan and the evaluation of proposals for contract specialist services.[37] In fiscal year 2007, CCE obligated almost $1.8 billion in contract actions. Because nearly all of the contractor-provided contract specialists at CCE during the performance of our review were employees of CACI, our primary focus was on the CACI contract. CCE had also ordered a few contract specialists from another firm, The Ravens Group. In all, CCE had established blanket purchase agreements (BPA) with four contractors in September 2006, under General Services Administration (GSA) schedule contracts, to provide contract specialist services.

To determine the extent to which and the reasons CCE is relying on contractors, we obtained contract specialist staffing levels in fiscal year 2007. We reviewed CCE's task orders issued under schedule contracts using the agency's BPAs for contracting support services and agency billing information. We also interviewed CCE's commander and contracting, training, and human capital officials and spoke with officials from the Army Contracting Agency (ACA), which is CCE's parent organization. We analyzed information from the Federal Procurement Data System-Next Generation to determine trends in CCE's use of other agencies' contracts from fiscal years 2005 through 2007. To identify the roles and responsibilities of the contractor contract specialists, we randomly selected 42 contract actions worked on by contractor contract specialists during fiscal year 2006 and fiscal year 2007 through June 13 to determine what work they perform on a daily basis. The intent of this file review was to understand the contractors' day-to-day duties; we selected the files randomly to avoid selection bias. We interviewed management officials from CACI and The Ravens Group. We also interviewed CACI's contract specialists at CCE, but The Ravens Group management would not allow us to interview their employees. We did not consider this to be a scope limitation because of the small

[37] *LEADS Corporation*, B-292465, September 26, 2003, 2003 CPD 197 at 1. LEADS Corporation challenged the Defense Contracting Command–Washington's (now known as CCE) acceptance of CACI's organizational conflict-of-interest mitigation plan and the evaluation of proposals. GAO denied the protest.

number (2 to 3) of The Ravens Group's contract specialists at CCE during the time of our review. For comparison, we interviewed government contract specialists at CCE regarding their roles and responsibilities. We also interviewed government contracting officers about the roles and responsibilities of the government and contractor-provided contract specialists. To obtain information on the general demand for contract specialists in today's marketplace, we interviewed contractor management representatives, and we reviewed a Defense Acquisition University report on contracting out the procurement function,[38] an Air Force-sponsored study to assess the status of contracting out procurement functions within DOD and federal agencies. We also looked at job postings on USA Jobs, the federal government's Web site for job vacancies.

To determine what actions have been taken to mitigate the risks associated with using contractors in contract support roles, we interviewed CCE managers and contracting officers and CACI contract specialists at CCE. We reviewed CACI's organizational conflicts of interest (OCI) mitigation plan and interviewed employees about their knowledge of policies and procedures regarding OCIs. We interviewed CACI officials regarding the company's policies and procedures to mitigate personal conflicts of interest, and we examined related documents—such as CACI's Standards of Ethics and Business Conduct—and the ethics training provided by CACI to its employees. We also reviewed other documents, such as the Acquisition Advisory Panel's 2007 report.[39] In addition, we reviewed sections of the Federal Acquisition Regulation (FAR) pertaining to organizational and personal conflicts of interest, as well as those related to personal services contracts. We conducted a legal review of CCE's performance work statement, BPAs, and orders for contract specialists and compared the elements of personal services contracts in FAR Subpart 37.104 with the environment in which contractors are working at CCE as contract specialists.

To compare the cost of contractor contract specialists to their government counterparts, we reviewed CCE's fiscal year 2007 task orders with CACI and The Ravens Group and agency billing information to identify the hourly labor rate the government is paying for these positions. Because the orders issued pursuant to the BPAs are time-and-materials contracts, payments to the contractors are based on the number of labor hours billed at a fixed hourly rate, which includes wages, benefits, overhead, general and administrative expenses, and profit. We identified the number of hours purchased from each contractor during August 2007 and calculated the weighted average hourly cost for contract specialist II and III positions.

[38] Defense Acquisition University, *Contracting Out Procurement Functions: An Analysis.* DAU Research Report 06-001 (Fort Belvoir, Va.: Defense Acquisition University Press, November 2005).

[39] Acquisition Advisory Panel, *Report of the Acquisition Advisory Panel to the Office of Federal Procurement Policy and the United States Congress.*

We reported the weighted average hourly cost because the agency used two contractors at two different rates in August 2007. To compare these costs to those for a government contract specialist, we identified two groups of CCE employees that perform the same tasks and share similar qualifications, those who were GS-12s with Defense Acquisition Workforce Improvement Act (DAWIA) II certification—which are equivalent to contractor-provided contract specialist II positions—and those who were GS-13s with DAWIA III certification—which are equivalent to contractor-provided contract specialist III positions. We obtained the actual salaries and the government's contributions to the benefits of those contract specialists during the pay period ending on August 18, 2007.[40] We used data from one pay period to capture the costs of government contract specialists because CCE has had turnover in these positions, making it difficult to capture costs throughout the year. From those data, we determined the average hourly rate and costs of benefits for these two groups based on 68.3 productive hours[41] during the pay period. To determine the government's overhead costs, we used the actual costs of support services—salaries and government contributions to the benefits of human capital personnel, manpower personnel, and other support staff as identified by ACA during the pay period ending on August 18, 2007. CCE also provided the agency's expenditures on travel and training during fiscal year 2007. We then determined the average travel and training costs per person per hour for only those government employees who were directly associated with these costs. This average travel and training cost estimate was applied to all government contract specialists supporting CCE and may be higher than the agency's actual cost per person. We excluded from our analysis the costs for supplies, information technology, and communication services because the government pays these costs for contractors as well. We also excluded the costs of facilities and utilities because the Director of Resource Management told us that ACA could not specifically identify these costs (which the government also covers for contractor employees). We compared the average hourly cost—actual salary, government's contribution to benefits, and overhead—of the two groups of CCE contract specialists to the weighted average hourly rate paid for the respective contractor positions. To determine how CACI and CCE employee contracting experience differs, we reviewed available résumés of contractor and government contract specialists. Résumés were

[40] We included CCE's contributions to employee benefits. These are Thrift Savings Plan, Thrift Savings Plan Basic, Civil Service Retirement System, Federal Employees Retirement System, Social Security, Medicare, Federal Employee Health Benefits, and Federal Employee Group Life Insurance.

[41] Office of Management and Budget Circular A-76, which establishes federal policy for the competition of commercial activities, states that staffing of federal civilian employee positions shall be expressed in terms of annual productive work hours (1,776) rather than annual available hours that include nonproductive hours (2,080 hours). For the purposes of this analysis, which analyzes the costs during one pay period rather than a full year, we are using an equivalent 68.3 productive hours per pay period to determine the hourly rate.

available for six CACI contract specialists who have supported CCE for at least 6 months and were identified by CCE officials as doing the same work as government contract specialists. Five résumés were available for CCE contract specialists hired in fiscal year 2007, who were identified by agency officials as doing the same work as the contractors. In reviewing these résumés, we considered previous contracting experience to be the time spent in jobs related to the field of contracting.

To determine whether the contract vehicles used to acquire the specialists were appropriate, we reviewed CCE's contracting strategies to determine whether new contracts were awarded to obtain contract specialists or whether interagency contracts through other federal agencies, such as GSA's schedule program, were used. We analyzed CCE's BPAs with four contractors—CACI, The Ravens Group, Tai Pedro & Associates, and Government Contracts Consultants—and their underlying GSA Mission Oriented Business Integrated Services (MOBIS) schedule contracts to which the BPAs were tied. We also reviewed CCE's performance work statements and analyzed the task orders that have been issued for contract specialists. We reviewed the contract files to obtain documentation, such as legal reviews and compliance with DOD policies on interagency contracting. We interviewed CCE officials and GSA officials, including the Director of GSA's Management Services Center, Region 10, who is responsible for the MOBIS schedule. We reviewed reports by GAO and others concerning the use of interagency contracts. We also reviewed FAR Subpart 8.4, which sets forth the regulations pertaining to GSA's schedule program.

We conducted this performance audit from May 2007 through March 2008 in accordance with generally accepted government auditing standards. Those standards require that we plan and perform the audit to obtain sufficient, appropriate evidence to provide a reasonable basis for our findings and conclusions based on our audit objectives. We believe that the evidence obtained provides a reasonable basis for our findings and conclusions based on our audit objectives.

Appendix II: Comments from the Department of Defense

OFFICE OF THE UNDER SECRETARY OF DEFENSE
3000 DEFENSE PENTAGON
WASHINGTON, DC 20301-3000

ACQUISITION,
TECHNOLOGY
AND LOGISTICS

MAR 24 2008

Mr. John Hutton
Director, Acquisition and Sourcing Management
U.S. Government Accountability Office
441 G Street, N.W.
Washington, DC 20548

Dear Mr. Hutton:

This is the Department of Defense (DoD) response to the GAO Draft Report, GAO-08-360, "DEFENSE CONTRACTING: Army Case Study Delineates Concerns with Use of Contractors as Contract Specialists," dated February 20, 2008 (GAO Code 120654).

We fully concur with the recommendations provided in the report. Recently, I testified at House Armed Service Committee Subcommittee on Readiness on the matter of inherently governmental responsibilities. I expressed my concern that we had a small number of contracting organizations that had contractors performing as contract specialists.

I view this to be a matter of grave concern. I plan to meet with the Army's Senior Procurement Executive in an effort to accelerate the transition of contractors out of the contract specialist role. If we can not eliminate the role of contractors acting as contract specialists within 180 days, I plan to urge the Army to transfer the workload within that office to other DoD contracting agencies or sister federal agencies so that contract specialists function are performed solely by Government employees.

Detailed comments on the report recommendations are attached. The Department of the Army Contracting Agency, Contracting Center of Excellence (CCE), provided a response for each recommendation directed to the Secretary of the Army.

We appreciate the opportunity to provide comments on the draft report. My point of contact for this issue is Janice E. Sullivan who is available at (703) 614-4840 and janice.sullivan@osd.mil.

Shay D. Assad
Director, Defense Procurement,
Acquisition Policy, and
Strategic Sourcing

Attachment:
As stated

GAO DRAFT REPORT – DATED FEBRUARY 20, 2008
GAO-08-360 (GAO CODE 120654)

"DEFENSE CONTRACTING: Army Case Study Delineates Concerns with Use of Contractors as Contract Specialists"

DEPARTMENT OF DEFENSE COMMENTS TO THE GAO RECOMMENDATIONS

RECOMMENDATION 1: The GAO recommended that the Secretary of Defense issue guidance to clarify the circumstances under which contracts risk becoming improper personal services contracts and to provide direction on how the risk should be mitigated.

DOD RESPONSE: Concur. DoD concurs with the need to provide guidance regarding the appropriate use of personal service contracts and how to mitigate the risks of unauthorized personal service contracts. We are in the process of developing such guidance.

RECOMMENDATION 2: The GAO recommended that the Secretary of the Army direct the Army Contracting Agency to work with their Contracting Center of Excellence to identify the appropriate mix of contractor and government contract specialists over the long term and develop a plan to help fill positions to achieve the desired balance.

DOD RESPONSE: Concur. The Army advises that the Contracting Center of Excellence (CCE) long term goal is to staff the organization solely with government contract specialists. We have put forth an aggressive recruitment effort to fill all vacant government positions with highly qualified contract specialists. Towards this goal, CCE decreased the number of contractor personnel from thirty-one in 2007 to seventeen currently (as of February 26, 2008). Today, however, CCE still needs contractor personnel who, on average, possess greater experience and/or expertise than available in the government workforce. We anticipate the continued reduction of contractors in the CCE workplace over the next two years as the Gansler Commission recommendations are implemented; improving the Army's acquisition workforce and developing Government acquisition personnel who are better trained and more capable of handling the complex requirements of our customers.

RECOMMENDATION 3: The GAO recommended that the Secretary of the Army direct the Army Contracting Agency to work with their Contracting Center of Excellence to implement a training program designed to ensure its permanent employees develop and maintain needed skills.

DOD RESPONSE: Concur. The Army advises that CCE has implemented the recommendation that will ensure Government employees receive training and needed skills as outlined:

a. In-House Training: All managers are required to meet with their employees to discuss career goals and objectives and to ensure that all Individual Development Plans are updated and reflect the desired and required training to remain current. An assessment of major trends and weaknesses in the organization is made and a determination on how to best utilize limited funds available to improve or update the skill levels of all of CCE contracting personnel. Training is conducted through various methods to include lunch time sessions, train-the-trainer, on-the-job training and mentoring. Some of the in-house training provided in FY 2007 included Team Building; Continuous Learning Course (CLC) 033, Contract Format and Structure; CLC 007, Contract Source Selection; Cost and Pricing; lunch time training on various subjects provided by acquisition professional, and monthly luncheons with speakers from National Contract Management Agency (NCMA); and Small Business Training.

b. Defense Acquisition Workforce Improvement Act: Certification requirements are reviewed annually to ensure all personnel are certified at their required level. Over 97% of CCE's personnel meet or exceed their required level.

c. Formal Training: Formal training is conducted at least once a quarter. Four formal training sessions are scheduled for FY 2008. Additional training include web-based courses and paying for personnel to attend outside training. For example, CCE hosts a monthly NCMA professional development opportunity. CCE also established an on the job training and mentoring program within the CCE Directorate of Contracting. On the job training and mentoring provide unique opportunities to our specialists who already possess some job-related skills and the knowledge to learn from their peers. Training schedule for FY 2008 includes Best Values and Source Selection, Performance Based Contract, Performance Work Statement, Commercial Contracting, and Review of Contractor Cost and Pricing Data. When available, CCE funds college tuition for courses related to acquisition or contracting.

RECOMMENDATION 4: The GAO recommended that the Secretary of the Army direct the Army Contracting Agency to work with their Contracting Center of Excellence to implement formal oversight procedures to ensure that contractors identify themselves as such in all interactions external to CCE, including telephone communications, emails signature lines, and documents, as required by the Federal Acquisition Regulation (FAR).

DOD RESPONSE: Concur. The Army advises that CCE recently provided all CCE Government personnel and the CCE support contractors with an information paper which, among other topics, explicitly re-enforced the long-standing policy that contractor employees identify themselves as required by the FAR. A copy was provided to GAO in February 2008. Consistent with Army policy, CCE has always required contractor employee email addresses contain the contractor's company name. Most correspondence (electronic or hard copy) leaving CCE is signed by warranted contracting officers. Those

2

documents and emails signed by contractor employees will be reviewed to ensure that the contractor's identity is evident. Ensuring contractor identity was added to CCE's contract file checklist. In addition, telephonic spot checks will be conducted monthly. Finally, CCE took additional steps to ensure that contractor employee identity is known, including having the contractor program manager assign all work to his/her contractor personnel and physically assigning all contractor personnel to the same work area. CCE's legal office also prepared policy documents on the duties and responsibilities of the contractor specialist to include contractor personnel.

3

Appendix III: Comments from the General Services Administration

GSA

GSA Administrator

March 19, 2008

The Honorable Gene L. Dodaro
Acting Comptroller General of the United States
Government Accountability Office
Washington, DC 20548

Dear Mr. Dodaro:

The General Services Administration (GSA) appreciates the opportunity to review and comment on the draft report, "DEFENSE CONTRACTING: Army Case Study Delineates Concerns with Use of Contractors as Contract Specialists" (GAO-08-360). We also appreciate the Government Accountability Office's (GAO's) acknowledgement of the actions GSA has already taken as a result of the report findings.

The GAO draft report includes one recommendation to GSA, namely that GSA strengthen internal controls to guard against situations where contractors advertise services on the GSA Advantage! website that are not in their underlying GSA schedule contracts. We agree with the recommendation and will take appropriate action.

Technical comments that update and clarify statements in the draft report are enclosed and incorporated herein by reference. If you have any questions, please contact me. Staff inquiries may be directed to Mr. Kevin Messner, Associate Administrator, Office of Congressional and Intergovernmental Affairs, at (202) 501-0563.

Cordially,

Lurita Doan
Administrator

Enclosure

cc: John Hutton, Director, Acquisition and Sourcing Management

U.S. General Services Administration
1800 F Street, NW
Washington, DC 20405-0002
Telephone: (202) 501-0800
Fax: (202) 219-1243
www.gsa.gov

2

Government Accountability Office Draft Report, "DEFENSE CONTRACTING: Army Case Study Delineates Concerns with Use of Contractors as Contract Specialists" (GAO-08-360)

GSA Comments

Page 22, paragraph 3: Beginning at "GSA agreed that CCE's orders for contract specialist were issued out of scope ... but a senior official stated ... it is only able to perform limited oversight of the orders issued under the schedule contracts."

GSA Comment:
The report correctly notes that GSA performs limited oversight. However, GSA does take extensive action to educating customers in how to best use Schedule contracts. In managing the schedules, GSA:

- Develops and manages Special Item Numbers (SIN) descriptions to ensure that they clearly convey what services are covered and what services are not covered
- Operates GSA Advantage!
- Provides guidance on best use of schedules via many channels
- Leads regulation in Federal Acquisition Regulation (FAR) 8.4. This provides ordering procedures for agencies to use schedules appropriately
- Evaluates contractor performance and compliance with scope through the Customer Assessment Initiative (CAsI) Report Card
- Delivers regular customer training courses, in person and via webinar
- Publishes Multiple Award Schedule (MAS) Owners Manual (updated edition coming soon)
- Consults to advise customer agencies on best way to use schedules
- Conducts annual compliance surveys to identify on-going opportunities to improve schedule usage
- Issues Frequently Asked Questions (FAQ's) for all of our schedules
- Conducts scope review, consultations and assists with acquisition planning to customers when requested

Nonetheless, it is the responsibility of the ordering activity to follow ordering procedures and stay within scope. It is also the responsibility of the contractor to follow Terms & Conditions of its contract.

Page 24, paragraph 2: Because of the demand for contract support services, GSA recently implemented a revised Special Item Number category—"Acquisition Management Support"—under the MOBIS schedule.

GSA Comment:
We appreciate GAO's acknowledgement of recent actions undertaken, but we note that the information GSA posts on its website also provides guidance that is directed to ordering activities, as well as contractors, to ensure that both parties are aware of their responsibilities and limitations under the regulations. As a result of the change to MOBIS last month, contracting for contract specialist work is now within the scope of the schedule.

Appendix IV: GAO Contact and Staff Acknowledgments

GAO Contact

John Hutton, (202) 512-4841 or huttonj@gao.gov

Acknowledgments

In addition to the individual named above, Michele Mackin, Assistant Director; Erin Schoening; William Allbritton; Timothy Carr; Daniel Chen; Justin Jaynes; Kenneth Patton; Charles Perdue; and Sylvia Schatz made key contributions to this report.

GAO's Mission

The Government Accountability Office, the audit, evaluation, and investigative arm of Congress, exists to support Congress in meeting its constitutional responsibilities and to help improve the performance and accountability of the federal government for the American people. GAO examines the use of public funds; evaluates federal programs and policies; and provides analyses, recommendations, and other assistance to help Congress make informed oversight, policy, and funding decisions. GAO's commitment to good government is reflected in its core values of accountability, integrity, and reliability.

Obtaining Copies of GAO Reports and Testimony

The fastest and easiest way to obtain copies of GAO documents at no cost is through GAO's Web site (www.gao.gov). Each weekday, GAO posts newly released reports, testimony, and correspondence on its Web site. To have GAO e-mail you a list of newly posted products every afternoon, go to www.gao.gov and select "E-mail Updates."

Order by Mail or Phone

The first copy of each printed report is free. Additional copies are $2 each. A check or money order should be made out to the Superintendent of Documents. GAO also accepts VISA and Mastercard. Orders for 100 or more copies mailed to a single address are discounted 25 percent. Orders should be sent to:

U.S. Government Accountability Office
441 G Street NW, Room LM
Washington, DC 20548

To order by Phone:	Voice:	(202) 512-6000
	TDD:	(202) 512-2537
	Fax:	(202) 512-6061

To Report Fraud, Waste, and Abuse in Federal Programs

Contact:

Web site: www.gao.gov/fraudnet/fraudnet.htm
E-mail: fraudnet@gao.gov
Automated answering system: (800) 424-5454 or (202) 512-7470

Congressional Relations

Ralph Dawn, Managing Director, dawnr@gao.gov, (202) 512-4400
U.S. Government Accountability Office, 441 G Street NW, Room 7125
Washington, DC 20548

Public Affairs

Chuck Young, Managing Director, youngc1@gao.gov, (202) 512-4800
U.S. Government Accountability Office, 441 G Street NW, Room 7149
Washington, DC 20548

SUBJECT INDEX

Doc/Pg

Iraq

Legislation – Federal

Military – Role of

PATRIOT Act, USA

Regulations – Federal

Terrorism Legislation – U.S.

Terrorism – Criminal Prosecution

www.ingramcontent.com/pod-product-compliance
Ingram Content Group UK Ltd.
Pitfield, Milton Keynes, MK11 3LW, UK
UKHW051048150926
475595UK00005B/177